Sisters in Sorrow

Sisters in

VOICES OF CARE IN

Sorrow

THE HOLOCAUST

Roger A. Ritvo
and Diane M. Plotkin

Foreword by Harry James Cargas

TEXAS A&M UNIVERSITY PRESS
COLLEGE STATION

The paper used in this book meets the minimum requirements

of the American National Standard for Permanence

of Paper for Printed Library Materials, z39.48-1984.

Binding materials have been chosen for durability.

∞

Library of Congress Cataloging-in-Publication Data

Sisters in sorrow : voices of care in the Holocaust / Roger A. Ritvo and Diane M. Plotkin ;
foreword by Harry James Cargas.

p.   cm.

Includes bibliographical references and index.

ISBN 0-89096-810-1 (cloth);   ISBN 0-89096-970-1 (pbk.)

1. Jewish women in the Holocaust.   2. Holocaust, Jewish (1939–1945)—Personal
narratives.   3. World War, 1939–1945—Medical care.   4. Holocaust survivors—
Interviews.   I. Ritvo, Roger A., 1944– .   II. Plotkin, Diane M., 1942– .

D804.47.S57   1998

940.53'18'082—dc21   97-46013

CIP

Preface

My mother
she was hands, a face
They made our mothers strip in front of us

Here mothers are no longer mothers to their children.

—Charlotte Delbo,
"None of Us Will Return,"
in *Auschwitz and After*

We came together to write this volume through coincidence. When Trudy Shakno brought me her sister Ellen Loeb's memoirs, she informed me of the request Roger Ritvo had made in some of the Holocaust center journals for any information regarding medical care in the concentration camps. I responded to his inquiry, sending him the translated narrative. While Roger had been researching physicians and medical care in the concentration camps, I had quite an important and detailed memoir, too short to publish by itself but too long to submit as an article.

Both of us had already spent days in Holocaust museums, from the National Archives and the United States Holocaust Memorial Museum in Washington, D.C., to Yad Vashem, Amsterdam, Auschwitz, Majdanek, Theresienstadt, Mauthausen, and Sydney, Australia, to name a few. Roger had compiled quite a list of people with whom he had spoken, in the United States as well as overseas. Since he had already conducted much of the preliminary research and spoken to many of our interviewees over the phone, I conducted the personal interviews both here and abroad. When we began to call the women to request these interviews, some were willing to share their experiences, while others were relatively unapproachable; one was even quite hostile. Still others agreed to speak to us, only to change their minds when it came time for the actual interview. Some agreed to share their experiences but allowed only their initials in the completed text. The reasons for their various reactions gradually became more understandable, as we found that many women did not feel they had done enough or had been in positions to provide adequate care. Others still suffer from memories of the abortions they had to perform, or worse, of the babies they had to murder in order to save the lives of the mothers. Two interviewees already had contracts to publish their memoirs, while a third was honored to be included in our study. A fourth, although initially willing to give us her memoirs, later decided to publish them herself. As still another began to talk, she became so immersed in the memories and horrors of the past that it was impossible for her to continue, thereby necessitating a second interview.

After I had conducted the personal interviews, Roger's secretary would transcribe them. Following that we spent many weeks reviewing the tapes and meticulously correcting the transcribed texts. When questions arose, we would phone the interviewee, which is why some notes read "Telephone Interview." Next we converted each interview to a narrative, scrupulously endeavoring to retain the "voice" of the survivor. As a result, however, we are aware that the text may contain some grammatical errors. The narratives were then sent back and forth and discussed over the telephone until the interviewees and we were both satisfied. In addition we obtained chronicles and permission to publish them from the United States Holocaust Memorial Museum, the archives at Auschwitz, *Le Monde,* and the United Jewish Federation Virginia News. The chapter about the work of Dr. Hadassah Rosensaft, however, is based entirely upon research, although she, too, was given the opportunity and graciously consented to comment upon and correct what we had written.

The book is organized into seven sections, five of which are preceded by an overview of the individual camp pertaining to that section. In as many narratives as possible we have included the experiences of each interviewee prior to her imprisonment, as this gives us a better picture of the person as well as information regarding any training she may have had in medicine and/or nursing. The oral histories of the women in the first three narratives proceed from their experiences in transit, extermination, and work camps, up until their liberation. The chapter about Lenzing bridges the experiences of two survivors who were imprisoned in Theresienstadt and Birkenau, as well as that particular work camp. The three narratives which follow the description of Bergen-Belsen lead from memoirs regarding the care of children to a third, which proceeds from the survivor's incarceration to her liberation. Completing the book are short chapters about one American nurse's postwar experiences caring for former prisoners immediately after their liberation, followed by a more recent article about the memories that continue to haunt the survivor.

This preface[1] and some of the short ones that follow are written in the first-person singular, not because either of us did any more or less work, but simply in order to give better insight into our interviewing process as well as the face-to-face interaction between interviewers and interviewees.

—Diane M. Plotkin

Contents

Illustrations

Foreword

Historical accounts of tragedies are both moving and necessary. We must know the truth of what happens; causes, effects, the impacts, whatever "meaning" there is to be gleaned from reflection and analysis. But an overview, regardless of its excellence, must be reinforced by a microview—what happened in the details? There is much that must be recorded about the events of the Holocaust; we must learn of the millions of victims, of the traumatized survivors (who are also fully victims though they still live), of the killers, the torturers, those who planned the overall attack on women, men, babies. *Sisters in Sorrow: Voices of Care in the Holocaust* preserves some of those details. This volume helps to fill a gap in our understanding which, alas, must necessarily be incomplete.

One almost despairs in trying to comprehend the meaning of the tragedy that exploded on the Jews in World War II. Even though the monstrous blot on the record of humanity can never really be apprehended, we would be failing in our efforts as humans if we did not try. When we read of a mastectomy performed without an anesthetic being administered; that prisoners carried on even when they lost toes or fingers due to freezing; that ten women in a single bunk had to share but three blankets in the winter; when we are told of terrible tortures at the hands of laughing persecutors, how are we to comprehend any meaning? Does any of this fit into some pattern of history that we had hereto accepted?

Calling what the killers and pain-inflictors perpetuated a kind of collective madness is irresponsible, a conclusion that is too facile and clearly incorrect. But for some there seems to have been a mob psychology in effect. How can we explain the 1,798 camps for internees (according to the Polish Encyclopedic Summary of Camps) without considering the massive number of victimizers? As I have said repeatedly, "It takes a lot of people to kill a lot of people." Jews were betrayed by neighbors, robbed, beaten, removed from their sources of income, deported, starved, tortured, murdered—and still some survived.

This book is about some of them.

It is clear that the women interviewed in this volume do not consider themselves as heroes. Yet they are. Merely surviving under the extreme circumstances that they experienced was remarkable. Victor E. Frankl, the Austrian Holocaust survivor, psychiatrist (developer of logotherapy), and author, has written that regardless of what is done to a man or woman, that person has the freedom to determine his/ her own mental attitudes towards those experiences. This is echoed in this book by Magda Herzberger who recognizes that "the only freedom I had in that camp was my spiritual freedom. I could think what I wanted. In my imagination I could be everywhere I wanted to be. I could see myself liberated. I could see myself at home. I could see my mother lighting the candles on Shabbat, on Friday night. They can kill you physically, but they can never take away that spirit of freedom. Spiritual freedom has the most value. You can change in the course of your life; you go through different stages, but this is something that never ages. It always stays with you; it's always fresh." These are the insights of a hero of the imagination.

We can envision individuals wondering, on occasion, "How would I have acted in certain situations? If most of my neighbors were anti-Semitic would I have stood up for Jews? Had it been easier to cooperate with the Nazis than resist them, would I have done so? Given the power to torture, the orders to kill, how would I have behaved?" Some will answer such questions too facilely. A great many men and women were treacherous when given the opportunity to be. Perhaps I, too, under certain conditions . . .

But the only answer need not be a negative one: there were those who showed the best side of humanity. This applies to the victims as well as their potential (but not actual) tormentors. We need their stories desperately. If we concluded that all victims "caved in," lost their wills to live, surrendered to an evil "fate," we would betray the memories of those who acted heroically. We could also deny ourselves role models for our own responses in times of great crises.

Reading how women banded together to protect those who were pregnant, how medical practices were carried on without disinfectants, without hot water, without sterilization of instruments, how primitive dentistry was performed without anesthesia is frightening. People are able to do this to people. And some people are able to survive! We have to know that.

Doctors became licensed murderers, expectant mothers were severely abused, prisoners were burned alive—the stories are endless, unfathomable from any philosophic perspective. But life had to go on. Life did go on. And all of us, non-Jews as well as Jews, must know that Life did go on and we must understand, as best we can, how and why it did. We can all learn from that. We *must* all learn from that.

Therefore we are indebted to Diane Plotkin and Roger Ritvo for the compilation of these chapters. It is clear that an enormous amount of intellectual and emotional labor went into this book. For this we can be grateful because the insights recorded here add another dimension to the unsolvable but ever-challenging mystery of the Holocaust.

—Harry James Cargas

Acknowledgments

This book fulfills a dream we share, yet it could not have resulted without the help of many people. It represents a woman collaborating with a man writing about a universal horror for an audience of both. In many ways, our teamwork defies the history of the women we meet in this volume. They were separated from their husbands, lovers, friends, teachers, rabbis, and acquaintances. This book represents a joining, a combining, and a continuity. We share a common heritage, possess the energy to make this book a reality, and have found ways to reconcile our differences. This work reflects the spirit and values of Judaism, higher education, our intense interest in Holocaust studies, and our belief that cooperation makes a better product.

Behind every volume there are many people whose contributions helped shape the ideas, whose suggestions helped form the context of the work, and whose encouragement guided the writing and editing process. We have thanked them individually and privately. This is our way of thanking them formally. We especially wish to thank Professor Harry James Cargas and our other reviewers for their careful reading of our manuscript and their helpful suggestions.

Both for their early telephone conversations and their later advice, the following current and former professional staff members of the United States Holocaust Memorial Museum deserve a public thank you: Henry Mayer, Joan Ringelheim, Brewster Chamberlin, Aaron Kornblum, and Dr. Robert Kesting. JoAnn Rudolph of the Yale University's Fortunoff Collection provided access to names as well as survivor narratives. Reba Karp, of the United Jewish Federation of Tidewater, provided the material regarding Marie Ellifritz, the American nurse. Bonnie Gurewitsch and her staff at the Museum of Jewish Heritage in New York allowed us to spend days rummaging through their tapes and files of survivor narratives, leading us to pursue and attain permission from Mme. Marie Odile-Masson of *Le Monde* to print "Militante du souvenir."

While fifty years ago Auschwitz was a place of death and desecration, today Mr. Jerzy Wroblewski and his staff, who work in its archives, were most helpful in allowing us to realize our goal. So, too, were Dr. Jan Munk of the Terezin Museum, and Mr. Jan Ooms of Westerbork, who supplied us with information regarding this transit camp and the Loeb family.

Dr. Hadassah Rosensaft deserves special mention, for it was she who contacted Hela Jafe and attained her permission to utilize her narrative. Dr. Rosensaft also corrected errors in translation and edited our section about the *Kinderheim* in Bergen-Belsen.

Paula J. Sarette transcribed many oral history tapes with exacting patience. Christine M. Hamann prepared the manuscript with energy and enthusiasm; she learned about the book's content while instructing Roger Ritvo on the intricacies of Word-Perfect! Barbra Fagin, librarian at the Dallas Memorial Center for Holocaust Studies, was never too busy to look through all her books to research some obscure fact. Joanne E. Clendenen and Kay K. Schlembach carefully created a thorough and functional index.

For those readers who have never written a book, patience and persistence replace weekends and evenings. For that reason, our families deserve special mention. Diane's mother-in-law, Sara Plotkin, has always provided encouragement. Mikki Ritvo, Roger's mother, was a pioneer in working with nurses eager to humanize the practice of medicine and reflects the themes in this volume. Our spouses and adult children meant it when they said, "We know why you cannot join us today." For this reason we appreciate the patience and understanding of Allen Plotkin and Lynn Ritvo.

As educators, we seek truth in the academy. The fact that *liberty* and *library* share the same Latin root provides inspiration for both our learning and our teaching; one informs the other. Society's liberties can be found on the shelves of its libraries. Yet Hitler's rise to power was fueled by the energy created when the Nazis burned the books of Germany's Jewish population. The women whose narratives appear in this book were denied their freedom. We hope this volume honors and reaffirms their liberty.

Each of these survivors has our respect and admiration. Their contributions to society have made this world a better place for future generations. Our desire is to honor their lives and words by re-creating their biographies as accurately as possible. We apologize in advance for any errors or omissions.

Sisters in Sorrow

●　　　●　　　●

Chapter One

Introduction

• • •

"ABANDON HOPE, FOREVER, YOU WHO ENTER."[1] So states the ledge above the gates of Hell, an inkling of what lies ahead for the souls of the damned. Dante the Pilgrim enters with Virgil, the voice of Reason, to learn the way to return to the True Path. In similar fashion, the gates above the concentration camps read, *Arbeit Macht Frei* (work makes you free), not the truth for sinners but rather a mockery for the millions of righteous, still living but damned only because of their identity, who were forced to pass through these gates on their way to suffering and death. Thus, while Dante's journey was to be a medieval quest for learning and salvation, a Holocaust survivor's journey had become a quest for life itself, but a life that could never return to the path from which it was so cruelly forced to stray.

The women whose biographies we are recounting in this book were forced by an evil beyond their control to stray from lives of health and happiness to ones of sickness and misery in camps that had, contrary to any voice of reason, been constructed for the sole purpose of their extermination. Whether through gas, beatings, starvation, disease, hopelessness, suicide, or outright murder at the hand of the SS guards, all knew and faced the same grim reality. Even at Theresienstadt, where the facades may have fooled the International Red Cross, people died, if not in gas chambers, from starvation and disease. For some, however, even within these compounds of horror, there remained glimmers of hope. Those who were capable and willing were sometimes able to help others live, thereby retaining a measure of value in their own lives as well as contributing to that of their fellow prisoners. In this way they were able to maintain a semblance of their own humanity. As Terrence Des Pres relates, "Nobody survived without help. Life in the camps was savage, and yet there was a web of mutual aid and encouragement, to which many of the survivors testify."[2]

How, then, did this come to be a book devoted to the memoirs and narratives of women? According to a 1994 article by Andrea Dworkin, the subject of women and questions regarding their imprisonment and survival patterns has not been adequately studied as a topic in itself. She contends that there is little gender-specific data, even at the United States Holocaust Memorial Museum, and few answers as to what happened specifically to Jewish women in the concentration camps of Europe.[3] Similarly, Holocaust historian Sybil Milton maintains that "women have been largely invisible in the current historiography on the subject. . . . Although both men and women were victims of the organized state system of terror, the experiences that separated female from male prisoners have remained unexplored."[4] Dr. Joan Ringelheim, too, has argued that the experiences of women have largely been absorbed into and obscured by descriptions of men's lives and that there is a paucity of literature which deals with life experiences exclusive to women, such as sexual victimization, rape, and vulnerability through their responsibility for their children.[5] Since the publication of their articles, however, there has been a significant increase in the number of papers and books regarding the sufferings and experiences peculiar to women in the camps.

Accounts by and about women in both the ghettos and the camps began as early as 1945 with *Warsaw Ghetto: A Diary by Mary Berg*[6] and the 1947 account of the early years in Auschwitz entitled *Smoke Over Birkenau*, by Seweryna Szmaglewska.[7] In addition to such autobiographical accounts as Anne Frank's diaries, there are those written by Etty Hillesum regarding her life in Amsterdam as well as her journal about conditions in Westerbork.[8] Topics regarding women and their concentration camp experiences have also been explored by Marlene E. Heineman in *Gender and Destiny: Women Writers and the Holocaust*,[9] by Vera Laska in *Women in the Resistance and in the Holocaust: The Voices of Eyewitnesses*,[10] by Ruth Schwertfeger in her study entitled *Women of Theresienstadt: Voices from a Concentration Camp*,[11] and by Carol Rittner and John Roth in *Different Voices; Women and the Holocaust*, the latter of which was written in response to Rittner's question, "Where were the women during the Holocaust?"[12] after she had read Roth and Michael Berenbaum's *Holocaust: Religious and Philosophical Implications*, in which they reprinted Holocaust reflections exclusively by influential male writers.[13] Other notable chronicles include Fania Fenelon's memoirs of her experiences as a female musician in Auschwitz entitled *The Musicians of Auschwitz*;[14] Charlotte Delbo's *Auschwitz and After*, an artistic and poetic account of women's experiences;[15] and the sad memoirs of Isabella Leitner recounted in *Isabella: From Auschwitz to Freedom*.[16] Sara Nomberg-Przytyk's narrative *Auschwitz: True Tales from a Grotesque Land* provides an interesting perspective of a young girl's concentration camp experiences,[17] while *Hannah Senesh: Her Life and Diary* records the experiences of a Zionist heroine.[18] Interestingly, there is a more recent anthology of women's experiences by Liana Millu, which, like Szmaglewska's work, is entitled *Smoke Over Birkenau*.[19] Gerda Klein, who frequently lectures about the Holocaust, also recalls her ordeal in the camps in *All But My Life*,[20] while Corrie Ten Boom's memoir *The Hiding Place* provides fascinating insight into the heroic actions of a righteous Gentile.[21]

After reading these texts, we would certainly have to agree with Milton that, when discussing the Holocaust, the subject of women as a unified whole is impossible to conceptualize or explore, as there are enormous differences and variations in their backgrounds and personalities. Nonetheless, although it is inaccurate to generalize, some common threads do emerge. Milton quotes Commandant Hoss as remarking that " 'general living conditions in the women's camp were incomparably worse [than in the men's camp]. They were far more tightly packed in and the sanitary and hygienic conditions were notably inferior,' "[22] as the memoirs of Ruth Reiser and Magda Herzberger attest later in this work. However, Milton relates that, despite this, as a rule women exhibited survival skills and techniques in adapting to their horrific environments which differed significantly from those of men. Although concentration camp inmates—both men and women—did what they could to resist, some women managed to survive through their ability to remain inconspicuous, while others obtained lifesaving food, clothing, or medicines by using sex as a form of bribery.[23] Many were able to gain some degree of control over their space by utilizing housework as a form of therapy. Frequently their knowledge of homemaking skills enabled them to refashion clothing from the rags they were given and to stretch their limited food supply by inventing new "recipes."[24] We have found this to be true in the few narratives, memoirs, and testimonies we have attained. The women we interviewed and whose oral histories we have included in this work did indeed exhibit remarkable survival skills, which frequently resulted from their backgrounds as homemakers and caregivers.

Milton goes on to say that women appeared to have been more physically and psychologically resilient to the effects of starvation and malnutrition.[25] Although we would be hard-pressed to prove or disprove her contention, without exception the women we interviewed managed to exhibit remarkable strength in the most horrific situations. Many gave their all for one another by such acts as attempting to conceal their friends' pregnancies from the SS, by offering their last crust of bread to a starving friend, or by preventing a fellow prisoner from committing suicide by offering a kind word and a comforting hand. By contrast, some men were reported by women in Gurs, Theresienstadt, and Bergen-Belsen to have been " 'selfish and undisciplined egoists, unable to control their hungry stomachs and [who] revealed a painful lack of courage.' "[26] Interestingly, none of the women we spoke to had anything negative to say about their male counterparts; in fact, several spoke of being given food and/or aid by the men they encountered. Therefore, it is obvious that one must be careful in the use of such statements. Indeed, Ringelheim points out that there is an inherent danger in beginning from a position of difference, as this has led some authors to conclude mistakenly that "women in survival skills, values, and even biological makeup, are superior to men!"[27]

Although some women tended to bond, forming networks of friendship within which they were able to help one another to endure the unendurable,[28] Ringelheim contends that this bonding was "limited and exclusive. It wasn't a bonding against the enemy in solidarity with other women." But within this bonding, she puts forth an important rhetorical question: "Did the terror of isolation and death *not* affect the women because they bonded?"[29] To this we must reply that it goes without saying that women suffered just as horribly as men, despite this tendency to bond. Many retain memories of terror that manifest themselves when world events bring to mind the horrors of the camps. For example, during the Gulf War, one female Holocaust survivor suffered from nightmares of the gas chambers when she saw the news reports of Israelis wearing gas masks. Rocking back and forth as we spoke, she sang lullabies her grandmother had sung to her in the ghetto and recalled her experiences during the horrible years of her imprisonment. As a result of our conversation, she began to speak to groups and now addresses them frequently. Some years later, however, when I began to interview her for the Shoah Foundation, despite the fact that she was by now quite an experienced speaker, she was again unable to speak about her experiences because of the bright, glaring lights of the camera, which reminded her of the searchlights in the camps. As with other survivors, not only does she remain affected by her memories of isolation and death, but she also speaks of the terrors she experienced during her pregnancies and retains horrible memories of rape and other forms of physical and verbal abuse. She does not recall any medical care being available to her or her fellow prisoners during the entire three years of her incarceration.[30]

There are a few books written about female caregivers in the ghettos and camps, such as Adina Blady Szwajger's *I Remember Nothing More: The Warsaw Children's Hospital and the Jewish Resistance*, a sobering account of the children in the Warsaw Children's Hospital,[31] and the experiences of physicians in Gisella Perl's *I Was a Doctor in Auschwitz*,[32] Olga Lengyel's *Five Chimneys: The Story of Auschwitz*,[33] and R. J. Minney's *I Shall Fear No Evil: The Story of Dr. Alina Brewda*.[34] There is generally a dearth of published information, however, specifically devoted to the details of women's health care or lack thereof. Simha Naor's memoir entitled *Krankengymnastin in Auschwitz: Aufseichnungen des Häftlings Nr. 80574* is available only in Europe,[35] and Lore Shelley's important compilation of twenty women's experiences, *Criminal Experiments on Human Beings in Auschwitz and War Research Laboratories*,[36] which has not been given the recognition it deserves.

Many of the works regarding physicians are about medical experiments carried out by the Nazi physicians, for example Philippe Aziz's four-volume *Doctors of Death*, which details the atrocities;[37] Walter Poller's *Medical Block, Buchenwald: The Personal Testimony of Inmate 996, Block 36*, an eyewitness account of the inhumanities committed at Buchenwald;[38] Albert Haas's *The Doctor and the Damned*, a chronicling of the atrocities committed in the camps;[39] Miklos Nyiszli's horrifying book *Auschwitz: A Doctor's*

Eyewitness Account, in which he writes about his work as a pathologist;[40] Michael Kater's *Doctors Under Hitler,* a history of the medical profession in the Third Reich;[41] Robert Jay Lifton's *The Nazi Doctors: Medical Killing and the Psychology of Genocide,*[42] a psychological study of the biomedical perspective under which physicians became killers; George Annas and Michael Grodin's *The Nazi Doctors and the Nuremberg Code: Human Rights in Human Experimentation,* a study of the lack of medical ethics that led to the development of the Nuremberg Code;[43] and *Doctors of Infamy: The Story of Nazi Medical Crimes,*[44] by Alexander Mitschlerlich, which describes in horrifying detail the Nazi medical crimes. Other works written by physicians are, for the most part, about the experiences of males. For example, although there are such statements as "Women were in a considerably worse state than men . . ." in "Role of the men's hospital camp at KL-Auschwitz II (Birkenau),"[45] two chapters are specifically devoted to the men's hospitals. In addition, neither Louis J. Micheels's *Doctor 117641,*[46] Christian Bernadac's *Doctors of Mercy,*[47] nor Frank Stiffel's *The Tale of the Ring: A Kaddish*[48] specifically addresses women's medical care per se. It was, therefore, with great interest and enthusiasm that we responded to the query of Trudy Shakno (the sister of Ellen Loeb, the nurse who had cared for patients in Westerbork, Theresienstadt, and Lenzing) when she asked whether or not her sister's memoirs, which had lain in a bank vault for the past fifty years, would be of any academic value.

This book does not, however, purport to be, nor can it be, a comprehensive study of the medical care rendered to women by their fellow female prisoners, although regarding female caregivers Carol Gilligan asserts that "women not only define themselves in a context of human relationship but also judge themselves in terms of their ability to care."[49] This morality of caring and responsibility defines the women in this book. Nevertheless, regarding *all* prisoner-doctors, male as well as female, Anton Gill states, "the best off psychologically were those whose work had some meaning."[50] Women, however, faced adversities that differed from those of men, such as danger of rape, loss of menses, pregnancy, abortion, and care and/ or murder of newborns and young children. Thus, although we are not able, in a study this limited in scope, to compare the behavior and survival mechanisms of men and women in a gender-specific manner, we are able to point out some behavioral mechanisms of female doctors and nurses which resulted from these problems. Still, it is difficult to generalize because none of us knows what he or she would do in similar circumstances. Just as not every woman bonded or attempted to render care, most men were not lacking in courage or unable to control their hunger.

It was a nightmarish world that those who were not there can never fully comprehend. In the ghettos and camps, words such as *courage* and *hunger* took on other meanings than those we understand. Following a description of the daily effort to survive, Primo Levi states, "in the face of driving necessity and physical disabilities many social habits are reduced to silence."[51] There are hundreds of stories of men who, even in the face of such adversity, contributed significantly to the survival of their fellow prisoners when they themselves were at the point of death.

Reading, listening to, recording, writing, and editing these women's accounts has been a historic, professional, and personal journey. One cannot help but become touched by and involved with the process. Their memories cry out for others to read and encounter, even though we can never fully comprehend or understand. Nonetheless, we hope that by presenting the narratives, testimonies, and memoirs of a few, we can make clearer the picture of life for the millions of women who struggled not only to remain alive, but to bring aid and comfort to their comrades in the hell that was the Holocaust.

Chapter Two

Women Trapped
within a Medical Paradox

· · ·

It was only at the juncture of two developments that doctors became licensed murderers and publicly hired torturers: where the aggressiveness of their search for truth met with the ideology of the dictatorship. It is practically the same thing seeing a person as a "case" or as a number, which is tattooed on the person's arm—a double facelessness of a merciless age.

—Mark Wand, trans.,
The Value of Being Human,
Medicine in Germany 1918–1945

In the ghettos and concentration camps of Europe, murder and mutilation, on the one hand, and mercy and care, on the other, contradicted one another in a dreadful paradox of the macabre. Nazi physicians who had trained under the most noted professors and worked in some of the most modern and best-equipped institutions of the time induced horror and death as they performed their medical experiments on innocent men, women, and children. By contrast, there were many doctors and nurses among the women prisoners, many of whom had not even completed their education, who worked under unimaginably horrible conditions in filthy, unequipped or ill-equipped infirmaries lacking medicines and supplies. They attempted to comfort the suffering thousands who came for help. To quote Florence Nightingale, "Every woman, or at least almost every woman . . . has, at one time or another of her life, charge of the personal health of somebody, whether child or invalid,—in other words, every woman is a nurse. . . . It is recognized as the knowledge which every one ought to have—distinct from medical knowledge. . . ."[1]

Physicians in the camps practiced a profession which had been based upon the principles designated in the Hippocratic Oath, but which, of necessity, had been altered to meet the perverse conditions within the concentration camps. Ironically, so did their professional counterparts in the SS, for as Heinrich Himmler stated, "'In a camp, there are only the able-bodied or the dead. The sick don't exist.'"[2] Contrary to the vow made by a graduating physician, *"I will follow that method of treat-*

ment which, according to my ability and judgment, I consider for the benefit of my patients,"[3] Miklos Nyisli commented, "In my role of sonderkommando doctor, I was making my morning rounds. All four crematories were working at full blast."[4] Furthermore, while physicians promise to *"abstain from whatever is deleterious and mischievous,"* Nyisli writes about the dwarfs who "were housed in barracks 14 of Camp F. From there they were taken by their guards to the experimental barracks of the Gypsy Camp and exposed to every medical examination that can be performed on human beings."[5] While the practicing physician is exhorted to *"give no deadly medicine to anyone . . . ,"* those who cared for their fellow prisoners did just that in the name of mercy, as Mme. Vaillant-Couturier testified during the Nuremberg Trials: "One day the German Schwester, Martha, arrived in the block and distributed a powder to some 20 patients. The patients subsequently fell into a deep sleep. . . . During the night the snores gradually ceased and the patients died."[6] Contrary to the pledge physicians make that they *"will not give to a woman an instrument to produce abortion,"* women in the camps were aborted in order to prevent mothers from being sent, with their unborn children, to the gas chambers. Finally, although the new physician vows, *"With purity and holiness I will pass my life and practice my art,"* Dr. Olga Lengyel remembers just the opposite, as she comments: "[Dr. Josef Mengele] was the tyrant from whose decisions there was no appeal. Nor did the state of health have anything to do with his selections. . . . How we hated this charlatan! He profaned the very word 'science!' How we despised his detached, haughty air, his continual whistling, his absurd orders, his frigid cruelty!"[7]

While female prisoners suffered from conditions particular to their gender, there were women who were in a position to function as physicians and nurses within the ghettos, transit and labor camps, and extermination camps, and even after liberation they served as caregivers in the camps that had become repositories for the thousands of homeless refugees. Prior to the transportation of Jews to the camps, thousands poured into ghettos created by the conquering German armies. In these overcrowded, unsanitary prologues to the infernos which were to follow, conditions went from bad to worse in the few hospitals where Jewish patients were allowed to be treated. Writing about her pediatric patients in the Warsaw Ghetto hospital, Adina Blady Szwajger describes the ever-growing number of "flea-ridden, lice-infested, fungus-diseased children. More children emaciated from hunger with the eyes of adults; more and more tuberculosis."[8] As conditions worsened and food became more scarce, she and her colleagues treated children suffering from typhus, rickets, meningitis, and *"Durchfall—*the bloody diarrhea of starvation."[9] She writes of seeing children with frostbitten toes and fingers, "black with gangrene, amputated on the bed without a table or even gloves—we'd simply wash our hands. And the stench—the terrible stench."[10] Overwhelmed by the tragedies she and the other doctors saw daily, the only way they could face the horror was by fortifying themselves with liquor. Finally the day came when the children in the hospital were to be deported to their deaths. Rather than see them suffer, she and her colleagues poisoned them with morphine, telling them that "this medicine will make the pain disappear."[11] Then, no longer able to bear the agony, she unsuccessfully tried to commit suicide.

Similar situations took place in other ghettos. In Lodz doctors were brought by the so-called "Department of Health" as early as 1941 to try to control outbreaks of typhus, dysentery, diphtheria, and other communicable diseases. Dr. Esther F. recalls that this "health department" was ordered to fight contagious diseases. Since the ghetto was located in the dirtiest section of town, where people were crammed into tiny apartments that frequently lacked plumbing, this was often a losing battle. There was little medication, and rations were far below the minimum for sustaining life. People were so starved and desperate that families frequently kept members who had died in their apartments in order to collect their food rations. Typhus, tuberculosis, and dysentery were rampant; by July 2, 1942, there were about sixteen hundred patients in hospitals and many others waiting to be admitted. Of these conditions Dr. F. states, "That was the tragic realism of desperation."[12] On December 22, 1943, severely ill Jewish patients were discharged from the hospital on Dworska Street in order to make room for Polish children suffering from typhus.[13] In July 1944 the last *Daily Chronicle Bulletin* listed 68,561 inhabitants still remaining in the Lodz ghetto. Most were deported to Auschwitz-Birkenau. Despite the efforts of this "health department," life in the ghetto was extinguished.[14]

In the Kracow Ghetto, Rosalie Schiff recalls that her mother, Helen Baum, who had breast cancer, was forced to undergo a mastectomy without benefit of anesthesia. Rosalie was sixteen at the time, her sister was fourteen, and her brother was ten. Rosalie relates, "Dr. Frisher did not put her to sleep. She was screaming and yelling. I don't know what he gave her. We were waiting outside. There was no need for the pain. They had ether." Rosalie and her mother, brother, and sister were taken to another town. "My mother was very ill. The doctor was gone already, so my sister and I had to remove the stitches. They locked us up in a room with no food, nothing. It was horrid."[15]

The Vilna Ghetto had a hospital with departments of internal medicine, surgery, gynecology, pediatrics, communicable diseases, X ray, and a laboratory. There were over 150 physicians, nurses, and technical personnel on the staff. In 1942 they treated over three thousand patients. Hitler had said: "There are many means by which a systematic and comparatively painless extinction of undesirable races can be attained, at any rate without blood being shed."[16] Thus, following a decree issued on February 5, 1942, which forbade Jews to procreate, deliveries were conducted in secret and newborns hidden. A secret delivery room functioned in the gynecological department at the hospital. Newborn infants were hidden in an area inside the hospital where the mothers could nurse their babies. When the children grew older, they were registered in the Judenrat offices as having been born prior to the date of the ban.[17]

Abram Gerzevitch Suzkever has a somewhat different recollection. According to him, the decree had been issued at the end of December 1941.[18] Regarding his personal experience, Suzkever related during the Nuremberg Trials that after his wife had given birth to a baby boy, he went to the hospital in the evening, after the Germans had left, and found her in tears. After the Jewish physicians had received the order that the Jewish women were not to give birth, they had hidden her child as well as other newborns. When members of the German commission returned to the hospital, however, they heard the newborns crying. Suzkever continues, "She saw one German holding the baby and smearing something under its nose. Afterwards he threw it on the bed and laughed. When my wife picked up the child, there was something black under his nose. When I arrived at the hospital, I saw that my baby was dead. He was still warm."[19]

After the second half of 1942, when the Germans learned of clandestine births, there was an increased number of abortions. In Vilna the Sanitation-Epidemiological Unit was responsible for combating contagious diseases and epidemics. The ghetto was divided into sanitary sectors, each with its own physician and team of nurses. Every sector had a number of women who were in charge of cleanliness and who offered programs and lectures on hygiene and prevention of contagious disease. Restaurants, public kitchens, and bakeries were supervised as well. Despite these measures to improve the quality of life, the ghetto was liquidated in August/September 1943.[20]

Jews in other ghettos underwent similar experiences. Efforts to prevent epidemics and control disease contrasted with the realities of malnutrition, overcrowding, suicides, abuse, and selections. Random killings by the occupying German forces continually increased the number of corpses lying in the streets, leading ultimately to liquidation.

From these ghettos Jews were shipped first to transit camps, then east to be exterminated. Upon arrival, a mother in Westerbork would realize all too soon what it meant if children were allowed to remain with their mothers, whereas in Auschwitz, as Seweryna Szmaglewska notes, "During the sorting [upon the arrival of a transport], the youngest and the healthiest Jewish women in very small numbers entered the camp. Women carrying children in their arms or in carriages, or those who had larger children, were sent into the crematory together with their children."[21] Mengele had a "reasonable" explanation for this:

When a Jewish child is born, or a woman comes to camp with a child already . . . I don't know what to do with the child. I can't set the child free because there are no longer any Jews who live in freedom. I can't let the child stay in the camp because there are no facilities . . . that would enable the child to develop normally. It would not be humanitarian to send a child to the ovens without permitting the mother to be there to witness the child's death. That is why I send the mother and the child to the gas ovens together."[22]

Most Jewish women, if not having first succumbed to the ravages of brutal treatment, starvation, and disease, were ultimately to be consigned to the gas chambers and crematoriums. Yet many survived because of the care given them by the nurses and physicians who were imprisoned with them. In the camps, as in the ghettos, there were primitive infirmaries in which a few overworked physicians and nurses attempted to help their fellow inmates. As Ota Kraus and Erich Kulka describe the conditions at Auschwitz, "One entire half of Camp B1a was used as a hospital. The treatment was the same as in the men's hospital—in fact all the hospital blocks were nothing more than supply centers for the gas chamber."[23]

This statement is supported by Madame Vaillant-Couturier's testimony at Nuremberg: "The Revier was the blocks where the sick were put. This place could not be given the name of a hospital, because it did not correspond in any way to our idea of a hospital." Describing the ordeal of attending sick call, she relates that the block chief first had to authorize a prisoner to go to the Revier. Then, no matter what the weather, the women stood in line for hours, and frequently patients died while waiting. In addition, the SS could come along and take the women who were waiting directly to the gas chamber.[24] Hence Szmaglewska's comment, "in the hospital each sick woman is examined by an SS doctor and when suspected of a contagious disease is exterminated. . . . It is generally accepted that: better to lie in the rain and mud than go to the hospital where only death awaits you."[25] Regarding their conditions, Vaillant-Couturier recalls that four prisoners occupied one bed "less than 1 meter in width." Because patients suffered from various illnesses, diseases passed easily from one to another. There was no possibility of sanitation, and lice were rampant. There were no medications or facilities for washing. Despite these circumstances, even in the infirmary, clever prisoners sometimes managed to elude death. For example, Micheline Maurel recalls, "One morning the *officerine* beat me . . . shouting that she was going to send me to my death. After she left, the *blocova* hurried over and took me into another ward. She put me in a bunk with the light behind me and pinned a new chart at its foot. In this way I was able to pass for another patient."[26]

In Birkenau, Dr. Olga Lengyel became a member of an infirmary staff that was to set up barracks 15, "probably the most dilapidated in the camp," as a new "health facility." According to her description, "The rain leaked through the roof and the walls had enormous, gaping holes. To the right and to the left of the entrance were two small rooms. One was designated the 'infirmary' and the other the 'pharmacy.' A few weeks later, a 'hospital' was installed at the other end of the barrack."[27]

Although there were thirty thousand to forty thousand internees in the camp with her, the infirmary staff consisted of only five women. She describes their day: "We rose at four in the morning. The consultations began at five. The sick, of whom there were often as many as five hundred in a day, had to wait their turns by rows of five. . . . Although we lacked everything, even bandages, we proceeded with fervor, spurred on by our consciousness of the great responsibility."[28]

Szmaglewska recalls a massive typhus epidemic in the women's barracks that killed Jews from Belgium, France, Holland, and Germany. Thus, in the winter of 1943–44, the average mortality rate was about three hundred per day. She states, "The virulence with which typhus has again exploded into epidemic proportions is terrifying. Some go to the hospital and die there, others conceal their illness and remain in the blocks, spreading the disease to the healthy ones, forcing themselves to attend roll calls and dying among their sleeping neighbors. Those who have not already been through typhus will not escape it this time. At night the blocks are filled with moans and delirious cries. . . . Death follows in twenty-four hours after the first symptoms appear." Regarding the appearance of the camp, she relates, "Each morning and evening, a small stack of dead bodies appears outside of every one of the fifteen Revier barracks."[29]

Once in a while, however, if a woman knew the right people, she could receive a modicum of treatment, but this was the exception rather than the rule. For example, Susan Beer came to Auschwitz with her mother and father, who had been a general practitioner before the war. She recalls that as a physician, her father was allowed to receive packages from the non-Jewish prisoners. She relates that once, "I had a terrible infection due to avitaminosis on my leg, and my father treated it through the fence with lotions and salves. Because he was a physician, he was able to get medications from non-Jewish patients who received packages. He even brought me a cup of chicken soup!" These logistics were arranged through a network of nurses and doctors. "Later on, when I had typhus, my father stole the slides confirming my condition from the lab so no one would know my diagnosis. Otherwise, I would have gone to the gas chambers." She remembers that her father did not have to go through roll calls. In addition, because patients sometimes shared food with him from their Red Cross packages, he was able to trade cigarettes for food and could occasionally send his daughter "real white bread, a tomato, an onion. . . ."[30]

While prisoner-doctors attempted to bring comfort to their patients, women who were untrained in aspects of medical care frequently attempted to help one another. For example, because in most cases pregnancy meant certain death, women, often aided by their companions within the barracks, attempted to conceal their enlarged abdomens from the SS. Dr. Gisella Perl states that when she came into Auschwitz, pregnant mothers were urged by the SS to step forward so they could be taken to a different camp where they would receive better care. They were subsequently "beaten with whips, torn by dogs, dragged around by the hair and kicked in the stomach with heavy German boots. Then, when they collapsed, they were thrown into the crematory—alive." Subsequently she delivered babies "on dark nights, when everyone else was sleeping—in dark corners of the camp, in the toilet, on the floor, without a drop of water." After a delivery she would bandage the mother and send her back to work or, when possible, place her in the hospital with a diagnosis of pneumonia.[31] In addition, women imprisoned in Birkenau, when due to deliver, were not taken to the infirmary; births generally took place in secret, in complete silence, in the women's blocks. Afterward many babies were killed by injections. According to the testimony of Madame Vaillant-Couturier, other newborns were "drowned in a bucket of water," and the mothers were told that the babies had been born dead. As Vaillant-Couturier relates, "After dark, the baby is thrown on a pile of corpses, and in that manner we save the mother."[32]

Susan Beer has a slightly different recollection. She spent a year in the Staatsgebeute, a special show camp for Red Cross inspections, which was about an hour away from Birkenau. In this camp there were about a thousand women who did such work as sorting linen, hairdressing, and washing laundry for the SS. The hospital there was clean, and what is interesting, due to their improved nutrition, women regained their menstrual periods. Even there, however, mothers were not allowed to keep their newborn babies. She remembers that when she had typhus and was in the infirmary, a woman's baby was delivered by candlelight. "The nurses left the baby with the mother until they fell asleep. Then they took the child away. It was the kindest thing to do or they would both be killed."[33]

Ruth Elias, three months pregnant, was transported to Auschwitz from Theresienstadt in December 1943. She gave birth on August 4, and the baby was allowed to live in order to provide fodder for Mengele's experiments. Wishing to see how long a newborn could survive without nutrition, he bound the mother's breasts. After seven days a sympathetic physician gave Mrs. Elias a syringe filled with morphine; she killed the suffering infant before Mengele had the opportunity to send them both to the gas chamber. Regarding her memory of this, Mrs. Elias comments, "I didn't want to live anymore."[34]

In an effort to stop the "inferior races" from further procreation, Hitler ordered men to be castrated[35] and women to be sterilized. As early as May 30, 1942, Dr. Carl

Clauberg had appealed to Himmler for "procurement of the necessary equipment" (i.e., Jewish women) to carry out sterilization experiments on female prisoners.[36] With horrifying regularity, Danuta Czech documents the selection of these women as well as male prisoners. During the Nuremberg Trials, Abram Gerzevitch Suzkever, reading from the Russian text entitled "Experiments on Living Persons," related that special hospitals, surgical suites, laboratories, and other departments intended not for treatment but for extermination had been set up within the camps. He continued to testify that other experiments had been carried out as well on women in the hospital blocks of Auschwitz.[37]

According to Czech's entry for November 2, 1942, Dr. Horst Schumann conducted experiments to determine whether or not men and women could be sterilized inexpensively. In barracks 30 of the women's camp in Birkenau, section B-Ia, in block 21, and later in block 10 of the main camp, he tried both X rays and castration.[38] Fifteen of these were girls between the ages of seventeen and eighteen; only a few survived. Regarding these experiments, Suzkever describes how electrodes were placed on the victim's body to burn the ovaries. "A month later . . . the reproductive organs were removed for study. As a result of the destruction of hormones the girls completely changed in appearance and resembled old women."[39]

Madame Vaillant-Couturier told of having been sent to Ravensbruck, which contained a section known as the "'NN' Blocks," *"Nacht und Nebel"* Blocks, "The Secret Block" from which no one was supposed to emerge to see daylight. In these were Polish women identified by the number 7,000 and called "rabbits" because they were to be used as experimental guinea pigs. Selected from convoys specifically because of their straight legs and good health, they were submitted to vivisection by physicians from Berlin who operated in their uniforms, in nonsterile fields, without so much as washing their hands. Because of the high mortality rate, young women refused to go to the Revier and had to be forcibly dragged.[40]

For those there, however, medical care was almost nonexistent. Madame Vaillant-Couturier recalls the experience of her young friend Marie Rubiano, who suffered from tuberculosis and, at the point of exhaustion, obtained permission to go to the Revier. Because the German nurse, Erica, was not quite as evil as some of the others, the young woman was x-rayed, and both lungs were shown to be severely infected. Marie was then sent to block 10, in which tubercular patients were confined. Because these patients were not considered to be "recuperable material," they received no care and remained unwashed. Vaillant-Couturier continues, "There were many patients—several to one bed in three-tier bunks—in an overheated atmosphere, lying between internees of various nationalities, so that they could not even speak to one another. . . . the silence . . . was broken by the yells of the German asocial personnel on duty and, from time to time, by the muffled sobs of a little French girl thinking of her mother and of her country. . . ." On February 9, 1945, along with seventy-two other consumptive women, Marie Rubiano was selected by Dr. Winkleman, "selection specialist at Ravensbruck," to die in the gas chamber.[41]

In the camps physicians differed in their treatment of the women in their care. Dr. Adelaide Hautval, a non-Jewish psychiatrist, had been imprisoned for wearing a yellow star as a protest against the Gestapo's treatment of Jews. Even in Auschwitz she continued to protest against the horrors the prisoners suffered, believing that there were more important things than one's own personal safety. But sometimes she felt that even she had to compromise her professional integrity in the interests of survival. Of this she wrote to Ima Spanjaard many years later, "Nobody could live during the nightmare years who in some instances was not forced to break the rules of traditional behavior. To be or not to be, that was the question. All of us, including myself, were sometimes in situations in which we had to make abnormal decisions. The impossibility of living without 'dirty hands' belonged to that phenomenon."[42] Nonetheless, Pola Plotnicka remembers Dr. Hautval as a noble heroine. In block 10 Dr. Hautval refused to perform hysterectomies, although she cared for the sick day and night. "She did not care what was going to happen to her."[43]

Opinions of Dr. Alina Brewda, however, are more varied. Before being transferred to Auschwitz, she had been a physician in Majdanek. There, although medications and supplies were extremely limited, patients were cared for by a medical staff that was less controlled by the SS. There were no pseudomedical experiments conducted at Majdanek on a mass scale, although some SS physicians conducted some on their own. Hence, female patients were cared for by a dedicated staff, albeit one which still did not work under the best of conditions. According to Jozef Marszalek, "the conditions of treatment at the women's hospital were . . . more bearable from the beginning. What contributed to a better frame of mind of the sick was the smaller number of selections than at the men's hospital."[44]

Ms. Spanjaard's memories of Dr. Alina Brewda in Auschwitz, however, are of a woman who was "clever and quick, but cool and not interested in us" as well as "drunk at times and living in luxury."[45] Dr. Brewda's response to this is, "What can I do when people give it to me?"[46] She was appointed to be the medical head of block 10, where one of her professional duties was to examine the prostitutes. She also tells of having sat at the heads of the young girls who were subjected to operations in order to calm and soothe them. During a court case in which Dr. Dering, one of the physicians involved in the sterilization experiments, claimed that he had been libeled by Leon Uris in *Exodus* (April–May 1964),[47] Dr. Brewda as well as several of the girls she had cared for were called as witnesses. Typifying the way they felt about their treatment was one girl's recollection: "I felt the warm hand of Dr. Brewda. She told me, '*Encore un peu, mon enfant*' (just a little more, my child). I cannot forget it. If it had not been for Dr. Brewda, I should not have lived."[48]

Compared to other prisoners, doctors received relatively favorable treatment. In fact, a doctor became a "favoured prisoner."[49] Dr. Lengyel writes that she and her coworkers no longer had to sleep in the "filth, lice, and stench" of the koya or bunk. They had a room, a basin for washing, soap, if of dubious origin, and blankets. Dr. Albert Haas recalls: "I had finally become a respectable member of the concentration camp society. This did not mean that I could not be hanged, gassed, electrocuted, shot, or beaten to death, but it meant that if any of these ends should befall me, the camp commandant would have to report my death. Now, discounting the unforeseen, I had a reasonable chance of surviving the next several weeks. It was no mean achievement in my circumstances."[50]

According to the recollections of Dr. Haas, the ultimate irony of his survival lay in the fact that his death would necessitate more paperwork for the SS! Nevertheless, going from being an esteemed member of French society to a number must have taken a heavy psychological toll. Life should be worth more than the forms required to record death. "While we waited in the hospital, [*Doctor 117641*] told (a friend) that I believed this assignment would save our lives. He did not seem convinced, but I was. Maybe this is what the SS physician on our arrival had meant when he told us to get in touch with him."[51] This same reprieve from death may have saved his wife Nora. "She said that as a nurse she was supposedly safe from Clauberg's experiments. She lived with fifteen other nurses . . . in a separate room on the first floor."[52]

Another medical practitioner in Auschwitz notes: "When I began to know more people in and around the hospital, I realized that as a doctor-nurse I was sort of upper middle class in camp society. As a member of the staff I received a double ration of soup and occasionally some extra bread. The better fed I looked, the more authority I seemed to have."[53] Even at the end, when Auschwitz was being abandoned, because he was a physician, Susan Beer's father was spared from going on the Death March to Ravensbruck. Nevertheless, even for the Jewish inmates who served as medical personnel life was far from desirable, and most recall their years in the camps with horror.

Whether physicians, nurses, or patients, each of the women in this book endured the unendurable, and they shared experiences which are beyond our comprehension. Many helped others to bear their suffering as well, and to those who were beyond help, they brought, if nothing else, a measure of comfort in their last moments of life. Those who survived, despite efforts to snuff out their lives, bore a new generation that was never to have been born.

The Talmud tells us, "Whosoever preserves a single soul . . . scripture ascribes [merit] to him as though he had preserved a complete world."[54] The same can be applied to each of the women whose narratives we relate and so many others like them, whose voices and acts of compassion contributed in measures both great and small to the survival of their sisters in sorrow.

Theresienstadt: The Limbo of the Damned

there were no wails but just the sounds
rising and trembling through the timeless air,

The sounds and sighs of untormented grief
burdening these groups, diverse and teeming,
made up of men and women and of infants.
—Dante Alighieri, *Dante's Inferno*

Theresienstadt ghetto, the "model" camp, had been termed "Hitler's Gift to the Jews." So-called "privileged" Jews from Germany, Austria, Holland, and Denmark were sent into the limbo of Theresienstadt, where, rather than being actually exterminated, prisoners died of hunger, torture, beatings, and disease.[1]

Following the Nazi occupation of Czechoslovakia, Jewish leaders, hoping to avoid deportation to Poland, aided SS leaders who wished to stay in Czechoslovakia rather than be sent to the Russian front in their attempt to ghettoize Czech Jews within the country. Although Jewish leaders wanted the ghetto to remain in Prague, the SS rejected the idea, and Hans Guenther, overseer of the Protectorate Jews, ordered Jewish leaders to look for another site with fewer than six thousand inhabitants.

Although not the choice of the Jews, the decision was made to place the ghetto in the small community of Theresienstadt. Thus, SS Colonel Reinhard Heydrich established the Terezin concentration camp on November 24, 1941.[2] Almost scenic, with broad streets, a large square, and two large and two small parks, Terezin consisted of a small town and a former Czech prison known as the Small Fortress, just two miles away. The area had been named after the Austrian empress Maria Theresa. Encircled by a double layer of embankments and containing dark, dank chambers, Theresienstadt had a high level of underground water, as the Eger River, a tributary of the Elbe, flowed just outside. There was no industry to speak of, and the SS planned to house eighty-eight thousand Jews in its 219 houses and fourteen military barracks and administrative buildings.[3] By mid 1942 all of the original population had been moved out, and the town became a prison for the Jews. Theresienstadt served three purposes simultaneously: as a transit camp through which Jews of Bohemia and Moravia would be sent to the death camps of Poland; as a death camp in and of itself, as nearly one fifth of its prisoners died there; and as a site for propaganda, which the SS would use to show the world that Jews there were being treated "well," thereby hoping to cover the reality of the ultimate fate of the inmates.

From the time of its inception until April 20, 1945, approximately 140,000 men, women, and children from Czechoslovakia, Germany, Austria, the Netherlands, Denmark, Slovakia, and Hungary had been deported to Theresienstadt. At the end of the war, another 13,000 prisoners were sent there from the abolished camps of Poland and Germany.[4] Regarding the fate of those who passed through the camp, Konnilyn Feig writes, "34,000 Jews perished in Terezin from 'natural causes.' As the ghetto became a funnel to the killing centers, the Nazis sent 83,000 Jews, including small children, to the extermination camps in the east."[5] The camp was liberated by the Russian army on May 8, 1945.[6] Of those who had left on transports, fewer than 4,000 survived.[7]

The conditions in the various infirmaries and the sacrifice of those who volunteered to care for the sick are reflected in the oral history of Hana Muller Bruml, which follows.[8] Her narrative was constructed by interweaving a previous interview conducted for the United States Holocaust Memorial Museum, a telephone interview conducted by Roger Ritvo, and a personal interview I conducted at her apartment. She spoke with assurance and intelligence of her experiences as she went from Prague to Theresienstadt, then on to Auschwitz and finally to Nachod, where she worked in an ammunition factory until she was liberated on May 6, 1945.

D. P.

Chapter Three

Hana Muller Bruml

"I WAS A NURSE IN THERESIENSTADT"

· · ·

I was born in Prague, Czechoslovakia, on May 30, 1922. I was the only child, the first grandchild in the family, and my mother's only live birth. A child due a year before me had died just before delivery. My mother had at least five or six miscarriages after me. She was a rather sickly woman who had frequent pneumonia. She was very shy, very sickly, and had enormously heavy, thick glasses because she was so near-sighted. I was very independent, almost compensating for her. My character was much more like my aunt's, my mother's sister, and my father's, who were much more outgoing.

I was very fortunate because we lived with my grandmother and grandfather. All my first warm memories are about my grandfather who died three months before my third birthday. My grandmother was with us as I grew up. Her birthday was five days before mine, so we celebrated together. She would also tell me stories, fairy tales which I had heard about fifty-five times but wanted to hear again from her. When I started going to school, she would cross the street to help me cross back again. I was more concerned about her crossing safely, but she was concerned about me. She was, in many ways, the mother on whom I patterned my life. She was bedridden most of the time, but her mind was fine. She had a very orderly closet in which she kept a bag with her white shroud. According to Jewish custom, she wanted to be buried in this shroud, in the same grave as my grandfather. Although we sent it with her to Theresienstadt, she never had a chance to use it.

I had scarlet fever at age seven; I was in the first grade. My parent's house and the whole schoolroom had to be fumigated. I was the only Jewish child in a children's hospital run by nuns in Prague. People couldn't visit me, although my mother was with me the first week in a private room. After the first three days, the strep was gone and I felt fine. I was up and around and bored stiff. I saw the children down the hall playing and having fun, so I said, "Mother, please go home, go home, go home," and she did. I couldn't see my parents for six weeks, although I could see them from the window. I really preferred being with the other children, most of whom were quite poor. Because I had more than they did, I was in charge of lending them my toys. In the evening, the children had to kneel and pray, but I refused to do so. I said, "I'm not going to go out and kneel, but if you want I will pray by myself in bed." In a way, the nuns respected it.

In the fifth week, I got an ear infection for which there were no antibiotics. It was a very distinct pain. I was up all night, thinking it was teeth, but it turned out to be my ear. They let me go home after the drum burst from the infection; that was a relief.

For the first five years I went to a Jewish school, which was more Zionistic than religious. After that I went to gymnasium, which was the academic level. Then I went into a business school and started working.

As an eleven or twelve year old, I went to collect money from my father's builders so he could make his payroll. In the beginning they looked at this little girl who came to collect money and would call to my father, "Is that on the level?" He said, "Yes, it's okay." Nobody knew that I was collecting money for the payroll. I gave them a receipt and signed it. At that time I read a book about the Marranos. I remember so clearly telling my grandmother, "Aren't we fortunate that we live in the twentieth century in Czechoslovakia, that such a thing cannot happen to us!" Six short years later, it happened to us, but much worse. One doesn't realize how vulnerable one is.

I was fortunate that we were able to have some social life and go to dancing schools—with the long dress and formalities. At that time, I was going with a student named Rudolph (we called him "Rudla," or "Rudie"). I was about sixteen and he was nineteen. We got married November 14, 1939, at the city hall. Because there was no separate housing for us, I went home and he went home in the evening. His family lived a couple of blocks away from us, so it was no big problem.

When I was seventeen, things were starting to get bad. I remember the day the Germans came. I remember the place, the street where I stood. It was a cold, snowy day, and they were pulling in. I was by myself. It was not far, maybe three-quarters of a mile from where we lived. We were watching them on their wagons, with their tanks, their half-tracks, with guns pointing to the rooftops. We knew that the screw was going to become tighter. We knew what was happening in Austria, but somehow we still had some foolish idea that we were safe in Czechoslovakia. Nevertheless, when the Germans came, they went to the Jewish *Kultusgemeinde*, the religious and cultural community, and wanted the names of the Jews. From there they got the names for the transports. We were so stupid! We went and registered!

We had to give up our jewelry, radios, and so forth because if we listened to the radio, it was dangerous. We tried to hide a few things with friends. Some were very cooperative and kept them. Others were afraid. Some friends decided that if we didn't come back, they would keep our things. It very much depended on the person.

Hana and Charles Bruml, Alexandria, Virginia, June 14, 1993.
Photo by Diane Plotkin.

My father's workshop was taken away, and he didn't have any other means of support. My parents' maid, who had worked with us for ten or eleven years, was my mother's age. She was very helpful and undemanding. She went shopping and did what she could, but her ration tickets were regular ration tickets, while ours were marked with a "J," so we couldn't shop when there was food in the stores. We could shop only at certain hours for certain things. Nevertheless, she was very instrumental in helping us.

We had all kinds of difficulties during that time: getting supplies, buying food, working, and going places. I remember going on the street and meeting one of my school friends. By that time I had the star. As we came closer to each other, we walked slower, thinking, "Should I stop? Should I talk? Who was it worse for? Her? Is it worse for me? What should we do?" So we slowly came together, looked at each other, winked, and passed again. It was that sort of situation. You had to think, "Wait a minute. Is today Saturday? Saturday, I cannot go to this place. Friday, I cannot go to that place." The restrictions were getting tighter.

As the Germans closed in, we had to go into increasingly cramped quarters. Rudie's parents had a big subdivided apartment. Each bedroom was given to another family, so there was really nowhere to go. Then one of the families was sent to a camp, so for a couple of months we had one of the bedrooms. In the meantime, he got scarlet fever. At that time, when you had scarlet fever, you had to go into a hospital for six weeks because they thought you were infectious until your skin started to peel.

Hitler closed all the universities, so I couldn't go on with my studies. Rudie had a brother, Karel, who was finishing his M.D. degree. Only two Jewish people were allowed to get their degrees. Although they awarded the degree to everybody, they gave the two Jewish fellows their diplomas in the bathroom.

At that time, I had an infection in my finger, which radiated up my arm. Of course, I couldn't go to the hospital; at that point we were not allowed to use the hospital. Later there was one private hospital which was very crowded, but Jews were able to use it. But at that time, there was none, and the infection was worsening. The Aryan, non-Jewish fiancée of my brother-in-law, Karel, took me without my star into the regular hospital. She was a physician. At great danger to her, she had me operated on and took me home by taxi. We were not allowed to use taxis. Otherwise I wouldn't have been able to get help.

I worked in what they used to call a Palestine Office. There were still people able to move, to emigrate. When you signed your paper for emigration, if I was Hana Schiff at that time, I had to sign it as "Hana Sarah Schiff." All women had to take "Sarah," and all the men "Israel" as a middle name. They had to give a list of all the property they were going to take in their suitcases. They had to pay that much for this and that much for that. Jacob Edelstein was the head of the Palestine Office and knew some people there, which later became very important to me.

We listened to the orders to go and register people so they could be sent by transport. When you went depended on what you did and where you lived. You were continuously threatened: "Am I going to be on the next transport?" We knew daily how many left. We had lists of people printed in the newspaper. Lists of people who were shot or hanged were posted. A friend of mine was among them. The screw was tightening with more regulations.

At one point, Heydrich, the protector of Czechoslovakia, was killed when two paratroopers from England threw a hand grenade under his car. Lidice was the Czech village where, as revenge for the affair, the Germans went and killed the men and many of the women and some of the children. Those who were left they sent to

Ravensbruck. I knew some of them. It was not known that some men from Theresienstadt were commandeered to go to Lidice to clean up the sheep, goats, and cows. At the same time, in Prague, the Germans were looking for someone on a bicycle. They came around us, looking and confiscating bicycles.

My parents went to Theresienstadt at the end of July, 1942. They got their suitcases and left in a transport. I went with them as far as I could before the collection place. I was saying goodbye to my father and to my mother, but much more emotionally to my father. I really knew in my heart of hearts that I was never going to see them. Our maid, Maru, was in touch with them through some gendarme and sent them packages for a while, but I knew that I was not going to see them anymore. My grandmother went with them. They carried her down the staircase on a litter and put her with the other old people on the bottom of a moving van. Her last words were, "Love each other. Be good to each other." As they carried her down the steps, there was no complaint, just kind of a blessing. From my mother, I know that when she came to the gathering place, she became confused with all the commotion and all that craziness. She didn't know what was going on, what was happening to her. She died three weeks after arriving at Theresienstadt. I was told she was begging for a cube of sugar from somebody who came to see her. The original records showed where she was buried in one of the last mass graves at that time. We went to the field; you could still see where they dug the furrows, put the bodies in, and put the soil over them in heaps and valleys. The Germans registered which row it was in, so we could count the rows, figure out about where she was, and put some flowers on it.

Rudla and I were living with my in-laws. I remember it so clearly. We were in bed reading John Steinbeck's *The Grapes of Wrath* when the knock on the door and our "invitation" to the transport came. I don't think I ever finished reading the book. We packed the suitcases very carefully because these were the only possessions we were going to have. We were at the collection station for a couple of days before they organized everything. This gathering place used to be exhibition hall. Over the PA system came, "Anybody who has money on him or gold or cigarettes or matches will be shot." In the lining of my coat, I had a metal box of Yardley talc. In that box I had some jewelry. Although we heard all of this, we had to protect ourselves somehow.

When we fifteen hundred people came to the gathering station, we were told only a thousand will go. All the women will be pulled out. Then they pulled us back. They took the person next to my husband and gave me another number. Through all the years in Theresienstadt I went as "Transport BA, Number 1101."

We came to Bohusovice, the train stop for Theresienstadt. My parents had already been there for three weeks. My husband was rather weak and sickly at that point. We carried a big bag—each tried to hold one handle—in which was mostly food. We each had a bed roll. On our backs, we each had a knapsack with just a few things. As it turned out, what we carried with us were the only things we had for the next few years.

We had to walk about three kilometers from Bohusovice to Theresienstadt. We carried just the knapsacks on our backs and the hand luggage. After we came to Theresienstadt, we never got the suitcases. Our transport gave these suitcases as a "gift" to the German nation for the "bombed-up" people. I was so glad we contributed something! So the precious fifty kilos we were allowed to take, which we put together with great care, were all gone. All I had for the three years in Theresienstadt was in a knapsack on my back. After that I had less and less, and finally only my body, but you were glad you had your body, for it meant that you were alive.

When we came off the train in Bohusovice, I happened to see Jacob Edelstein, the head of the ghetto government. He said, "Try to get yourself approved for work as soon as possible." I didn't know what it meant, but I went with all possible speed in order to protect us.

At that time, all the former citizens of Theresienstadt had been evacuated, and it was a Jewish ghetto. Therefore, we were able to move around. It had once been a military town with barracks. Each *kasserne*, or barrack, was named after a German town. There was "Dresden," and "Magdeburg." "Hohenelbe" was for the older people and sick people. When I went by this hospital, a doctor was leaning out of the window. I said, "You need some help?" And he said, "Yes, get yourself a permit." Without any further training, I started working as a nurse. I was always fairly well rated.

When we came to Theresienstadt, all the nurses who worked with the infectious diseases lived in a former brewery. We had two little rooms in the back of the building. If you went to the last room, you had to pass through all the other rooms. The first room was very small, but there were eight people living in it. All the nurses who came in from the day shift and the night shift were in eight bunks. Because the nurses lived together in these very tight quarters, intimacy with your husband was very difficult.

In my room, which was the second, there were three bunks. I remember in the room ahead of ours was Sister Miriam, a kind, gentle soul. She was a nun from Vienna, Austria, of a Jewish background. She had converted to Christianity and had been a Catholic nun for about thirty years. Because she was of Jewish origin, they brought her to Theresienstadt. She was in her fifties when she came. In the beginning she was very embarrassed because she was bald headed. She was shaven and wore a wig when she went in public, but all of a sudden she had to show herself without hair. Later we were all bald in Auschwitz. For her, it was shocking, destroying her life. Nevertheless, in spite of everything, she showed a great gentleness and kindness towards everybody. She worked as a nurse, the only one who really had some training in nursing. None of us nurses had training; we just went there and the doctors trained us. She was a very kind, calm, sweet person. From what I have heard, she eventually died of cancer in Theresienstadt.

At that time men could visit. We got sheets as a little curtain, and privacy was minimal. When you washed your hair, you used water you brought from somewhere. On the second floor there was a kitchen, and behind it, three or four rooms. In the kitchen were old ladies from Vienna who tended the oven, warmed up things for us, and heated what they could. Nice little "old ladies," they were probably much younger than I am now, but for us they seemed like little old ladies.

We got rationed soap of horrible quality, like a little stone, but every little bit of that soap was precious. I remember being in the yard, washing my laundry with this little bit of soap, and there was a little left over. At one point we were issued money and could buy things with it. One of the things you could buy was a little bit of mustard, a little bit of ketchup, or another piece of this terrible soap, if it was available.

You could leave your laundry in a certain place, and maybe three weeks later you got it back again. There was also a shoe repair, where you could get some shoes fixed because we could not replace anything, but they were only open when we had our work hours. It was very difficult, but we worked together; our life was there.

There were hearses which had been brought from all over Czechoslovakia, all over Bohemia, from Jewish cultural groups. They brought corpses to the cemetery in hearses. Everything was transported in these hearses: sick people, bread, wood. These were the only wagons.

There were two small houses right opposite of the main *kasserne,* where the leadership was. The Germans, in their organization, took away all the names of the streets. Because Theresienstadt was built as a grid, they called the lengthwise streets "L" (for "Lang") and the crosswise ones "Q" (for "Quer"). Typical German. So these two houses were L-17 and L-19, Q-17 and Q-19. These were two smallish villas that were joined together. That was to become a hospital. The lower floor, one big room, was where the doctors lived. Six doctors slept in the same room. They were all males. One of them died of a kidney infection. The administrator of the hospital had the room behind them, and across from the entrance, on the other side was the hospital. There were about four rooms, one after the other.

The children were in iron beds, one next to the other. There were not even little aisles between them because there was no space. If laundry was possible, maybe it was changed every week, maybe every two weeks for these children. We slept in the other house around the corner, not very far away.

At first we had children with whooping cough. Then came a very big epidemic of scarlet fever. The whole hospital was converted to a scarlet fever hospital. At the time, it was thought that scarlet fever is contagious for six weeks. I worked at that hospital because I had had scarlet fever and felt I had enough immunity to safely be in a hospital with scarlet fever patients.

It took about a good nine months to a year before the scarlet fever epidemic ebbed, and eventually there was typhoid. We did get typhoid shots in our shoulders, not in our arms, so we could work. We had a little group of children who had scarlet fever and abdominal typhoid.

There were two little rooms in the back of the building. We had two teenage boys and six little girls, three little girls in one room and three in another. The oldest was sixteen, and the youngest one six. One day they had brought in a little feverish girl. I said, "What's your name?" She said, "Misha." I said, "Misha Lausher!" She was my cousin's daughter, a very bright child. She was only six years old, but she knew what her temperature had been for the last three days.

Misha drew a picture of a garden and a tree with a bird on it. The bird had an open beak and out of it came letters. I said, "What is this?" She said, "It whistles," and gave me the note. I kept her drawings. Her parents couldn't see her; I was her only contact with the outside world. I would take what she had written or drawn, iron it out, and carry it out to them. She survived in Theresienstadt because her parents were making toys for the Germans. It was just luck. Most children recovered only to be killed with all the nurses I knew who went with them. This was such a terrible tragedy.

We didn't have any disinfectants. All we had was us, kindness, and trying to bathe the children. You were supposed to contain these children who were basically all right after the first fever was gone. Many children got impetigo, and we painted them with gentian violet to neutralize it. That was the only thing we had. These children had all of these violet spots on themselves and the bed sheets. They were trying to play and that helped them. Bathe them, entertain them, and maintain them so they wouldn't scratch themselves and fight. We were lucky if we changed beds every week or two because there were no facilities.

I had sort of a black sweatsuit and a white apron. We had only one advantage in that infectious disease hospital. There was a small bathroom, and we had a container. We were able to make a fire and heat water, so two of us could take a bath at the same time. Then we put the same clothes on because we didn't have much else. I was in that hospital for quite a while.

There was quite a bit of TB and a big TB ward. Alna Schtreizer had a brother who was sixteen, a beautiful, smart young kid. He had a very pervasive TB, and he died in that first hospital we were in. I remember his beautiful long lashes. Kids with TB had long eyelashes. He was in the room with everybody else, but they just put his bed a little bit towards one side. I remember Hana; I can't think of her last name right now. She was my age and had TB. Everybody from her family brought her food, trying to maintain her, but she's gone forever too. We had one beautiful bright thirteen year old die of TB. His brother's still alive and is a friend of mine.

It was hard work with the children. We worked twelve-hour shifts. We had to do everything. That means we had to serve the food and wash the dishes and the floors. We had to make the fire. We had to wash the patients. We had to take out the urine and the feces. We knew the only infection from typhoid is through excretions, so when we dealt with excretions, we put Lysol in the water and washed our hands. That was the only thing we had. There was always some sort of a container with Lysol where we put our hands when we carried anything out. All the time hands in Lysol. I actually liked the smell; it's a clean smell. Lysol did help.

For parents it was heart-breaking. They were outside and didn't know what was happening to their children. There were no visiting hours. Mothers could visit only through the windows because it was so crowded and many of these things were infectious. They didn't know how their children were. We were the only contact. In the meantime, they were afraid they would be called into transports and the children left there.

They brought us food from the central kitchen in big kettles, and we put it into smaller containers for the children. Twice a week we got some sort of dumpling, and once a week this caramel sauce. That was a big deal. Otherwise we got some sort of soup; it might have had some vegetables in it, but that was still very good. In the morning it was black coffee. We used to say, "You take one bean, put it on a string, wave it over the pot, and that's what makes coffee." Of course, it was not coffee at all, but it was warm and black. Once a week we got some sort of tiny piece of bakery. It was not much, but for us it was great, and there was a little bit of milk. I remember that because we worked as nurses in infectious diseases, we got a little bit of extra milk. Otherwise we wouldn't have gotten any milk at all. We did get a little tiny bit of extra food. But it was very little, and because my husband was sickly and he couldn't work, I gave him the extra.

The first doctor was Hans Schauffer, a pediatrician from Brno. He was very good with the children. Eventually he had three young doctors with him. The irony was that he was deathly afraid of typhus, not typhoid. He worked with typhoid all the time. Typhoid is an intestinal disease, which is different.[1] Typhus is transferred from person to person by lice.[2] He died of typhus later in the camp. It was like he had a premonition. He was always afraid he would die of typhus, and he did.

At that time there were no antibiotics, no vaccination. We did get a sulfa drug made by Bayer called Prontosil. It was good, but it was red and dyed everything red. The urine was red, the children were red, we were red. Because the children were throwing up, even their vomit was red. Then we got Cibazol, one of the first antibiotics made by CIBA. That was precious, but very rare. Some people got it for exchange from outside and smuggled it in.

We had a few people who had measles. With measles you can get complications of pneumonia, so for that the Cibazol was very helpful. We didn't know how much to medicate and didn't know the strength of these broad-based, primitive antibiotics. We also had *heilgas*,[3] glycerin and ammonium chloride. They put it on wounds. It was very primitive and haphazard.

When there were fewer children, they brought in the grown-ups. I left that hospital and worked for a while in a clinic with two urologists. In Theresienstadt's Hohenelbe, in urology, they had an EKG instrument and could give people EKGs. I learned quickly. One of the gentlemen who had to come in was Professor Alfred Cohn, from the Czech University. He was the one who had identified and discovered the function of paratyphoid. Until then, people knew about typhoid but not paratyphoid. Many people, after an operation on the thyroid gland, got tetany. He discovered that the paratyphoid gland controls the calcium in the body. He was a gentleman of eighty years of age, and he had problems with his prostate because an older gentleman with an enlarged prostate retains urine, so he came in to have a catheter inserted for his bladder to be emptied. Mostly older gentlemen came in with infections, but again, there was not much medication available.

There was a woman who had scarlet fever. Then she got measles and pneumonia. She got mostly aspirin because that is what we had. The doctors did all they could to help her, and she did survive, but her heart was damaged.

There were people with all kinds of illnesses. I remember this one particular woman from Germany with some internal problem. I don't know what it was. She was a nurse in Germany, so she knew what was going on. Twenty-four hours a day she would not move from her bed. She squirreled away the little food she got to give to her husband, who was much older than she. Yet she needed it so urgently. She was in a pitiful, debilitated condition. I talked in German to her, and I got her at least to the point where she put her feet on the floor. But all we could do was move her body to the other side of the bed so we could make it. I felt a real victory that I got her to move. Holding on to her, I got her to be a little bit more alive, to walk three steps in front of the bed and three steps back. She gave me the big plastic apron she had brought with her from Germany. She would never need to use it again as a nurse. I didn't want to take it, but I had to because for her, it was the best she could give to me. I took real personal interest in her. I don't know what happened to her or to anybody else.

In that room, there were at least twelve beds in one tier about six inches apart. We had another woman who had some sort of an internal problem and another woman with dysentery. That's where I learned about it. There were no medications for it at that time.

Across the yard there was a laundry where a mother and child lived. They didn't want them anywhere else. The child was severely retarded. He was six years old and about two feet long. He couldn't sit up or respond to your gaze. He was a total "it," and for six years, the mother had loved him and taken care of him. I'm sure she went to Auschwitz with him and no further. When they took "it" away, they took away her whole life anyhow. The child was so pitiful, and she was so pitiful with that child. In the same hospital we had a fifteen-year-old girl. She was big and strong, but her mind was like that of a five year old. You had to take her to the bathroom and wipe her off. Her parents brought her these little children's books for two or three year olds, and that's what she read. She was severely retarded, but she was still a human being who responded to you and looked at you and laughed at you. But this other was a total nothing.

In that house we had a young boy aged sixteen, who had a kidney disease. He became very weakened. I was still strong; I put him on my shoulder and carried him to the yard so at least he could see a little sky. These were the kinds of things we could do.

There was one *kasserne* for old people. They had the worst medical care. I had duties with the older people, but it was pitiful. They were treated terribly because whom do you care for first? They didn't have enough food or care. Older people didn't have anything to exchange; they died from hunger. The hunger was particularly bad in 1942 and 1943. For them it was the most difficult part. There I found my grandfather's sister, Antonia, who was in her eighties at the time. One day I was allowed to give out food, some sort of boiled potato. She was so happy because I was able to give her an extra one.

Through my entire time in Theresienstadt, I remember only one female doctor. She was with the old folks. If somebody was dying, we had to bring in a doctor. Every night somebody died. To enter the main door of the older patients' kasserne, you had to walk across a big yard with big trees. She was scared stiff to walk across that yard, afraid of the shadows. I had night duty, so I went. I, who was about twenty at that time, walked her across the yard so she could fill out the papers for the Germans.

Then I worked in a hospital where there was encephalitis. They had wooden beds and people slept most of the time. There was nothing. We just had to wait until the infection was over, until the body healed itself. Jewish doctors examined them and could diagnose them, but that's about all. There was nothing much we could do.

There were some emergency operations. I remember a lady who had scarlet fever and got a terrible infection in her hand. One of the children's doctors opened her hand, drained out all kinds of pus, and closed it again. He did an extremely good job. I don't remember what kind of anesthesia they used; maybe it was ether, one of those sprays that stinks. I was very excited to see how an operation was done.

We had people coming to the clinic after surgery for care. We had one woman who had a breast removed for cancer. From the infection after surgery, she got erysipelas.[4] It was horrible. She had to be bandaged because there was pus, but you couldn't give out new clean bandages. She was a wonderful, cheery woman with a great attitude. In spite of the pain and the horror of the infection, in her state she took these bandages to whatever home she had, washed them herself, brought them back, and we put them on again. She was getting some medication, but I don't remember what it was. It was minimal because whatever medication we had was minimal. As a matter of fact, I touched her and got erysipelas on my earlobe, so I was all bandaged. I also got hepatitis. I had yellow eyes (from jaundice) but I got over it.

If somebody got pregnant and they knew what was going on, they had the baby aborted. The abortions were performed by Dr. Hahn and Dr. Polak from Brno, who were gynecologists. They were very skillful doctors who really did wonders under impossible situations and who tried to be very humane and as kind as possible. Nobody talked about it, but it was a sheer necessity because it meant survival for the mother. I was in gynecology in the Hamburg kasserne one time and saw a couple of them done. I don't know how much I assisted actually; at the time I was a total novice. He would have told me, "Give me this, that." You took increasingly larger instruments to open the cervix. Then they took long prongs and delivered the baby. After a couple of hours, the mother went back to where she lived. We had one woman who was pregnant. A few weeks before the end of the war, she was taken to another camp, but they had to do a high forceps delivery. The child was brain damaged and didn't live very long, but the mother had gone through the whole pregnancy in the camp and we sort of protected her. We didn't have very tight fitting clothes; you did what you could.

There was a big ward for mental patients. They had bars on the windows. When you went by, they were screaming and hollering. In the old mental hospitals, the only thing they could do was to wrap them in cold sheets; that was all that was available. I knew a sweet, dear, gentle lady who was working with them. Of course, that unit was cleared out very quickly.

At one point towards the end, in one of the special rooms we had two men, Rudy Cohen from Germany and Robert Kohn from Czechoslovakia. They both had scarlet fever and typhoid. First they were upstairs. When they brought Rudy in, he was not so bad. At night he walked around, bending over the other people, and probably infected somebody else. That's how Robert got typhoid. Robert, who was still sick and had high fever, was a human being you could talk with. But as Rudy, the German, was just getting worse, his fingers were split and full of pus. He was just full of pus all over. I don't know what he had besides the typhoid. One morning, when we were coming off duty, we said, "Is Rudy still alive?" We expected him to die any moment. I came on duty and he was still alive, in terrible shape. Robert had a pocket watch hanging on the wall. Rudy was on the right and Robert on the left. Robert asked me, "How much longer can he live?" I just had to tell him something because I could hear the labored breathing. It was getting shorter and shorter. We could see it was coming to an end. So, just off the top of my head, I said, "Half an hour." He died in half an hour, the first death from typhoid we had in the hospital. Robert would never forgive himself. He got well and Rudy died. After he got well, Robert worked in the kitchen, peeling potatoes. Once in a while he brought me an extra potato. He did not survive.

There was a man who was sent from Theresienstadt to a campsite in some woods to do something which he found terribly obnoxious. So he thought it would help him if he drank some sort of a disinfectant or something. He drank it so it would make him sick for a while and they would take him away, but it completely ruined his intestines. He had continuous bloody, watery diarrhea. Whatever he ate went out, and he just got weaker and weaker and couldn't make it to the bathroom. He had one of those night potties next to the bed, and that's where he sat. He really ruined himself completely. I don't know how long he lasted. He defecated himself to death. It was just one tragedy after the other.

At that time, they started sending transports of the older Germans. They told them they were going into a sanitorium. It was cold in winter and hot in summer, but they came from the train in fur coats and big hats. The ghetto had sixty thousand people instead of the six thousand in normal times. They were put under the roof of the big kasserne. These were huge roofs with huge wooden beams. You didn't know if they were sleeping or if they were dead already.

Most of the work in Theresienstadt was done by young Czech Jews because we were the main occupants. I was delegated to go and help out, and they would say, "If Hitler only knew what the Czech Jews are doing to us!" The hygiene there was impossible. There were no bathrooms, but they still couldn't comprehend it; they couldn't put it together. The survival rate was very small.

We were forever living under a threat: Who is going to be in the next transport? My aunts came through Theresienstadt in the beginning of October, 1942, and then went on. My aunt Eva was closest to me; we were four years apart. She had two children: Raymond was sixteen at that time and Joe was twelve. My aunt was very near-sighted, just like my mother. She was legally blind. Because I was a nurse, I was able to go with her to the gathering place, but they wouldn't even let them come into Theresienstadt. They kept them there in the gathering place as they arrived, immediately prepared for a transport to go on. We did everything to get them out, but we couldn't. So I took Raymond and Joe out of there, brought them to where we lived, and put them in my bed. They had boots on. I put the two pairs of boots under my bed. They slept together so they would at least get some rest. My aunt told me, "I know I'm not going to survive. I know I'm not going to be back, but I know that you will take care of the children." And I would have, had they survived.

On the way to Auschwitz Eva threw a card addressed to Jiri Pollack my schoolmate out of the window. After the war, I met him; he told me that he had the postcard. Somebody had picked it up and mailed it. They were the first transport to Auschwitz from Theresienstadt. No women or children and not too many of the men survived. They arrived on the 27th of October, 1942.

In Prague, they had brought in a darling three or four year old, little Frankie. The parents were Polish Jews who had escaped from Poland and were going to go to France. They were poor people escaping with this little child who got scarlet fever and had to go to the hospital. They were not allowed to take him out of the hospital, but they had to go in the transport. They were sent away, and this little child was left alone in the hospital. My sister-in-law, who didn't have children, befriended him. We were already in Theresienstadt, but she was not, so he finally had another mother. Then they sent him by transport from Prague by himself, just with a number. When he came to Theresienstadt, my husband and I went to visit him; he was just totally confused. "What's going on? "Who are we?" My sister-in-law was transported to Auschwitz holding him by the hand, and therefore, she went to the gas with him.

In October, 1943, we heard that this transport of two hundred children from Poland was going and they were looking for nurses to go with them. They were to be deloused, washed, bathed, dressed, and prepared for a trip to Switzerland. For volunteering, they were supposed to protect our families. I was still with Rudolph, but I volunteered and was accepted. I had my few things packed, but was told that anybody who was married cannot go—only single people. I knew some of the nurses who went. They went to Auschwitz where the children were annihilated. They went straight to the gas.[5]

The worst part was that we were continuously in uncertainty. There was a Damocles sword hanging over you all the time. You never knew how much time you had for what. Daily life was difficult. We lived so close together. As crowded as we were, hygiene was poor and laundry was impossible. In summer, it was suffocatingly hot, so sometimes people tried to sleep out in the yard. Fleas were a pain in the neck. They were multiplying and biting, which made it difficult to rest. It was hard to get rid of them because people in the barracks lived in three-story little cubicles. If you were able to kill a few, more came. You couldn't go and air your stuff or disinfect. Then came the bedbugs.

There were periods, like windows of permission, when you were able to get packages, and some people were getting packages from abroad. The Danes were the best off; they were able to get a monthly five-kilo—not a pound, but eleven pounds—package with salami, butter, and cheeses from Denmark. That was the gift of the Danish government to the few Danish Jews in Theresienstadt. There were also a number of prominents, Germans and Austrians, who during the First World War got either the Iron Cross or one of the very high medals. For some reason, they were protected in Theresienstadt and not sent on. During the time Edelstein, who was a wonderful man, was *Judenältester*; he did what he could. But he himself was deported, and we had other *Judenältester*, which made things worse. Nevertheless, there was this tremendous, vibrating cultural life. I remember seeing a whole production of *Die Fledermaus.* I remember going to a poetry reading. There were philosophical debates and concerts. There was this need to live very intensively. I think this was the essence of Theresienstadt. You had these few years, so you had to live them so intensively. You had to use every minute.

Then I was hospitalized with pneumonia. I just remember that I was in a hospital, and Ruth [Reiser] was with me. Upstairs was a men's department and her husband—I don't know what he had—was there. I remember that I borrowed the book *Fleur de Mal*, by Baudelaire, from him.

I had middle ear infection, and they had to trepanate my ear drum. I sat in a chair while they punctured it. Things of that sort one had to endure. You either got well or you didn't. There were not many choices. I would have gone in September, 1943, but it saved me; I was taken off that transport.

My husband was in the men's barracks and was really going down the drain. He didn't wash properly. It was always a very bad sign when you didn't keep up your personal hygiene. I had to go into the *kasserne*—the men knew me—and clean up his bed. He was sickly and really couldn't do much. It was getting worse and worse. In many ways, he was resentful that I could work. When I came after work on the night shift, I wanted to sleep during the day, and he woke me up.

The marriage was getting very difficult. I was seventeen at that time and naive. As time went on, I realized more and more that the marriage could not last. Things got so bad that I really couldn't tolerate it anymore, and the marriage ended. Even if my husband had survived, the marriage would have ended. He went in the September transport with his parents and his brother to the *Familienlager* in Auschwitz. He had a sister and a brother-in-law, but none of them returned. My father-in-law died in the transport from Theresienstadt to Auschwitz. My mother-in-law, a very energetic woman, and my brother-in-law were in the family camp. I was told they knew what was going to happen to them. Rudla was with them, and I understood he was quite sick. He probably died of encephalitis before he went to the gas chamber. I heard that he was asking for some mashed potatoes, for something to eat, which was, of course, impossible.

I made friends with, and then became the wife of, Bruno Mandel, one of the young doctors in the hospital. He was an internist. He would have trained for cardiology and been very good at it. I could see that he was very involved with his patients. We worked together day by day in the hospital. He was very kind to me, which was very different from Rudie.

He was ten years older than I. He came from Prostejov, Moravia, with his mother. Officially, we couldn't get a divorce and get married. There were all kinds of obstacles. But within the jurisdiction of Theresienstadt, we got our papers changed so that I would be divorced and married to Bruno after the war.

There were two private houses which had a small garden. We had a tiny little plot where we could plant little radishes, which was the only fresh food one could get. He spoke English, and together we read *Lady Windemere's Fan* by Oscar Wilde. I tried to read and translate it because he wanted to help me learn English. We also went over all the bones, so I would know anatomy in Czech, German, and Latin. He taught me a great deal, and I knew he valued me a great deal, too. Don't forget, I was there by myself. At that time, his mother very much wanted me to be with him, but Rudla's parents were asking what I was doing. Besides working twelve hours a day, six days a week, I was under a great deal of pressure. Nevertheless, in the evening we went to lectures that were held under the roof of the barracks. We went to every cultural situation we could. It was such an intensive life, all this work, the social things, the personal things, and all the diseases around you.

There was constant pressure; transports kept going. Are you going to be on the next transport? Are you going to be saved from the next transport? With whom can you stay? Who is going to go? There was pressure on the people who made the lists as well. Are you going to save your family? My father's cousin, whom I was very fond of, came through. I knew he was going. How do you try to keep any kind of normalcy and somehow still stay a human being under these circumstances? With very great difficulty!

The tendency was to try to maintain as normal a life as possible. How do you replenish the few things you brought with you? The inventiveness of people under the circumstances was incredible. At one point I was able to make a contact. First, I used up my money on the black market to buy extra food smuggled in by the Czech gendarmes. We bought as much as we could. Finally I sold my wedding ring for half a loaf of bread—exchanged it through the gendarmes. I thought the bread was more important. A slice of bread, a small loaf of bread was a wonderful birthday present. Somebody saved it up or had connections.

Misha's father had access to a little bit of grass. He planted some tomatoes so that Misha would have some fresh food. There was a group of women who worked in agriculture. They were sometimes able to smuggle something in.

Misha's mother, Irma Lausher, my cousin, was teaching children in the youth home. She had an incredible memory and wrote me books of poems for my birthday. Even under these circumstances we tried to celebrate birthdays.

My parents went with one of the transports and could have gone to any of the camps. I don't know what happened to my mother. Somebody told me they saw my father in Auschwitz, working in some laundry. Even though he was in his fifties, he was still in fairly good shape. As far as I could trace, I found out that in February, 1945, he was in one of the ships that was loaded with prisoners and sunk in the North Sea. Just to get rid of prisoners, they took old German ships, loaded them with explosives and prisoners, and just sunk them in the cold sea. My uncle was on one of the ships. Just by sheer accident, he survived, the only one of his family. By coincidence, the British were trying to help the people who were sinking. It was very humane.

I was in Theresienstadt when the Red Cross came through, a comedy organized and directed by Germans. In May we started to beautify the city. The main street was painted, made beautiful, and we got a coffeehouse. The "coffee" was chicory mainly, but it was warm. The miracle was that the water was somehow blackish, but we got better food for a week.

They made one house as a sample—one family can live together in one house. The houses were painted only outside, where the inspection was going to take place. They loaded people on a truck, like they were coming from a harvest. We all knew it was total make believe. It was for a propaganda film which was completely false.

Seidl was the SS man there.[6] The children were told that if somebody came to interview them, they were supposed to get a box of sardines and say, "Uncle Seidl, Uncle Seidl, sardines again!" That became the joke. Of course, we never ate or saw sardines. When the Red Cross came through, they didn't come to the clinic at all. We just kept away from them.

Then there was the counting of the people. One day all the people had to go to this big meadow. This counting was documented in films. We were in the hospital with the children, so we didn't have to go; we spent that lovely day in the hospital. We didn't know what was happening to everybody, what was going on, or what was going to happen. It was a terrible day.

I was in Theresienstadt from 1942 until 1944, for two and a half years. Then I volunteered to go to Auschwitz with Bruno. In September of 1944, they were saying the transports were going to labor camps in Poland. The front was moving. They needed labor groups with shovels, with spades. There were five transports of men. In the last transport, they allowed five hundred women, so I volunteered to go along. What else was I to do? We packed our things, and miraculously we were not in a cattle wagon. We were in a regular wagon, sitting on top of our luggage, crowded. We were on a transport of fifteen hundred people. To be sure he had them, Bruno carried our marriage papers with him.

It must have been early afternoon when we arrived in Auschwitz. We got out of the train and were told, "Don't touch anything. Leave everything as is." But we still carried some things. I had come from Prague to Theresienstadt in ski pants, good boots, and a winter coat, which was fortunate, and I had the coat through all these bad winters. This is how I came to Auschwitz—with a beaver collar. I had kept it for the transport. I was still pretty strong, more husky because I'm big-boned. We were supposed to stand outside of the train, always in fives because Germans can count easier that way. Women here and men there as we got off the train. We were standing there with a young soldier in camouflage uniform. All around us were camps with wires. Out of one camp ran a woman yelling (I don't remember if it was German, Polish or Yiddish) at us, "They will take away from you everything. What you have, throw it to me!" One of the girls had a knapsack and threw it to her over the fence.

I have this scene so much in my memory. This young guy was talking to us, and I saw this woman running about to catch the knapsack. At that moment, he took his gun and "psht," shot her. That was our welcome. This young man, who chatted with us in German, just took out his gun and "psht!"

We were standing in fives, and I was in one of the first rows. In front of it came a man in an SS uniform and white gloves. Mengele! I didn't know at the time it was Mengele, but I knew there was something very ominous about him. He was standing there with his gloves, and as every person came by, he pointed with his finger either right or left. Men went first. As my Bruno went by, he was yelling at me, "I'm not going to see you again! I'm not going to see you again!" I didn't want him to say that, but that's what he was saying. As they went by, Mengele shoved him.

When the men were gone, we started to go. When we came there, Mengele shoved me on the other side. So I stepped up and said to him, in German, "My . . . my . . . my husband went on this side. I want to go there, too." He said, "March on the other side!" There were soldiers with guns around us. I just saw this one shoved, so I went to the left. One was to gas, and the other was to work. How did you know? Fate. Total fate. We were so incredibly naive. When we got off the train, we saw the SS men or other older prisoners taking the carriages and the children off the train and putting them beside it. We said, "Well, they are not so bad. You see, they are helping." My foot! They were put to death!

That was our welcome. By this time it was getting dark. This is the end of September in Poland. They marched us first to where we had to undress. I had a can of oil and a can of sardines in my pockets, and I still had a good Swiss watch. There were women prisoners as guards, who already had short hair. We had to undress. I thought I would be very smart. I went to one of them and asked her, "What is your name?" She said, "Hana Muller." That was my maiden name! I said, "Look, in the corner I put my watch and the can of sardines and the oil. Keep it for me when I come through." Of course, I never saw her or anything else.

We were supposed to strip completely except for our shoes, so I still had my good shoes. As we undressed, we had to go through a hallway, naked except for the shoes. The SS came by and looked at our breasts and bellies; some of us might be pregnant. If they saw anybody pregnant, they pulled them out. Then we went to a room where they shaved us. I remember sitting there, seeing someone I knew with long hair. At that point, half of her hair was shaven and half was still long. I had a few bobbie pins and kept them. I thought when my hair grows, I will have the bobbie pins. When you suddenly see bald-headed, completely shaven women, everybody looks like a monkey. With that German thoroughness, they also shaved our pubic hair—hundreds of people with one blade. No cleanliness!

In the next building there was a cold shower. I was still holding the bobbie pins when we went to the shower. When I went for my shoes, they were gone. This is the first time I started to cry. The shoes were the last thing I had. We went into the next room and were given some old rags. I was given an old summer dress, some pants, and something. This was in cold weather. The wooden shoes we were given were absolute killers. In the mud of Auschwitz, there were no socks in the cold. The wooden shoes rubbed our feet. When you had a sore on your foot, it would never heal. They also got stuck in the mud, and you couldn't pull them out.

We were marched into the barracks and saw the fire from the chimneys. We wouldn't believe what it was. I didn't eat for three days; I was in a state of shock. How could you believe that the fire was from burning our families? It was incomprehensible. How could you believe what was happening? The last bit of humanity was taken away. We were given one big pot with five scoops of soup. Everybody slurped like an animal. At one point, I saw somebody dragging a bag of spoons; one was hanging out. I pulled it out, so I could be more civilized. (I kept it throughout and gave it to the United States Holocaust Memorial Museum.) It's an old scarred spoon, but it's special. It was part of becoming less than a human when you have to slurp like a dog.

We slept five to a bunk and didn't have any blankets. It was cold, but we warmed each other. We were five friends who stayed together. The dehumanization continued when you went to the toilet—benches with holes in them. You didn't even want to sit down, but if you didn't, all of a sudden somebody came and pulled you down because the women who were in charge of those holes wanted them clean. They just pulled you down very gently. You couldn't wash; you couldn't clean. But you had to wash the floor every day in the barrack. We had to go through the shower. We stood there naked, waiting. These were portable showers, again cold, no soap, no towel, nothing. One girl had a very heavy beard and had to shave. Of course she couldn't. We didn't have anything. We were just as we were born. These young soldiers, SS men, came and looked at us. One came to her very kindly and said, "One of us has to shave." Kindly!

Disinfectant was poured on our clothes. When we came out of the shower, we got somebody else's rags. This was the last time I menstruated for many months; we lost menstruation. Very carefully I washed out the pants but couldn't hang them. I couldn't do anything with them because they would be stolen immediately. So I carefully folded them and held them under my arm so my body warmth could dry them. Then I folded them the other way and held them under my arm for about three days, hoping they would be clean and dry. Finally, I was able to wear them, only to lose them and get somebody else's dirty pants. All the time there were these kinds of dehumanizing things.

I didn't see any medical facilities in Auschwitz. We had a dentist, a Polish one; all she could do was pull teeth because there was nothing.

We had to be shaved again, with all the people walking around. We heard shooting because there was a "selection." Older people were selected. They were running around or shooting while we were in the barracks. It was terrible. In our barrack I happened to run into two women whom I knew from Prague before the war. One went to the same school I did. She came to the religious classes from another school. Hanka Narastrukova is now a physician in Switzerland, and Jera, with whom I went to gymnastics, is in Prague now. They were in the Lodz ghetto. They happened to be in the same barrack. It was awful there.

The woman in charge of our huge barrack was from Slovakia. She learned that the man who was going to come and look for labor was pretty good. At that point, labor was needed, so various factory supervisors or directors used to come to Auschwitz to select laborers. We were told that this man had a pretty good set-up, so they directed him to our barrack. They took 200 women, 120 Slovaks, and 80 Czechs. We were five friends together, and he took four of us. One of the oldest he rejected, but she survived. She was an aunt of Bruno's.

They took the four of us from the *Familienlager* in Birkenau to another transit

Lager. We were there about a week. The leader of that barrack was a Ukrainian. The Germans had a high stack of blankets, but she wouldn't allow us to have them. There were also Ukrainian female prisoners who had long hair and were better dressed. Instead of a toilet there were two buckets. We stood in line to use the buckets. A lot of people had diarrhea, but when a Ukrainian came, she pushed us away and went immediately—never mind the line.

One of the lower leaders in the hierarchy was a woman, Jana; I don't remember her other name. She came from Ruthenia in the easternmost part of Czechoslovakia. She lived in Nachod and had a boyfriend there, but she had been in Auschwitz for a long time, ever since they had to go work with the dogs barking at their feet. She was telling us about it one evening. It was pretty awful.

There was an antisocial woman prisoner wearing some sort of uniform with a black triangle. She had a gun. While waiting for a transport, she was shooting rats in front of us. She could have shot any one of us just the same. It was fun for her!

We had to stand in rows of five for hours in *Appell*. By this time it was October, and it was cold. Somewhere I saw a big bag with a sock hanging out. I ran and got it—just one sock. The five of us would use the sock. The one who had it would stand in front because she was getting the coldest air and was sort of protecting the others. Later I cut that one sock in half and made two gloves out of it.

They did give us some better clothes. I had a striped skirt, a sweater, and a big black, heavy winter coat. They didn't give us caps, so I took a piece of the lining and made a scarf because, if you have no hair, it's very cold. Then they gave each of us a piece of bread and something else, and we were loaded on cattle trains. There were also men on this train who wore striped outfits, but they got hats.

We watched the stations and knew we were going westward from Auschwitz. Then we stopped for a long time. God, we had been going for thirty-six or forty-eight hours. All of a sudden, we started looking at where we were standing. To our absolute horror, we realized we were going back again. If we were going back to Auschwitz, we knew what it meant. Then they uncoupled some wagons and moved us again.

Two hundred Polish and one hundred Czech women arrived in Kudowa-Sackisch, a subcamp of Gross-Rosen located in Lower Silesia. It was a small camp. There were so many camps. You met people and all of a sudden found out about all these camps. They told us, "This is a spa, but not for you." We were walked to the wooden barracks. There were already three hundred women there, mostly Poles and Hungarians.

From October, 1944, to May, 1945, until liberation, we were twenty women between eighteen and thirty-five who knew each other from Theresienstadt, all together in this one room with double-deck beds. In this last camp, there was also a woman who had five or six children, and they took them away. At night she screamed, yelled, and hollered, so they put her into a room by herself because nobody could tolerate it.

The German *Lagerälteste* from Sudetenland was miserable. She had an *Unterscharführer*, a noncom official. When she was angry with somebody, he had to beat the women. She didn't allow people to peel the potatoes for our soup; they had to be thrown in as is. But she was removed, and we got an older *Lagerälteste*, which was a great advantage. Hanelle didn't want to be an SS woman; she was drafted. She warned us before an inspection and was in many ways much kinder. She allowed the potatoes to be eaten, and when an SS man came for inspection, she always slept with him so that he didn't bother us. She escaped before the end of the war and became a civilian in Czechoslovakia, but they knew who she was. I know she was hanged after the war.

In December of that year, my husband's friend Hanna Klein, who had worked as a nurse in Buna, which was part of Auschwitz, became sick with a high fever. We didn't have a doctor, but I was convinced she was dying of typhoid because I could hear her labored breathing. There was a certain smell about it too. I recognized it because I had worked with typhoid and saw the symptoms. She was moved into one empty room, and I volunteered to stay with her overnight. I really thought I was immune. After so much typhoid, nothing could happen to me. This was not unrealistic; I was pretty much immune. I stayed with her until she died on the 19th of December, 1944. That was a really low point for me.

Then a very peculiar thing happened. Miraculously, this last *Lagerälteste* allowed me to have a flashlight for her at night, which was unbelievable. She ordered a plain wooden coffin for Hanna. I washed her, dressed her in newspapers, and laid her in the coffin. People asked, "Are you crazy? Why are you doing it? Nobody does that." I said, "That's the only piece of dignity I can give her. I treated her. If I washed her when she was sick, why shouldn't I wash her now?" I didn't realize until years later that this was the Jewish tradition: visit the sick; wash the dead; comb them, clean them, dress them before they go. But that was not conscious at all. She's buried in that camp.

This was an enormous experience for me. People were dying all around us, but I was alone with her when she died. That was the last decent human thing we could do. It was nonsense, but that was the tradition. The women in my room didn't want to let me back in because they were convinced I was crazy for washing a body.

In that area there used to be big textile factories which were changed into ammunition factories. We were making the part of airplanes in which the propeller sits. In one of the camps next to us were Russian prisoners of war, mostly the Mongolian mustachioed, heavy-set Soviets, working on the propellers. There were all kinds of groups in this factory; it was a tower of Babel. There were German soldiers who had gone AWOL and were like prisoners under guard. They moved heavy machinery. There were French, Italians, Danish, Dutch, and, of course, the Poles.

I started working on a big turning place (a lathe). An Italian by the name of Antonio Pezutto taught me how to do it. There's a very sharp knife that goes to the metal and cuts what needs to be cut, but they didn't have enough material, so they put only the edge in the metal. Of course we were breaking the knives, and they were very angry with us. Then they took us to a classroom and taught us how to use a micrometer. The man who taught us was a German *Meister*, a foreman. I knew how to use a micrometer, but we had to do that. They wanted to know if we knew fractions and things like that. We sat on school benches. I looked, and in one I found a core of an apple. Somebody had eaten an apple and left the core. I didn't care who ate the apple; I ate the core. My goodness! That was fruit!

We were there only a few days. One day the master said to the five of us, "Look, if you would like to bathe, I will let you take a shower." That was very dangerous for him to do. He took five of us to the shower room and let us shower. We didn't have a towel; we didn't have soap. We had to put the clothes on that we had, but just to be under water, to shower, was such a relief! It took years before I finally allowed myself to remember why he did it. He stood in the corner and watched five naked young women taking a shower. He got his jollies!

Antonio Pezutto sometimes brought me a piece of bread. He was one of the Italians who had fought in Italy with Badoglio, who turned against the Germans. They came in as prisoners, but they were better off. They could move around and got more food. Once in a while, he brought me a roll or a piece of bread. He hid it somewhere and I could take it. Some of the other women also got food from the *Meisters.*

At Christmas time it was cold as could be. The screws on the inside of the barracks were white with ice. All we had was a bowl and a spoon. It was so cold at that time that we put them under our coats and put a string around us because we didn't have gloves. Mimi was thirty-five, and she was the oldest of us. She was also the most flat-chested of all of us. She was going with the bowl, and one of the Mongolian guys stepped out of his line to touch her because he thought it was a breast. But instead he touched the dish. It [stepping out of line] was very dangerous for him.

At that point we were working twelve-hour shifts again, seven to seven. We walked in the snow and ice three kilometers to the factory and three kilometers back. Today three kilometers isn't much, but in those conditions it was terrible. We walked through the village at night; we never saw daylight. There were lit windows, and at Christmas people had Christmas trees. There were people living normal lives in those houses, but we were like animals, going back and forth. Once my terrible shoes were sticking in the snow and I couldn't get them out. The women absolutely dragged me to the factory. I was out of breath for about a half hour.

When we came to the factory for the twelve-hour shift, we got two little metal triangles with DMV, which is actually documented in the Nazi records as the *Vereinigte Deutsche Metallwerke*. When we went to the john, we had to put one on. We could go twice in the twelve hours, and since we had diarrhea, it was terrible. The *Lagerälteste* just sat there.

Some of us had to carry the big metal containers with soup, which we had at midnight. They didn't know we had lost menstruation. The craziness was that when they thought we had menstruation, we didn't have to carry it. Never logic!

We tried to celebrate New Year and do some fun things. One tried to be human even under these circumstances; it was very important to us.

Slowly we were running out of material. Because the eastern front was coming, shipments were not arriving. At the end they loaded all the material, all the machinery, on trucks and took them to Germany. They were bombed on the way, which we were not sorry for.

When they had no more material, they shipped the machines away and made work, such as taking bricks from here to there, then bringing them back. I had to sweep with one of these big brooms. It was horrible to sweep for twelve hours. The only good thing was that it made it possible for me to move a little bit around the factory, and I made contact with a Czech guy. At that time, we had some very sick people. I asked him if he could get some pudding, and he did. He hid it in some material. I went in, got the pudding, put it in my pocket, and brought it to this girl who was very sick. I sent him a thank you letter after the war. His father answered that he got the letter on his birthday: "That was the best letter I could get, to find out how well my son behaved."

I made contact with other people as well. Once the Italian boys had a whole big can of soup that got sour. They said, "Do you want it?" Of course we ate it. We said, "Well, we will think it's potato salad. That's why it's sour." We got sick. This time I cried for hours because, with the work, with everything, I was getting more and more desperate.

Together we had one needle. It got lost, which was a tragedy. Once an SS man came and asked us, "What is the thing you want the most?" We said things like a toothbrush. A toothbrush was so basic. He promised us toothbrushes, but of course we never got them. This was a kind of teasing. I had repeated dreams about taking a bath and having a nice towel because we were not able to clean ourselves. I remember sitting on the bed and finding my first louse, an absolute downer. The last drop of civilization was gone. We had to look for lice every day. In that camp there was a group of people who had to wash the laundry for the SS. They also had lice. They said they had lice even in their handkerchiefs.

One day, I didn't eat the bread; I exchanged it for some sort of a contraption out of which I could make a bra. I wanted a bra so badly. These were the sort of leftovers of civilization.

We needed to read. Not being able to read was a deprivation. One of the girls had read *Gone with the Wind.* I never read the book, but I remember her because she told us the whole story. I knitted a pair of socks for one of the SS women because she gave me printed material—one of those Harlequin romancelike things. She was a woman who could blow hot or cold. Once in a while, she talked to us; her boyfriend was at the front. On the other hand, sometimes she would beat up people. But she did give me a piece of soap for the socks. We had a game. You had to make a menu card for a whole day, and then the next woman had to make a menu card. You couldn't repeat it until everybody made all the menu cards for the week. We told jokes. We recited poems—anything to keep our minds going.

I trained myself to go to the bathroom every second day to save strength. I walked very slowly. I had these horrible shoes to walk in, but they were shoes. As camps go, this one was by no means the worst; this one was pretty good. Even so, we were getting pretty desperate about what was going to happen.

Toward the end of April, 1945, I didn't think I was going to survive and became very depressed. I talked so slowly that people didn't have patience to listen to me. Then the hills started to be green; spring might come. We knew the end was near, but we didn't know when. The front was coming. There was a pocket of resistance around Breslau, and we were close to it. We could hear the shooting and were happy. "Maybe the end is coming."

One of the girls was able, through somebody else, to make a contact. They were going to build a railroad from Nachod, across the border in Czechoslovakia, to make a connection. Some of the Czech women from the village got together and, even though it was rationed, got food and bribed the SS women by giving them more food for our group to eat. They were wonderful. They did it at great risk, but the SS women took the bribe of food because they didn't have that much either. Bozenna Levitova was one of the women. Her husband was Jewish, and she protected him. Her three children were all in camps, one in Theresienstadt and two in Dachau, and she was doing this. She was a great woman.

Out of five hundred, thirteen women died between October and liberation, which was the beginning of May, a short time for normally healthy young women. But comparatively, thirteen was very few. They were buried in coffins because, miraculously, Hanelle had ordered them. It was unheard of.

We were liberated on the 6th of May, 1945, in Nachod, in Upper Silesia, three kilometers from the Czech border. When the Russians were coming, the SS just opened the gates, said, "Go," and disappeared. So we went. There was a tremendous crowd of people, all going in cars, wagons, motorcycles, bicycles—you name it— from east to west, escaping from the Russians. Going westward, I just walked out on the street. I had a different shoe on each foot. We walked to the border, into what was Czechoslovakia, to Nachod. Nobody told us what we were going to do. Totally spontaneously we stopped and sang the Czech anthem. In that moment, singing that anthem and crossing the border, I was normal. I spoke normal. I walked normal. Everything was normal.

Everybody knew we were prisoners. That's how we were dressed. We had no hair. A man whom I met on the street, who knew Jana, gave each of us some money. "I know you just came back, but did you happen to run into Jana?" I told him, "Your name is so and so." I remembered him. She gave us his name in October, and I just remembered it in May. I told him she had survived. She did survive and returned, and they married.

I went to Mrs. Levitova. All her three children had survived. She brought us thick Czech bread with a half inch of butter on it and honey. We bit into it, and you could see the imprint of the teeth in the butter and the honey. I will remember the bread with butter and honey—the first meal. That was a marvelous meal! Our teeth were singing! Mrs. Levitova let us have a bath. She put us in a bed with pillows and covers. Trude, a friend of mine, and I pinched each other at night. Is this a dream, or are we really sleeping in a bed? Mrs. Levitova fed us for a few days, then her three children returned.

We walked into Nachod, and that very first night of liberation I volunteered to work at the Red Cross shelter. The Germans were coming through, and the Russians were chasing them. There was still shooting going on. On the streets, they took down the swastika and put it on the floor. For one crown, everybody was allowed to clean his shoes on it.

On the first day the trains ran, I went to Prague, to my parents' maid. I slept in her kitchen for three days. Then, after the war, I studied nursing, but I left it because I had a chance to come to the United States. When I came here, I had to go to work to pay for my education. Once I was able to, I went to the university. I earned a bachelor's degree in three years and a master's in a year. I am a clinical psychologist, a Ph.D. from George Washington University. I did my internship at St. Elizabeth's Hospital.

When I'm in Prague, I always go to my grandfather's grave and put little stones on it. Since we were not able to bury her there, I had my grandmother's name put on the same gravestone. My relatives in Prague maintain the grave, even though so many others are neglected. So she is there, at least in memoriam, as she wished to be.

Every survivor has a different story to tell from a different point of view. Because I was a nurse in Theresienstadt, I saw things from the point of view of the nurses and doctors. You had to learn how to protect yourself. That was most important. Later we talked it out. When I talk to some of the people who didn't talk about it, who kept it inside, it was much worse. I feel like it's a part of my life that I have pretty much dealt with.

• • •

Dr. Hana Bruml lives outside of Washington, D.C., with her husband, Charles Bruml, an artist. She frequently speaks at the United States Holocaust Memorial Museum, where her testimony is available to the public.

Chapter Four

Margret Lehner

"IF ANYONE HERE MENTIONS HUMANE TREATMENT . . ."

•   •   •

And now, down there, we found a painted people,
slow-motioned: step by step, they walked their round
in tears, and seeming wasted by fatigue.

—Dante Alighieri, *Dante's Inferno*

Similar to the textile factory in which Hana Bruml worked, Lenzing was a labor camp in Austria where prisoners were utilized as slaves when they were brought from Auschwitz, rather than a transit camp from which they were transported to their deaths. Despite this, we have introduced it early in the book because it was there that Ellen Loeb and Ruth Reiser cared for their fellow inmates. Margaret Lehner, a young Austrian woman, now lives in an apartment adjacent to the grounds on which their barracks stood during the war. At that time there had been a wall of silence regarding the fate of the Jews, which was maintained by euphemisms and camouflaged language. Although all Jews were to be expelled, it was not stated, even in internal correspondence, that they were being executed; instead they were termed to be "re-settled," "evacuated," "removed," "deported," or given "special treatment."[1] Because of this, because of fear, and because they simply did not wish to admit the obvious, many Germans denied any knowledge of the Holocaust. Typical of the reactions of many were those of the *Burgermeister* and his wife in the town of Ohrdruf when the Americans liberated the camp on the outskirts of the hamlet on April 4, 1942. As Lewis H. Weinstein recalls, "their faces were ashen; she was sobbing and he repeatedly denied any knowledge of the camp or even of its existence. . . . 'Our hands did not shed this blood; nor have our eyes seen.'"[2] Although the Burgermeister repeatedly stated that he had no knowledge of what had been occurring, he could not explain why people from the village had been working in the camp or how the citizens of Ohrdruf did not smell the stench of death and decay which emanated

Margret Lehner, Vöcklabruck, Austria, March 11, 1994. Photo by Diane Plotkin.

from the area. Nevertheless, both he and his wife committed suicide after having been forced by American troops to view the carnage.

Fifty years later, not only is there an increase in anti-Semitism, but, according to opinion polls, it is stronger in Austria than in Germany, France, or the United States. Some surveys have shown that about 75 percent of all Austrians privately express some anti-Semitic views.[3] This plus an intellectual climate of historical revisionism, which has increased since the mid 1970s, have resulted in a movement that denies the reality and actuality of the Holocaust. To quote Deborah Lipstadt, "What claims do the deniers make? The Holocaust—the attempt to annihilate the Jewish people—never happened."[4] Margaret Lehner and her co-authors combatted this distortion of the truth as they conducted their research and published their book about Mauthausen and its subcamps. On March 11, 1994, her thirty-ninth birthday, the cab driver, Margret, her son, and I sat in a noisy restaurant in Vöcklabruck as she told me about the history of Lenzing and the surrounding camps and their attempt to fight denial and revisionism. As she describes her feelings regarding their research:[5]

I am working with about twenty other young people to prevent our children from making the same mistakes our fathers made. We are making a little bit of history; we are responsible for the monument [commemorating the women's camp at Lenzing] within our district. We were the initiators of this monument. On the first weekend of every May, we make great celebrations to remember the people who worked there, who worked for a terrible regime. We make these celebrations to remember what it was like and to prevent them from doing such things again.

I do this because my father was a soldier of the German army. He was stationed in Paris, where the Austrian Resistance was imprisoned. He had to take care of these prisoners but was sent to the Russian front because he helped the prisoners by giving them extra food or telling them the date or time. Since he was a silent man, he never told me about his special history. Nevertheless, my father told me to take care to keep history alive, so I feel responsible for doing this. The former mayor told me that our generation should let the memories fade. Since Lenzing is a nice town, the next generation should be allowed to forget, and the following generation should be free of all such thinking.

I disagree. It's not possible to do too much alone, but we have a group of twenty or twenty-five people. We are in contact with the former prisoners of Mauthausen. We go to schools and teach the children about this history. We show films about Mauthausen to make history alive. We are also writing a book documenting the subcamps of Mauthausen: Lenzing Pettighofen, Redl-Zipf/Schlier and Vöcklabruck.[6]

According to the statements given to Ms. Lehner by people who lived in Lenzing during the war, citizens were indeed well aware of what was happening to the women in their midst. Some of their memories are quoted in the following section. The initials rather than the names of the women are as Ms. Lehner recorded them. The following is according to her testimony.[7]

In April, 1938, some leading functionaries of the SS and the police founded the *Deutsche Erd und Stein Werke* (German Earth and Stone Works). Many SS firms thought of the possibility of using prisoners as cheap labor and, at the same time, "unwanted to work to death." For the building program for the "Renewal of the *Reichschaupt statt*" Berlin (so-called "buildings for the Führer"), a great demand for natural and gravel stones developed. Stone quarries also had to be acquired for the setting up of the concentration camps near Flossenburg, Mauthausen, and Gusen. The KZ Mauthausen existed from August 8, 1938, until the liberation on May 5, 1945. It was the only KZ in the whole *Reichgebeit* with Step III, which meant that political enemies here were liquidated without a trial, i.e., the building of a death camp. The lifetime of a prisoner in Mauthausen lasted between fifteen months in 1938/39 and five months in 1945; the average was approximately six months. Approximately 206,000 women and men were imprisoned in Mauthausen between August 8, 1938, and

May 5, 1945. More than half were gassed, beaten to death, shot "while fleeing," or murdered in other cruel ways.

All together they had forty-nine regular subcamps plus a few that existed for only a few weeks. Eleven of those were in Oberosterreich (at that time "Oberdonau"), three in the district of Vöcklabruck:

Vöcklabruck/Wagrain: June 6, 1941–May 14, 1942

Lenzing: November 3, 1944–May 4, 1945

"Schlier"/Redl-Zipf: October 11, 1943–May 3, 1945

All instigators, troublemakers, *Phaffen*, German-hating Czechs and Poles, as well as communists and similar low-life were supposed to be put into concentration camps per order of the Reichführer-SS dated August 27, 1941.[8]

After Hitler's troops occupied Austria on March 13, 1938, all the possessions of the Republic of Austria and any land and furniture were now owned by Nazi Germany. Among other resources and available assets, the defense armament industry also had a lot of "potential workers" available in Austria, which enabled the defense industry to expand. These strategically protected sites inside Austria also made it possible to plan great projects, such as the ones next to the Hermann Goring factories in Linz (which today is Voest), the gas factories in Linz, the aluminum factories in Rahnsofen, and the *Zellwolle* factory in Lenzing. On May 28, 1938, the already existing factories were purchased from a Swiss firm.

In 1938 the *Zellwolle* factory became the property of the *Deutches Reich*. It was in a strategic position midway between Salzburg and Linz. They were producing good

Factory, Lenzing, Austria, March 11, 1994. Photo by Diane Plotkin.

material called "viscose," a kind of suede which is nearly like cotton. The factory is now called Lenzing-AG—Lenzing because of the place, and AG for the form of association. In former days it was called *Zellwolle*-AG, and after the Second World War, it was changed to *Chemichwolle* Lenzing-AG. Chemical products were made there, and there was also a factory producing paper.

In order to increase production in textiles, women were brought to Lenzing where they were housed in barracks which, since November 3, 1944, had been a new satellite or subcamp of Mauthausen. Helena Dorner, Dr. Lotte Springer, Berta Kusolmann, Henriette van den Bergh, and Olga Zwickar survived and provided sworn testimony to Investigating Officer Eugene S. Cohen, Major, OM Corps. on May 16, 1945, about the conditions they had endured:[9]

> On October 30, 1944, about 500 women were transported from concentration camps Auschwitz and Theresienstadt to this camp at Lenzing. We came in cattle cars, about 60 to 70 in each car. We had nothing but the rags on our backs. Among the women were Hungarians, Austrians, Czechs, Poles and Russians, and Dutch.[10]
>
> We were greeted by the SS and told we would be put to work in the chemical works. Food was scarce and terrible. No one was killed here by the SS, but there was no payment for the work and we were insulted regularly and beaten quite often by the SS men and women.

The persons in charge were *Lagerführer* Karl Giseler, chief overseer Gretl Freiburger, and an Austrian overseer, Maria Kunik, who beat the prisoners regularly. She carried a revolver and threatened to shoot anyone who did not work properly. Maria Shelko was another Austrian overseer who beat and threatened prisoners. Dr. Brauer, the head doctor, relayed orders from Mauthausen. It was he who threatened to send the sick to Mauthausen, stating that fifty sick people was the maximum. Everything was carried out under the orders of authorities at Mauthausen.

Worker Conscript[11]

The women in the KZ were put to work in various areas, despite their poor health— in the factory, gardening for the general population and in parks, in street construction, and air raid shelters, and, towards the end of the war, trenches to defend the place—of course everything without pay.

All was carried out per order of those responsible for running Mauthausen. The camp at Lenzing was about three kilometers from town. Here, approximately 565 women were put to work in the textile factories. They had to walk to the factory every day, early in the morning, in their thin clothing and wooden shoes. Most of them didn't even have any shoes; they rolled paper around their toes and their feet.

Of this, Anna Benjamin (Hanna Kohner), prisoner #469 in the Lenzinger satellite, writes:

> *We then marched through the little village of Lenzing with its typical, Alpenlike houses. The sun came through the clouds and fresh air slowly penetrated our weakened bodies. Surely it was a change for the better. The inhabitants of the village of Lenzing clearly showed their compassion for us.*
>
> *The day went like this: at six o'clock the counting of people, a slice of black bread with some brown liquid, the march of the morning shift in the direction of the factory. They went through the brick paved streets of Lenzing, passing fields of grass, dense woods, and a small stream. After crossing the railroad tracks, we finally arrived at our workplace. Our guards were heavily armed SS men and women who treated us like a dangerous band of criminals, not like the walking skeletons that we really were. The factory was a modern textile factory and weaving factory and produced synthetic yarn for parachutes. The employees consisted of a few people from Lenzing, foremen, foreign workers, who were deported from their countries by force, and us, who looked as if we stepped out of a picture of Hyronimus [sic] Bosch.*[12]

There is a small local train which goes from Attnang-Pucheim to Kammer-Schorsling, a small place, four kilometers from the Attersee. This line was very important because it transported the woolen and cotton bales to the great towns, to Linz, where things for the army were produced—clothing made from the cloth, the fabric, the viscose bales—from Lenzing. Every day the women marched in a long line, crossed

Railway crossing, Lenzing, Austria, March 11, 1994. Photo by Diane Plotkin.

the railroad tracks to the south in Lenzing, walked along the tracks, and crossed over them in the direction of the factory. One day there was a bad accident. At six o'clock in the morning, a train approached silently from the direction of Vöcklabruck. The SS woman, Elizabeth Sturm, made the women cross the railway before the train had passed, and it drove right into the column of workers. Five women didn't make it to the other side; they were killed. We think the parts of their bodies were taken to the crematory at Mauthausen. Nothing much was mentioned at the workplace, but five years before that, when a train (Kammerer Hansl) had collided with a busload of workers and nineteen workers were killed, they had been recognized with full Nazi pomp. There are no names within the books of the people who died here. Elizabeth Sturm was allowed to go free after the war. In 1945 she was living in the Attersee.

Lenzing was a top secret camp. Some of the women who were working for *Zellwolle* were also working to produce a special bomb, the so-called "super bomb," for the German army. They were bringing scientists, like Werner von Braun, and prisoners from the concentration camps in northern Germany to work here because the British army had bombed the camps of northern Germany. There was a beer brewery in Zipf, and the weapons were being produced there, under the earth because it was not possible to see the factory from the air.

One day there was a great explosion and forty people died. Women studying to be engineers, who had come from Germany to work here, were killed in the accident. Their graves are still in Vöcklabruck, graves with no names and no dead people under the crosses because the explosion was so great there was nothing left to bury. People told me they heard the explosion fifteen kilometers away. The SS said the prisoners caused this by sabotage. Because of this, four prisoners were hanged, and one prisoner was cooked in a water pot. These were only men—engineers.

There was resistance within the population. The winter of 1944 was very harsh, and some of the villagers hid some food, such as potatoes, under the grass for the prisoners. But as a general rule, treatment of them was inhumane.

"If anyone here even mentions humane treatment" [13]

Frau H: Four or five prisoners and an SS woman came into the kitchen and picked up the food. This was the first time I saw them when they arrived. I'll never forget it . . . I went and said to Mr. W. (The kitchen chef, H.Ch), "If anyone mentions the word humanitarian treatment, it makes a mockery of it." I said, "They can't help it that they are Jews. . . ." When a human body is already so emaciated that they can hardly stand on their feet, that person is put to work.

Frau H: When you saw them standing or walking, you were wondering how it was possible for them to work because they were mere skeletons. . . .

Frau P: During winter, I saw long columns of them in the street pushed close together. They were dressed in long gray uniforms and jackets and head scarves. With bowed heads—like a herd of sheep—they moved along. . . . I tried to figure out what crime these women committed that they deserved to be incarcerated in a KZ.

Meals

The imprisoned Jewish women received the worst possible category D and an average of 1,000 calories a day. These calories were mostly soup—consisting of well-cooked kohlrabi or rutabagas and black flour—and whole grain bread, and in the morning, some kind of fruit tea with nothing else. The food was wheeled out of the kitchen under supervision of four or five women and most likely consumed in the camp. For those women who worked in shifts or in a dangerous or poisonous environment, there was an additional something added. That was a special meal on Friday night which they shared with the others.

"They were the last ones . . ."

Frau H: . . . and the Jewish women, they were the last ones. . . . They were starved. The rutabagas were cooked to a very soft death and then thickened with black flour that was salted. Aside from that, the cook was not permitted to give them anything else.

Frau H: I know once we got a small pig, which had sickness which was released from the free bank, and that the prisoners received [some].

Frau H: Whenever one gave them something—no one was allowed to see it. There were supervisors around. . . . When it [a parcel] came, they turned around and looked out the window. And whenever one gave them something, they took it home and distributed it—for those that needed it more. They had sick people there.

Supervising—Guarding

The ones in striped uniforms—a rough, hard material of Mauthausen—and wooden slippers, very, very hardworking women, were supervised by twenty to twenty-five SS women. Toward the end of the war, most of them were conscripted into doing these jobs and had an aversion to it. They passively supported the KZ women. But according to testimony from some women prisoners, quite a few enjoyed their jobs and threatened the Jewish women with deportation or beat them.

The following "Statement of Mrs. Holzweiser" illustrates this point clearly:

> *At the end of 1944, I was appointed as shift leader in a* viskosekeller. *No natives were available for that job. One day the Jewish woman Edith, who was assigned to me, came and told me she was sick and can't work. I allowed her to lie down in the cloth filtering room. Unfortunately, my boss, Mr. Grohganz, came by and saw her lying down. He reproached me and wanted to know why the Jewish women were allowed to sleep. The shift supervisor, Alfred Hollerman, found out about it, showed up in his SA uniform, which he always wore at work, and ordered me to Herr Groghanz's office. He warned me that this incident will have other consequences. Herr Groghanz was standing in the office with his back turned towards me and I was looking out the window. While I was telling him the events and describing the physical condition, with the side remark that the Jewess was also a human being, no answer was forthcoming and I left the room feeling very uneasy. But evidently, no one was about to punish me, neither Mr. Groghanz nor Herr Hollerman.*
>
> *I remember another case. The German Jewess Judith hoped she could trust me and asked me whether I would help her escape. She had a chance to go to a hiding place. I handed her my Red Cross uniform and my identification papers, but it was up to her to figure out how to get past the exit of the factory. Once she is that far, she should board a train from the Red Cross in Attnang in order to get out of the penal zone. My papers should disappear as soon as possible. She made it and wrote to me from Aachen after some time had passed. I had a new Red Cross uniform made in our sewing section. Ironically, the seamstress was also a Jewess. That was so I didn't have to show up without my uniform to the Red Cross* appell *during that 14 days.*

The women of the camp were eventually discovered by a French physician, Dr. Paul Le Caer of Deauville, France, who was a former prisoner in Zipf, one of the nearby POW camps. When the U.S. Army was coming from the west, the POW camp had been freed, but the prisoners were taken to Ebensee. This was a long march, and many prisoners died. Two doctors escaped and hid within the woods. They stole a bicycle from a farmer and while riding around the mountains, found the women in Lenzing. These doctors contacted the U.S. Army, and Dr. Le Caer said, "There are women. They are not going to be able to get away from the camp because they are so sick they cannot get out of the factory. There are no SS there."

Although the factory buildings in Lenzing were supposed to have been destroyed by a bomb under order of *Gauleiter Eigrubers*, it was possible to turn over the factory to the U.S. Army in May, 1945, without any defense. There were about ten people concentrated within the factory, as well as some local population, who had formed a special resistance group and gave the plans of the factory to the British army. The American army liberated the prisoners in other KZ satellite camps on May 4, 1945, and the women were handed peacefully to U.S. troops as well in early May, their first contact with the U.S. Army.[14]

"From now on we have no camp anymore"

Frau H: The W. Camp came down and said: "Frau H, from today we have no more camp. Everything is here for everyone. There is no such thing anymore as Camp A, Camp B. Everything is the same. And when the kitchen needs anything, give it to them. . . ."

Frau P: Since they had nothing to wear, they were permitted to make clothing from the plaid, woolen bed covers and from linen towels. Because of that, I got acquainted with them and I sewed for some of them. My first question was: "What kind of crime have you committed to deserve to be punished like that?" Answer: "We were housekeepers, seamstresses, etc. We did not do anything wrong. We were taken out of our homes because we were Jews and put into camps." I could not believe it. . . .

The former KZ women were then housed in Kammer, a former Nazi party labor camp, and were taken care of from the labor kitchen. Their spokesperson, Frau Lichtenstern, was put in charge by the American occupation officers to make certain that the women had a specific area and were properly taken care of. They gave the women vitamin tablets and organized beds from a youth camp, a former Hitler *Jugend* in Seawalchen, near Attersee, only four kilometers from here, where children from ages ten to sixteen had been educated. The women were being cared for by a medical student who had been in the French resistance.

Today it is a leading factory in helping to clear up pollution in the air and water. On April 1, 1992, a stone was placed here in Lenzing, on the area where the barracks of the concentration camp were, to commemorate the prison camp that was here. It reads as follows:

AUF DIESEM AREAL BEFAND SICH VOM 3. NOVEMBER 1944 BIS 4. MAI 1945 DAS NEBENLAGER PETTIGHOFEN DES KONZENTRA-TIONSLAGERS MAUTHAUSEN MIT 565 WEIBLICHEN HAFTLINGEN ZUM GEDENKEN UND DAS SCHICKSAL ALLER ANDEREN DIE MART-GEMEINDE LENZING IN JAHR 1992
[Translation: On this area there was from the 1st of November, 1944, to the 4th of May, 1945, the subcamp Pettighofen of the concentration camp Mauthausen, with 565 women

Commemorative stone, Lenzing, Austria, March 11, 1994. Photo by Diane Plotkin

prisoners. In memory of their pain and the lives of all the others. Made by the community of Lenzing in the year 1992.]

Dr. Le Caer, who returns every year, gave the following moving account of his memories to those who attended the commemoration:[15]

My Very dear Mr. Burgomeister
My ladies and gentlemen!

First of all, I'd like to tell you the reason why I am here in Lenzing, a former subcamp of KZ Mauthausen. After I left the column in the march which took place after the evacuation of camp Redl-Zipf/Schlier, I walked on foot to Ebensee. After that I settled in Weyregg.

On Wednesday, the 8th of May, one of my comrades from Zipf, who escaped a few hours after I did, said to me: "Hurry up. There are women who are living in a factory and they haven't got the strength to leave after they are liberated."

Arriving in Lenzing, it was difficult for me to keep going. Everything was very dirty, and the smell was so sickening that even a person like me, who experienced similar things, was nauseated. I spoke to an old female doctor, but she did not have the strength anymore to make decisions.

As fast as I could, I made contact with the Americans and the French military attaché, Captain Chatenay, who gave me the necessary papers.

In Seawalchen I discovered a Hitler youth camp at the sea. The next day, all the women had a bed with clean linen. I made contact with American doctors and received vitamins for all camp inmates. My assistant and I were the only males in the camp. A few days later we evacuated a young woman who gave birth to a baby in the hospital in Vöcklabruck. The mother and grandmother remained in the camp.

• • •

In their letter granting permission to publish these materials, Margret Lehner and her co-authors wrote: "We are glad to help you . . . make a good publication of [those] terrible days during the Second World War."

Like Hana Bruml, Ruth Reiser, originally from Prague, was taken to Theresienstadt, where she served as a nurse. From there she was transported to Auschwitz, and then to Lenzing, where she assisted Ellen Loeb until the camp was liberated. Because she and Ellen, as well as the women in Margret Lehner's testimony, talked about the terrible starvation in that part of Austria, we have included copies of letters from the German government regarding the manufacture of an experimental mushroom sausage called *biosyn wurst* with which they attempted the appease the hunger. Unfortunately, this would-be sausage only made the people ill.[16]

As Ruth and I sat in the conference room at the Sheraton Hotel in New York, she slowly and thoughtfully recounted her experiences, once even calling London to confer in Czech with her sister-in-law, Zuzka, for confirmation of a few details. Unfortunately, although Zuzka also had recorded her memoirs, they were not available for this book because she was already working with a publisher in London. After we had converted Ruth's interview to a narrative, both Roger and I spent many hours going over it with her until it read satisfactorily to all of us. We hope we are able to do her justice, for, like the others, she gave of herself while caring for and nurturing many of her fellow inmates.

D. P.

Chapter Five

Ruth Reiser

"THE ONLY MEDICINE WAS CHARCOAL"

• • •

I was born in Prague, Czechoslovakia, now the Czech Republic, in 1926.[1] I was an only child. My father worked in a bank. My mother looked after the household, as was the custom at the time. My early childhood was very secure and happy. Until 1939, when I was thirteen, it was a very normal, pleasant way of life. I think it's the only normal life I've ever had. I went to a primary school, and then for three years to a high school for girls.

On the fifteenth of March, 1939, Germany occupied Bohemia and Moravia. Soon restrictions and anti-Jewish laws started, and our lives became increasingly difficult. I don't remember in what succession it happened, but one restriction after another came into effect. My father, like most other Jews, lost his job in the bank where he had worked all his life. Within a few days we had to vacate our apartment when a German family wanted to move in. We were not allowed to find another place for ourselves, but had to move in with other Jewish families already living in the designated area of the city, which was in the old part of town, mainly within the boundaries of the old Jewish ghetto. I remember how devastated my mother was to have to share the kitchen and the bathroom with strange people. It was hard for my parents and for all the others. Our room was full of our landlady's and some of our own furniture. We could hardly move. Every so often Jews had to surrender something: first the radios, then bicycles, all musical instruments, fur coats, pets of all kinds. I had to give up my cat, my skis and ski boots. These are just the things I now remember. Warehouses were designated for collecting the goods, and I remember having to work in one of them to sort and number the items.

Sometime in 1941 all Jews were ordered to wear a Star of David, and a curfew from 8 o'clock until the next morning came into effect. Our ID card, which all the population had to carry at all times, was stamped with a "J" for *Jude*. "Jews Not Admitted" was a sign in most shops. Of course we were not allowed to go to theaters, concerts, cinemas, or libraries. We were not allowed in parks, gardens, or on the embankment. At some point Jews were no longer permitted to walk in certain

Ruth Reiser, New York, May 3, 1994. Photo by Diane Plotkin.

streets or use the streetcars except for the last car. Trains, buses, and cars were out too. There were not many places you could go. I do remember sometimes meeting a few friends in the old Jewish cemetery. Today the cemetery is part of the Jewish museum. All this was, of course, very disturbing and stressful, but most families could still face it together. Nobody knew as yet how trivial this was compared to what we would have to endure in the near future, when the transports started.

In 1940 no public or private school was allowed to admit Jews, and so my formal education came to an end. I was not yet fourteen years old. About that time, the Jewish administration, together with the Zionist Youth Movement, managed to get permission to open an *Aliya* training school, which was to prepare people for emigration to Palestine. My parents were always devoted Zionists, and I was brought up in that sense. I was a member of *Macabi* [an athletic group] and *Hatzair* [a youth movement], so naturally I was enrolled in the *Aliya* school. Hebrew and Jewish history and some crafts were taught there. The teachers tried as best they could to give us a more general education, but when the school was in its second year, all education for Jews was prohibited.

After the school was closed, I started working in the Jewish hospital. It was run only by Jewish doctors, and everybody on the staff was Jewish. The hospital was located in the ghetto. It couldn't have had more than sixty beds because the building wasn't that big. Surgery had to be performed in another small hospital where my appendix was removed. The Jewish hospital was run as well as possible, but by today's standards it was poor. There were not many medications, but a few were still available. There were no antibiotics and none of today's treatments. There were no MRIs and such, but there was a lab working normally. We had patients who had eczema and other skin problems which were treated with special rays called Bucky rays.[2] It was a small apparatus, and you put your hands under the rays of the lamp. At one point I was working for the X-ray department. The apparatus was not built as safely as today's; the technician's only protection was a lead apron and a screen. I did not see any other X-ray departments, so I did not know whether ours was more antiquated because it was a Jewish hospital.

I very much wanted to become a nurse, but I was very young. My parents were not delighted with the thought that a very young girl should go into nursing. At that time it wasn't done. But I didn't want to do anything else. So, in the end, my father said they wouldn't help me, but if I could find a way to become a nurse in this Jewish hospital, he wouldn't stand in my way. I think they thought that I would never succeed. But I did; I became a student nurse. I was the youngest there. I had a good time because everyone was extremely nice to me. That was my first nursing experience, and I was more and more keen to do it. I worked in this hospital until the deportation to Theresienstadt. The transports started in 1941. I was taken to Theresienstadt in June, 1943.

Theresienstadt, or Terezin in Czech, was a garrison town. Before the ghetto was established, the population of the town, civilians and soldiers together, was about seven thousand. When we arrived in Terezin, fifty thousand people were living in the ghetto. The overcrowding was unbelievable. The Germans chose Terezin for building a ghetto because it was well suited for the purpose. The emperor Joseph II had built the garrison in the late eighteenth century and had named it for his mother, Maria Theresa: Theresienstadt.[3] It had fortifications, a moat, and ramparts. It was easy to seal off without building many fences. The ramparts had six gates, which were, of course, locked, leaving little possibility for escape. The ghetto administration, called *Altestenrat* (Council of Elders), was entirely Jewish and worked under the supervision of the German authorities. The Council of Elders had no easy task.

They tried their utmost under extremely difficult circumstances, and on the whole, they were successful. The head of the SS command was camp commander Seidl. In 1947 he was sentenced and executed in Vienna.

When I arrived in Terezin, there were over fifty thousand people crowded there. The first week or so we lived in a loft. Our "family place" was between two beams of the roof. Two of my teachers from the Prague *Aliya* school, Gonda Redlich and his wife Gerti, helped me get a place in a house for teenage girls. There twenty-one of us lived in an average sized bedroom. We shared good and bad times together, the transports changing the inhabitants every so often. Recently I tried but could not remember more than eleven of my roommates. Only about half survived. I'm still in touch with a few of them, although we live in different parts of the world. In Theresienstadt, my mother eventually moved into a barrack for women, and my father to a different one for men.

Zionists had leading positions in the administration of Terezin. They had great influence in the labor and education departments. By the time I arrived in the ghetto, the administration had managed to take over some farms and vegetable gardens around the city. It was a great privilege and advantage to be assigned to work in agriculture. Besides getting out of the ghetto walls, you were in the open all day, and sometimes you could find a way to smuggle vegetables under your clothes into the ghetto. Several times I was offered this as a special privilege, but refused with no regrets. All I wanted was to work in a hospital again. In our dormitory, I was the only person working as a nurse.

I was assigned to a small hospital, which might have been an office building before. The rooms had been converted into sickrooms. I don't know how many patients there were at the time. I guess about sixty. The hospital had two stories; one of the rooms was made into a morgue. I worked on the men's ward, which consisted of five or six rooms. The small rooms were used for infectious diseases; the others had eight to ten beds in each. In a corridor was the nurses' station with one benchlike seat.

We had a small place where you could boil the syringes and sterilize a few things. There were some bandages available, but not much medication. The rooms would look overcrowded in a normal hospital. Some had six beds, or at the most, eight beds. We tried to keep infectious cases isolated in smaller rooms.

The name of the chief physician was Dr. Salus. Another doctor was a Dr. Lohr. I remember him very well. I remember the chief nurse, the head nurse, or the *die-Oberin,* who was German-Jewish. She was very disciplined. I can't remember her name. She was stocky and small. I can see her in front of my eyes. To me she seemed much older, but she was probably only in her thirties. She was very nice, but she ran the hospital like an army sergeant. We had normal shifts. For the night shift, we had to have a pass for walking in the streets after curfew.

There was also a children's hospital where everybody liked to work. The facilities for the old and the mentally ill were very poor. I had never been in that hospital, but I know it existed within the walls of the fortress.[4] It was cold and damp. Many died there, not only from pneumonia and starvation, but their existence was hopeless. Most of their families, who might have helped them, were gone, and they lost the will to live.

There was also a large hospital in Theresienstadt. My husband's mother was a patient in that hospital for a long time, and was looked after quite well. Other medical facilities were in various buildings where only a few beds were available.[5] There was always a need for them, as the transports were constantly bringing new people to the ghetto and sending others away.

One day a nun arrived from Austria in her habit. She was an extremely nice young woman who had no idea of her Jewish origins. She had been brought up in a convent. When they found out that she was partly Jewish, they transported her to the ghetto as she was, in her habit. She became a good friend of mine. Her name was Mirly, but I don't know whether it was her real name or her nun's name. I don't know her other name. I don't know whether she was a nurse in the convent, but she was certainly nursing in Theresienstadt. We worked together a long time. She did not survive.

Among the patients, I remember a middle-aged man who had such severe lupus erythematous[6] that several times every day he had to get up, and we had to shake his bedclothes to get all the skin off. Nothing else was done for him other than keeping him clean. I don't know whether there was any medication for this condition, but at the time, it was certainly not available there.

I also remember a big man who was a grave digger in Theresienstadt, a Jewish man from Germany who suffered from tetany.[7] His attacks were due to a lack of calcium. At times it made him absolutely rigid, and he had to get a shot of calcium very quickly. Calcium was available; syringes were available, but they were not disposable ones. I remember that he got the calcium because I administered it. I remember him because he was an enormous man; he must have been over six feet tall. I am a small person and was slim then. I can remember that holding him when he was rigid was always difficult. I had to find somebody quickly to hold him and to get that syringe and inject him. He was a very gentle man and after a seizure was very apologetic, as if it had been his fault.

There was also a young man from Moravia, who suffered from elephantiasis.[8] He was in his twenties then, and his thighs were enormous. I have no idea what happened to him later. Then there was a room of elderly people who suffered from heart disease. In addition, a lot of people suffered from various forms of tuberculosis.

I can't remember many women, so I must have been mainly on the men's ward. Men and women were segregated as much as possible. Some rooms were for women; some were for men. A different hospital catered to the old people. It was a much worse hospital where not much could be done for them.

At the time, there was a great danger of typhoid, and after I left, typhoid fever broke out. We had some cases of infectious meningitis. One of my colleagues died of it. Her name was Eva. I was with her when she died. There were as yet no antibiotics. There might have been some sulfa drugs, but I don't know how they were distributed or administered.

In the Theresienstadt hospitals there was one patient per bed. I don't know how that worked in old people's homes. There were some linens, hardly enough, but everybody was allowed to bring with them twenty-five or thirty kilos from home. A lot of people came with bed linens when they left home on the first transport, but even this was confiscated upon their arrival and did not end up with them. It ended up in Theresienstadt. Once you left the ghetto in another transport, you didn't worry about linens anymore.

It's very difficult to visualize our situation. My parents, for instance, who were used to living in one place all their lives and having everything there, had to move twice to smaller and smaller quarters until we were in a ghetto in Prague. But people still had a lot of possessions they didn't want to lose or get rid of. You had to choose twenty-five kilos, or only as much as you could carry. Nobody could carry it for you. What do you choose to take with you? Is it your shoes, or is it your linen, or is it your clothes, or is it something you can barter with or sell later? You don't know where you are going. I know, for instance, when I left Prague, I had a duvet with me which we would have made into a sleeping bag. That was important because the winters were very cold there. Everybody had his own quilt in my room in Terezin.

There were people assigned to do laundry, and in the barracks—many had been military barracks—there were washrooms with troughs and water taps, and the linen was washed in these. Some women were assigned to do only washing. They did the laundry for many people. You brought it there as if to a laundromat. Of course you couldn't pay. You had it done the best that person would wash, but it wasn't washed as often as it should have been.

At the hospital the linen was changed when it was necessary. It wasn't changed every other day, but I can't remember that anybody would have been in a very dirty bed. Most of the people were very careful to be clean. What was terrible, and that was really a problem, were the bedbugs. There was nothing anybody could do because the rooms were so overcrowded and there were no pesticides. You could sit at night in the nurses' station, and the bugs were just crawling up the walls and ceiling.

Later lice were the biggest problem because of the typhoid, but in Terezin we could control them. But the bedbugs in this hospital and everywhere else in Theresienstadt were terrible. In summer we used to try to go and sleep outside on a balcony or terrace, where we were not bitten to death by all these bugs.

We washed the patients with hand basins. There was no bathroom facility because the bathroom was used for the lab. There were a few showers in the ghetto, but not in the hospital. They were in some of the barracks, and you had to get permission to use the shower. I remember being in a shower a few times. You could keep yourself clean—you still had your own clothes—maybe not much; maybe occasionally you sold something for food, but you still owned your things. In the hospital, too, most people had their own pajamas. They had come from very civilized places, so they were trying hard to keep clean.

We even had a little soap. It was not given out, but people who came in brought soap with them, and you could barter it for something. As far as toothbrushes go, you had what you brought in.

Toilets were available in the barracks. It was a good thing that barracks were prepared for many because a lot of people lived in them. There were people especially assigned to the toilets, to keep them reasonably clean and to be nasty to people who didn't keep them clean.[9] And there were toilets in the houses. There were not many, but at least they were functioning.

Some doctors brought medical instruments. Specialists brought what they needed. The ophthalmologist brought his instruments, as many as he could, in his little bag. In the hospitals I worked in, there was no surgery performed, but I know there were operations, and there was ether anesthesia administered by the doctor. My husband's brother had a middle ear infection which would not heal, and tuberculosis set in. He had a trephination[10] done. But because there were no antibiotics, the surgical wound never healed, and he died after surgery. He was sixteen.

I have a friend who had terrible problems in her sinuses. She also had surgery in Theresienstadt. They opened the bone above the eyebrow and cleaned her sinuses, and I think it helped her. She still has a big scar. I know there were also a lot of abortions done there.[11]

Every day two meals were given out. It was the same food for everyone—mainly soup, and we had rationed coupons for it. Patients got reasonable portions, but certainly not more than anybody else. To be honest I can't remember exactly what food they were given.[12] The meals were brought for all the patients from the kitchen. Nobody could cook for themselves, so every day you had to go and line up for your rations. It was mainly potatoes and a few other things.[13]

At that time, during the war, the whole population of Bohemia and Moravia, which was then a German protectorate, had not much food either. Certainly the ghetto had less food than the general population. The non-Jews in the province could grow something, or they could have their own chickens or their own livestock, which was highly illegal. Nevertheless people did risk it.

We had our own bakery in Theresienstadt, and it was a great thing to work in the bakery. Out of the bakery came bread for all the fifty thousand people. The bread was wonderful if you were hungry—any kind of bread, dark or light. They also made some light breads, but these weren't distributed to the general population. Only the dark bread was distributed.[14] The bakers did bake something on the side, like a *barches* or challah, which is always used for Friday evening. It was good challah. I know that because I had a boyfriend who worked in the bakery, and sometimes he would bring me a small *barches* for my mother. Work in a bakery was extremely difficult. In the end most people died because it was so exhausting. But it was a big break for anyone to work near some food or be a cook in the kitchen.

I didn't live with my mother; she lived in the barracks. She always kept bits of bread from her ration, and once in a while she made a little cake from it. You were given a bit of margarine every week. You got a ration of bread, a little bit of margarine, and a little bit of sugar. She used to save it—not eat her portion—and then make a little cake out of it. Everybody was supposed to have the same rations, but it didn't work that way. In the end those who were working harder got bigger portions. Of course, the older people had very little food. Most of them were very malnourished.

As far as our duties went, we had to wash the patients; we made their beds; we brought their food in; if they needed medication, we had the roster for administering the pills. When I saw that our grave digger was going to have a seizure, I knew what to do. The work was as near to normal hospital duties as it could be under the circumstances.

The hospital was very overcrowded.[15] There were very few things which a normal hospital would have. For example, there were no bathrooms. If you had night duty, you couldn't have a break even for a short time. In spite of this, everybody tried to do the best for the patients. Dr. Lohr even did research on people with malnutrition; he weighed what people ate and what they excreted.

I was there during the beautification of the ghetto, before the Red Cross came through on June 23, 1944. My hospital wasn't on the inspection route for the Red Cross.[16] Because the Red Cross inspection team was not expected, nothing special was done in that hospital. I don't know which hospital they visited, but they probably went into the children's hospital because everybody always tried hardest, even without the Red Cross coming, to do the best for the children.

We had to make big rearrangements in our living quarters for the Red Cross visit. We had three tiers of bunks to accommodate twenty-one girls in a not-too-big bedroom. Within half a day, we had to remove the third tier and make it into two tiers. As we were all young girls, we all had boyfriends. Some were working in work-shops and had access to bits of wood. The boyfriends came, and together we took off the third tier and made collapsible bunk beds that could accommodate every-body in the room. Our windows were facing the main street, where the Red Cross delegation was to go. We were ordered to make curtains, but I couldn't tell you where the material came from.

The Red Cross Commission didn't visit the inside of the houses, and I think that was their biggest mistake. They never looked in to see the overcrowding or the old people's dormitories, but of course, the pavement was scrubbed and everything was done wonderfully. Everybody was briefed. In case somebody asked you if every-thing was wonderful, you had to say you were having the best time of your life.

The children were told what to say, and the saying is still with us today. The children had to play on the playground, which had been put there for that day only. It included a merry-go-round and swings. A few children were briefed to say to the SS man, whose name was Rahm, "Oh, Uncle Rahm, do we have to have sardines again?" Still today, when we eat sardines, we say, "Oh, not sardines again." It was a big one-day show. Even a ghetto currency was invented for the occasion. But it reverted quickly to the old ghetto life. It was completely useless. They couldn't find anything wrong because they didn't really look. Why they did not want to see where and how people lived none of us could understand.

For all purposes of transportation, hearses were used which were pulled by people. They were used for carrying everything from provisions to dead people. When the Red Cross came, the people pulling the hearses had to wear white gloves, and they had bread on the wagons. A few hours before, these hearses had been full of dead people.

Then came the transport of a thousand children from Bialystok.[17] It must have been 1943. One day there was a big curfew during the day, and nobody was allowed to go out. There was a big hush, and then over a thousand very small children—from ages four or five, up to about ten—came into the ghetto. They had already come through many camps, and they knew much worse camps than Theresienstadt. Why they were brought to Theresienstadt I don't know. It was the eeriest, absolutely unforgettable event. There was not a sound from these thousand children. They were walking absolutely silently, ushered to some area where nobody was allowed to come near them, except the very few people who were to look after them. Nobody was to know what these kids had already been through. They were walking in fives, holding hands. Everybody volunteered, wanting to look after the children because they were so scared; it was terrible to see them. There were other children in Terezin. Of course they were not free, and they couldn't do what they wanted, but they still could speak to each other, with their teachers, and they were in little classes. People tried to look after them. But these kids wouldn't utter a sound. It haunts me still today. Some of my friends and other people volunteered to look after them.

They must have been there two or three weeks. The Germans said these kids were going to go out somewhere into freedom. But of course they went straight to Auschwitz and were all killed along with the escorts who volunteered to go with them.

I was in Theresienstadt until the 1st of October, 1944. Then I went to Auschwitz. A lot of transports left Theresienstadt at that point, but none of us knew where they were going. We knew that they were transports to the East, that they were going somewhere into Poland. But nobody wanted or dared to believe it when some news filtered through about the transports ending in Auschwitz. Sometimes, when people arrived in Auschwitz, they were ordered to write a card which was postdated. By the time the cards arrived, all the people who had written them were dead. But the SS wanted the cards to arrive so the people in the next transport would not make any fuss about going. They wanted everyone to believe that the transports went to a labor camp. That way people on the next transport would think that they too were going to a labor camp.

Everybody knew it was a bad thing to go to the East, but nobody suspected what was waiting for them, even when they had hints from the people who wrote in the cards in Hebrew words that there was a lot of death here. Nobody could grasp the real thing. They would say, "All right, it's hard work; you could die from work, from malnutrition," but nobody could believe they would be killed straightaway in the gas chambers.

I went in a transport on the first of October with my mother; my father had already gone before us. My father worked in Theresienstadt for the administration, and I suspect he knew more than he ever let on. I don't think he knew about the gas chambers. I'm nearly certain he didn't. But he knew there was very little chance to survive. He left about a week or ten days before me and my mother. When he parted from me, he suspected he would never see me again. That must have been very hard for him, but at least we said good-bye, and he gave me his blessing. I wonder whether he did know what was waiting for him. I'm sure he hoped I would stay in the ghetto with my mother. I don't know what happened to him. I think he got out of Auschwitz. He went with a transport which went afterward to Kaufering,[18] but I'm not sure because when I asked after the war, everybody said, "Just don't ask."

My father was in the transport with my then boyfriend, on whom I was very keen. The last time I saw them was when we said good-bye to each other. My boyfriend was quite optimistic, thinking that we would see each other again, but he died six weeks later of tuberculosis. After the liberation, when I came back to Prague, I met a few people who had come back from Kaufering, and when I asked them about my father, all said that I should not look for him.

My mother went with me on the transport from Theresienstadt. We went on the first of October. There were four more transports after us which went from Theresienstadt to Auschwitz. There were about a thousand people in each, and the railway was, by that time, extended into Theresienstadt. When I first came to the Theresienstadt ghetto, there had not been a railway going all the way. It went only to the nearest small place, and then you had to walk, not very far, but a few kilometers. By that time, because they had so many people—they wanted to deport fifty thousand people, and they wanted as little commotion as possible—they had extended the railway all the way to the front of some of the barracks.

We got new numbers. They were made out of a piece of cardboard which we had to tie around our necks. My number was EQ936. I didn't remember the number, but I got it years later out of a register from the archives at Terezin. In the German way they were very organized. There were no more names; everybody went by a number. We were put into the trains. Again they said we could take as much as we could carry. They wanted us to take as much as we could because they knew they were going to take it all away from us on the other side. But of course we didn't know, so once again we went through the trouble of deciding what we would take and what we wouldn't. Not that we had much, but it was fall, and we knew we were going into the winter somewhere in Poland. It was very cold, so we needed boots, a warm dress, and other things that seemed important at the time.

I met my future husband in Theresienstadt. He was a patient of mine in Dr. Salus's hospital, on my ward. He had glandular fever and tuberculosis. They just let him rest. We knew each other quite well. I don't know whether I fell in love or whether we just understood each other very well. He had somebody else and I had somebody else, but we understood each other and could talk a lot. At night he didn't sleep well, and when I was on night duty, he usually visited me at the nurse's table. We talked about various things. He left in a transport after me. He was still in Theresienstadt when I was leaving, and he brought me—I don't know how he got to have them—a box of sardines, the famous sardines which had been provided for the Red Cross inspection. They were supplied in great quantity. That was to show how well the Jews were fed in the ghetto. Before he fell ill, Arnost had worked for a short spell in the bakery. Anything could have been bartered for bread. He gave me this one box of sardines, which my mother and I took for the transport.

Sometime in the afternoon we were supposed to report to one of the barracks for the transport. My mother was very depressed, of course, because my father had left, and I don't know how much he told her. I think she was well aware that we were not going into a sanatorium. After my father left, she was pretty broken. She was young, forty-eight years old, but she looked tired, and she had a head scarf on which made her look much older.

The wagons in which we went were normal wagons. Many transports were already going in cattle wagons, even from Theresienstadt, but we went in a normal old passenger car. We could actually sit down; we were pretty squeezed, but not suffocating. Later I was to travel in much worse conditions. In the wagon I went in with my mother, there were seats—actually benches. Five people sat on a bench on one side and five on the other. Behind us it was open, although not the entire wagon was open. About fifty people went in that wagon. Most of the people in my vicinity were sitting on the floor.

There must have been some bathroom facilities, and we had what food we took with us. It was not supplied specifically for that, but we took the sardines with us. Nobody was very interested in having food at that moment. People were facing the unknown, not knowing where we were going, yet knowing we were going to something much worse.

Now everybody says to me, "My God, if you talk about Theresienstadt, you think of it with fondness." I do because we still had our families around us. We didn't live together, and these were very difficult circumstances, but compared to what came after that, Theresienstadt seemed like heaven. There was still a certain dignity allowed to you; you were dressed in your own clothes; you could speak with others without restrictions; you tried to read, to think. You had a very overcrowded but in some way reasonable life, in hope that this was to be only a transition until the end of the war. And I think that's why, thinking back, I forget the terrible things about Theresienstadt. It was no fun to be there, but I was very young, which helped a lot. I was with a lot of people my age, so we tried our best to overcome the bad times. We didn't have luxuries. I can't remember ever having decent food or anything like this. We didn't have a lot of food, but we were not absolutely starving. There was bread; there were potatoes. But there was a war, and everybody had a very hard time. We had a few possessions of our own. Even with the fewest of things, you still feel somehow yourself. But I still feel as long as I have something of my own, I cling to it. In the evenings after work, we could talk about boyfriends or hopes or what would we do after the war. So from that point, I still feel that for me Theresienstadt was not the worst. I agree that for old people, people over sixty, there was no chance; there was no hope even in Theresienstadt. It was different. But for me, it wasn't that bad.

We settled in the train. We still didn't know where we were going. I can't say exactly how long it took. We rode all night. They used to run the trains mainly at night. Not many people knew what was happening outside. It's not that terribly far from Theresienstadt to Auschwitz. I don't know in miles how long it is, but it couldn't have been more than a twenty-four-hour journey, even if the trains were just standing in various places where other trains were allowed to go.

We arrived during the day. It was not yet dark. I don't know if it was morning or afternoon, but I would expect it was during the late morning because it remained light for a long time. When we arrived, we saw the inscription, "Auschwitz." And then, of course, everybody was absolutely out of their minds. We knew we had come to the last place we wanted to, and nobody believed that this would really happen.

When the train stopped, the prisoners came on and started to get people out very quickly and say, "Leave all the luggage, leave everything. Just you get out and you get out very quickly and everybody—we will get your luggage" and all this sort of thing. All this happened very fast. A young man came, looked at me, and said, "How old are you?" And I said, "Seventeen." And he said, "You are not; you are twenty-one and don't forget it." And he said, "Have you got any food?" I said, "Well, I have sardines here," and he said, "Eat them, eat them very quickly, and get out." So I opened these sardines with scissors and ate the whole box. I think that saved me for a few days afterward.

I didn't understand. The whole thing seemed so unreal. We didn't know what was happening. My mother couldn't swallow and couldn't eat anything, understandably, because she was worried about me. It's a different approach to danger, to everything. You are looking after your parents and you are worried, but your parents are much more worried about you. I have never had my children in the camp, but I have nightmares about losing my children in the camp. Never the other way. I think it's a very different feeling. My mother must have been completely out of her mind. Anyway, I ate these sardines.

Then I got out with the whole group of people. We were very quickly ushered onto the platform in groups, the men on one side, and the women on the other side. There were only the two of us, my mother and I, standing with a few young women who had come with us and who used to live with my mother. My mother had this head scarf on and looked worried. We came in front of this guy we didn't know, a big officer in a uniform. There were a lot of soldiers with rifles and dogs and sticks around him. He said for me to go to the one side and my mother to the other side. I went in front of her and I said, "No, I go with my mother. It's my mother. I want to go with my mother." I never knew why he didn't say go with your mother. He wouldn't let me go with her. He sent some soldiers who pushed me to the other side, and they said, "Oh you will see her soon enough. Don't worry." So I didn't even blink. I didn't say good-bye or anything to my mother.

We were taken through the camp. I remember very well because the way it looked was something you couldn't imagine in your wildest dreams. They took us between the fences, electrified fences, away from the platform. There were dogs, and there was screaming, and there were people behind these fences who thought we still had some food. They were begging, "Have you got any food? Give us food." And the soldier next to me had no hesitation. A woman came very near and wanted some bread, but he shot her. Another person came to the wires, touched them, and was dead. You came to a point at which you really didn't know what happened to you at all.

We walked, and I was thinking; I prayed that my mother didn't have to go through this. Maybe the young people would be taken to harder work and she would have an easier time. Then they got us to the barracks where they stripped us of our clothes. We were naked. They took our hair; they shaved our heads. They shaved everything, but the rest doesn't worry you as much as your head. It's something you are unprepared for; it all was done in a very rough way.

Everything you still had on you was taken: your watches on one pile and whatever jewelry you still had on you on another pile. I had two things. I had a ring which was just a metal ring. It was made in Theresienstadt. It was not made out of precious metal, but it was a nice ring that somebody gave me. It must have been from my mother, and I didn't want to part with it, so I left it on my finger. Also, for my last birthday, my boyfriend had made me a little lucky charm which had the biblical Ruth, a woman with sheaves of grain. I know exactly who designed it. It was very nice. It looked like a large coin. Somehow at that moment, it was all I cared about. I thought if I lose that, that's it. I have no hope anymore. So I put it in my mouth, put the chain on the pile, and left my ring on. Nobody noticed it.

Then we were naked. They had big bunches of clothes, and you quickly took what you could. You just grabbed something; you didn't know what it was. I got somebody's long johns and a handkerchief, which was wonderful. Then you went on and you got two shoes which didn't match. They were certainly not your size. But nobody cared. At that point, they were normal shoes, a pile of normal shoes, but not matching pairs. Later the shoes were changed for wooden clogs, which stuck in the mud all the time. You just grabbed what you could because they were chasing you, "Quick, quick, quick, get it, get it, get it, get it." So you got something. You still didn't believe that it was the real thing—you thought maybe you were somewhere else, and that you were not naked or you were dreaming.

Then a woman who was in charge there realized I had this ring on and said to me, "Give me." She took the ring off. "How can you still keep it? Were you not told to take everything off?" And my ring was gone. It was my least worry, but this lucky charm of mine was not going to be taken from me, and I managed to get it through many selections. And they looked all sorts of places. But I managed to keep it. (Unfortunately I was mugged and lost it from my purse many years after the war. I'm very sorry I lost it.) So then again we were naked; we had nothing on; we had no hair; we looked terrible. You looked around for somebody you knew, but you didn't recognize people when they seemed so different. Somebody looked at me and said, "Oh you look like an ugly boy."

Then we were taken to the barracks. The first night was absolutely unbelievable. When we got to the place we were supposed to sleep, there were some sort of planks we had to use as beds. I don't know how many we were, but there was so little space that we fit like sardines. When one person wanted to turn, about twenty people had to turn with her. Of course, we had no blankets, nothing like that. The only good thing was that all those people kept you a little bit warm. I stayed together with a woman who was my mother's age. She had lost her son when we arrived, the same time as I had lost my mother. I think she felt she had me around, and I felt I had her, and we spent this night together.

The whole night it was raining. That part of Poland in the late fall is foggy and mud, mud, mud. Nothing but mud, fog, and rain. We were getting all wet with the little clothes we had on, and nobody cared a hoot. I don't know what happened to that woman after that first night. I don't even remember her name.

That night, when we arrived in the barracks, everybody asked the inmates who had been in that camp for a long time, "What happened to the other side? Where are the people? When will we see them?" And they were very cold and cruel—at least some. "They are already through the chimney." This is not what I wanted to know. We were there, and we still didn't believe that it was possible.

At that point I didn't see the chimneys; I saw them later. Even if you would have seen the chimney, you wouldn't have believed what they were used for. When you come somewhere, and you see a big factory chimney, do you believe that the smoke is from burning bodies? You wouldn't. You could smell the stench, especially a few days later, when there were a lot of transports and when they were in full operation. But you are shocked in such a way that you don't know what you are seeing, what you are feeling, what you are smelling. You just don't know. And if somebody tells you your mother, whom you had seen three hours earlier, is already dead, you just don't want to believe it, and you don't believe it. You say they are just saying it because they have been here a long time, and they are envious that we came only now. You find various reasons why you don't believe the truth. Of course that woman who was with me, the same was said about her child because it was a small child. That's why the guy on the platform told me, "If somebody asks you, never say you are seventeen." You were always older because when they wanted you for work, they didn't want children, although children were kept for experiments.

What happened in the next few days is a sort of blur. We stood for hours being counted, but not for food. We were always standing outside now with no hair, and it was very cold. You are much colder than if you have something on your head, like a handkerchief. It helped me a little bit because I could put a handkerchief on my head. But you get very cold and tired and absolutely out of your mind standing for hours and hours. They had no intention of letting us work in the camp, so all we did was stand, or if we were allowed to go into the barracks, we had to lie down on the planks.

A few days later, I stood with some people I knew on one of these *Appells* and looked into a window of a barrack and saw my future husband's sister, Zuzka. I knew her only slightly as I had met her two or three times before. At the next *Appell*, we tried to stand with each other and decided that we would stay together as long as possible. We did stay together till the end of the war. It was not always easy because they played so many psychological tricks on you, knowing that people had nothing else, maybe a friend or a mother, or someone else they don't want to part from. The minute they knew, they tried everything possible to separate you. They were really tricks. For instance, sometimes you were walking somewhere or were marched somewhere, and a big military truck was standing in front of you—a military truck with the Nazi insignia on it. As you always walked in fives, somewhere two had to go this way and three had to go the other way. If you were lucky, you were standing with your partner. If you had to part, you never knew whether you would see each other again. These trucks were an absolute horror because you never knew where these lines would part and where, or whether at all, they would come together again.

Whenever you lost something in Auschwitz, you never found it, whatever it was. It might be as insignificant as a handkerchief, but you never saw it again. Whenever you got used to it—if you had a shirt which was maybe sixty times bigger than you needed, in two hours you would be stripped naked and would never see it again. That was terrible. It seems like nothing looking back, but when you were going through it, it was pretty awful.

When we got to another barracks, things were a little bit different. Again we didn't have much space, but there were two-tiered bunks. All night the rats were running across that particular barrack. They were so tame that they could do whatever they liked. They would even walk on your head. That was the only barrack in which I encountered rats, but that was terrible. It was absolutely infested. There were a few nights of just rats around you. They didn't bite me. I don't know if they bit anybody else, but that was not funny.

Then I met a friend of mine from Theresienstadt, who had already been in Birkenau for some time. She had survived the extermination of the family camp shortly before we came.[19] Although most had been killed or gassed, a few survived. She was looking for somebody else but found me and Zuzka. She really was the first one I believed when she told me where we were and what was happening. There was no chance of surviving in Auschwitz because by that time they were starting to just destroy the people and not send many people out for labor. So the crematoria were working to capacity, and I had no hope of surviving. She was working there, so she knew more about the life in the camp. She even brought me some bread. It was unbelievable to get a bit of bread in Auschwitz. But she did bring me bread. She said she probably could never find me again because it was very dangerous to go somewhere far. But I did believe the things she told me, what was happening and which of our friends had died. She told me all that. I didn't see her again until after the war. Her advice was, "If you ever can get out, don't hesitate." A lot of people, when a rumor came that a transport would be going out, started to hide under the bunks and behind a corner. They all thought they would be going into the gas.

Zuzka and I said we couldn't survive here; there was no chance. There was no food; we were not supposed to be working. We were just a mass, waiting for nothing and treated that way. It was very cold; it was dreadful. By then we had clogs on our feet, the wooden clogs, which of course didn't fit either. If you had clogs which were too big and were sticking in mud, you had a hard time getting them out. We were very cold; we were hungry and generally miserable. So we decided should there be any possibility, anybody breathing the words "A transport is going out," we would not hesitate. Not that you could volunteer for it, but you could make sure you got there quickly. It is hard to describe, but if you were in a barrack and they said, "Go quick, quick, quick, you have to be out, you have to be out," and a column was formed, and these capos or somebody said, "It's for a transport out; it's a working transport," a lot of Hungarian girls and other girls started to scream that they didn't want to go. It would be to the gas. Zuzka and I went. We stood in the line in fives. We must have been in the first twenty-five rows, among the first hundred people. We said, "We are in the first part of the column, and so whatever happens we are out."

We were really marched to a platform, to everybody's surprise, not to a selection. We had already been through at least seven selections. Each time we had to be completely naked and run around some officers who looked at us and said, "You go this way, you go that way." When we both ended up on the same side, we were extremely relieved that at least we were together. You knew very quickly whether it was for life or for gas because the older people, people who looked a bit less fit, would be there. We were both very young and were still very fit.

Every time we went through a selection, we were stripped of whatever we had. We then went naked to another barrack where they would throw some other old shirt and other things at us. We were no longer human beings. We had no names. We had numbers, but the numbers didn't mean anything. As long as we had the tattoos we were a particular labor force, but if we didn't, we meant absolutely nothing.

We were not in Auschwitz that long, only four weeks. We were marched in a column to a platform where a train actually would be arriving, and we were all feeling elated. We didn't know where we would go, but wherever it was, it couldn't be worse than here. Whatever happened could be only better. There must have been about two thousand people, so we always stood in long columns of fives. Then a big officer came, as usual with bloodhounds and with his stick, and said, "About turn." We were the last hundred. We never thought this could happen. We still didn't know what was happening, but then, after the count, they needed exactly two thousand slaves for some labor camp.

As it happened, this transport went to Bergen-Belsen, and they had a very tough time, but I had friends who saw me standing there not getting on. When they saw me after the war, they couldn't believe their eyes because they were absolutely convinced that we had gone to the gas chambers. Anyway, they got on. The Germans counted, and between one hundred and two hundred people were left standing on the platform. I don't know exactly how many. The man who was in charge of the count said to another one, "*Eins gas.*"

By that time, I don't know whether we still had any feelings, whether we were relieved, or what. They did take us off the platform. All of us who were there have a little different memory of this, but all pretty horrible. They put us into something which you would use today as a kennel. It was not big—it wasn't even a barrack. We couldn't stand up; we couldn't lie down; we could just about sit. It was right in front of the gas chambers.[20] We could see the columns of people waiting for the gas chambers. We could see the smoke. We could smell everything. There was a big commotion because a lot of the people who were already waiting for the gas chambers were praying and wailing, and it was dreadful. I was in this kennel, and all night I could hear the wailing and the praying and the dogs barking if somebody moved out of the line a little. I don't think we spoke much at all. The flames from the chimneys never stopped.

The worst—maybe not the worst—but a very bad thing was not having anything to drink. We were hungry, but thirst is much worse than hunger. We became dehydrated and were practically in a coma. We would have given anything for a drop of water and begged for water from the people passing by, but nobody was allowed to help us.

I don't know how long we were there. Zuzka has a different view of how long it took, and somebody else has a different view. We were certainly there more than one night. I don't have any recollections that we had any last thoughts. We were completely numb. That's what I was, and Zuzka felt the same. I think also you know what's happening. By that time you are physically pretty beaten down. The psychological things, the selections and the people around you and the screaming—you become completely dehumanized. And you feel that, well what has to come has to come. I think the feelings that you are alone, that you don't have anybody to worry about helped me. My mother was no longer around. It must have been terrible when a mother and daughter were together and couldn't help each other and thought how the other suffered.

How long we were there I don't remember. Then they needed a hundred more people for another transport. They got us out, we didn't know for what. They got us to the platform, brought us to another column of people, and that's how we got out of Auschwitz. It must have been fate. I can't think of anything else. Certainly we couldn't do anything about it. Nobody dared even to whisper the question, but it was on everybody's mind: where are we going? How long shall we stay alive? It was not a long way, and we stopped on a railroad platform again. About one hundred women were needed to complete a labor transport. We were pushed into a cattle car and locked in. We were on the way out of Auschwitz.[21]

Apart from Zuzka, I did not know anybody around me. There were women from Hungary, Poland, some from Holland, and some Czech. They all spoke in their own languages if they spoke at all. We were not allowed to speak at a *Zehlappell*. At the *Zehlappell* you're not allowed to utter a word. At one of the *Zehlappells* in Auschwitz I fainted, and I only wanted to die. That was the only time I thought I just cannot go on. They can do whatever they like with me. But there were two or three girls around me, and they started to revive me. They just pushed me up and held me standing up. Then they put my head up and down. I thought, oh, if they only would let me go. That was the only time I fainted in Auschwitz. Whether it was from hunger, or whether it was that I was cold—it was a combination of everything. That was the only time I thought I really didn't want to go on anymore. The girls got me through the *Appell*, and my will to survive never left me again.

We got on that train, which was pretty awful. They were the cattle wagons, and about a hundred women were pushed into a wagon. Only a few people could sit down in turns. We were squeezed together, standing. I had a corner with Zuzka and some other people. At that point we were relieved to be on the way out of Auschwitz. We were given a bit of bread and a piece of very spicy meat. It was something to preserve the meat, but to have that after being so thirsty and having no water for another three days was unbelievable.

In each wagon they left two buckets, one bucket for a toilet and one with water. But the wagon had no windows; it was very dark, and very soon the two buckets were identical. So there was no water, and at intervals of approximately ten hours—I can't be sure exactly how many, but at long intervals, we were allowed to empty the buckets when they stopped the train somewhere, but by then it wasn't enough because then they let only a little bit of water in, and we never got more. We actually got less because by then people were crazy for water. Being thirsty is really much worse than being hungry.

It was dark; it was unpleasant; people were ill. People were everywhere. There was no space to sit; we didn't know what was happening. But in these wagons there were narrow slits near the ceiling, little openings between the planks, so people with good eyes who were near the wall could see through.

We realized that we were going through Moravia. At one of the stops somebody recognized exactly where we were. I know it was on the 28th of October. It used to be a national holiday in Czechoslovakia. We were delighted to be going through our home country on that day. We, of course, didn't know where we were going, but it was not bad, at least, to know where we were.

It took us three days to get to Lenzing. I thought that was fantastic, to be coming from Poland, from this mud bog, to the Austrian mountains. You could see a big mountain then, which is called the Traunstein. It's behind a big lake, over the Attersee. It's a very beautiful part of the world. The mountain peaks were already under snow; the sun was coming out. This was fantastic air, which you could breathe and didn't breathe any smoke. Everybody thought, "Oh my God, here we can survive. It can't be that bad."

After about seventy-two hours, when they opened the wagons in Lenzing, we were awaited by some SS women. There were a few men around with bloodhounds, but mainly women were waiting. When we got out of the wagons, they were absolutely aghast. They had never seen anything like this. They didn't know what to do with us because they thought they were going to get laborers, and they were digging out skeletons—of course in a terrible state, no clothes, no nothing.

A man came who was from the factory where we were supposed to work. He apparently said—I personally don't remember it—but I was told that he asked, "Where is the luggage?" And the soldiers who had come with us as escorts on this train said, "There is no luggage." And the man said, "Well, where have they got some clothes? You know they can't work like that." And he wanted to send us back. He didn't want to accept or sign for five hundred bodies. But these people who escorted us—they must have been some SS officers—were worried that they would be encumbered with us longer, so apparently they just got on the train and took off and left us there. "That's what we were supposed to deliver, we delivered it, and that's it."

We came straight to Lenzing. We were sold to this factory. In Lenzing was a *Zell* factory. It's called *zell,* but it was *zellwolle,* a wool which was made from some sort of synthetic fiber. They thought it was very important. I don't know whether it was or it wasn't. I don't know if that is still made, but this factory did exist for a long time.[22] It was quite a big factory.

The women didn't know what to do with us. They gathered us in the usual fives. They were women who used to look after prisoners in Mauthausen, but they were still not prepared for what they saw. They marched us about four kilometers, from the factory. I don't know whether it was bombed or burnt out. There was an old paper mill that was to be our habitat. It was an enormous hall with windows. Half of them were broken; half of the roof was broken. It was fenced in on three sides, and on the fourth side we faced the river Ager. On the river side was a big washroom that had a long pipe with faucets which brought water straight from the river. An unrestricted water supply was absolute heaven, and the women went wild and drank and drank.

The SS ushered us into the hall. There were bunk beds, two-tiered bunk beds. I don't know how many slept on each bunk. People who knew each other started to crawl into the bunks together, and the *Aufseherinnen* (supervisors) were absolutely out of their minds, saying, "Well, where do you think you are? If ever we see two in one bed together, you will be shot." These women had no idea of the space we were used to in Auschwitz.

We actually were assigned two to a bunk, and we had a so-called mattress. It was actually a sack filled with shredded paper, but it still was something to lie on. We each got a horse blanket, and they supplied us with long trousers woven out of paper and the striped prisoners' jackets. Some of us got hats, but I don't think I had one. We got our own new numbers—put on a metal strip, which we had to have on our wrist. We also had to put the numbers on the front of our jackets. Then they left us doing nothing for at least three or four days because they couldn't see that we would be able to walk as far as the factory. It was a wonderful rest, and we started to dream of survival.

They made a labor force the first day. Then, when we were put into this factory, they made some divisions of who would go to work where. They asked who spoke German. Few people volunteered. People were very reluctant to volunteer for anything. From them they chose helpers for the Germans. A few people stayed where we lived. Some of them didn't have to go to work but looked after the so-called administration of the place—to see that people went and brought the food to the camp.

Every day, four or five people had to go for food. An hour before everybody else got up, they had to get up, which meant at two o'clock in the morning, because we got up at three, and went these four kilometers there and four kilometers back with a kettle of so-called soup, or in the morning it was some sort of liquid. I don't know what it was. It certainly wasn't coffee. We had a slice of bread a day, which was getting smaller and smaller because in that part of Austria there was very little food. Generally even the Germans themselves had very little to eat.

Of course the citizens of Lenzing knew about the camp. We walked through the town twice a day, and there were many other camps around. There were few people from town in the factory. There were some people, such as the foreman, who were very nice to prisoners. They behaved nicely in hopes that they would get a good testimony later. Nobody was allowed to have anything to do with us. It was under death penalty to help a prisoner in any way. I had once a terrific toothache. I have always suffered terribly with teeth. One of these SS woman took me to the surgery of the factory, and with me standing, the doctor extracted my tooth. He told me to spit the blood out when I was outside. I spit it out, walked away, happy as anything, my pain gone. After the war, I nearly died from extractions with all the anesthesia and sterile conditions.

After the war, when we compared the rations with those in other camps, ours were the smallest. We had fifty grams of bread, a little bit over four ounces, for a day's ration. So in the end, we ate grass; we ate anything we could possibly find. The hunger was that bad.

One room of our barrack was made into a sick bay, where we had a Czech doctor whom I knew quite well from before. Her name was Charlotte Springer. She must have been in her late thirties, or around forty. She was a slight woman, but very energetic. I don't know how they got the nurses. They had two or three nurses at the beginning. One, who was a staff nurse, was Illa Loeb, a Dutch girl who was originally from Wuppertal, Germany. She had studied medicine for a semester or so. Another was Margot Weil. She had been a nurse before. Our friend, who was from Prague, and who managed to get her twelve-year-old sister through Auschwitz with her, came with us. The young sister was physically a big girl and managed to get through the selections. In order not to endanger her, because she was a child, they made her a nursing assistant in the sick bay. She wasn't a nurse, but she managed to work there in order not to go out on assignment, which was hard.

The walks to the factory were very difficult. You had to get up at three o'clock in the morning, and it took till six o'clock to count all the five hundred people. When it came to breakfast, we were given our ration of bread and liquid, and then we marched over an hour the four kilometers to the factory. At seven o'clock, the shift started. We were assigned to various parts of the factory, so everybody worked in a different place. I'm familiar only with the part where Zuzka or I worked. Zuzka went straight into the start of the manufacture of *Zellwolle*. It started as a liquid which contained sulfuric acid. It was terribly painful to breathe the fumes, and you got burned easily. Of course all the foremen and the Germans had protective glasses and gloves. We had nothing. Zuzka worked in this part, and I was assigned to the very end of the operation. The finished product looks and feels like glass cotton-wool. If you touch it, you can cut yourself badly. I had to move around and stack the bales, which were bigger than I was. We had a little two-wheeled trolley, and I had to put the bales into rows and pile them on top of each other.

I don't know how long I would have lasted there—not very long because it was very difficult for me to do. I don't remember how I got away from this work. I think what happened, from what other people said, is that at one point they ran out of raw material and had to stop the factory for two weeks. At that point I got away from the factory floor, and I was assigned to clear the floors and everything in the SS mess, in the cafeteria.

Every day I scrubbed the floors and the chairs. Every chair had to be scrubbed because they didn't have enough work for us, so they made us scrub the chairs underneath, on top, and everywhere else. To keep myself sane, while scrubbing one chair after another all day long, from seven o'clock till five o'clock in the evening, I pretended they were my own chairs in my own kitchen. I am back, and I have my own apartment or house, and I am doing it for my own family. I got through all of it quite well because I was fantasizing, never speaking to anybody.

That didn't last very long. Sometime in March, Zuzka's friend, who became one of the translators between the SS and the rest of us—she was called a *Schreiber*, somebody like an administrator, with power in the camp—took pity on me and managed to change my assignment to a potato peeling commando. About five or six people went to peel potatoes in the SS canteen. This was a stroke of luck, a great assignment. We peeled raw potatoes all day long. Of course, secretly we could eat the raw potatoes and not be seen. We could manage to hide and take the peelings from there. On top of that, every day I had an extra ration of soup, which was from the factory kitchen and not our camp soup. On arrival in the camp, every prisoner was given a gray metal soup plate and a wooden spoon. In order to get the soup to Zuzka, I had to carry an open soup plate these four kilometers. Apart from the time that the soup was frozen, when it was easy, it wasn't very easy to carry and not to spill for four kilometers. But I did it till the end. Sometimes I managed to share the carrying with Zuzka if I was anywhere near her in the column.

I had just a little bit more food on this assignment. We were not allowed, of course, to bring even the peelings home. Once they caught me. I had stuffed them in my pocket or somewhere. They made a body search when we came back. My peelings were found, and I had to go to a mock trial. I will never understand why and how I got away. I was sure that they would send me back to Auschwitz because that was a terrible crime. I was brought in front of three soldiers, the Wehrmacht or SS, I wouldn't know, and they asked me, "Why on earth do you do this?" I looked at them in absolute astonishment and said, "Well, we are hungry." And they said, "Well, why didn't you say so?" They pretended not to know how little food we were given. It was unbelievable; they let me go.

There was no heating whatsoever. In the mountains it is not warm during the winter, and we had come to Lenzing at the end of November. There was a stove in the sick bay which was lit every day. I knew the doctor. I got very friendly with Margot, and through Margot with Ellen Loeb.

I can still visualize her. She was short, not too small; she was bigger than me and a bit stocky. She was always fair, and she was good. Whenever I could, I went to the sick bay and had some hot water and a bit of warmth and helped out with whatever was needed. They didn't have many beds there, but they tried to do the best they could. There were a lot of things which were happening. One memorable day was on the 11th of January. It's Zuzka's birthday, so that's why I know the exact date. Dr. Springer let her stay home. She was ill. Her hands were in a terrible state from her work in the *Duesen kolonne*.[23] The doctor could always leave somebody at home one or two days, so Zuzka was staying home that day. Because it was her birthday, I worked it out to be sick too so that we could be together for her birthday and not go out to the factory.

At three o'clock in the morning it was the *Appell,* and about six o'clock everybody left. The days were still relatively short. It was early morning, completely dark, and it was snowing very hard. The women walked close together to fight the driving snow. It was a long column when five hundred people were marching. In front was a soldier with a dog, and in the back was a soldier with a dog, and in between were the SS women who looked after us every day. The guards changed around. They never let these SS women stay with us longer than two or three weeks, in order not to get used to individual prisoners and be nicer to them. That's why they rotated the guards all the time.

The route to the factory crossed an unprotected railroad track. It was snowing very hard, and the guards in back were screaming, "Go faster, go faster." The column mustn't be split on the railway because they were always worried that somebody would escape if anything unusual happened. So we had to cross before the train came.

It was foggy; because they tried to rush all the prisoners quickly across the railroad tracks, they didn't see the approaching train until it was too late, and several of the women were killed.[24] There was a great commotion because they had to leave the injured and the dead women on the spot. Several bodies were dismembered, and all had to be cleared away. The rest of the prisoners were marched to the factory to work as usual, and one of the guards came back to the barracks and reported what had happened. Not even thinking, five minutes later, I volunteered to go with blankets to help to get someone in case somebody was injured and needed help. Of course the guard said, "How come I could be allowed to stay home sick but could still go?" But they needed somebody to clear the bodies, and they let me go.

We needed to bring a sled and blankets in order to carry all the bodies back. I don't think there were many survivors. I don't know how many people died, but that was one day all of us remember.

The next day I remember happened later in January, when Auschwitz had already been evacuated. A lot of people had been evacuated from other camps in death marches in the snow. There were about twenty girls who survived one of these death marches and who came to Lenzing. One of them was a Yugoslav girl called Nadja. I forgot her other name. I was still in touch with her after the war. She was about fifteen when she came, and her feet were frostbitten and frozen. They were completely black. Her friends had carried her the last stage of the walk to Lenzing. She was taken to the sick bay. The SS doctor from the factory used to come to inspect the sick bay, see whether things were going right, and make sure the Jewish doctor was not doing anything against the rules. Unfortunately, he was a surgeon who loved to cut or amputate. It was always a big worry of our doctor how to hide people who would look like possible surgery cases. Nadja was hidden from him for a long time because he would have amputated both her legs. She was in excruciating pain, and the doctor had nothing much to help her. All we had was charcoal for diarrhea, dysentery, or typhoid. Charcoal powder was used on Nadja's feet. In some way it must have helped because new skin grew on her soles after a time.

Every day, late at night, we had to take off the bandages. Every time one of her toes stayed in the bandages, and she screamed with pain. Somebody was always needed to help change her bandages because somebody had to hold her head to help her not to scream. She was in excruciating pain. But she survived. She walked again, but not very easily because she had lost all her toes. For many weeks we had to hide her the night the doctor came so he wouldn't see her.

I really didn't work in Lenzing as a nurse, but at that time I used to come to the sick bay every night to see Nadja. I did not get much sleep. We had to get up at three o'clock in the morning, and it was not until after eight o'clock in the evening that we were free to move around the barracks. Only then could I sneak to the sick bay.

By that time I was really getting very exhausted, and Zuzka helped me a lot. She got our ration of bread in the morning. I would have eaten the entire piece at once, but she managed to hide part of it for me to eat in the evening, when we came back. She was right, but I could not have done it on my own. I was not as disciplined as she was.

At one point Lenzing became infested with lice. We got no sleep at all because we were itching. We couldn't get rid of the lice. I have always suffered from insect bites, and I got terribly allergic. I got bloated like a balloon, and I was very scared that they would ship me back because it looked like I had scarlet fever or something terrible. I was bitten on absolutely every part of my body. With the lice came an outbreak of typhoid. Luckily it happened not long before liberation, and only a few of the women died. The rest were treated after the liberation by the Americans.

One woman was pregnant, and she had either a stillbirth or an abortion. But that too had to be hidden from everybody because she wouldn't have survived; she would have been shipped back to Mauthausen.

There was another very young girl who was pregnant and who carried the pregnancy secretly, possibly because our loose jackets hid her. She delivered the child the day after liberation. It must have been our doctor who delivered the baby girl on the 6th of May. There wasn't any more necessity of hiding the child. Formerly the child would have been killed straightaway because in the camps newborn babies, even if they were healthy, were killed at once to save the life of the mother.

I can't remember the details of the sick bay anymore. A friend of mine, who was a sister of this very young girl, and I have terrible disputes as to whether the window was on the left side or on the right side. She thinks it was on the right side; I think it was on the left side. It's very irrelevant, but I can't say that I remember exactly how things looked.

What I do remember very well is that the sick bay was not a very big room; actually there were two rooms. It was a wooden barrack which adjoined the old factory, but the factory was abandoned when we came there. It seemed to me that these rooms could have been offices while the factory was still in operation. We lived in a big hall. There was a long corridor, and across the corridor were various little rooms. One of them was for the SS, one for the Wehrmacht. Two rooms were the sick bay. One had a stove; it was used more like a surgery; there were no beds, but people came there and the doctor saw them, even though, in fact, there was very little she could do for them at all. If somebody was cut up badly, they had some bandages.

The only medicine that was available was charcoal. At that time iodine was available, and if you were cut, you could put iodine on it. The charcoal was available if you had diarrhea. If you had a high fever, she let you stay at home two days. That was about the only remedy. How she managed the miscarriage—I know it was done there, but what instruments she had I wouldn't know. It had to be done in secret.

There were very few bandages available for people who injured themselves in the factory. There was large machinery there, and people did become injured. There were times when some of the commandos went out and had to bring some stones from one place to another. One labor unit worked in the salt mines near Salzburg.

There were few medicines in the sick bay, but the doctor invented a fantastic thing. She realized that a lot of people need to believe they are treated, so she managed to find little bottles or a bottle which we put water in. And with an eye dropper and a little spoon, she administered a few drops of just plain water and said, "Don't tell anybody I gave you this. I've only got a little of it." And she administered this water and people got better. We used to call it *Udenol*. It was nothing, but even after the liberation, when I worked with her in a different hospital, she still used *Udenol* and people loved it and went around saying, "You didn't give me my medication for six hours now; I need it." That was a good invention. It didn't do any harm.

Illa Loeb was a very nice person. She was the one who tried to be very fair to everybody. She somehow realized that she had a bit of privileged position there. She didn't have to go out; she got her food delivered—not that it was any food, but at least she didn't have to fight for it. Everybody was very careful to be nice to her because occasionally you needed a day off if you were completely exhausted. Of course she worked very closely with Dr. Springer. I knew her very well, but I was much more friendly with Margot because Margot was nearer to my age. Illa was a little bit older than I am, but she already had, I think, a semester or so of medicine. At least she pretended to have.

I lost touch with Illa the day she left. In the camp I had been with her very often, mainly regarding Nadja, the Yugoslav girl with her frozen feet.

During some of my free time with Zuzka we joined my friend and her thirteen-year-old sister. She desperately tried to provide some little education for the sister. So if we had any Sundays we didn't have to go to work, the four of us sat together and made quizzes. We tried to remember streets of Prague, which shops are on the streets. Just to do something, we tried to learn Hungarian. (I still can count to ten in Hungarian.)

Another pastime, which was more than a pastime since it was an obsession of practically everybody, was exchanging recipes for food. We had terrible quarrels because if you said this recipe needed three eggs, somebody else said you need five eggs. We argued whether you need hot water, hot milk, or cold milk—it was an obsession. We couldn't think of much else other than food. We exchanged these recipes at night. We woke up somebody saying, "Do you remember your mother's recipe for this or that? Tell me. It's a very important thing." That happened in all of the camps. Somehow, there's some things which you can't help.

Near the end, in April, it started to be very bad. There was no food, so on the way to work we used to collect some grasses, like dandelions, which we knew were edible. In the spring the snails came out, so we collected and ate the snails. (I can't eat snails even today. I can eat sardines; that I like.)

In April, both fronts were coming nearer. The Germans started to be a little bit more nervous. Air raids were more frequent, and at that time planes, low flying planes called *Tief fliegers*, were flying over most of the territories.[25] They were flying so very low that the pilots could see the people on the ground. They bombed whatever they found, so when the sirens sounded, the SS guards used to get us out into the open, make us take off our striped jackets and put them on the ground to show that there are prisoners there. Sometimes they even put them over their own uniforms. They were so scared that the Allies would target the SS uniforms. They thought nobody would go for the striped prisoners' uniforms. Of course we were glad and knew the end was coming. The rumors started to go around that they wouldn't let us survive, that they would get us to these salt mines or another quarry and blow us up. Whether it was true or not I still don't know, but some of the girls who were working in the salt mines said they knew; they had seen the charges there, and the mines would be blown up.

We didn't know what was happening. We knew through the grapevine that there were a lot of prisoner of war camps around. A Russian camp was near, and there were some French civilians who had been deported there as forced laborers. They were not prisoners and were free to walk around. I couldn't speak any French, but Zuzka was very fluent in French. One day two Frenchmen on bikes appeared near the fence and told us to remain calm. They promised to try to find the Americans and tell them about us. We could hear the shooting at the front, and the Germans were saying, "If the Americans come we are all right; if the Russians come we will commit suicide because they will kill us." Nobody knew who would arrive first. It was chaotic on the road. People were going in all directions.

The front was coming, and it really came to the crunch there, where the Russians and the Americans met.[26] The number of the air raid sirens was a code about what was going to happen. Either there were low flying airplanes or a big air raid of many planes. We were told that when the sirens go on for many minutes—I can't remember now how many times—the Germans are allowed to abandon their posts and flee. So everybody was counting the number of sirens furiously whenever the air raids sounded.

At last the air raid came, and the sirens were hooting and hooting. The SS woman who was in charge of the whole camp called another *Appell* and said, "The enemy is near, and we have to abandon our posts. You will be locked in the camp until somebody else will take over." She got on her bike and disappeared, and in a little while she came back because she forgot her iron. She collected her iron and disappeared for good.

In a short time, two trucks of Americans arrived. The commander was a Jew, and shortly afterwards came black soldiers. They were the first black people I had ever seen. It was the 83rd Division of Patton's Army.[27] I don't know whether there was another white division with him, but I remember that these black men came. They were the only ones who came to Lenzing at that moment. The commander told us he was making a diversion just to liberate us because he had been alerted by some French men that we are in great danger of being killed soon. I never knew the name of the commander. I know that it was part of Patton's Third Army.

The soldiers were surprised and shocked. I think that was the first time they had seen something like that, and, unfortunately, they left whatever food they had—

the K rations with bacon in it. Many women ate everything at once, and the bacon had bad consequences. Many got bad diarrhea, and tragically, a few died on the very day of liberation.

The American soldiers were friendly; they gave us all their rations. But they disappeared very quickly. They weren't stationary anywhere. They were moving on. Because the war wasn't over, they locked us in our camp again. People were, of course, very happy and praying and singing, but it took another day before the army came and opened our gates. If we wanted to, we could go out of the camp. We couldn't go very far, though strangely enough, as prisoners we could walk eight kilometers a day, but when we were free, we couldn't walk very far. It was somehow overwhelming to go where you wanted. I went out a little bit with Zuzka and returned again.

When the American army came, they took over the sick bay and left Dr. Springer in charge. Another small hospital which then served the main Lager was in Ebensee. Dr. Springer was allocated wooden barracks which would serve as a small hospital. She asked me to join her as one of the few nurses. Zuzka didn't want to nurse, but we didn't want to part because we were so close by then, we wouldn't have survived without each other. And, as many people found, there were times when one couldn't go on anymore and the other one said you must. When life was at its worst and other people couldn't go on, you had to talk them through it. Because Zuzka and I wanted to stay together, Dr. Springer found a job for her looking after the linen and all the supplies. It was a lot of work. A lot of people were just exhausted. Many had tuberculosis; a few had died of typhoid. Many had dysentery. When the Americans came, they tried to contain the typhoid.

The Americans provided whatever medical facilities they had. A lot of people were X-rayed for TB. Everybody had blankets; we had sheets and soap. We were given food which we had not tasted for years from the United Nations Relief and Rehabilitation Administration. That did more for us than any medication. Most of the camp was quarantined. There was a place where people were quarantined for some time because they didn't know what diseases we had. Whatever Dr. Springer asked for and they could supply, I am sure they did supply. The army was not prepared for anything like they found. I think they were shocked to see people in the state we were in and really didn't know what to do.

Before we left for home, I went to one of the U.S. commanders and asked him if we could use the civilian car for driving home some of the seriously ill women who would have had difficulty traveling in the open trucks. He agreed and signed the papers for the car in mine and Zuzka's names. After our arrival in Prague, our car disappeared with the driver, never to be seen again. After the war, a car was a big deal.

After the liberation, of course, we all had two thoughts: to get home and to have enough food. It was unbelievable the amount of food that we could consume. Then the Americans supplied us with UNRRA rations. There were tins of condensed milk in it, and we consumed I don't know how many tins of that milk each night.

After the liberation, Ellen Loeb and the Dutch people left for Holland. They were the first ones to be repatriated. A plane arrived to fly them home. It was wonderful. But we had to wait about five weeks before we were transported back.

We stayed in Lenzing to work with Dr. Springer; then the Czech government together with the Red Cross rescue operation organized our repatriation. Every day on the radio was a broadcast announcing which people will be collected from which camp and where they will be going. Shortly after the liberation, several young men came to Lenzing trying to find surviving family members. One of them said he would be going back to Czechoslovakia. We begged him to let the Red Cross know that we were still in Lenzing waiting for transportation home. We were listening to the radio every day. Then the radio announced that we would be collected the next day. It was sometime in June. The trucks would come to collect us. And sure enough, they came and we drove home.

After five weeks of waiting, I arrived in Prague. That was more traumatic than I had expected. For several years you have in your mind, you only think to be back to your hometown, to everything. Now you arrive on a lorry in the middle of your town, and you don't know where to go. You are truly and absolutely homeless. I knew my mother wasn't coming back. I guessed my father had not survived either. I knew within a day that he was not coming back. So where do you go? To some people you know? I had a distant relation who married a gentile, and they lived in Prague at the time. So I went to them, and they were very nice to me. But you feel nobody can ever understand what you went through. They look at you a little bit like at somebody from the zoo. We had no clothes; we were still in the striped jackets. We were at home, but we were strangers.

I knew that my parents had put some of our belongings with people for safekeeping, and all of them denied it. All of them said, "Oh, we were so badly off we had to sell it." I could see my parents' belongings in their apartment. I was nineteen; what could I do? You can't say it's not true. So you go away. I knew my father had been working for one bank all his life, and I knew he had life insurance there. I was told I was entitled to his pension and insurance.

I had nowhere to go. I couldn't go back to school because I had no money. So I went to the bank, and they gave me two hundred crowns as charity but said all the documents of Jewish employees had been destroyed, and they did not want to know about the life insurance. So again, what are you going to do? You have no idea whether you have a right to do something or not. A lot of people tried to emigrate very quickly because our welcome wasn't overwhelming. I wanted to stay, but it took a long time to settle down.

At first I worked for the Jewish Civic Center. It was a registration office for survivors. There were lots of books which had been stored by the Germans in our synagogues, and they were trying to restore the library from what books were still around. So for a little while I worked there in this book storage to register and catalogue the books. I had no way of finishing my high school education. I applied and was admitted to a nursing school in a big hospital and started nursing.

During that time there was a transport of children from deprived countries going to England for three months. They were looking for escorts for these children, and I took the chance and went. The children were quarantined in a camp for four or five weeks before they were taken by foster parents. I didn't know what to do, so I went as an au pair, a girl who looks after children. I decided it would be nice if I could stay in England, so I got a work permit to see if I could do midwifery. I couldn't do nursing because I had not matriculated and had no money. But they took me and said I could start to work with the students. In the last two days I decided I didn't think I could stand it there, and I went back to Prague.

Two years after our liberation I married Zuzka's brother, Arnost Reiser, who is now a professor of chemistry. I started to work in a hospital, but not as a nurse. I worked in the medical laboratory. Still, I was working in a hospital. But coming back was very traumatic, and I think, even till today, very hard to get over. I never felt at home there after that. I never felt I could relate, and I always tried to somehow get out.

Zuzka survived and married a British soldier in a Czech division. He was a journalist, and she started to work as his secretary. In 1960, I emigrated to London via Denmark.

• • •

In 1982 the Reisers moved to the United States. Dr. Reiser became a professor at Polytechnic University in Brooklyn, New York. Mrs. Reiser has been a volunteer for the Metropolitan Museum. They have two sons, one born in 1952, the other in 1956. One is a pediatrician in England; the other is a violinist in Philadelphia. They have three grandchildren.

Westerbork

JOURNEY TO THE UNDERWORLD

How hard it is to tell what it was like,
this wood of wilderness, savage and stubborn
(the thought of it brings back all my old fears),
a bitter place! Death could scarce be bitterer.
—Dante Alighieri, *Dante's Inferno*

After the Blitzkrieg of September, 1939, when the Germans conquered Poland, most of the German Jews who had not yet emigrated were shipped to ghettos in the Polish cities. Other Jews living in western European countries that were occupied shortly thereafter, such as the Netherlands, were transported to transit camps, which were then to become sluices to the extermination camps in the East. One of these transit camps was Westerbork, situated in northern Holland in the province of Drenthe, eleven kilometers south of Assen. It had originally been built in 1939 by order of the Dutch government to provide temporary shelter for Jewish refugees from Germany. Never intended to be an extermination camp, when the war broke out, it was soon taken over by the Germans. Between July 15, 1942, and September 13, 1944, ninety-three trains deported more than one hundred thousand people to their deaths in Germany and Poland. Run by SS-Obersturmführer [First Lieutenant] Albert Konrad Gemmeker, the camp operated smoothly and without incident. As long as the train left every Tuesday with its weekly quota of deportees, Gemmeker "acted the part of a decent gentleman, who treated the Jews correctly." Running of the camp itself, however, was by and large left to an organization of German Jews.[1] The commandant maintained that he had no idea where the prisoners were taken, although when asked one time if a child could be spared the trip because he had a temperature of 104 degrees, he replied, "No, the child will die anyway."[2]

Westerbork was a camp of contrasts and contradictions. There were no bellowing, murderous SS guards. Prisoners themselves maintained order within the camp; they were assisted by Dutch military policemen, who later took over watch outside the camp as well. Food was relatively good, although the water was not fit to drink. Commandant Gemmeker, a "gentleman soldier," was said to have "no patience with brutality, was approachable and, above all, incorruptible. Compared to other camps, where torture was a daily pastime, Westerbork was positively 'civilized.'" Nonetheless, he was said to be "devoid of natural feeling, capricious, and, in short, incalculable." He never screamed at anyone, and as long as he filled the weekly quota, he gave the Jews "the best treatment that was permissible under National Socialism." After the war it was said that many wanted to hang Gemmeker, albeit "with a velvet cord."[3]

At first glance, it would seem that life in Westerbork was not all that bad. Indeed, inmates as well as officers there enjoyed music, ballet, theater, an excellent cabaret, and sports.[4] Children attended school. In addition, there was a *Legerwarenhaus* (warehouse) and a well-provisioned canteen, where inmates could make purchases with camp money that had been exchanged for hard cash. Inmates were also allowed to receive packages, and at times some were even allowed to go home on "leave."[5]

Medical facilities in the transit camps varied. In Westerbork, for example, there was a 1,723-bed hospital staffed by twelve hundred physicians, and patients were free to choose their own doctors. The staff included pediatricians, who were in attendance from 2:00 to 4:00 P.M. every day. Physicians held medical conferences at "the highest scientific and clinical level" every week.

A general staff of over one thousand included dieticians, hairdressers, photographers, chaplains, dentists, messengers, pharmacists, photographers, and porters. There were such special areas as isolation units, a psychiatric ward, a diet kitchen, stores, a section for making anatomical diagrams, an orthopedic clinic, laboratories, a welfare department, first aid clinics, a hygiene department, dental clinics, a postal service, and operating rooms. An outpatient clinic was open from 7:30 to noon and from 2:30 to 5:30 P.M., and there were special sessions for workers at 6:30 A.M. and from 7 to 8 P.M. Visiting hours in the hospital were from 7 to 7:50 P.M. daily. All inmates were X-rayed for tuberculosis, immunized against typhoid and paratyphoid fever, and tested to determine their blood groups, which were then kept on record.[6]

Despite the facilities, however, medical care often left much to be desired; Philip Mechanicus relates that the infant mortality rate was high. Children suffered from pneumonia, scarlet fever, and dysentery. Although care given by doctors was excellent, nursing care was generally not up to par.[7] Etty Hillesum relates that people suffered from chronic colds due to the climate, and that the worst problem was lack of hygiene. Women, moreover, did not have sanitary napkins, and there were no rolls of bandages available.[8]

Hildegard Grau recalls Westerbork as being "massive" and "overpowering." Similar to others, she remembers a pervasive odor of Lysol. Functioning as a pediatric nurse, she recalls that there was an ample supply of physicians but a shortage of food and medications.[9]

The head of the Medical Service, Dr. M. Spanier, and the camp commandant, Gemmeker, had an unusual relationship. Dr. Spanier seemed to have such a great influence over Gemmeker that he was not required to stand up in Gemmeker's presence.

Although there were no gas chambers there, prisoners faced the certainty of deportation and death. Hillesum, writing about some of the people she encountered in the hospital, gives a graphic description, typical of the heartbreak of a mother who confronts the inevitable: "She looked deranged. A flood of words poured over me, 'that isn't right, how can that be right, I've got to go and I won't even be able to get my washing dry by tomorrow. And my child is sick, he's feverish. . . . And I don't have enough things for the child, the rompers they sent me are too small . . . oh, it's enough to drive you mad. And you're not even allowed to take a blanket along, we're going to freeze to death. . . . do you think they'll leave the children with their mothers . . . ?' "[10]

The misery of life in Westerbork was reflected in its gallows humor. For example, the main street of the camp was called *Boulevard des Miseres* (Boulevard of Miseries), *Rachmones* (Pity) Street, or *Tsores* (Trouble) Avenue. One riddle going around camp asked, "What is 'a privileged position'?" And the answer was, "a front seat in a cattle truck for Poland."[11] Inmates had to endure noise, filth, heavy labor, a total lack of privacy, and the constant threat of deportation. These bitter realities are perhaps best seen in comments made by the prisoners themselves. J. Cahen describes the miserable condition of the prisoners upon arrival: "approximately 17,000 Jews came to the camp at the beginning of October (1942). And what we saw defies any description. They arrived pushed along like cattle. . . . Sick women, lifted from their beds, dressed in thin nighties. Bare-footed children still in their pajamas, old people, sick people, lame people, the stream of newcomers went on and on and on."[12]

Etty Hillesum tells of the miserable living conditions. "Most appalling, they are ramshackle and overcrowded sheds with draughty lathwork where iron beds are piled up three layers high beneath the drying laundry of hundreds of people. One lives and dies in the same bed as one eats, lies ill or awake in, due to the crying of so many children through the night, or because one is wondering time and again why almost nothing is heard from the thousands of people that already left this place."[13]

But the strange paradox of life in Westerbork is perhaps best contained in the words of T. Van Reemst-deVries. After she had given birth to a premature infant, Commandant Gemmeker ordered an incubator from Groningen and sent for a professor of pediatrics to discuss what could be done for the child. No efforts were spared. She relates:

> Gemmeker frequently came to have a look, whenever I was tending the baby. . . . To us
> this meant that this child would stay alive, and that they were fighting for its life. Even with the

help of Gemmeker who was, after all, our enemy. We clung to this hope and to this tiny human being. And this little human did stay alive. The flame of life was growing stronger. One day he could drink from the bottle. And when he weighed five and a half pounds, he was even let out of the incubator into a cradle. . . . We thought that we had made it, that this proved that there was hope, that there was a future. But when Michael weighed six pounds, he was transported to a labor camp. . . .[14]

The inconsistency and ever increasing misery of life in the camp is reflected in the letters of the Loeb family to their friends in Amsterdam, as there were "writing days" when the prisoners were allowed to post mail. At first no one knew what was to become of them, as indicated by their first postcard as well as in the first section of Ellen Loeb's memoirs, which describe her life and her efforts to nurse the sick in Westerbork.

Chapter Six

Trudy Shakno

"ICH WEISS NICHT WAS SOL ES BEDEUTEN"
[I DON'T KNOW WHAT THIS ALL MEANS]

• • •

The conditions in the various infirmaries and the sacrifice of those who volunteered to care for the sick in Westerbork, Theresienstadt, and Lenzing are reflected in the memoirs of Ellen Loeb. In these memoirs the reader can feel the day-to-day emotional suffering in what sufficed for an infirmary. In essence, she found herself in a position of virtually holding the power of life and death over the women in her care. Her sister, Trudy Shakno, painstakingly translated the single-spaced typewritten memoirs Ellen had written and which had remained hidden in a bank vault for fifty years. Trudy stated that she had recently come across these diaries as well as a collection of postcards from Westerbork to the Strauss family in Amsterdam, who were friends of her parents.[1] She relates her recollections of her own family as follows:

My father had been a physician in the German army, Battalion #65, during World War I.[2] He raised chickens where he was stationed in order to have eggs and chicken soup for his patients and sent eggs to me when I was sick. In 1916 my grandfather was run over by Kaiser Wilhelm's carriage in the spa of Kreuznach in the Hunsruck region of Germany. My father was allowed military leave to attend the funeral and was discharged in 1918. He was awarded the Iron Cross on July 13, 1934, on a document dated March 18, 1935.

He was a political liberal whose sympathy was with the working class and felt that as a physician he could contribute to the physical health of the community. He chose to live in Wuppertal, an industrial city in West Germany. It was the twin city of Barmen and the headquarters of Bayer Medical, Solingen Steel, and Bemberg Rayon. Barmenia, named after Barmen, was the very first medical insurance company in the western world. Credit unions also originated there.

After World War I, my father taught volunteers to administer first aid in case of disasters. The young German students who were his make-believe patients later turned against him when they joined the Nazi Party. When I was seventeen years old, my father was informed by Jewish agencies to prepare as many Jewish teenagers as possible to leave the country and go to live with Jewish families in Italy. Later he was allowed to take about fifteen girls there. His Dutch cousin also offered whatever help we needed, and by March or April, 1932, my cousin and my parents arranged for me to go to Holland.

In 1934 my father, who had studied under Dr. Semmelweis[3] in Vienna, was sued for having performed an abortion which was allegedly complicated by infection. Although he was judged innocent through the intercession of the dean of the medical school in Berlin, my father's medical license was revoked, and my mother found him in his office contemplating suicide. In 1935 she had him taken across the border into Holland by a young Christian man. My father came to live in my apartment in Amsterdam.

My mother had stayed in Germany to dissolve the household and later came to Amsterdam with our maid. They couldn't bring any money, but because I had emigrated before the time of Hitler, I was allowed to bring a dowry: my parents' ten rooms of furniture and household goods. By then my father was too old to get a license to practice medicine in Holland. My mother, a dietician, utilized her training to create a sanitarium for people who needed to be on special diets. This flourished so well that three years later it had spread out to three adjoining suburban two-story homes and had a staff of ten.

During *Kristallnacht* my father, hearing about the burning and destruction in Germany, suffered a cerebral hemorrhage that left him totally paralyzed. The Dutch cardiologist began immediate therapy. The morning after the stroke, my father was visited by a therapist who brought flash cards and began to work with him to restore his speech. He had to be in a sitting position most of the day. The therapist's aide moved my father back home and slowly trained him to talk, write, and walk once again. The only residue was a juxtaposition of the laughter and crying responses.

My husband and I immigrated to America on August 15, 1939. During the week we were on the ship, Hitler invaded Poland. My parents and sister had planned to go to England and from there to South America, but they lost their nerve before they crossed the channel and went back to Amsterdam.

My sister was picked up by the SS and disappeared for a bit, but came back. At first she was put into a hiding place between the ceiling and the second floor. Then the Jews began to be transported to Westerbork. A few of their friends went in each transport. In 1941 the family began to suffer harassment, and in 1942 they were listed for transport. My father's cardiologist did not feel that my father could make the trip and wrote the following letter:

September 4, 1942

I herewith advise the authorities that Dr. Julius Loeb is suffering arteriosclerosis. He suffered a stroke, and his mobility and ability to communicate are very limited. He needs the constant attention of his wife and daughter, and I consider him unable to survive transport to Westerbork.

Dr. J. Groen

Specialist for Internal Disease

It didn't help; they had to go anyway. They were transported to Westerbork on November 8, 1942.

My Dear,

Ich weiss nicht was soll es bedeuten [I do not know what all this means].

December 24, 1942

In a great hurry.

Dear Strausses,

Our thanks for the wonderful package. So much love and compassion. Our friend Mr. Karpf, who was allowed to return to Amsterdam, offered to send us, through you, a package each week. The towels and handkerchiefs were so welcome.

I'm working in the hospital. Dr. Spanier from Dusseldorf is the administrator. I hope that my parents will soon be allowed to work there too. Many regards.

Yours,

Illa

In all the letters the Loebs addressed friends formally because in Germany, no matter how good a friend, one was still addressed by his or her last name.

The next letter was written on two sides, one from Mr. Strauss's mother after the death of her husband, the other from Julius Loeb:

Dear Children,

My sorrow is still a frightening dream. The thought that our beloved father is now free from pain and delivered of suffering and anxiety is my solace. Do not worry about me, my dearest.

Your mother

April 4, 1943
Dear Richard,

Please accept my heartfelt condolences and be assured that your father has been spared much future suffering. My family will look after your mother. My daughter still suffers from scarlet fever, and my wife is still hospitalized. Only the hope of an end to all this keeps us alive. Very heartfelt regards.

Yours,
Julius Loeb

Trudy's mother-in-law was still in Amsterdam at that time, making hats. Sometime later she too was transported to Westerbork. She had been depressed ever since her emigration from Berlin and had attempted suicide shortly after her husband passed away on March 21, 1937. Although she was treated for her depression, Trudy and her husband were advised that she would probably attempt suicide again. As predicted, she killed herself in Westerbork shortly after her arrival.

Later postcards describe the worsening conditions, as well as deaths in and transports from the camp. Despite these circumstances, however, inmates were allowed to receive packages every six weeks. Ellen and her family received them regularly from friends of theirs who had a mixed marriage. On one card thanking this family for a package, they wrote:

May 1, 1943
Dear Mrs. Pincus,

Please do not think that I forgot you, but I suffer a bone infection on my right hand, and my daughter has been isolated in the hospital with scarlet fever for five weeks.

Would it be possible for you to obtain some summer clothing for us? There will be a group from the Jewish Community Center visiting here.

My husband's health is very precarious. Six weeks ago my daughter's mother-in-law died very suddenly here in Illa's arms.

Many regards.
Yours,
Dina Loeb

And another to the Strauss family reads:

May 1943
Dear Strausses,

You made us so happy with your package. I'm wearing your sweater day and night. It's freezing here at the North Sea. We have no blankets. When we left, all our blankets had been taken by our rest home guests. Could you find us some?

Illa works in the hospital. I will soon work in the diet kitchen. Your parents, Mr. Strauss, are doing reasonably well. Your dad still enjoys his food. We need towels, toilet paper, and maybe some apples. Where is our son-in-law's mother?

Oh to be with you and just talk. And how we wish for a piece of meat. Do not forget us. Many, many regards.

Your,

Dina Loeb

It seems that everyone from Amsterdam had someone sending them something. There was a collection station for clothing and other necessities at the Jewish Community Center in Amsterdam, where people could be supplied with the bare necessities.

May 12, 1943

Dear Strausses,

Again, many thanks for the wonderful package. It lifted my depression. We are now all recovered from infections, scarlet fever, and my ear infection. Illa is working again in the hospital, and my wife is starting to work there. She is in the dietary department. I myself work in the pharmacy.

We could survive here, but how long will we be allowed to stay? Meanwhile, all our clothing is wearing out. I have no shoelaces for myself or my wife. Please try to get us some. Also, could you get me a steel writing pen? Your mother, Richard, whom I see periodically, is doing reasonably well. We hope that you are all in good health.

Yours,

Julius Loeb

July 1, 1943

Dear Strausses,

Many thanks for your post, which arrived in time for me to answer today, the assigned day for letter writing. Regarding your Aunt Hedwig, I forgot to tell you in my last letter that I immediately contacted a teacher who takes care of the deaf and dumb. He sleeps near me. I asked him to keep an eye on her. Unfortunately he has not yet been able to find her. I myself went to the administrator and got a document saying she has not arrived. I will be notified if she comes here and will help her as much as I can.

Many thanks for the razor blades. Could I ask you to send my wife a steel fountain pen and either a scarf or a handbag for her birthday, July 12? Please tell me what I owe you, but I hope maybe one of these things will arrive in time. Otherwise, we are doing all right.

Yours,

Julius Loeb, Barrack 17
Lager Westerbork

July 6, 1943
Dear Strausses,

I have just returned from the camp administration. Mr. Phillipp has not arrived here. You need to inquire in all the hospitals. Many of our acquaintances have arrived here lately. Some have been allowed to return to Amsterdam. One of them is Mr. Karpf.

Could somebody send us some summer clothing?

Julius Loeb

July 7, 1943
Dear Strausses,

Since my wife and daughter work all day and there is little for me to do, I do the writing. Thank you again for the packages, especially the food, the first in a year's time. You cannot imagine what a treat this is. We have enough vegetables, but no meat.

Many of our friends are arriving now. Since the time we came, we came on November 8, 1942, only ten of this group are still here. I pray that we can stay. We only have you left in Amsterdam.

Thank you so much for the buttons for my suit.

Yours,

Julius Loeb

Because Dina Loeb's birthday was on July 12 [born 1894] and Julius Loeb's was on July 10 [born 1881], the next letter thanked their dear friends for birthday presents.

July 17, 1943
Dear Strausses,

With what love you have surrounded me for my birthday. We celebrated in spite of these sorrowful days. We tasted your wonderful cake and shared it with friends and co-workers.

We do not know what the future will be. Hopefully we can stay here. I will try to bring some flowers to your bereaved father as soon as I am allowed to. Again, all my love and thanks.

Dina Loeb

Other letters, such as the following, relate the fact that friends had been sent on transports to death camps in the East:

September 23, 1943

My Dear Mr. Strauss,

I am very sorry that I have bad news for you. Your mother went totally unexpectedly on a transport today. When I saw her last, she looked well. I feel for you. Hopefully all will be well.

I have a lot of work, but the diet kitchen is an interesting place to be. Warmest regards.

Yours,

Dina Loeb

September 25, 1943

Dear Strausses,

The arrival of your package provided a holiday for us. We are so needy. My wife and daughter join me in gratefully thanking you for the razor and the shoes. They are somewhat big, but so what.

I sent a poster to you about the site of your father's burial plot. If you make contact with the Jewish community, they will arrange to have the urn sent to you for burial.

My wife has been sick in the hospital again; very high fever, but no diagnosis. But she is improving. Somebody stole the buttons off my gray suit.

We hope to be able to stay here for some time. Please be thanked for all you're doing. We hope to be able to reciprocate in the near future.

Yours,

Julius Loeb

Barrack 17, Lager Westerbork

September 28, 1943

Dear Strausses,

We do not hear from you anymore. I am sitting on the kitchen floor to write. I am free till 4:00 P.M. Then diets for supper, then infant formula. Dr. Mosberg is with us quite a bit. He is hospitalized.

We hear nothing from Amsterdam anymore. Would you have some discarded, mended hose you could let us have? Many regards.

Dina Loeb

Dina Loeb smoked two to three packs of cigarettes a day and did not hesitate to ask for more.

October 22, 1943

Dear Strausses,

Many thanks for your card and package. You are the only ones thinking of us. My husband is hospitalized. I am concerned. Illa and I have lots of work, but providing some nourishment and a proper diet to patients boosts my morale.

We have no money at all any more, and I must ask you for some soap (and cigarettes). How is your little boy?

Yours gratefully,

Dina Loeb

My father died of pneumonia on November 2, 1943, and I received this in 1944 from the Netherlands Red Cross:

19 Juli 1944

Rud., Schachnow [sic], 2720 Oaklawn, Dallas,

Texas, U.S.A.

The Correspondence Bureau of the Netherlands Red Cross wishes to inform you that Mr. Dr. Julius Loeb, born 10 Juli 1881 died 2 November 1943 in Westerbork.

A letter to their friends, the Strausses, reveals the fact that they had expressed their condolences:

November 1943

Dear Strausses,

Thank you for your letter of friendship. We discouraged condolences from our new friends here. Your letter was our loved one's eulogy.

We have a lot of work and are tired by evening. Then we sleep and start over at 6:00 A.M. Through my work I can help people somewhat, and that is my satisfaction.

Does Mrs. Van Zuylen know that my husband is not with us any more? She relied so much on his judgment. I am so glad that everything is going well for you. You are the only ones to help us. Hopefully we will see each other again. Many regards from our hearts, and many thanks.

Dina Loeb

According to his death certificate, he was buried in Province Drenthe.[4] I never found the grave, but feel it is somewhere near the North Sea.

As life in Westerbork continued for Dina and Ellen Loeb they wrote:

December 6, 1943

Dear Strausses,

Your package made us very happy. We are doing all right, having already been here thirteen months. I now have to tell you something very important. From now on we can receive one package every six weeks, one for Illa and one for me, not more than two kilos each. We would prefer butter, cheese, and sausage, but no bread. We will send you food stamps to be put on top of the package. If you have a few guild-ers left, we would be very grateful.

I receive very little mail and do not hear from the children in America.
The new package rule starts December 15, 1943.[5]
Many, many best regards,
Dina Loeb

December 25, 1943
Dear Strausses,

We are sorry not to hear from you. Nobody but some of Illa's friends are thinking of us. Our health is good. I even gained some weight.

It's very cold here, but when I work, I do not feel it. I am in the kitchen from 7:00 A.M. to 8:00 P.M.

My daughter Illa and I are so close; we live so peacefully together and hardly need anybody else. Our beds are next to each other, and our belongings are with us, so we get along.

Dina Loeb

Finally they too were scheduled for transport, as they wrote:

Dear Strausses,

After a long time I can write again. This will probably be the last time, as we are scheduled to go to Theresienstadt. We thank you for all your love. Please write. Please write to our daughter in America and tell her where we are. We would be so grateful if you would continue to help us.

Since yesterday I have been sick with gallbladder trouble, and I fear tomorrow's trip. But it will be okay. Again, many regards, also to our daughter in America.

Your,
Dina Loeb

Trudy never heard from them. From Illa in the same letter:

Dear Strausses,
It really is not going well with mother. I just hope that she survives the trip.
Your last package has not yet arrived.
Best regards.
Illa

After they were scheduled for transport to Theresienstadt, my sister was offered a reprieve in Westerbork but elected to go with her mother. This established a tremendous bond between them which carried them through their misery and remained until their deaths. My husband and I never knew what had happened to them until we received a letter in 1945, which was written on a gray envelope.

After the war my sister began to write to me of all the terrible things she and my parents endured. She began with a letter but stopped in the middle and recorded her experiences more completely in a diary. Although she said that neither she nor my mother wanted their story told, I believe I'm actually following her wishes by publishing her diary, for she wrote at the beginning, "A book should be written about this." Chapter seven is her story as she wrote it.

Chapter Seven

Ellen Loeb

LEIBE TRUDE, LIEBER RUDY
[DEAR TRUDY, DEAR RUDY]

• • •

To do justly is joy to the righteous,
But ruin to the workers of iniquity.
—Dante Alighieri, *Dante's Inferno*

Dieses wird das letzte mal sein,
dass ich uber meine Erlebnisse in K.Z. . . .

[This will be the last time that I will talk about my experiences in the concentration camps. . . .]

It is really strange to write to you. What we went through in these terrible times is difficult to put on paper. A book should be written about this. First I have to tell you that unfortunately, but also miraculously, only Mother and I have survived. You cannot imagine what this means. You know that we were in Westerbork. We were sent there on the 8th of November, 1942. I worked as a nurse in the concentration camp at Lenzing. Before I came to Lenzing, I was in three other concentration camps. I think I should recall it one more time so I won't forget.

On the 8th of November, 1942, our parents and I were aroused at 2:00 A.M. by the Gestapo and had to join all the other Jews to be transported to Westerbork. Had Father applied for legal exit visas, we never would have been brought here. The only way to get them was through a Mr. Puttkammer, who stamped our papers for legal immigration. You had to pay money to authorities in Amsterdam, and then you were safe for a time. The papers for our legal immigration did not arrive until an hour before we had to board the train in Westerbork for transport to Theresienstadt, but they saved us for a while.

There was terrible trepidation at the station; you cannot imagine how it upset Father. Our neighbor had succeeded in getting a car to bring us and what little we could take with us to this meeting point. Father, who had a massive heart attack and a stroke, could hardly walk, but we got to the station and were at Westerbork in a couple of hours.

Westerbork was a Dutch transport camp located near Zwolle, one of the most northern points of little Holland. The big barracks had no lights; everything was fenced in. Inmates were brought there for transport to Auschwitz. When people came there, some were lucky and, for some reason, got to stay longer. Others had a shorter stay. Some, who were luckier, were then transported to Theresienstadt. Others, who had exit papers to other countries, were sent to Celle [Bergen-Belsen], and some just stayed in Westerbork to keep the camp and a very big hospital going. Sick people could go to the hospital. In the beginning that was a fantastic way of being safe for a time, but later it no longer worked.

Father and Mother, by showing Father's military discharge papers as a physician in the Kaiser's army, were taken out of immediate transport. I myself, now being older than sixteen years of age, was not eligible for this status, but Mother, as always, saved me. She said, "And what about my child?" I looked young, and I escaped transport that time, but this lasted only eight days. Then we were scheduled for transport again, but the head doctor, Dr. Spanier, talked to the Nazis and got Father another reprieve. There was a transport to Auschwitz every week, and you could just never get it out of your mind. You might be on the next week's list; you never had a minute's rest.

Ellen Loeb's ID card. Courtesy Trudy Shakno.

One time I didn't feel very well and was put on the transport list, but I took twenty ephedrine tablets. My pulse went up to 120, and I was declared untransportable because I couldn't work, and they didn't know what was ailing me. All the other people were going directly to Auschwitz.

On the 23rd of April I contracted scarlet fever, and Mother had an infection on her thumb. Poor Father, who could not help himself, had to take care of both of us. At that time we still got little packages from old friends in Amsterdam, and this helped us. Of course, these friends were not Jewish. Before the end of the six weeks, pretty unexpectedly, we were put on the transport list again. The scarlet fever helped us because the six weeks isolation period were not up yet. Mother was taken back into Westerbork, and Father was so sick that they put him into the hospital, so we were safe for a little while.

A few weeks later I was scheduled to go on transport again, but this time I took castor oil and had such diarrhea that they could not take me. After that time we got some respite. But eventually we were taken to Theresienstadt. I can only tell you, my dear sister, that God meant well to take Father and save him from Auschwitz.

We lived there in barracks with three hundred people. Mother and I were next to each other on the third floor. Mother started working in the kitchen; Father worked just enough to keep him off the transport lists; and I was lucky, I worked as a nurse. Poor Father was usually alone all day. During this time we were on the list to be transported to Auschwitz seven times. You cannot imagine how upsetting this was. On the days there were transports, we had to get up at 4:00 A.M., dress all the sick people and ready them for the trains. It was more than a person could do—to put these people in those cattle cars. It was so awful. I can only say that we did not know where they were going. We thought they were going to Theresienstadt, which was not thought to be all that bad because the Red Cross made periodic visits there. If anybody would have known where they were really being sent, nobody would have had any hope, and they would not have survived.[1]

That's when I started to be a nurse. I knew absolutely nothing, but I acted as if I knew everything. I just watched everybody wherever I could, and pretty soon I'd advanced to being a friend of the head nurse. After observing her for a short time, I learned how to take care of my patients.

In the beginning, the hospital in Westerbork was very primitive. There were no instruments and no medicine, but later it got better. In fact, we even had a modern operating room. At first I worked in women's internal medicine; then, for a short time, I was in surgery. I was then assigned to the children's ward. After that I was in charge of pediatrics.

One day I heard that there would be twenty very sick children from another concentration camp arriving in Holland.[2] We were to make them well so that they could either go to work or at least be brought to Auschwitz to be done away with. We tried to be ready for them. We prepared a room with big and little beds. We didn't have any linens, or at least we had very few. The only thing to give this room a friendlier appearance were some wonderful blue flowers we had been picking in the meadow outside that we put in water glasses all around.[3]

At 5:00 the next morning the train arrived, and pretty soon came the gurneys with the children. Great was our horror, and we were frightened of what we were seeing because the line of carts just didn't stop. There were more and more, sometimes three children on one stretcher. Many were babies under one year old. We were not prepared for those. There were also children of two and three years of age up to fourteen, all of them very, very ill. They were half naked or wrapped only in a thin blanket. Most of them cried miserably and were totally exhausted and hungry. More and more gurneys were being brought into the room until eventually we had a total of forty-five children with all kinds of diseases. Most were scantily dressed. Many had pneumonia after having had measles. Others had otitis media, chicken pox, whooping cough, and many other children's diseases. Almost all the children had terrible diarrhea. You were actually fighting for each child.

At first we had to put them into some kind of bed, so we separated them, as far as possible, according to age and disease and put two or three in one bed, one bunk on the top and one on the bottom. But it didn't work. Little ones, many under three years of age, didn't even know their names. They had no parents and many were too weak to talk. But we tried to do the best we could. You just cannot believe what went on. I could write for hours about their misery.

In Westerbork we were able to help them. To a large extent, many really got better. Almost all recovered. I think five children were beyond saving. I'm so sorry that these children had to go on transports. I cursed the parents who had left their children alone in the underground instead of staying with them, but I'm sorry to say, I understood it later because this was the better of the choices left to them. If the mothers had stayed with their children, in most cases they would have gone on transports, usually to Auschwitz or Theresienstadt, and been taken immediately with their mothers to the gas chambers.

We tried to keep the children unable to travel as long as possible so you could postpone the transport day. We hoped that for each child there would be some change in our situation. There was one child in particular we could keep from being transported only if he became ill, and that might save his parents as well. He had been in the punishment barracks for people who were in the underground and had been found by the SS. So we gave him a milk injection. The poor boy developed a high fever, but that saved his family. The parents didn't know about it, but it was a terrible responsibility for me. I worried and was frightened. The head of pediatrics tried to pacify me. He didn't feel that there was such a terrible risk.

So, from June, 1943, until February, 1944, I was very, very busy with the children. It was wonderful and thankful work, but I knew that in the end they would be taken to Auschwitz.

In October, 1943, our father got very sick. First he had an inner ear infection, and later he had pneumonia. The last few days and nights, we were with him. He was lying on an operating table in the hospital. The illness lasted three weeks, and we were able, thanks to Mother's working in the kitchen, to give him what he needed. I can only say that it was very lucky that our father did not have to endure the rest of all this.

Mother and I were put on the transport list again, but through her work as a trained dietitian, we were rescheduled for a later date. The same worked for me. We were actually among the last thousand in Westerbork. The parents in this group were to be sent to Theresienstadt, but the young people were to go to Auschwitz. So my number was not up yet, but Mother was to be transported on February 23. I just volunteered to go with her.

The transport to Theresienstadt was not so bad: two days and two nights in a normal train compartment with whatever belongings we had left. We did not have a bad trip. We got through the Gestapo, which was very difficult. All our belongings were locked up for two weeks. Everybody went through them and stole whatever they could, but especially what little food we had left. We also had to be stripped and checked. I had some money, but it was found. You just cannot fathom what it meant when they took what little money we had. It's a miracle they did not put me in a special prison. I was really frightened for the first two weeks.

Theresienstadt was a former military station. Now only Jews and the Gestapo lived in this city. The Jews lived in barracks and private homes. The rooms held ten to twenty people, and the barracks as many as sixty. There was no heat. The people who had a room did not always have beds; they slept on straw mattresses. In the barracks they had cots, one on top of another. We had to borrow coats and thin blankets from other inmates since ours were locked up.

In 1943, the circumstances had been terrible in Theresienstadt. Hunger was especially bad in 1942 and 1943. The hygienic facilities were impossible. There were no toilets or running water, no facilities of any kind for health or cleanliness. People died, hundreds at a time in one day. They just lay there, thousands of them, on the floors of the barracks and warehouses, covered with lice and terrible diarrhea, totally neglected. The food was not too bad, but there was not enough, so the old people who could not work just died from hunger. If you had to have anything else, you would have to barter. Hanukkah 1943, we received a letter from you through the Red Cross. This was the only light in all that we went through. The lipstick you sent me bought us half a bread. Some of the Czech Jews got big packages from friends in Czechoslovakia, and they did very well. Others were poorer than we were, especially old people who could not work and didn't have anything to barter.

In 1944, suddenly everything started to get better. There were fewer people there. We had hospitals and even some old age homes. In May the Germans began something new—city beautification.[4] We were expecting the Red Cross to come to Theresienstadt, so everything looked great. We even had a film company, and they made a movie to send to other nations. So, by the time we came to Theresienstadt, it wasn't all that bad. There was a physician's control office, and everybody, at regular intervals, would be checked for health.

Mother immediately contracted a bad case of flu. In Theresienstadt you had to pay for everything with food. For half a bread we bought a bed for her. After three weeks we were assigned to a room with eight other people in a huge military barrack, but it was well located. We got a little rest here and had the feeling that for the foreseeable future there would be no transports. This made a great difference. I again was employed as a nurse, this time in the surgical department in a pretty big hospital. It was well supplied with everything. You would almost think you were in a normal situation. Pretty soon I knew what I was doing.

After three months I was assigned to a new unit for Germans for a modern treatment of blood diseases. They called this treatment *heilgas*.[5] Only three nurses and three physicians worked in this unit. There were twenty patients. I was called to see the head physician who had come to see what these experiments were. The new medicine was very interesting. It was made out of perubalsam,[6] glycerin, hypermangan [potassium permanganate, a disinfectant], quinine, quinosol [used to disinfect the mouth or throat], sodium iodide, ammonium chloride, and hexamethyltetramine [a disinfectant]. All of this would be heated to 300°F., and the resulting gas would be applied to purulent wounds. The condensed water was applied to serious cases of stomatitis[7] and sores. The results were at least partially successful, but we were surprised at how well some of it worked. I worked there until October, while Mother worked in a doctor's office.

In September, 1944, the transports started again. Our name was again on the transport list. First, five thousand men were to go, and then the women. We were scheduled to leave October 11. I could have stayed in Theresienstadt but did not want to leave Mother, so I volunteered to go with her. Whatever I tell you now cannot describe what we went through, so I will use few words. The transport was terrible. We traveled in wagons, seventy people with whatever they had in one compartment. We sat on top of and underneath each other. The trip took three nights and two days. Nobody knew where we were going, but the more we traveled, the more we knew what our destination was to be. In the end, we came to Auschwitz.

Auschwitz was probably one of the worst places. It was called *vernichtungslager*, which means "killing ground." There I could not work as a nurse. You saw nothing but fences and barracks. When we arrived, everybody had to get out of the train. Your belongings stayed on the train. We never saw them again. Then we had to line up—men on one side, women on the other. The SS came and looked us over. Old people, mothers with children, and sickly looking women would all be sent to one side, and that meant the gas chamber. Mother should have gone too, but she said, "I'm going with my daughter. I can walk for six hours." By some miracle this saved her life because they believed that she could walk.

They sent us into a shower room where they took all our clothes. All our hair everywhere was shorn off. We were given one pair of pants and one dress of rags. We had to stand in line for hours. Then we were put into a barrack. We had no dishes, forks or spoons. Six of us ate out of one pot with our hands. There was no place to wash, no soap, and no toilet. If you needed to go, you had to take pieces of your clothing to clean yourself. You could only go once a day. We could not drink the water. Everybody was terribly thirsty, so we discovered that if we exchanged one slice of bread for raw cabbage, the cabbage would help the thirst.

Ten people had to sleep on a wooden plank three meters wide. Eventually we got three blankets for the ten of us. You cannot believe what that meant. Everybody in that situation thinks only of himself; everybody is fighting for life. Everybody wants a piece of the blanket. One time we changed barracks and were very tired after a whole day's work in a wet barrack. The *blockältesters*—these are the worst and most brutal of any people I've ever seen—they are the ones who either gave us or deprived us of favors; they steal what you have; they give you only half of your food and are worse than the Gestapo—she promised us blankets if we would get them ourselves. Everybody went and carried what we could carry, but this woman had us put the blankets at the barracks entrance, and nobody got them until the next morning.

If you lost weight you went into the gas chamber. You could not get sick because if you did, you would be killed. A physical exam meant only that you had to strip and the physician looked at you. Old, sickly, and thin, meager looking people went immediately to the gas chamber. The others went to work. People would go to work with a temperature of 40°C, which is 103° or 104°F. If somebody fainted, he would be beaten back to consciousness, mostly in the face.

We belonged to the group who could work, and ten days later we expected to be on a new work transport. Everybody was elated to get away from Auschwitz and the always threatening gas chamber. First we had to be examined by a physician who would judge whether or not we were able to work. If we had been thin, we would not have had a chance. Once again Mother's heavy legs saved her. She probably had edema from heart trouble. But when the doctors looked at my legs, they saw that both of us had heavy legs. Because we were able to establish the fact that heavy legs were a family trait, we got on the transport to the new work station.

We had to stay in Auschwitz four more days and it was a terrible wait, but at least we knew we would get out. Of the two thousand people who had come with us, there were only fifteen left. Those days in Auschwitz were an eternity. We slept in terrible quarters—they had been stables before we slept in them. There were Russian female prisoners in those barracks who were very upset that we had been brought to their quarters and made it hard for us whenever they could. We asked them if they knew where we would be going on transport, and they said we would probably go to heaven.

We had to be checked out one more time, and when Mother did not dress herself quickly enough, the doctor said, "*Mussulman*, you come to my attention. I'm getting terrible doubts about you again." But eventually the train came, and we got out. Seventy of us were put into one cattle car with two SS. Everybody got one bread, a little piece of sausage, and a slice of margarine. There was one bucket of water and one bucket to use as a toilet. Eventually the drinking water was mixed up with the toilet water and neither could be used anymore.

We traveled for three days and two nights without anything to drink. We could not get out. There was no more food, no light, and no windows. Seventy people were standing up. You cannot imagine what the conditions were. People would vomit right onto the floor between us and on us. We just were not human any more. The air was impossible to describe. We were totally *kaput* when we eventually came to Lenzing. This is a place not far from Linz, Austria.

We belonged to the concentration camp of Mauthausen and were the first women in Mauthausen. There we were put into an old factory, but we were overjoyed when we heard that we each would get a wooden bed. They were actually bunks, but nobody cared. And everybody got two blankets. We got a basin, a drinking cup, and one spoon. After what we had been through in Auschwitz, this was good for a time and made us happy. We got prison clothing. All of it had lice in it, so our whole camp was full of lice.

The commandant of the factory asked for a physician. There was one. She had no hair, just like us, and wore rags. As it was, we had traveled together in the same compartment and I had talked to her for a while. She was an internist and had never done any surgery. Since I told her that I had worked in the surgical unit, she asked for me to be her assistant. I didn't know much, but we acted as though we knew something.

The women here had to work very hard. Most of them worked in a rayon factory, and there was a lot of sulfuric acid. It was really work for men, but the women were glad to do it. The men wore gas masks, but the Germans didn't give the women any. People were blind for days at a time because they didn't have any goggles. Others had stomach poisoning and were vomiting. Many could not eat. Many had wounds on their hands which immediately developed into purulent sores. Other women worked in a mine, digging an underground tunnel a hundred meters below the surface. They brought up the stones in little carts.

The women got up at 3 o'clock in the morning. We would be counted at 4 o'clock, 560 of us. Then we got breakfast: a cup of coffee and 200 grams of bread. Later that was reduced to 100. At 5 o'clock, after breakfast, they went to work. It was an hour's walk, and in the winter it was terrible. We wore wooden shoes and not enough clothing. They worked until 9 o'clock in the evening. For lunch and dinner we got 70 cc. of watered down soup with one potato. We were very hungry.

The work in the factory was in three different shifts. The other shift was from 6 o'clock in the morning to 6 o'clock in the evening with half an hour of rest. Mother worked as housemother because she was one of the oldest women in the house. The oldest at that time meant about forty-eight years old. The older ones had either died or been gassed. She had to clean up everything and wash it. I was then made the supervisory nurse of this particular barrack. I was lucky because I shared my room with a physician and the room had a little stove. We cooked edible flowers that we found in the fields. We also sometimes found potato peelings in the trash cans, and we would bake them. Also, we found snails, and they made a pretty good meal. The only light in this terrible time was one man who, at Christmas time, brought us a little piece of cake. This was a great, great favor. Out of all these horrible people, there was one person who had that one bit of compassion. If the SS had caught him at it, he would have been gassed. Afterwards, a couple of times he brought us a slice of bread and even a cup of coffee. And later on he did even more for us. He came over at night and told us what he heard on the radio. That helped give us some hope. He really knew where the Americans were. In fact, he told us to hide in his house when it became necessary to flee the barracks. But we didn't know who would reach us first. Happily we didn't have to do this because you never knew what would happen, but it gave us some peace.

My work as a nurse was very difficult. Sometimes we had no medicine and no instruments. There was only one room where we could treat patients. The women were all suffering from terrible diarrhea, many with fever. Then we received a few provisions of medicine—mostly charcoal, forty tablets for three hundred women with diarrhea. The women would actually fall on me to get these tablets. Of course, it didn't help. But just getting something gave them the feeling that they might get better. Many had purulent infections and came for help. We had nothing to help them, not even a piece of linen to put on their wounds. They didn't want to believe it. Then they helped themselves. The older ones from Hungary knew what to do with the plants that they could put on their wounds, and truthfully, it sometimes helped a little bit. After a week we got some bandages and eleudron [a sulfa drug], some charcoal and ichthiol ointment.[8] Our physician did get a stethoscope, one thermometer, one syringe, two pair of forceps, and two scissors. The thermometer was probably the most valuable and also the most potentially problematic instrument of all, and we were careful not to break it. It was the only one for 560 women. When things went well, the thermometer lasted for three weeks. When that broke, we often went for weeks without any. We did not even dare to ask for a new one. Sometimes we waited four or five weeks so they wouldn't know how many sick people we had. We hoped something would happen to end this misery.

The worst thing was that only a certain percent of my patients could be sick. Of the 560, I had 120 ill. Only forty were allowed. The others had to go to Mauthausen, and that meant gas, so I had to declare them fit to work if they were at all able to work, and that was one of the worst things. The women who were sick were too weak to send to a factory, but everybody knew they had to go if they wanted to live. A German doctor came to see that nobody pretended to be sick.

We put them in a sick room, which was actually a room with two beds, one on top of the other, and three single beds. It had a stone floor, a heater, and one window that you couldn't open. Usually it was very dark, and eventually they painted it black on account of the blackout. We had only some artificial light. We had one table, and that was the examining table. Many came to get their wounds dressed, to be examined, and to get their medication. There was no rest. They were coming all day long with all kinds of complaints, and it was hard to tell if they were really sick or not, especially during the times we did not have a thermometer. Their pulse was usually normal or just a little rapid, but we didn't have a real watch to count it, so we just had to estimate. We could not bear to write that they couldn't work, so, sick as they were, we sent them back to work. The worst was to certify somebody unfit for work. Everybody would have liked to stay one or two days, but only a small percentage could be sick. Sometimes we could keep them for one or two days, but then they had to go back.

One of the most frequent illnesses was a series of red, very painful spots on the legs. It was something between erysipelas[9] and erythema nodosum.[10] We took care of them with ichthiol ointment and salicylic acid or sulfonamide. We had a lot of people with diphtheria and other infectious diseases, but we just had to keep them going to work. You cannot imagine what the beds looked like. We had no robes or gowns to give them, so they just lay there in their rags on the straw. One half blanket was available, and we used it on those who needed to be covered and borrowed clothes, most of them torn, for the others. The trouble was the toilet. We had one bedpan. All the other patients had to go in a bucket which was under the table. There was no water in this room. You had to go up three stairs to get some water. Nothing was sterile. There was not even any talk about that. After a while we got a small piece of soap to clean our hands. The syringe could not be boiled. Occasionally we just heated it, but usually it took all morning to get some water heated. You ask what did we do with the syringe. Since we had nothing to inject into these patients, we just used it to make the women feel better. Everybody was so nervous; it was difficult to tell whether or not they were really sick. They wanted something for their suffering, so we gave them water injections.

We had some aspirin and gave it all kinds of medical names so that they thought we had some miracle medicine. We also dissolved it, and that made some miracle drops. We called it *Udenol.* Water with a little bit of salt, one aspirin, and a tiny bit of alcohol was the medicine of choice. Many women came for that every day for their heart or for their stomach or to sleep better or for other diseases. We just had to be careful not to give too much because we didn't know what the end result would be. It was absolutely nothing, but sometimes it helped.

To give an injection was much more difficult. You had to use a lot of persuasion to convince the patient that it helped. We did not actually give them injections; we pushed the needle under the skin and took it out again. Sometimes, when we gave them these injections they got better. I don't know why, but I think it was something they imagined, and then, when they came back for more, we had to perform the same sad procedure again.

We had two women with ulcers. With one we actually succeeded with our everyday injections. She was so convinced that for two months she was okay. Then she came back for more injections. We had another woman with asthma and heart disease. She was heavy and elderly. She had pretty severe episodes of asthma, and we had to give her our famous water injections. That was terrible. Sometimes she got over it when I gave her one or two of these injections.

Our patients were never allowed to have surgery. A German doctor who came from time to time to check on us would drain the worst abscesses. Even when an amputation of the finger was done, he just did it without any anesthesia on our examining table. If there was a big wound, they often got wound diphtheria, but the Germans were so afraid they would get diphtheria that they gave us some serum, and it healed quickly.

On the 1st of January, a woman had to have an abortion on a fetus of five months. The woman doctor who was my boss had never seen a birth. One of our women had, and she and I performed the delivery. We did the best we could. I asked for some linens because this was a special case. They gave me a package of dressings, some sterile forceps, one pair of scissors, and some yarn so that we could bind the umbilical cord and hope to God that everything would be okay. But nobody can understand the fear and agitation. We tried to be as sterile as possible, but we didn't even have a bedpan. The mother was very weak, but she had no complications, and she went back to work. The doctor saw all this and was absolutely astounded. Sometimes you don't know how you get through these things.

January was our worst month. A short time after the abortion we had a very sad railway accident. There was high snow, and it was very dark. The supervisor had forced the women to go on despite the darkness and high snow. No one had heard the oncoming train. Lots of women had been hurt. Five women were caught by the train and pulled along. Four died immediately; one was very seriously wounded. She was brought to us in terrible condition, but after two days she got a little better. She could even have taken a little nourishment if our dear German doctor had not interfered. He came to check on her but did not do much for her because he was convinced that she was not likely to be able to work for us, and with that, he gave her an overdose of morphine intravenously. The next day she died.

The drug of choice, and it was called the wonder medicine, was hypermangan. We used it on everything from impetigo[11] to eczema and furuncles.[12] We smeared a ten percent solution of the hypermangan on and just let it dry. In many cases it helped. Many women had stomatitis, and we were successful with eleudron.

For two months the doctor with whom I worked and from whom I learned was very, very ill. She had three weeks of high fever, and every night she had convulsions. No doctor looked at her, and I did the best I could. For several weeks the German doctor didn't come, so there was no doctor at all. During that time, I had to judge everything by myself. During this time, Mother became ill with a fever higher than 39°C. I never knew what she actually had. There was hardly any medicine for her. Sometimes there was not even a thermometer. You cannot imagine what worries I had. I was responsible for 560 women. I had a lot of people with high temperatures and laborious breathing. It looked like pneumonia, but I could not make any diagnosis. I tried to give them eleudron, but I didn't have enough to give them a therapeutic dose, so in most cases I didn't have much luck. I also gave them novalgin[13] or quinine,[14] and that was better. As much as possible I tried to talk it over with the sick doctor. Two of the cases had a continuous temperature of 40°C., or 104°F., and were delirious. All of them had all the symptoms of typhoid. It was impossible to isolate them. We had to give them cabbage soup. Later, when the doctor was better, she was able to establish a diagnosis of typhoid. They called it "stomach typhoid." We didn't have more than five of those. How all those people got well without medicine or diet I cannot understand. I think it was their will to live.

In the sick room, we also had people for whom there were no beds. We had sixteen patients in a room that was meant for five or six people. Then we put them in a room of 15 feet by 20 feet, where they had to sleep in the cold, without enough covers and with no shoes. We had too many sick people. I didn't have enough hands to help them. We just took turns on the night shift. That meant that we stayed with the patients and slept only every third night, as we had to work the next day.

One day I had 120 girls who were unable to go to work. Then the German physician came and insisted that within eight days there would be only forty people who were allowed to be sick, or else I had to send thirty back to Mauthausen. So I wrote letters saying that they could work and sent them to Mauthausen. I was so depressed I just couldn't think. I didn't know what to do because this meant that the people would be gassed. But the patients knew this, and they helped me. Anybody who could walk at all went, and eventually, after two weeks, we had only forty that we could not send off.

Some patients had very large, painful, abscessed axillary glands. The German doctor would just incise the glands and drain them. He himself had only one scalpel and just a little bit of chloroethyl,[15] and that way he opened up the infected glands. There was nothing else. I had to learn to do it, and I did it. It worked.

One day a transport with sixty women came from Auschwitz. They had walked one hundred kilometers through the snow, then were in an open train for eight days. They came in their bare feet. One woman had walked with no shoes, and both her feet were frostbitten. They had tried to bandage her in Mauthausen. I didn't have any room for her and, for the first two days, had nothing to help her feet. After three days, I was able to make some room for her, and the two of us had to look at those feet. It was terrible. I could hardly take it. I cannot imagine how the poor woman lived. One foot was totally black; the toes were dead. The other foot was partially black. We had nothing to help her pain. That poor woman suffered so. I didn't know what to do. I'd never seen anything like it. The physician didn't know what to do either. I thought we should amputate her feet, but we just put some ointment on them and hoped maybe something would help. After four days, the German doctor came again. We let him see what we had done, and he put some warm hypermangan on and also some marphanyl prontalbine[16] powder. Every second day we'd change the bandages. That medicine was unbelievably good. After terrible pain she got well. After five months, her feet were almost normal.

The same day that this girl got better, another fell on her arm. She had such pain that I could only think that her arm was broken. Her lower arm was fractured. Never in my life had I set and stabilized an arm fracture, but I did succeed in putting it back together and telling her not to move it. I put it on a piece of wood, connected the bone at her elbow, and made some kind of splint. Then we put a sterile solution of boric acid on linen rags and wrapped her arm in them. Next we put wood pieces on it so she could not move her arm. After four days the doctor came, realigned the bones, and wrapped her arm in a cast.

While I was busy with the cast, one of the girls who had just arrived from Auschwitz came to me and said, "Don't tell anybody, but I'm a physician. I want to get into the camp, and I do not want to practice as a physician, but you can talk to me." I was so glad that I could now talk my problems over with somebody, and my responsibility was not quite as heavy. I told her that our doctor was sick and she just had to help me, and she did. Then, once again during visiting hours, somebody had an underarm abscess. I didn't have to incise it. This new girl did it for me. I thought it was a poorly done job, but my patient got better.

The other doctor was still sick with high fever. She had lost all her will to live. The new young doctor said immediately, "I can see what's the matter. She has tuberculosis." When the one who was sick mentioned some symptoms that were not indicative of tuberculosis, the new physician said that if it wasn't tuberculosis, it might be malaria. Then she left. Then the older doctor said, "This woman is not a physician." In Auschwitz many claimed to be physicians or nurses, which exempted them from heavy manual tasks or the gas chamber. This was so unethical as it involved patient care. These were irresponsible people, for they had to pretend when they treated people, and the patients were harmed even more. This also meant that my hope to get some help was fading. Nobody wanted to be a physician. In Auschwitz, if you were a doctor you were not in such danger of going to the gas chamber. In Mauthausen, you didn't want to be a doctor because you wanted to work. To me, these were people without a conscience because if they were doctors, they should have helped take care of the patients.

On the same evening, I had a very difficult case. One girl who already had a kidney infection started to run a high fever and was out of her head. I had no idea what to do and got this doctor who didn't want to practice medicine, but she didn't know what to do either. We took the girl into the clinic and just gave her hot compresses, and after a few days she actually got better. But in all these things we had more luck then sense.

A new disease developed which they called "hunger edema." The people had swollen legs and red, swollen faces. Eventually their stomachs and backs swelled. Those poor people were in terrible condition. There was nothing we could do for them but talk to them, try to give them a little support, and tell them that it would be over pretty soon. They cried. They cried in the clinic and always asked me, "How long can we live?" It was so difficult to give them an answer because there was no hope for these people. It could not last much longer. Pretty soon these people got diarrhea, and then the swelling would recede some. Then they looked even worse—nothing but skin and bones. When the diarrhea stopped, the edema came back. The ones that were in bed did not have hunger edema as often, but we could not put them all in bed.

We had one who had a perinephritic [surrounding the kidney] abscess which bulged out the size of a baby's head. The patient had a very high fever. The doctor, who was now better, tried to drain it, but without success. The condition was terrible. It was so awful! One day the German doctor came. He punctured the abscess again and got a lot of pus out. He promised he would come back the next day and drain it again. He said he would bring everything. What he brought was a scalpel, a little bit of chloroethyl, and a little bit of sterile bandage material. In his winter coat, the way he came from the street, under a local anesthetic, he made a ten centimeter incision into the abscess and the pus was drained out. We got two liters. He covered it with sterile gauze and disappeared. Further treatment he just left to us. One doctor wouldn't help; the other was too sick, and as our doctor did not like to bother with surgical cases, I took over the care. Nobody wanted to help me. The next day I drained the wound and put a new bandage on. The patient was always swimming in pus. Then I tried to sterilize some water and clean her up. After four weeks, the pus stopped. The patient still had fever, but eventually it healed, and after six weeks was totally clear.

We then got two more rooms to take care of sick people. That helped. We obtained some pajamas for the patients, but most of them were full of lice. We also got a few bedpans; that was so necessary. A hepatitis epidemic started, but it didn't spread too far. We had five cases. One had pneumonia as well. The people cut themselves in the factory, and that, along with the sulfuric acid[17] that was being used there, made for terrible purulent cellulitis[18] that, not infrequently, led to blood poisoning. The people perspired in the factory. Those who had infections on their hands actually needed surgery, but as I've said before, the Germans did not want to do anything for them, so all we could do was drain the infected areas. This took a lot longer and hurt more. It was also hard on the patients who had to go to work. They sometimes went for days with fevers.

Now came the big moment. We were freed. The plan had been to shoot us or gas us all, but I heard that the manager of the factory took his car and met the American Army and told them of the women in his factory. This influenced the high command to get to us two days earlier than had been planned. On Friday, the 5th of May, at 6:00 P.M. we heard the alarm. After silence of five minutes, we knew we were free. The SS ran away, and on Saturday we were given over to the Americans. You cannot imagine what that meant. Most of us were at the end of our strength. A few more days, and we would not have made it.

The Americans' first concern was for the sick people. They brought us food for these poor sick patients. After four days we were all put into a real hospital. We had thirty beds, linens for everybody, pajamas, water, medicine, anything we needed. It was a dream. How quickly these Americans took over. Everybody got an x-ray. Unfortunately, the results were very bad. Most of the patients had active tuberculosis. Only five people were healthy. The other women, about twenty, were not too bad. All the others had some tuberculosis. The twenty worst cases were immediately put in a sanitarium in Austria.

They all took care that we got clothes and dresses and brought us into better places to live. On the 3rd of June we started on our train back to Holland. After all we had gone through, it was like a fairy tale. First we went with seventeen Dutch women in a cattle car to Horsching, which is an airport. From there, the French Red Cross took us over. One of the physicians told us to take a train to Switzerland, and they would take care of us. That's what we did. We went to Konstanz-am-Bodensee and were received there with everything you could think of. We were brought into a hospital where we stayed for two days of rest and then went to the very best hotel in Insel Reichenau. The Germans were all sent out, and we were told just to go into their houses and take what we needed. So we got some shoes, dresses, and a coat.

All the food yards were at our disposal. We hadn't eaten so much food in six years. We stayed there for one week and then boarded a Red Cross train and went all through Switzerland, from Geneva to Lyon, France. At each station people brought all kinds of food, chocolate, and cigarettes, and in Geneva, the Red Cross even woke us at night with flowers, cocoa, chocolate, and quiche. We stayed in Lyon three days and went from there to Valencienne. We stayed there one night and went from there in another car to Brussels, where we stayed three days. You could hardly tell that there had been a war in Belgium. From there we went to a monastery in Holland and got our first Dutch papers. The next day we joined our friends in Amsterdam.

Trudy Shakno continues, "The first I knew that my mother and sister were alive was in May, 1945, when I received this letter with the return address on a grey envelope":

May 1945
Return Address: T/5 Arthur C. Schwartz Jr. 8435217
576th Mtr Amb Co
A.P.O. 5 P.M.
New York, N.Y.
Mother and sister found:
Illa Loeb. Lenzing frauen krankenhaus ehemaliger Kranzentrationslager[19]

To Miss Freda Schackman [sic]
Brother and Sister Shop
2720 Oaklawn Ave.
Dallas 15, Texas
Mr. and Mrs. Trude Schakno [sic]
My mother is with me. Father passed away.

The rest of their correspondence provides an interesting view of postwar conditions in Amsterdam.

July 15, 1945
My dear family,

You cannot imagine what your letter meant to us, and it arrived here on Mother's birthday, on the 12th of July, and we celebrated in freedom. For the first few months we do not have enough money. Mother's jewelry has come back to us, and we have furniture for two rooms. But we don't have clothes and are waiting for your package. People get packages from Switzerland and we hope soon from America. Everything here is very expensive. I do not know what's going to happen to me, but I'm planning to work as soon as possible as a nurse. I won't make much money, but I need a diploma. After all, in the camp I practically worked as a physician. You might think I'm deranged, but deep in my heart, I would like to study medicine. . . .

July 1945
Dear Trudy and Rudy,

Just now we got your letter and package. Maybe things will get a little better for you now. With all the rice and bread and potatoes that we eat, we actually are gaining weight. I weigh now about 120 lb. Our doctor says that there is no residue from the pneumonia. . . .

I'm not as active now as I was. We prefer to stay home and read. Our room is full of flowers that friends sent us. Don't worry about sending us warm clothes. We are not choosy any more after we wore clothes that were alive with lice. We are so glad to have this room because there are no apartments for aliens without country. We are a little better off since we lived here so long.

I made some hamburgers out of vegetables, red cabbage, potatoes, and a little bit of beef. Not bad at all! We need some vinegar. A bottle on the black market costs 10 florins; butter 25 florins a lb. Coffee and tea are impossible to get. The tea that you sent we exchanged for fruit and cheese for their nutritional value. Do not worry about us. I am in good health, but I'll get a special ration of grits, tapioca, and bullion blocks. Thank you for the 260 florins you sent and the other money. We do not need this now, since we can not buy anything anyway. I have only one wish: to see you and be with you and talk to you.

Many, many kisses from your old one.

On August 16, the Shaknos heard from their friends, the Strausses, regarding Ellen and her mother:

Amsterdam, South   *16-8-45*
Oostertebautlaan 38
My Dear Shaknos,

We thank you for your loving letter. It was for us an unforgettable moment when Dina and Illa one nice evening suddenly appeared in our door. Even the day before they were positively identified as being dead. I am so glad that I can assure you that your mother is unchanged. Illa is naturally much more mature. My wife and I admire her positive thinking and her positive appearance, but also the energy with which she immediately starts to prepare her and her mother's future.

We are so happy that we can be their hosts for the first few weeks. Even in these terrible times we were able to survive. We will try to help them to forget the terrible experience that they have been through, and with our modest means, help them to get established. Unfortunately, there's no transportation from here to Amsterdam. This is very difficult for Illa, as of now, we were able to find them a very nice room in Amsterdam.

We made a contact with the lawyer Karlsberg, who still is the most knowledgeable, to help them to get to the U.S. . . .

The Strauss Family

September 18, 1945
My Dears,

We are now leading a real quiet life. Your sister is back home, as she is still too tired to work. There is not too much to do in our small home. I'm cooking our linens in a small cooking pot as there are no laundries available. Nothing works here, where in Belgium everything is normal. The harbor workers are on strike. Money has no value; only the black market operates at ridiculous prices. That's where the strikers make money the easy way. Some matches can be bought for one florin; a package for 25 florins. It will be some time before things are normal here.

You won't believe that anti-Semitism has increased. We, who are stateless Jews, feel it every day. Haven't we suffered enough? Dutch Jews and other Dutch people who returned from the concentration camps receive double rations and special food, but we'll make it.

There is a chance to be reimbursed for the contents of our home. Since you actually are entitled to one third of what Father owned, see if you can help us to get some money back for what has been stolen. The Germans stole everything, and we are trying to file this under "war debt."

Mother

• • •

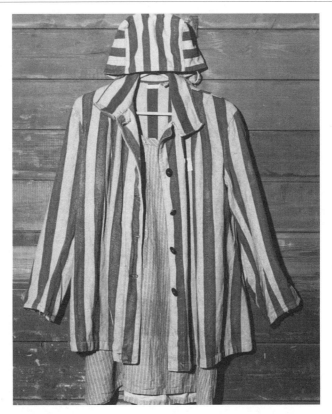

Ellen Loeb's concentration camp uniform. Photo by Dr. Paul Greenberg.
Courtesy Dallas Memorial Center for Holocaust Studies.

Illa (Ellen) and Dina Loeb immigrated to America in 1946 and came to live in Dallas with the Shaknos. Ellen Loeb received her medical degree from Southwestern University School of Medicine on June 2, 1952. While Dina Loeb worked as a librarian at Southern Methodist University, Dr. Loeb practiced hematology in the Wadley Center in Dallas. She was well respected by her peers until her death in 1980.

Dina Loeb died in 1986, at the age of ninety-four. Dr. Ellen Loeb's striped concentration camp uniform remains on display at the Dallas Memorial Center for Holocaust Studies.

Labor Camps

CIRCLES OF SUFFERING

And I saw people in the valley's circle
silent, weeping, walking at a litany pace
the way processions push along our world.
And when my gaze moved down below their faces,
I saw all were terribly distorted.

—Dante Alighieri, *Dante's Inferno*

Following the blitzkrieg, Germany gained seventy-three thousand square miles of land that had formerly belonged to Poland. It also annexed Danzig as well as thirty-two thousand square miles of land divided between East Prussia and Silesia. The western portion of newly acquired territory was divided into two districts, or *Gauen*. First was Danzig-West Prussia, commanded by Gauleiter Arthur Greiser. The rest of the thirty-nine thousand square miles of land was termed the General Government of Poland and placed under civil administration. This was commanded by Hans Frank, whose headquarters were in Kracow. This huge area was subdivided into four districts: Kracow, Lublin, Radom, and Warsaw, and was known as the "Nebenland" adjunct of the Reich.[1]

According to the *Polish Encyclopedic Summary of Camps,* there were 1,798 labor camps throughout the German occupied territory. Twenty-one of these were penal labor camps, and twenty-three served as "educational" labor camps. There were 437 forced labor camps for Jews and 2,197 labor camps for prisoners-of-war, which included nineteen Offeg (officer camps) and sixty-three Stalag (NCO camps).[2] In the area that was designated as the General Government, there were ninety-one camps for Jewish laborers.[3]

Living conditions in the labor camps were primitive, and there were few, if any, sanitary facilities. As a result, inmates suffered from lice, which frequently led to typhus, and itch mites, which caused scabies and impetigo. Tuberculosis was rampant as well. Sleeping quarters were crowded, and inmates slept on hard floors without mattresses or straw. Laborers worked seven days a week from dawn to dusk and were driven to the point of exhaustion. Food was meager at best, and clothing was distributed irregularly, if at all.[4] Hence illness ran rampant and death rates were high.

Benjamin B. Ferencz estimates that by the end of 1942 there were close to two hundred thousand Jews in forced labor.[5] Utilized in industry and armaments factories, the Germans made use of the Jewish prisoners until they died or were murdered. He writes of their condition, "The Jewish concentration camp workers were less than slaves. Slavemasters care for their human property and try to preserve it: it was the Nazi plan and intention that the Jews would be used up and then burned."[6]

As Dr. Edith Kramer relates, the conditions of the women differed from those of the men. For example, they were sometimes attacked sexually by the SS in spite of the fact that they looked strange with bald heads, shabby clothing, and wooden shoes. Although they were physically weaker than their male counterparts, it was more often the men who succumbed to the conditions, sometimes becoming almost as cruel as their Nazi guards. Explanations for this could include the facts that the men's lodgings were inferior to the women's, their punishment more severe, and their mortality notably higher.

It is an axiom in Judaism "that human life is of infinite value and that all efforts must be applied to heal the sick, to cure illness, and to prolong life."[7] Dr. Kramer's oral history, which was given to the United States Holocaust Memorial Museum, shows her to have behaved in accordance with this obligation during her imprisonment in the labor camps, despite the difficulties she faced in attempting to provide adequate care.

Interestingly, Dr. Kramer was one of a group of 1,210 Jews who were set free on February 7, 1944, a result of financial negotiations between Jean-Marie Musy, the former president of Switzerland, who apparently wished to hide his pro-Nazi leanings by showing some sympathy for the Jews, and Heinrich Himmler, to whom it did not matter what happened to the Jews as long as they were out of Germany.[8] The following chapter relates her experiences.

Chapter Eight

Dr. Edith Kramer

HELL AND REBIRTH—MY EXPERIENCES
DURING THE TIME OF PERSECUTION

• • •

In 1942 I still lived in Berlin.[1] I had to call myself "Medical Practitioner for Jews" and was no longer allowed to treat Aryans. According to a decree issued July 25, 1938 (RGBD1, 969), "A Jew could be a doctor provided that he confined his practice to Jewish Patients."[2] But many of my former patients came through the back door. On the other hand, there came also agents provocateurs who attempted to induce me to illegal actions, e.g. abortions.

Soon deportations of Jews started in Berlin, which of course caused the greatest anxiety. These were disguised as "Workers Transports," but nobody understood why people should be taken out of Berlin, where there was plenty of work to be done. Even Jews who had been working in essential industries were called up.[3] It was also alarming that children and old people were not exempt. Nearly every day patients who had received the ominous letters came to me. Many asked me to certify that they had contagious diseases and were not capable of work. Strangely enough, these certificates were taken notice of—until the next transport. Others asked for prescriptions of sleeping tablets and wanted to know the lethal dose. Very often I was called to certify the death of suicides or to arrange for transport to the hospital. There, their last wish was respected and no attempt was made to revive them.

It also happened that Jews faked suicide and then disappeared.[4] Amongst them was my friend Elsa Danziger, since deceased. She was lucky enough to share a house with an Aryan. This woman, Gerta Bartels (whom I am proud to count among my friends, and who is one of the unsung heroes of the Nazi period), hid Elsa Danziger for three years and protected her. Furthermore, she hid about fifteen Jewish men during the so-called "Crystal Night."[5] Such "crimes" were punished with death when discovered, and we knew of many frightening examples.

Many of my colleagues had already been deported to Birkenau when, in June, 1942, I received an order to report to the police. The call-up was one of the customary forms, used also for Aryan people. I was assured that my call-up was not a deportation order; in fact it would protect me from being deported. Berlin, I was told, would remain my place of residence, and I would have to find another doctor to take over my practice in the meantime. I was to report at once at the German Labor Front office at Posen (Poland), where I was to receive further orders. So I hurriedly packed my suitcase and took the train for Posen.

During the journey I was not molested by fellow travelers (mostly soldiers on leave), although I wore the Jewish Star.

In Posen I created some sensation as people were not accustomed to seeing Jews in the street without an escort of SS men. The trams had signs, "Only for Germans," while the trailers were for "Poles Only." I boarded one of the latter. All Germans wore Nazi Party badges, and children were proud of their swastikas and were conscious of their importance as members of the master race. They showed this by their reckless behavior towards elderly Polish people.

Having arrived at the German Labor Front office, I reported to the medical officer who was in charge of the Jewish Camps. He was courteous to me, although he wore the golden party badge, and informed me that there were twelve hundred Jews in work camps, among them six hundred women who had been without a doctor until now. He had visited the camps very seldom. Recently an epidemic of typhus had broken out in one of the camps, Fort Radziwill,[6] and it would be my duty to prevent the spreading of the epidemic to the population outside. Failure would have disastrous consequences for me. Later he asked me to look also after the two other camps where there were numerous cases of TB and other diseases.[7]

From the tram terminus I saw a red brick medieval tower on the bank of the river Warta surrounded by a barbed wire. This was Fort Radziwill. Inside I noticed women of all ages cowering on the ground, clad in old rags, wearing the Star of David—not only on the left breast, as all German Jews, but another one on the right shoulder so that they could be distinguished also from behind. When they noticed me they all jumped up and welcomed the doctor they had been longingly waiting for.

Crossing the drawbridge, I was at once taken to the camp commander by the guards. He was a Pole and had served in the Polish army, but after the German invasion had discovered his German origin. The Germans did not trust him and had given him charge of the Jewish camp as a test. He was tall, powerfully built, about forty years of age, and looked particularly brutal. This first impression did not deceive me, as I found out later. He was an unscrupulous slave driver.

There were girls and women of all ages in the camp, children twelve years of age, who looked not more than nine, and old women who were really not more than sixty. Only four weeks ago many had been taken from their families in towns of Western Poland and had been deported as "Volunteer Workers." Seldom were relatives left together in the same camp. Men and women were kept in different camps, and it was regarded as an extraordinary favor if they were allowed to see each other once every few months under guard at the barbed wire fence.

The whole camp smelled strongly of Lysol. The dormitories, arranged in a circle, had very small grated windows. There were sleeping bunks, three high, leaving no room for any other furniture. Each girl had only one thin pallet and two light cotton blankets; very few had any other bed clothes. To get warm, usually two girls crawled under four blankets. This accounted for the enormous spread of scabies[8] and other diseases. Typhus cases were isolated in a room that was even darker than the others. The patients were lying on straw without bed clothes. There was no possibility of making the patients comfortable. They had to use a convenience situated in the middle of the yard. The recovery of the few that got better took a very long time owing to the lack of proper food.[9] As they were not able to work, I had to report them as sick and they were listed for "Transport back home," to which I shall refer later.

When examining the girls, I found eighty percent were suffering from scabies. The camp commander insisted that he must be present at all examinations, but I was able to prevent this. Many girls were afraid to attend the examination; when they were forced by the camp police, I found marks of thrashing on their bodies. At last they would confess that the marks were inflicted by the camp commander himself for trivial offenses. Thus he could show his power and satisfy his sadistic inclinations.

Another room was reserved for cases like pneumonia, scarlet fever, dysentery, and scabies. In this infected room, which held dozens of dangerously ill women, I had to treat them and even operated. The only equipment was a raw wooden table and a bench. The operations had to be performed without anesthetics because those were not available for Jews. One can imagine how much the sick and feverish girls suffered when they heard the cries of the ones being operated on and what difficulties I had to do justice to all.

At first I had no possibility of sterilizing my instruments, but later I was able to procure a boiler. The chemist would not supply ointments, declaring that one was not allowed to cure Jews but only to prevent the spread of diseases. Later I bought the necessary ointments from my own money, the assistant chemist helping me very understandingly by selling medicines to me, which he was not permitted to do.

Food

Thin ersatz coffee without milk and sugar was given for breakfast. Lunch consisted of a badly smelling vegetable soup. For dinner the same soup, only a little thicker. In addition there was an issue of eight ounces of bread a day, one and one half ounces of margarine per week, and every few weeks six ounces of jam made of carrots and a little sugar. Sunday dinner consisted of a piece of tough horse flesh or similar. The food contained 1,000 calories per day, so little that it does serious harm to people doing heavy work. I found that the sick did not receive an evening meal and was told that the camp regulations did not provide for this. The evening meal was supplied by the Polish employers. This, however, did not apply to the sick who were unable to work. I succeeded in making the Polish contractors see that this policy was unsound and stopped this terrible hardship.

Originally the working Jews should have received the same amount of food as the Poles (1,400 calories), but the German Labor Front embezzled and stole most of the food, often working together with the camp commander. Unfortunately, even Jewish stewards made sometimes common cause with the Germans, benefiting themselves for some time. But they were soon dropped by their German friends. When, at sudden check-ups, prohibited food was found with them, they were hanged on the spot. So it happened that several bars of sugar were brought into the camp with the knowledge of the SS guards. When the sugar was unloaded, the SS confiscated the sugar and executed seventeen Jews for prohibited black marketing.

To prevent starvation the girls ate raw potatoes, barley, and vegetables. Cooking in the camp was strictly forbidden, so they collected roots and other inedible things on their way to work and potato peelings out of rubbish tins, which caused serious digestive troubles.

Camp Antonienhof

From Fort Radziwill the girls and I were transferred to Camp Antonienhof,[10] which was a former farm east of the city of Posen. Only a few weeks before, the family who had owned the property for generations suddenly got notice to quit, but was allowed to take their furniture with them. So the house was empty when the girls moved in. Sanitary arrangements suited a large family but not hundreds of people. Nothing would have shown that this old Polish family residence was now a concentration camp had it not been for the electrically charged barbed wire fence and the notices, "Property of the City of Posen" and "Strictly Forbidden To Enter." There was a POW camp nearby.[11] Sometimes English prisoners would meet Jewish girls on the road or came near the camp. They managed with great skill to give the girls much desired cigarettes, chocolate, bread etc. on which they wrote, "For our sisters."

Sanitary Conditions

I had been warned before that sanitary conditions here were much worse than in Fort Radziwill. However, I found things worse than I possibly could have imagined. The girls, their hair cut off, were in a dreadful state. They were pale, emaciated, and half of them had swollen legs and suffered from dangerous infections. There was TB and diarrhea, and young girls barely older than children showed alarming signs of starvation. Their frail bodies were susceptible to any infection; the smallest injury to their hands or feet became dangerous. So minor surgery became the most important part of my work. Major operations could not be performed owing to lack of assistance and instruments.

I had to watch a young person dying from appendicitis as I was not allowed to send her to an Aryan hospital in the city. Although one of the buildings had been turned into a hospital and sick girls from other camps were brought here, there was a complete lack of instruments, medications, disinfectants, and nursing facilities. One girl of seventeen arrived pregnant, after having been raped by a guard, and tried to conceal this. In spite of her condition she worked as hard as the others. Her camp mates looked after her most tenderly, sharing their meager food ration with her and hiding her from the guards. I admired this attitude of the enslaved and helpless girls. At last I had to keep her away from work and should have reported her to the Gestapo. Failing to do so was punishable by death, but fortunately a premature birth occurred. The child died after ten days, and I declared it a stillborn case, which saved the mother from being deported.

Health conditions in the camp had to be reported to the Gestapo daily. Diagnoses like "Starvation" or "Emaciation" were classed as atrocity propaganda and prohibited. More than five sick were not permitted; a camp doctor who reported a higher percentage was regarded as a saboteur and deported to the East. Altogether I had to attend to three camps, which were a good distance from each other. I was given a bicycle and certain streets were marked on a map which I was allowed to use. I was the only Jew who could move freely outside the camps without guard.

Where the Camp Inmates Came From

Early in November, 1941, it was announced in the Ghetto of Litzmannstadt (Lodz) that men and women could volunteer for work in Germany.[12] They were told that it would be work in a sugar refinery, that they would be paid and could send money back to Litzmannstadt. As conditions in Litzmannstadt were unbearable—people were starving and expected to die—one had nothing to lose, and a number of persons (mainly young ones) volunteered. They thought where there is work there will be food. However their destination turned out to be the collecting station for prison camps, where they had to stay for days without blankets and straw, even though it was November. Before leaving, everybody was bathed. This provided a good chance for the SS men to beat the naked girls with whips. The prisoners were then taken to Posen in cattle trucks and housed in camps.

When I arrived in Posen in June, 1942, this number had been reduced considerably by death and deportations. In Camp Antonienhof there were about 350 women at that time, the same number in Fort Radziwill, and only about 150 in the camp "Sedan" [*sic*]. The nationality of most of the women was Polish, but there were also German, Austrian, and Czech girls amongst them.

The Administration of the Camp

After they had arrived in Posen, the girls were summoned by a Gestapo man and told that they would be taught to work and, if they worked well, would be treated well. They also were promised payment, which they could spend as they liked. "Kapos" and other key positions like camp constables or camp stewards were chosen from the few German Jewish girls. The position of "Senior Jewess" (camp steward) was very important, and the well being of the whole camp could depend on that person. She was the connecting link between the Jewish camp mates and the German camp commander. Fortunately there were very suitable "Senior Jewesses" in the women's camps. They were of good morals, just and incorruptible. I must state that in the men's camp, unscrupulous subjects who had acquired SS manners and who were hated by their mates as much as by the SS itself had pushed themselves forward.

Second after the position of "Senior Jewess" came the Senior Police women, who had to see that there was order and no friction in the camp. When the girls returned from work, they had to queue up for the evening meal. It was one of the main duties of the camp police to maintain order there. They had to be on duty day and night and were made responsible whenever anybody tried to escape. In spite of the heavy duties, these positions were very much in demand. They were safe from bad weather, while the outdoor workers had to be in the open all day long.

Outdoor Work

The Jews were used for gardening the Board of Works, a Steel Construction Company, or in the Town Gardens. Nearly all the road repairs, new paths and improvement of scenery between 1941 and 1943 were made by Jews. The girls had to work as hard as the men. They had to dig holes into the wet ground, had to fill the wheel barrows with the heavy clay. Only the old and infirm were put on farm work. They had to work under any weather conditions. In the cold winter of 1942/43 the girls had to work without gloves. The results were countless frozen fingers, which had to be amputated. When I reported this to the German authorities, I was given the reply that the soldiers had to work outdoors too, at twenty degrees fahrenheit, in the frost.

The Polish firms employing the Jewish girls received large orders from the German municipal authorities. From records I happened to see, I understood that the Gestapo had placed these "Political Internees" at the disposition of the DAF (*Deutsche Arbeits Front*) Posen, and the DAF sublet them to Polish firms. These firms were assured that the workers in question were "young and strong." When reading the documents, one felt like being placed back in the times of slavery. The half-starved Jewish workers, of course, were unable to fulfill the demands upon their working abilities. But the Polish farmers, who received premiums for making them work hard, drove them on with threats and beating. It often happened that the Polish foremen knocked down the girls with their fists and nailed boots. Still this treatment was gentle compared to what the men had to endure. The men carried stretchers with them to work, as nearly every day they had to carry mates home who had been knocked to cripples or even knocked dead. The Germans cynically blamed the Poles for crimes like this, passing remarks about the "inferiority of this nation."

Remuneration

During the first months the Jewish workers received RM.36 per working hour, but RM.45 were deducted from their monthly wages for food and lodging. They were allowed to use their earnings to buy coupon-free articles in the camp canteen or else to send the money to Litzmannstadt. The sick ones who could not work, therefore, got involved in debt, which was the reason for their being put on the list (for return transports). However, after some time all payments stopped, allegedly to counteract the ever increasing endeavors to escape.

Timetable

Reveille was at four-thirty A.M.; then came making beds. In winter in the camps, there was no electric light. Washing took place in the yard at the water tap or in one of the few sinks. One piece of substitute soap was given to each person every two months. At five o'clock they had to queue up for "Coffee." There was a five-thirty roll call in the yard, everyone counting up and leaving for work (under guard). After one hour's march, work started at seven o'clock. At twelve o'clock soup was brought from the camp, mostly cold. Twenty minutes rest for lunch followed, but there was no possibility of spending them in a sheltered room, not even in winter or in bad weather.

At five o'clock P.M. they knocked off, returned to the camp, and again there was a roll call and counting up. Then followed lining up for the evening soup and bread, which often occupied time till late in the evening. In some camps they had so called "order calls" at night. This was a speciality of the camp commander at Fort Radziwill, who coming home late and being drunk, would go and inspect the dormitories. Whenever he noticed the least offense, everybody had to get out (without having time to dress), and he made them stand in the yard for one hour. On Saturday afternoon the whole crowd bathed in big wooden tubs. Four girls used the same water, as it had to be fetched from the river in buckets. Very often they were made to work on Saturday as well, so the girls hardly found time to mend their clothes and linen.

After work the girls used to sit together and sang Polish, Russian, and Jewish folk songs, or even some they had made up themselves and which described very vividly and, in spite of all the misery, even with humor, the camp life.[13] A book of these songs and short sketches which I collected myself unfortunately got lost with my other belongings.

German Administration of Jewish Camps

In spring 1941–42, the City of Posen took over the administration of the camps, as previously the DAF, by its mistakes and coarse bribery, had starved hundreds of people to death or let them be infected by epidemics. The responsible employees decided they would feed the Jewish workers a little better, not because they felt pity for them, but because they had to preserve the manpower which was scarce already. There was no chance of getting other workers. For a period the interest in manpower was put above the extermination principle of the Gestapo. There were many differences of opinion between the SS and the municipalities as far as this matter was concerned.

For the important position of the camp commander, deserving party members were chosen, for instance the men or faithful Germans who had lived in other countries but had "come home to the Reich." They were not subject to any controls, and the fate of hundreds of human beings depended on their good or bad will. A German woman from the Baltics was thus appointed commander of the camp Antonienhof.

Her saying at the Gestapo headquarters that she was an Anti-Semite was considered proof enough for her ability to be a camp commander. She had no idea of administration, but I was very much surprised when she told me that she had been enticed out of her country by Hitler under false pretenses and that she hated the Nazi system ardently. Her religious convictions would not tolerate any oppression of the church or persecution of Jews anyhow. I found out that these words were not empty phrases many times during the one year I had to be together with her. She always cooperated with the Senior Jewess and with me, thus saving many human lives.

This camp commander once helped me escape an unpleasant and dangerous situation; in fact, she probably saved my life. The camp was to be enlarged, and the girls had to erect the brick walls themselves. To inspect their work, a "building inspector" came from time to time; he did not shrink from attacking the poor girls sexually. He visited me also in my office where, except for an examination table and two chairs, there was no other furniture. He tried to persuade me with all sorts of promises to submit to his wishes. Of course, I was not only physically disgusted but also feared that he would try to get rid of me as an unwanted witness after having had his will. So I kept running around the table which served as a barrier from his attacks and cried, nearly out of my senses, "The Fuhrer doesn't want it." This only increased his greed and rage. He was not far from catching me when the good camp commander appeared and freed me from the situation. Later I heard that he was hanged by the Poles after the war as a collaborator.

Mail and Parcels

The camp inmates were allowed to write a card every four to six weeks. They also received replies from their relatives, mostly from Litzmannstadt, Austria, and Germany. These messages were subjected to severe censorship. However, in 1942, when people tried to escape, all mail was stopped. Any communication between the camps in Posen was strictly forbidden. It happened that people heard of the death of relatives as late as a year after, although they had lived in the same city, but in another camp.

Sometimes the camp commanders unscrupulously robbed the camp inmates of gifts that were sent to them. They would use any trick if it was to their advantage. For instance, the men in one camp were told to write to their relatives that they were allowed to receive money and parcels. When the food and clothes arrived, the camp commander simply confiscated them all. They even made the men sign for the receipt of the goods.

Return Transports

I was ordered to make a list every few weeks of those who were unable or would soon be unable to do hard work. This list had to correspond with my daily reports about the three camps. Also the number of persons recommended for "Return Transports" had not to be less than a certain minimum fixed by the authorities. We were told that the people in question would be sent back to the Ghetto of Litzmannstadt. This sounded true, as at that time there was a factory for military uniforms in Litzmannstadt, and many relatives of our girls were reported to work there. Therefore, at first, many volunteered for these return transports, hoping that they would meet their relatives again and also get rid of the hard laboring. The girls promised to write soon, secret codes were made up, even illegal communications with the aid of helpful Polish people were planned. However, no news arrived, not even after several of these transports had left. When letters from Litzmannstadt came, addressed to girls who had left, we became alarmed; there were rumors that the transports, instead of going to Litzmannstadt, were put onto a side track. Some of the Polish guards told us in confidence that they had been ordered to return before the trains were thus diverted. They had been told that new barracks had been built near a small station and nobody was allowed to enter these except the SS and Jews. They were called "Bathing Huts," but some said they were gas chambers. People in the neighborhood noticed that the chimneys were smoking for days after the arrival of every transport. These stories sounded so fantastic that one simply refused to believe them. However, I became very careful with my reports and tried to put in the name of people only whose lives were lost in any case. Nor did the girls volunteer any more but tried to keep from the transports with all their force. Even if it was beyond their capability they kept on working and, after the transport had left, collapsed altogether. Others were hiding and only reappeared later. But many were so weakened that they let themselves be lifted apathetically onto the trucks which stood ready. The SS guards even beat the miserable ones if they did not get in quickly enough. Thousands of Jews disappeared like this from the Posen camps and have never been seen again.

Partly through death, partly due to the "return transports," there remained after one year only the tenth part of the original number of 12,000 Jews. The Posen population had no knowledge of the events in the camps, as is illustrated by the following little incident: A new camp commander had, by mistake, instead of sending the list of the girls chosen for return transport to the Gestapo, sent the girls themselves, accompanied by a guard. Some of the girls collapsed on the way, and people in the street became attentive. A girl cried and called out to the bystanders in Polish, "For Heaven's sake, help me. They want to send me away. They want to kill me. I have always worked hard." Some people wanted to know more about these strange miserable beings, but soon Germans appeared who called the police, and the crowd was dispersed. They declared the girls were insane; the camp commander and the guard responsible for the incident were deported.

Escaping

In spite of the strictest measures, people often tried to escape, but these endeavors were mostly unsuccessful. The meager and bald shaved men and women looked too strange, even if they succeeded in procuring good clothes for themselves. But most of them had exchanged their last few good clothes in the Ghetto for food and wore utterly torn clothes and shirts. They also wore shabby wooden shoes, and this alone frustrated many endeavors to escape. The penalty for trying to escape was death; furthermore the whole camp was punished: depriving [prisoners] of meals, work on Sundays, beating every tenth [person], parading in the yard for hours in any weather. Most of the fugitives were captured and brought to the Gestapo. For many the lack of documents was fatal. If anybody was caught, his own mates were made to hang him.

The 5th of October, 1942

Often finding money in possession of Jews, the Gestapo thought of a way to take all the money from them at once. On October 4th an order was issued to assemble all inmates, sick or healthy, in the camp yard with all their belongings, ready to leave. A terrible panic broke out as we thought that we all would be sent to the gas chambers straightaway. Some tried to commit suicide, and nobody could sleep that night. After hours of standing in the yard in tense expectation, the Gestapo came, not in the notorious trucks for deportation but in stylish private cars. One of them addressed us smilingly, "Money would only make people mischievous," and he would keep it all for us. Everyone should surrender what he possessed, money or jewels. Those, however, who would disobey, he would have to punish most severely. Intimidated, most of us gave him our poor belongings, often only Pfennigs, and he collected RM.150 altogether. He also checked on a few girls to see if they had kept anything, but found nothing. Some were dismissed and glad to have a narrow escape. In the men's camp, things did not turn out so well. When searched, some men still had money and were hanged on the next tree.

Burying the Dead

The hearse came more often than the baker's cart. A horse wagon of a Posen firm appeared with a long undressed wooden box into which the body was thrown. Often the hearse came from other camps, having a sad load already to which a new body was added. All the bodies showed the same signs of complete starvation, right to the skin and bones. To prevent spreading of epidemics, all dead bodies had to be completely undressed, shaved, and handed to the driver without a shroud. The mates accompanied the dead to the gate of the camp. Death was no horror, rather liberation from a life that was too hard to be endured.

Men's Camps in Posen

The lodgings of the women were not suitable for human beings, but they were still heavenly compared with the conditions in the camps for men. In stables and ruined huts, the men slept on the ground without blankets or straw. In those dirty places, vermin and diseases of all kinds spread. The men had to work even heavier than the women while the food was equally insufficient. Correspondingly, the mortality was enormous, and some of the camps died out completely. Punishment was even harder than in the women's camps. Smuggling letters, stealing, trying to escape were punished with hanging. Executions took place in the *Stadion* and in presence of delegations of the other camps. After an execution, the women were ordered to dance around the hanged bodies. The condemned persons mostly died bravely. At one execution where I had to be present, the young fellows shouted at the gallows, before the rope was put round their necks, "Avenge us!"

A former staff surgeon who had served in the First World War was in medical charge of the Posen camps. His name was Dr. Sieburg and he came about once a week. Dr. Sieburg was not a member of the Nazi Party and was certainly not in favor of the way the Jews were treated. He had a leaning towards the German National Party; when I drew his attention to the terrible conditions, he tried to bring about some improvement. He suggested I write a report to point out the existing state of affairs, the hygienic defects, and the low allotment of calories. He promised to support the petition with his own comments. He further advised me to state malnutrition as cause of death in the death certificates. He was convinced that the dreadful conditions were not in the intentions of the government. Actually, after this report had been submitted, an improvement became noticeable. Food was more plentiful and work better organized. The prisoners of the Antoninek Camp thanked me for my help.[14]

Unfortunately, the improvement did not last long. After a few weeks an official came to arrest me and brought me to the Gestapo prison in Poznan. There an SS man accused me of "sabotage of German work," shook me by the shoulders, and threatened to destroy me. Everything else I would learn in Berlin, where I was to be brought for further questioning. My luggage was taken from me and also my diary, which I had kept during the fifteen months I had spent in Antoninek. I have never seen it again.

As far as Dr. Sieburg was concerned, I learned later that he was sent as punishment to the Russian front, where he fell.

I stayed in the Poznan Gestapo prison for about three weeks under wretched conditions. One of my co-prisoners (a woman) helped English prisoners-of-war to escape. In a wagon behind bars, the men were handcuffed. We were transported in a group of twenty to Berlin.

Before I describe my experiences in Berlin, I want to mention a woman in Poznan. Her name was Magdalena Nowitzka, previously housekeeper with the Stablewski family (the former owners of Antoninek). She used to give me and the other women of the camp food, although she had no abundant supply herself. Some time after I had been arrested, the whole camp was to be broken up and all inmates to be sent to Auschwitz into the gas chambers. At that time she hid three girls in the attic of her small cottage. There they were found by the Gestapo and arrested together with Mrs. Nowitzka. The girls perished but Mrs. Nowitzka was later released.

In Berlin we were put into Alexanderplatz prison at first. Very soon myself and other prisoners were brought in the green police car (so called "*Grune Minna*") to the Gestapo prison in Bessemer Street (now in the Eastern Sector) where I spent another three weeks. The inmates were women of all nations, some of them Jewesses who waited for their transport to the nearest concentration camp. We were twelve in one cell.

From the windows we could see the Gestapo police training dogs to jump at fluttering skirts fastened to wooden rods. At that time there were often Air Raid Alarms. Of course we were not allowed to go to the shelter. Later I heard that a bomb had hit the prison and there were many casualties.

One Sunday afternoon I was called before the woman supervisor of the prison. On the dirty floor of the corridor there lay a young Ukrainian woman about to give birth to a baby. I asked for a pair of scissors and thread and delivered the child. As a reward I received half a loaf of bread, which I shared with my co-prisoners. They wished I could deliver a baby every day.

Again I had to enter a green police car and was driven to the Gestapo at Alexanderplatz for further questioning. There I was asked what offense I had committed as no papers could be found. I answered cautiously that some administrative oversight might have occurred with the death certificates. Thereupon the official said with a cynical smile, "All your patients are already in a camp in the East and you are going to follow them." I could gather from his look what he meant; it was so obvious. Later the sad truth was confirmed: All my poor girls and men patients had been sent to the gas chambers after my departure. Up till now I have not heard of any survivors of the camps in Posen and I believe I am the only one.[15]

The next day I came into the collecting camp in the Grosse Hamburger Strasse. This building, an old school, was divided into two departments. The first floor housed all those who were to be transported to Theresienstadt, while those on the second floor were to be sent to the East. I fell into the second category; my name had already been entered on the list. I was desperate and near suicide.

Then, in a miraculous way, another incredible piece of good luck happened which undoubtedly saved my life. I met amongst the people around me the M. couple, who previously had been patients of mine in Berlin. They told me they would be released the same afternoon and intended to go to Sweden. They had bought their freedom through bribing a Gestapo man. They offered to help me and to bring me in contact with an intermediary. Did I have any money? I answered in the affirmative and gave them name and address of my sister in Berlin who was married to an Aryan and kept some money for me.

At the last moment, on the eve of the transport to the East, a Berlin advocate, Dr. J., appeared. I should go with him to the chief of the Gestapo and should leave it to him to answer any questions I may be asked. The first question was where was my husband? Dr. J. replied that my husband had died because of injuries received during the First World War and had obtained the Iron Cross, First and Second Class. Further questions referred to children and profession. These questions were truthfully answered. Obersturmfuhrer D. asked Dr. J. how many persons were listed for Theresienstadt. Dr. J. replied sixty-nine. "All right," D. said, "Let's make it a round figure." Thus, on August 4, 1943, I joined the transport to Theresienstadt. It comprised all the personnel, doctors and sisters of the Berlin Jewish Hospital. Everybody was wondering how I had managed to go with them, but I could not disclose the real reason. I made a note of the East-Transport number and learned later that none of the about two thousand persons had survived.

This is how I was sent to Theresienstadt instead of the East, which was the same as escaping certain death. After the war my sister told me that she had given Dr. J. three hundred marks and three hundred cigarettes which, so he said, he passed on to some official.

I stayed in Theresienstadt for eighteen months. Like all other inmates, I had first to join the so-called *Hundertschaft* (group of hundred), to perform physical work. For some time, I cleaned the office and bedroom of the notorious Eichmann, which was considered to be privileged work.

After about three months I was allowed to work as a doctor and was assigned to the *Genie-Kaserne*, in particular to the TB ward. This also meant that I received somewhat bigger food rations. Although Theresienstadt was considered to be a privileged camp, the nourishment was so inadequate that I still suffered from malnutrition and hunger edema.

At first I was housed in an attic together with three hundred women. New arrivals had to sleep on straw and to wait until beds became available through transport or death. Most of the window panes were broken, and there was no heating.

Since my reappointment as a doctor my social status improved, and I was housed in a room on the ground floor together with seven other women. All of these were Czech, and three were women doctors. It was understandable that they were not overjoyed about the new arrival. In addition, the Czechs had an aversion to anything German, even German fellow Jews. Later, when we came to know each other better, the situation improved and I became quite friendly with one of the doctors. Her name was Anna Krasa, and I shall mention her later again. Tragically, none of my roommates are still alive. They were transported to Auschwitz and ended in the gas chambers.

One day Dr. J. appeared in my room. Together with his wife and two children, he had been sent to Theresienstadt and immediately brought before the Ghetto court. He had acted as a Gestapo informer in Berlin. For instance, he made appointments with Jews to come to his office to pick up false passports, for which he had received money. When his poor clients came, they were arrested by the Gestapo who waited downstairs in the entrance hall. He approached me now with the request to speak in his favor as he had rendered a great service to me. I tried my best, but my intervention failed. Too much evidence had accumulated against him. Dr. J., his wife, and his children had to join a transport immediately and disappeared.

I stayed in Theresienstadt until February, 1945, when I was lucky enough to be liberated and brought to Switzerland by train, together with twelve hundred persons.

Let me try to describe the atmosphere during the last few months before this transport left. It was about four months since the last trains to the East had left Theresienstadt. It had become quiet and the streets were desolated. Where previously lots of men and women hurried to work, only few persons were seen. In the evening the little town seemed to be empty. The few remaining people missed their loved ones they used to visit after work. Everybody sought closer contact with each other; the thoughts went to the many who were absent.

When the last transport in autumn 1944, left,[16] we had been told it was for "work in Germany." Although we were generally suspicious of the SS, this time there was some probability of truth. Had not all privileges been canceled that otherwise applied to deportees? Even people with war decorations, cripples, and blind had to go. It is true the question arose, "What work could these persons do?" One consoled oneself and the deportees with the hope that, as in Theresienstadt, they would find some work in the kitchen or in an office.

Now all of them had been away for months. No news arrived, but could this be expected? The deportees were certainly in a closed camp and had no means of smuggling letters. We knew these difficulties from our own experience. We drew comfort from the thought that the war would end soon. The news that leaked through—we had two secret radio sets built into beds—sounded hopeful. The communiqués of the German army conceded defeat. The last offensive in the Ardennes had been repulsed.

Christmas was celebrated. Our Christian co-prisoners had gotten hold of some small trees. New Year's Eve came; would it be the last one in Theresienstadt? Or the last one altogether? One never knew what the Gestapo was up to, although they had solemnly declared that no further transport would take place.

Theresienstadt was to be "cleaned up." Actually, in the middle of winter, bed bugs were exterminated. This was certainly necessary, as even in the cold the insects continued their gay activity and tortured us, particularly the bed-ridden. It was difficult to transfer these poor people in the heavy frost from one part of the barracks to another. In the icy cold rooms the sick were even more miserable and would have preferred to stay in the heated, though bug-infested rooms.

Coal was now plentiful since 20,000 persons had been deported. New arrivals came, this time mixed-marriage couples from Moravia and Germany.[17] All of these were comparatively well-fed and optimistic. They confirmed the reports of the army communications we had intercepted, but nobody had heard anything of our deported mates. The new arrivals comforted us and said that Germany was in such a state of chaos, overrun with bomb victims, foreign workers, and refugees, nobody could get any news from anyone.

Almost every night new trains arrived. I was often on duty at the railway station; I had to examine the newly arrived for their health. Compared with our people, these were well-nourished. Nevertheless, each train brought some idea. Eichmann, who was frequently present, asked me eagerly about their number, and when I replied so and so many dead, he would acknowledge it with the single word, "Good."[18]

The Ghetto was to be replenished, so the rumor went. We were driven to work. New barracks were built, much to our astonishment. Wasn't there enough space in spite of the new arrivals? Had not Theresienstadt housed 60,000 people and now there were hardly 19,000? Why these remote barracks on the bastion which had such a strange appearance? It struck us as strange that they had no windows. Were we supposed to live in them? We were accustomed to many kinds of dwellings: garrets with dormer windows, attics that hardly allowed light to penetrate, cellars with broken window panes. But no windows at all?

Some said the new barracks were probably intended as store rooms for food. With increasing war danger the SS had brought their families to the safer Theresienstadt. Buildings and barracks were evacuated for them and renovated. Did they intend to store their coal and other provisions in these new barracks? Or perhaps ammunition? Mountains of files arrived from Berlin. Did they want to preserve the most important documents there?

Still, there remained little time for speculations. We were driven to work hard, and the remaining inmates had to cope with the additional tasks that had been previously performed by the deportees. Anybody who complained was pointed out the privilege of having remained in Theresienstadt. Therefore the work on the new barracks went on, and nobody knew their true purpose. Only after the collapse did it become known that these strange structures were to serve as gas chambers.[19]

A heavy, strenuous week had come to an end. It was the last of February, 1945, a great dull day as so many before. No new events were expected, perhaps some army reports or new arrivals. Then, suddenly, a rumor swept the Ghetto like wild fire: a transport was going to Switzerland.[20] This was received with scornful laughter. Another transport, although we had been assured that no more deportations would take place. Of course, three months had passed since the last transport. This was the usual interval. Nevertheless, the rumor persisted that this time it was different. This transport was said to have been organized by the Red Cross. Volunteers should come forward, women and children would be favored. But who would believe this?

It was not long ago that orphans had come to Theresienstadt, half-starved children who were housed in separate buildings.[21] They were cared for by selected physicians and sisters. All this was most mysterious; they were not even allowed to talk to others. A few weeks later they disappeared—allegedly to Switzerland. We never heard of them again. Would they not have written if they really arrived in Switzerland? Postcards from this country arrived, though with long delay; even parcels with valuable food were received.

At first volunteers did not come forward as nobody would believe this fairy-tale. Better to stay until the end of the war which was expected within the next few months. During this night hardly anybody slept. All Austrians, Germans, Czechs, and Dutchmen were called to report in the Sokolovna (where the administrative offices were) at three o'clock in the morning. Significantly, no Danes were included.[22] They always received special treatment, never had to join a transport, and received monthly small parcels with the sender's name, "The King of Denmark." The notice forms were differently worded from the usual notorious slips of paper of deportation orders.[23] Nevertheless nobody trusted the appeal. However, as one was used to obeying orders, all those who were ambulant went to the meeting place. We doctors were told to be prepared for duty on the departure of the transport.

The Sokolovna was brilliantly lit in spite of the existing black-out regulations. Jewish employees of the Gestapo sat at long tables and drew up records. No signs of SS men. We were asked, "Do you want to join the transport to Switzerland, or do you renounce voluntarily?" Most of the interviewed renounced.[24] The Jewish clerks themselves tried to dissuade us. Nobody had confidence in the truth of the destination. Besides, many had personal reasons to remain in Theresienstadt. Some did not want to be separated from their relatives who did not want to join. For many Czechs, the consideration was decisive that they did not want to leave their country, but would rather stay near home now that the end of the war was in sight.

For most inmates the old soldiers' motto prevailed, "Never report voluntarily." It had been estimated that 2,000 persons would join the transport, but less than half put their names down. The unheard of procedure that one had to choose whether to join the transport or to renounce in writing had different effects: many were set at ease; others decided it could only be a bluff of the Gestapo as usual.

As far as I was concerned, Rabbi Dr. Leo Baeck and his niece, Dr. Nelly Stern,[25] advised me to join. I took Dr. Stern's place; she had been appointed transport doctor but did not go as she wanted to stay with Dr. Baeck.

Those who had decided to take the risk were to queue up in the barracks yard. It was raining and bitterly cold. Still we had to stand in the yard from three A.M. until seven P.M. Names were called, numbers shouted, and the persons concerned led in groups to the camp commander Rahm.

As it was to be expected, the lists were not correct. Some who had refused were called up. Others who were prepared to go waited in vain, myself amongst the second group. It turned out that whole lists had disappeared. But without enrollment nobody could reach Rahm and, therefore, not depart. Some unyielding persons, amongst them myself, stepped through a window into the Hamburg barracks, which were closed that day and in which we suspected the lost papers to be. We were successful. The missing sheets were found and the numbers were issued.

In the meantime, it had become late and it was said Rahm had already enough and could close down. However in his office, the SS headquarters, the lights were burning. Long queues had formed before the building. It was still raining and we were wet and hungry. But who cared? The queue did not get smaller as people remained upstairs for a long time. Only two persons were allowed simultaneously. Many who had been refused returned. A Dutch colleague with four children had to stay behind, and no reason was given. A pale, care-worn woman in front of me also was rejected. She had asked Rahm to be allowed to go to Switzerland to inquire into the fate of her relatives who had been deported to the East. "Rather stay with us for another while," Rahm said to her.

Finally my turn came. In the large hall, which I had never entered before, two men sat at a large table: Rahm and Brunner. Eichmann stood behind them. In the door stood the "Race Researcher" Guenther[26] and his brother from Prague. I was also aware of other prominent personalities, but this time they appeared mild and nothing reminded [*sic*] of the savagery of past days. They looked at us with faint irony.

A supervisor called my name, and I was led to the table. Rahm asked my marital status. "Widowed." Your husband died in a concentration camp?" "No, of an illness before the war." This reply seemed to satisfy him. "How many children?" "None." "Have your relatives been transported to the East?" "No." I saw that Rahm stamped my papers, and I guessed that I was accepted. The passport was ready. Fingerprints had already been taken in the Sokolovna and a photo was attached, obtained probably from papers that were taken from us earlier.

I rushed "home" to pack for the transport was due to leave the next morning. For luggage, an "elegant suitcase" was prescribed.[27] My suitcase, which had been through two concentration camps, prison, and disinfection stations, looked anything but elegant, but was intact. According to orders, no rucksacks were allowed. What a nonsense! I never had traveled in Switzerland without my rucksack; why should I this time? I was sure I would miss it. I [packed] it in a great hurry and put in it all my warm things except those I wore. I did not possess a winter coat, only a worn out ski dress.

Soon the suitcase was packed. The few effects I had inherited from deportees—unfortunately all of us had to rely on such sad gifts—did not look too elegant.

Before the departure of the train on February 5, 1945, each participant received an extraordinary large helping of soup; in addition other provisions, such as a generous piece of bread and tinned food.[28] This came apparently from Swiss gift parcels that had not been distributed amongst us. Certainly it was intended to show the Swiss that the gifts had reached their destination and that we had been provided for plentifully.

We were 1,200 persons. At last we had settled in the wagons, a process which had taken many hours. The SS men cursed and called us names because the procedure was too slow. But how could the elderly people climb the high steps? It is true they were supported by the transport helpers, but the latter could not assist everywhere and had enough to do with stowing away the luggage. I was very proud because I had succeeded in smuggling my rucksack through the controls. Everybody's traveling gear had been critically inspected as on previous transports, but this time with a difference. On earlier occasions, one was not allowed to carry suitcases, only "soft luggage." This time suitcases were even prescribed. Surprisingly enough, some people were able to get hold of hand baggage of comparatively civilized appearance. As was to be expected, the luggage was mixed up and strange pieces were stowed over our heads.

I kept my rucksack on my knees, did not let it get out of my hands. It used to accompany me on my hiking trips in happier days and had remained faithful to me throughout the sad years. In prison it had served as a pillow; in attacks it stood the test in all the dirt. It had followed me through all the disinfection situations and had endured all that hardship. Now the outer pockets contained the provisions for the next few hours, also a small booklet, the parting gift from Nelly. In this I had entered the addresses I had been given by those who remained behind. I was to try to ascertain the whereabouts of their relatives and friends and get in touch with them. Outside, the eating bowl, which I had "bought" for half a loaf of bread some months ago, was fastened. It held about one pint. How useful it was; how many portions had I fetched in it from the kitchen, anxiously watching that it be filled at least half-full. This time there was a second helping. As farewell we received the usual goulash soup, which was given to all deportees before leaving, probably to cheer them up. This time the soup was tasty as never before. Allegedly the SS had ordered it in plentiful quantity. Some people started to eat from their traveling provisions before the train left. However their stomachs, used to hunger, could not digest the rich repast, and they became sick.

For hours the train stood in the railway station. It was a long one, but not Red Cross wagons as we had expected. In the last minute Dr. Baeck and Nelly came to say good-bye. Finally the train was locked and left, accompanied by SS men. For three days, until we reached the Swiss frontier, we actually did not know whether we really went to our freedom.

Although we were forbidden to look through the windows, we could see the rubble heaps in Germany. During the night the train stopped because of air raid danger. In Augsburg the order was issued, "All men out!" There was general panic. Everybody thought this was the end. However, we only had to change trains, and the men were to transfer the luggage to the other wagons.

Finally on the third day we approached the Swiss frontier. We were told by the SS men to take off the Stars of David and to "beautify." They even distributed lipsticks for this purpose. This was the last order the SS issued and this they admitted. They withdrew and wished us—to our enormous astonishment—all the best. Only now we realized that we were really going towards freedom. Married couples embraced; many wept and sobbed. It was unbelievable that we should be free. Only youth was not quite so sentimental; when the Gestapo went, a young girl sang, "Say softly servus [sic] as farewell" and "who will weep when we separate. . . ."

But once again our confidence was shaken. Shortly before the Swiss frontier the train stopped for hours in front of a barn. Many doubted we would be allowed into Switzerland. The Gestapo would lead us into this large barn and kill us there. The whole night we spent in terrible suspense, but next morning the train rolled slowly into Kreuzlingen station.

We saw the Gestapo discuss something with Swiss civilians, documents were handed over, a few wagons were opened, and obviously superficial tests made. We were free.[29] Swiss conductors entered the train, which seemed to us beyond comprehension. We asked them whether they really were Swiss.

From now on rows of people stood on the platforms and in the streets, waved and shouted, and threw chocolates, cakes, and bread into the train.[30] Our first stop was St. Gallen, where we were housed in a school. The two trains with wagons of the Swiss *Budnes Bahnen* (SBB), which had brought us from Konstanz, were directed onto a side track to the St. Fiden Station so that we would have only a short walk to our destination, the *Hadwig-Schule*. Most of us were able to cover this distance on foot, even though "we looked very worn out and dragged our luggage along laboriously," as the Swiss papers reported the next day.

In the school we were welcomed by the president of the Joint Committee, Sally Mayer, who delivered a short speech. He said how glad one was to know us to be safe and stressed that Alt-Bundesrat Musy, who stood by, had prepared our transport and that we owed our liberation to him to a great extent.

I had been introduced to Mr. Mayer as one of the doctors of the transport, and when he mentioned Musy, my first impulse was to step forward and to thank him. I was just wondering whether I could suppress my sobbing, when Mr. Mayer, who had apparently guessed my intention, held me back, saying, "Don't thank him. Mr. Musy would not appreciate it." A few days later I learned that Mr. Musy had initiated the whole action by negotiating with Himmler and other Nazi officials, with whom he stood on good terms. One suspected that he himself was financially interested.[31]

In the *Hadwig-Schule* we spent three days, sleeping on straw but in freedom. The first meal impressed us very much. We were given real plates filled from a bucket by Red Cross sisters. I was advised to throw my tin pot away, but could not make up my mind to do so. Postcards were distributed with postage stamps so that we could write to our friends in Theresienstadt. We were to tell them the journey had been very pleasant and that we were received with great friendliness.[32] We were advised to do this immediately as a further transport from Theresienstadt was expected. However this never arrived. Hitler was told about the matter, got an attack of frenzy, and forbade any more transports.[33]

It was pointed out to us that reporters would interview us about our experiences in Theresienstadt. In view of later transports we shouldn't say anything unfavorable. When the reporters finally came, we followed these instructions. Only an old granny, who was deaf and had heard nothing, told freely—the reporters shouted the questions into her ears—how much she had suffered and described the terrible conditions. All this appeared later promptly in the newspapers.[34]

Shortly after our arrival, thanksgiving services of all confessions were held. All compared our liberation with the miraculous salvation of the children of Israel from the Egyptian bondage. Then the Jewish and other Swiss population was led to us— naturally not very close lest any contagious disease was contracted. The disappointment of those who had hoped to find their beloved ones in the transport in vain was tragic.

Our next stop was a former hotel near Lake Leman, where we were put in quarantine. We were deeply impressed when, on our trip there, we saw lighted windows with curtains and people sitting at dining tables. All these were things which we had not seen for a long time.

Now we refugees—we had changed our status from that of a prisoner to that of a refugee—tried to prepare ourselves for a normal life. All these years we had waited for the moment of liberation and thought that now all our worries would be over. But hardly had the first excitement passed, when it appeared that the energy used so far for self-preservation would be necessary for a new struggle. This realization came quite unexpectedly to many and was a terrible shock to those who had thought they would receive preferential treatment as martyrs.

Many felt not to be up to the new struggle, and even amongst my four roommates two committed suicide, also victims of the Nazi regime. Others gained strength from past experience, a strength they had never been able to foresee. They continued the battle for existence.

Visiting Hermann and Ninon Hesse

Before I end my report I would like to mention a couple whose acquaintance turned out to be the greatest experience of my stay in Switzerland. I owe my acquaintance with the Hesses to Anna Krasa, who was a school friend of Ninon's. Poor Anna! What had she done to deserve her terrible fate while I was so incredibly lucky to escape the Nazi hell?

Anna and I met in 1943 in Theresienstadt, where we both were forced to work as doctors. Anna had a bed in a small room in which she lived with five other women. As there was no room for another bed, I was told to sleep on the floor. However Anna would not allow this and offered at once to share her bed with me. One lived in perpetual mortal fright, was forever subject to chicanery, suffered hunger, froze, and had still to work seventy hours a week to help the poor sick. Anna and I discussed our problems, hopes, and fears. Unfortunately the latter were only too well founded. On October 28, 1944, there was another of these dreaded transports to the East and Anna was "enrolled." This was all the more tragic, as it was the last transport to Auschwitz. The liberation armies were already advancing, and the gas chambers in Auschwitz were stopped on November 2nd.[35] Nearly four thousand unfortunate people were still gassed at the last moment.[36]

Before Anna left, we exchanged addresses of friends so that we should have some meeting place in case we both survived. If not, the other one should give the last greetings to the friends. Anna gave me the Hesses' address. At that time I did not realize how soon I would have the opportunity to comply with her wish. Not quite four months later I was liberated and arrived in Switzerland by the only train ever to reach freedom from Theresienstadt. We were about 1,200 persons[37] and were lodged in an abandoned hotel in Les Avants sur Montreux. I wrote to Ninon Hesse at once, gave her Anna's regards, briefly described my experiences, and apologized for not having stamped the letter. The reply came by return mail: A warm, heartfelt letter of welcome asking me to tell about Anna, whose fate worried her greatly. Ninon added greetings of her husband and expressed the hope that we should meet soon. A whole sheet of postage stamps was enclosed. This started a correspondence which lifted me tremendously, as I had neither friends nor relatives in Switzerland, and I gathered new hope and regained faith in the goodness of mankind.

A few months later I was transferred to a home for refugees in Brissago, beautifully situated at the Lago Maggiore. I was the doctor in charge. Lugano was not far away, and soon I received an invitation to come to Montagnola (where the Hesses lived). I took two days off and walked on foot over the mountains—partly for economic reasons, partly because I liked hiking.

Ninon came to meet me at the garden gate, a beautiful woman full of charm and dignity, and Hermann Hesse greeted me [just as] friendly and warmheartedly. He was dressed like a gardener and wore a big hat which protected him from the sun; he had just worked in the garden. His cat Schneeweisschen (Snow White) never left his side. The house was cozy, but simply furnished. Below [was] a large room with rows of books; upstairs the bedrooms and Ninon's studies. She was an archeologist and had a scientific library.

I was invited to stay the night. Soon after breakfast I had to report about myself, my experiences in Theresienstadt, and, above all, about Anna. While I still hoped for her survival, the Hesses at once feared the worst. Unfortunately they proved to be right. As I heard later, Anna had been sent to the gas chambers on arrival from Theresienstadt.[38]

Hermann Hesse asked me to report in detail, even such things as seemed unimportant to me. From his questions I gathered that he never missed anything I had already told him. He encouraged me to write down my experiences and said emphatically that these were quite exceptional and worth recording in all details. He was simply interested in everything. For instance, he produced a hiking map of the surroundings and made me point out which way I had crossed the mountain. He also discussed with me my work in the home and spoke about my future. He advised me to work in the Kanton Hospital—he understood at once that I had lost touch with the medical world for years and therefore had to brush up on my knowledge. I succeeded in obtaining the transfer to Zurich, where the Hesses visited me quite frequently. They helped me to find lodgings and invited me to concerts, to theater performances, and to friends.

This was the time (1946) when Hesse was awarded the Nobel Prize.[39] As his health was not the best, he did not go to Stockholm, but a celebration was arranged in Bern instead. He told me that a "friend" had donated an amount on this occasion. This was to be given to a refugee who wanted to continue his or her studies in Switzerland and Hesse recommended me. Thus I received monthly support. I suspect that Hesse himself was the friend, for he did not allow me to thank the anonymous donor. I visited the Hesses also from Zurich several times. One afternoon—we were just sitting at the coffee table—the maid brought a visiting card: RICHARD STRAUSS. However, to my regret, Hesse did not receive Strauss. He did not wish to be in contact with people who, in his opinion, had lacked backbone during the Nazi time.

In the meantime I had settled in Switzerland, worked in a sanatorium in Davos, when an old friend of mine sent me a permit to emigrate to Australia. At the same time it happened that I was invited by the O.S.E. (Organization Secour Enfants) to take charge of a transport of children to Australia. I asked Hesse's advice, whether I should venture such a risky step. I told him about my friend, a musician, whom I liked very much but whom I had not seen for many years. Hesse recommended at once to try a new life in Australia and sent me on this occasion his poem "Steps":

> . . . *The heart must ready be to part*
> *At every call of life and each new start*
>
> *To enter bravely without regret*
> *Into such tasks it has before not met.*
>
> *And each beginning bears a magic spell,*
> *Protects, and helps us on this earth to dwell*
>
> *Serenely we should step through space and space*
> *And shall not cling to any native place.*
>
> *World spirit does not want to hem us or to chain*
> *But lift us step by step to reach new heights again . . .*

I took Hesse's advice, married my friend, and set up a medical practice in Sydney—not without having passed a four year course at the Medical Faculty of Sydney University, for my German medical certificate was not recognized in Australia.

When today I lead a normal life again and have overcome—though not forgotten—the time of terror, I owe this to a great extent to the Hesses. They led me with superior understanding to settle again in human society.

Auschwitz

THE DEPTH OF HELL'S ABYSS

For when the faculty of intellect
is joined with brute force and evil will
no man can win against such an alliance.
—Dante Alighieri, *Dante's Inferno*

Of the nine women we either spoke to, interviewed, or whose oral histories we obtained, eight had been incarcerated in Birkenau. Hana Bruml and Ruth Reiser, natives of Prague, after having been transported to Theresienstadt, were then taken to Auschwitz. Ellen Loeb, living in Amsterdam, first went to Westerbork, next to Theresienstadt, and then to Auschwitz, while Magda Herzberger, originally from Hungary, was transported from a smaller transit camp in her native country to Birkenau. While Ruth and her friend Zuzka were at first left to die in block 25 before being transported to Lenzing, Ellen Loeb and her mother were transported to Lenzing after a short time. Magda, on the other hand, went with a work squad to Bremen prior to being sent to Bergen-Belsen. Dr. Ada Bimko was the only one of the women with whom we spoke personally who was in a position to render some medical care in Birkenau itself, although due to the conditions under which they worked, it could hardly be considered adequate.

Regarding the medical facilities, Danuta Czech contends that there were three phases in the development of hospitals in Auschwitz. During the first, from November, 1940, to the end of April, 1943, the "hospital" was actually the antechamber to the crematorium. Prisoners either died under terrible conditions, were killed by phenol injections into the heart, or joined the masses who went to the gas chambers.[1] Yisrael Gutman and Michael Berenbaum,[2] however, contend that during the first year, 1940–41, prisoners viewed the hospital as either a shelter from the inhumanities of camp existence or as a place to die peacefully. During this time prisoner doctors worked as camp nurses, the important positions held for the most part by German criminals. Because their sole concern was survival, they were either indifferent or hostile toward the patients. Medical care being insubstantial at best, the mortality rate was high. During this period the hospital barracks were located in Auschwitz I, the main camp, blocks 19, 20, 21, 28, and, for a time, block 9. Patients were separated into wards for internal diseases, infectious diseases, surgery, and a so-called *Schöningsblock*, or convalescent ward, in which Jewish prisoners unfit to return to work were selected for the gas chambers.[3]

Gutman and Berenbaum define Phase II (1942–43) as a time when Germany's need for manpower increased.[4] Hence, in an effort to enable prisoners to recover and return to the workforce, the SS began to use prisoner-doctors in the hospital camps. Between March and August 1942, approximately seventeen thousand female prisoners, most of them Jews, lived in ten blocks in Auschwitz I. Block 3 was designated as the hospital.[5]

As Auschwitz II, Birkenau, expanded, the Nazis established hospitals there for the inmates as well. The first, set up in May 1942, was in barracks 7 and 8 in BIb, the newly established men's sector. In late 1942, barrack 12 became a hospital as well. Barrack 7 came to be known as the "death block," since it was used as a dumping ground for moribund prisoners.[6] In August 1942, thirteen thousand women were transferred to Birkenau and placed in sector BIa. The ill were assigned to barracks 22, 23, 24, 25, and 26. During 1943, because of the ever increasing number of sick prisoners, more hospital barracks were added, with the result that nearly all the wooden blocks in sector BIa became hospital blocks. Berenbaum and Gutman continue: "Barracks 25, nicknamed by women prisoners 'death block,' which formally belonged to the camp hospital, served as a dumping ground for seriously ill and extremely exhausted women prisoners, mainly Jewish, selected in the camp hospital and labor squads, and doomed to death in the gas chambers. In this barrack, as well as the outpatient clinic located in the nearby barrack 28, women prisoners were killed by intracardiac phenol injections."[7]

Although these barracks were barely sufficient to hold 200 to 250 prisoners, there were often as many as 800 bedridden at a time. This made it impossible to isolate those with communicable diseases. The hospital barracks lacked electricity and had only one small stove for heat, four buckets to use as toilets, and a floor that was slimy from excrement and urine. Medication was scanty, and there were no bandages or antiseptics. Paper and placebos were used as substitutes. Mme. Vaillant-Couturier states that these blocks "did not correspond in any way to our idea of a hospital. . . . The bedding was so full of lice that one could see them swarming like ants. . . . The dead lay in bed with the sick."[8] Because ill patients were unable to work, they received less food than other inmates, thereby reducing hope for recovery. Regarding the food, Konnilyn Feig quotes one prison doctor as stating that patients received "rotten potatoes, weeds and without exaggeration one may state that it contained 20% rat feces."[9] The infirmary became the last stop before the gas chamber. After the camp resistance movement formed, those working within it were able to use the hospital complex as a cover.

Women gave birth to infants in wards filled with rats, mice, and filth. Until 1943 all newborns were drowned in a barrel. Mme. Vaillant-Couturier recalls that Jewish prisoners were forced to have abortions. "The woman in charge was a German midwife who was imprisoned for having performed illegal abortions. After a while, another doctor arrived, and for two months they did not kill Jewish babies. But one day an order came from Berlin saying that again they had to be done away with."[10] Babies received no food rations, and after 1944 many children were burned alive. Severina Shmaglevskaya recalls that, "Children were thrown in alive. Their cries could be heard all over the camp."[11]

Phase III lasted from April, 1944, to January, 1945. The Camp Resistance Movement was able to bring some improvement in the hospitals' conditions, and there was better sanitation. Non-Jewish prisoners were allowed to receive food from the outside, and more supplies were "organized" from the Canada warehouses. Those who were helped the least, however, were the prisoners, especially the Jews.

Margita Schwalbova, from Bratislava, Czechoslovakia, arrived in Auschwitz in March, 1942, and worked in several of the barracks mentioned above. Transferred to Birkenau in August of that year, she worked in both the hospital and experimental barracks. She also describes her activities with the Camp Resistance Movement. Her oral history, written in German, is housed in the archives at Auschwitz and is presented here with their permission.[12]

Chapter Nine

Margita Schwalbova

"THEY WERE MURDERED IN THE INFIRMARY"

• • •

Men tortured children.
Cleverly. Deliberately. Efficiently.
It was a routine job for them.
They worked hard, they tortured children.
                    —Naum Korzhavin, "Children of Auschwitz,"
                        in *Voices within the Ark: The Modern Jewish Poets*

I was born on September 29, 1915, in Bratislava. After I was no longer allowed to study, I worked in various occupations. I was arrested around the 21st of March, 1942, with about a thousand other young women, all of us under thirty years of age. We were ordered to assemble in a specific place. At first I did not want to report, but when the police threatened my brother with arrest, I decided to report to Patronka, a collection camp (*Stammlager*), in Bratislava. At this military compound, the women were assigned to various tasks. Women who were able to work were assigned to the Patronka Assembly Camp (*Stammlager*). The commanders of the camp were Slovakian Fascists called *Gardisten*. There were also Germans believed to be SS.

We were there for only a few days. After that we walked on foot to Lamacz, a village near Bratislava. We were loaded into four wagons, approximately a hundred young women in each wagon, for transport to Auschwitz.[1] The first transport, numbering one to two thousand, was sent on March 26th from Ostlowakia. I was in the second Slovakian transport to go to Auschwitz on the 28th of March. We did not know where we were going. According to rumors in Slovakia, young Jewish people were being sent to a work area.

The transport lasted approximately twenty-four hours. The wagon was locked, and we had nothing to eat or drink on the way. Although we had brought a few belongings, they were taken from us by the Slovakian Fascists before we were transported, so we left without any baggage. At the border, the Slovakian Fascists handed the train over to the Germans. We arrived in Auschwitz sometime late in the afternoon.

I can't remember anything, perhaps because of shock. I don't recall whether there was a ramp when we got off the train or whether it was at the railroad station. There was no selection, as we were all young people who could still work. We were led to the main camp of Auschwitz *(Stammlager)*, where we first had to be bathed. The bathroom was in a barrack. All personal belongings were taken away and our hair was shorn. In Auschwitz we received old Russian or French uniforms with pants.[2] I was allowed to keep my own shoes, but most of the others got wooden house shoes [*sic*]. We weren't registered until the second day. At that time we got our numbers; I was number 2675. We were not tattooed until later in Birkenau.

The women in my transport were assigned to block 9, a one story block in the *Stammlager.* We slept in wooden bunks. I remained there for three days. On the third day a call came for any doctors among the prisoners. I had studied medicine but had not yet completed my doctorate, but I was the only one who spoke up and was immediately transported to the Revier. SS *Arzt,* Dr. Bodmann, or von Bodmann, questioned me.[3] He asked some medical questions, and since I could answer them, I was accepted as a general practitioner. I was assigned to block 3, which was a one story building.

There were sick prisoners in some of the rooms, but I cannot remember how many. At first, there were no female prisoners other than me who were doctors or nurses. Only later, when other transports from Slovakia arrived, did we get medical personnel. I remember the names. For example, one was Edita Bokova from Zylina. She was gassed in 1942 along with her mother. Then there was Ena Wajsowa from Banska Szezawnica. She survived.

Prisoners worked in the Revier, which was in the basement in block 3. The female doctors and other personnel were housed on the first floor, while patients were on the ground floor. Even then we had a *Blockälteste* [block leader]. I believe it was Gertrud Frienke, a German political prisoner, who managed the office for the prisoners. Then there was Orli Reichert, who worked mostly as a nurse in the infirmary, and Annie Blumenauer, a cleaning lady. Angela Marie Autsch looked after the kitchen. Although the food was the normal diet, there was a special diet available for sick people. It was not cooked in block 3, only distributed.

During the first few weeks we got better medication than we did later in Birkenau. At first we received Prontosil in the form of tablets and injections, Eleudron in the form of tablets, and Tierkohle [charcoal] and Thanalbin for diarrhea.[4] We had only paper bandages. Most of the illnesses were diarrhea, phlegmon, pneumonia, and various injuries. No operations were performed. At that time, no dentist was available; only later, in Birkenau. I remained in the Stammlager until approximately the middle of August.[5] In Auschwitz, a special selection process took place between blocks 3 and 4, where there was a special wooden building in which those with less serious ailments were housed. That is where Camp Doctor SS *Lagerarzt* Bodmann made his selections. When the trucks arrived, Avmeyer, the camp leader, came with them. Because the selection process was too slow for him, he took all the women, approximately two hundred to three hundred, and sent them to the gas chambers. Most were Jewish and Polish.[6] Bodmann also started murdering prisoners in the infirmary who were suffering from inflammation of the brain[7] with Phenol injections, which he produced in the prison hospital. No doctor was present, and it was my duty to carry the dead into another room.[8] I don't know exactly where the dead women were sent from there. I know of two women who came back from working outside the camp, who were shot by the guards, one in the foot, the other in the stomach. The first one was from my home town, Okolicne, in Slovakia. Her name was Neufeld. They were still alive, but Bodmann killed them with phenol. Someone in the office must have kept records of those who died, but I don't know who had this responsibility.[9]

When Himmler came to visit the camp,[10] he watched how the women were beaten twenty-five times.[11] That was quite in the open for everyone to watch. I watched it from the window.

In the beginning, different nationalities were separated: Poles, Jews, and Germans,[12] but all ten blocks had women living in them. I believe the *Reichdeutscher* block was between blocks 3 and 4. Before the transfer of the women to Birkenau, counting was organized by the supervisory personnel and carried out by supervisors. Other selections were made, but not very often. Bodmann himself made a special selection of patients in the hospital whom he considered seriously ill. These patients were picked up at night.[13]

The sickrooms in the camp were normal rooms with three-level beds which, at that time, were furnished with straw and covers. One woman slept in each bed. There was also a washroom where the sick could wash themselves. There was no problem with the water supply. I can't remember if a change of underwear was supplied in the camp hospital. It was, I think, possible since Angela Autsch controlled the laundry and permitted the change of dirty for clean underwear. This was not possible in the main camp.

During summer 1942, I was sent to Birkenau. We, the personnel, walked to Birkenau. The barracks were not yet fenced. At that time only blocks 23 and 24 were designated as hospitals. They were wooden barracks with a sign on them: "Beware of lice." They consisted of three levels of bunks with an oven in the middle of the room. At that time, block 22 was still under construction. Later, after its completion, block 22 was designated a hospital barrack. Soon block 27, a stone building with an oven in the middle of the room, was also incorporated into the hospital complex reserved for Jewish patients.[14] I often worked in the infirmary shortly after arriving in Birkenau in 1942. Birkenau compared to the *Stammlager* was more primitive. In the *Stammlager* they had a laboratory, a room for doctors, and a place for the office *(Revierstube)*, while the infirmary barrack was mainly the *Revierambulance.* On the left side was an examination table and a closet with medication, which we gave patients while they were being examined. In the corner, a secretary kept records of the prisoners. In the closet were instruments, such as one to measure blood pressure. Trudi Millerova, who still lives in Prague, worked with me. I don't know who came to work there after her. In the Revier office were mostly files with records. As far as I know the following female prisoners are still living: Wanda Mende—Polish. I don't know what her name is now. Fran Ana Tytoniak, who now lives in Krakow. I talked to her yesterday [June 7, 1988].

We only had approximately four or five nurses in the hospital in the *Stammlager.* Some were caring; some were not. One of them, Nurse Frigda, was especially sadistic. She herself selected the ones to be gassed. She stood in front of the infirmary and whipped the patients who were standing there.

In the beginning, I worked in the infirmary in block 28. On one side was the infirmary, and on the other the office. Sick people had to go from the infirmary to the office, where they had to ask the *Blockälteste* for permission to stay. Whether or not they were allowed to stay was up to the female doctors. If the [SS] doctor was there, the women had to parade nude before him. At the time it was not Bodmann, but Meier.[15]

Bodmann was between thirty-five and forty. He looked like a meat inspector: a heavy set bald man with glasses, and behaved accordingly. He was crude, stern, and thought he knew it all. He only talked to the prisoners as servants. Meier was much younger, a tall fellow who seldom softened. He was possibly afraid of typhus, but he also made selections. As far as I can remember, he was blond.

In Birkenau I was the one who wrote the death certificates of those who committed suicide by throwing themselves into the electrified fences. There was a girl from Slovakia who yelled that people should not go to work for the Germans since they would be murdered anyway. She was shot by guards, and Bodmann said that was a warning for others who would behave like that. We were not even allowed to bandage her and had to put her on the ground and let her bleed to death.

There was very little water in the Revier because there was only one well in the camp which was almost impossible to get to. A water line led to the hospital complex, and the infirmary received water through this, so we did not have to carry water buckets. Toilets were not available, so the patients had to use pails. All the patients were together in the hospital, and infectious patients were not isolated. As far as I can remember, the only picture in the infirmary barrack was a portrait of Hitler. The floor was wooden. There was no heat, and no grass grew next to the barracks. The windows were not protected by any bars.

I can't remember how many female doctors and/or nurses were available. I remember some names: Edita Bokova, Elena Wajsowa. The Polish doctor's name was Jadwiga Wegierska. I believe others came later. Later male prisoners were called upon to act as doctors as well.

Before the fall of 1942, block 27 had been for sick people. Most prisoners suffered from diarrhea, typhus, and phlegmon. I was able to go there as a nurse/doctor. There were also Polish doctors whose names I can't remember, but who treated me quite well. Then the doctor let all the Jewish doctors and nurses go for no reason. A number were able to go to block 27, which was not a Jewish block any more. On October 3, 1942, all the Jewish patients in block 27 had been taken to the gas chambers—approximately three hundred to four hundred Jewish women. That particular day I wrote into my book.[16] After that block 27 contained Czech and Polish women.

In September or October, 1942, the assistant technician or aide by the name of Shulz called me to block 22, which was not finished yet. I worked in block 22 with Clauberg and in blocks 5 and 6, shifting back and forth between the blocks and the infirmary. In the front part of block 22 was an examination table. There were some healthy women there, and some were on stretchers. The women were called into the room and told they would be vaccinated. They were put on the table and got an injection of phenol directly into the heart, which killed them. No doctor was present, and it was my duty to carry the dead into another room. There I had an opportunity to meet some women and ask where they came from. They had come from Lublin. Some of them observed that while many women left the room, none came back. When we told them the vaccination story, they knew what to expect because they figured it was revenge for an act of sabotage in Lublin. We heard that men from Lublin were also killed. There was a total of forty-five, among them a grandmother, mother, and grandchild.

The SS nurses had supervision of all prisoners. Eva Wrigel and Erna Gobel were the *Lagerältesten* in the prison in Birkenau. Orli Reichert came after them. They were Germans and were responsible for anything and everything that happened in the hospital.

I remember the doctors. Meier was there from approximately August to November, 1942. Then came Dr. Vetter.[17] He was ruthless, and any woman who had a child was gassed along with the child. I especially remember Selma Haas, whom I knew from Bratislava. She was approximately twenty-two years old, and she was gassed because she gave birth to a beautiful, strong boy.

In 1942 a lot of transports arrived, and some pregnant women slipped through the selection process. They were Jewish women. I don't know how many. Pregnant women had no separate barracks. They tried to hide their pregnancies and gave birth in secret; they knew that mothers and babies would be gassed. In the *Stammlager* in 1942, Dr. Bodmann himself aborted every pregnancy, regardless of whether they were in the third or eighth month. About twenty women in block 3 were affected. They all died of blood poisoning while in the hospital. Later it was arranged that women who were in the beginning of pregnancy were aborted under more sanitary conditions, and they survived. These abortions were announced wherever possible, and pregnant women were advised to come forward.

When Vetter first came, some of the children were kept alive. Then the order came from Berlin that they all had to be gassed. Some of the children had died in the meantime, but the mothers were gassed anyway. Until spring of 1943, Aryan women and their children were gassed. Then, beginning in 1943, Aryan babies were not murdered; only Jewish women and children. I don't know whether that was an order. There was no special place for these children and no special nourishment. The Revier personnel tried to give them more food. Their diet consisted, for example, of soup that had a white color, and the bread was whiter than the usual bread in the camps.

In 1943 and 1944, a well-qualified Polish female doctor gave the pregnant women something to abort their babies in order to save the lives of the mothers.[18] No one knows how many children were born. From 1944 on, no more children were born. Women far into pregnancy were selected to be gassed, while those in earlier months were aborted.

In December, 1942, I left block 27 and went to the experiment block. That month an x-ray lab was established in block 30 in Auschwitz.[19] Someone was looking for Aryan women to work there, but none came forward so I told Nietzwicki that I had learned to be an x-ray technician. He said that since they could not find anyone else, they would take me. So at first I went to the sauna and was deloused. Then I worked in the experiment block with Dr. Clauberg.[20] Dr. Vetter was there as well.

Block 30 was divided into two parts. On one side was Dr. Schumann and his x-ray machine with which he sterilized people.[21] On the other side Dr. Clauberg had his machinery. There were ten or twelve beds for female patients. On that side, Sonja Fischmann (her name is now Sonja Fritz), from Vienna, who still worked for Dr. Clauberg, and a Polish woman were working. I believe her name was Kazia, and she also survived the war.

Clauberg came, at the most, two or three times a week. He was a short, stocky man and always had a bottle with some kind of white liquid.[22] The bottle only had numbers and no name. He injected the liquid into the womb of a patient, after which I had to turn the x-ray machine on and off. He told the patient she would get a fever. When I worked with Clauberg, I had very little to do since Clauberg came so infrequently. I lit a lamp because the x-ray room was dark. Once, when I was reading, Dr. Vetter came along and told me I was not to use the lamp because it wasted electrical energy.

We lived in block 30 with the machinery and were not allowed to leave. The personnel and female prisoners were moved to the *Stammlager* [main camp], but I was not. I worked there until March, 1943, at which time I was moved to block 10.[23]

In Birkenau the largest *Appell* took place in December, 1942.[24] It took place behind the chain link fence on a lawn. It was a *Generalappell* for all except *Bauabschnitt* [barracks] BIa; patients did not participate. The Germans drove out all the prisoners. Those who couldn't walk were beaten. Those who fell were stepped on their necks. The women stood on the lawn from morning to night. Then they were pushed back and had to leap over trenches. Those who were unable or too weak to leap were pushed into block 25, after which they were gassed. At that time all the Slovakian women were gassed. One was Tamara Grunberger, a nurse who had been fired from her duties by Vetter. Of all the Slovakian women, only three or four hundred were left. That was the way the *Appells* were conducted; often without any plan, selections were made. Even if women came to the infirmary sick, they could be selected.

In the spring of 1943, a new doctor, Dr. Kitt,[25] came to block 30. Ena Weiss, from Czechoslovakia, and Orli Reichert were the doctors there. In March or April a dental office was established. Danielle Casanova was the dentist. Casanova was a wonderful person.[26] She had a Polish woman, who died during the summer of 1943, working for her as a technician. I don't know who took her place.

In the summer of 1943, men from *Bauabschnitt* BI were transferred to BII.[27] The women were also in BI. Barracks 4 through 30 were taken over to be a hospital for prisoners. The entrance was where the infirmary was—opposite barrack 28. The barracks had no identifying signs and only had wooden bunks. Only block 27 had a stove. There was no pharmacy. Medication seemed to come from the *Stammlager* [main camp] and was delivered and distributed from the infirmary.[28] The doctors had to sign a register as proof that they had used medication and to name the sick prisoners to which they had been given. In 1944, the wooden barracks in *Bauabschnitt* BI were designated for sick people.

When a sick woman came to the hospital, she had to give her name and number. At first patients were allowed to keep their underwear and clothing. In the prison hospital the personnel kept several documents, but only later, in 1944, did

Medical records, Auschwitz. Courtesy Auschwitz Archives.

they keep fever charts.[29] Food was distributed by nurses. It was possible to get certain diets: for instance, soup with milk or white bread.[30] The diet kitchen was in block 22, where Angela, and later Annie Blumenauer, were working. We got our meals on tin plates. Each prisoner had her own dish, but there were no spoons. There must have been a fence around the prisoner hospital because I had been ordered by SS Dr. Vetter to stand guard at the gate.

In the camp for men there was an underground organization. When I did not want to work in x-ray any more, I started to make contact with the resistance movement in the *Mannerlager* [men's camp]. My main contact was David Szmulewski. I was told to leave the experimental camp as soon as possible because the SS wanted no witnesses. After that I worked in various blocks and dispensaries, such as blocks 22, 23, and 24, and later block 5 with Ljubow Alpatove, who was a surgeon. We made

Medical records, Auschwitz. Courtesy Auschwitz Archives.

contact when new transports came in and got the names of women who needed special care. Illegal medication was sent for them from "Canada."[31] The following people who worked in the hospital belonged to the organization: Orli Reichert and Daniella Casanova; Maie Politzer[32] and Marie Claude, both of whom died; Maria Erdeliova, Marie Claude Couterier, Eva Neuman, Bojka Takchnerova. I had contact with them because I was in the Revier. I also had contact with Alma Rose, who had been my good friend. Her death has never been explained. She snapped when she heard that the Czech part of the camp was gassed.[33] First it seemed to affect her mentally. Later she developed cramps and other problems and died in block 4.

There were also German female Communists with whom we had illegal meetings. We talked about political situations as well as what could be done in the block. It was important to go into the blocks and mention to the prisoners that there was an organization that could help. With the help of an SS man from Bratislava, I smuggled letters out of the camp. He also gave my glasses from home to one of the people in the hospital.

As a prisoner, I received regular postcards admonishing me to write more often. I mailed approximately six postcards to my family, and they received them. It probably was in May, 1942, that I was allowed to write to the Jewish congregation in Banska Bystrzyca. That is the date on the cancellation. I did not get an answer to this letter and can't remember whether I got any answers from members of the congregation.

In the beginning we were allowed to receive packages of food, but later, when mail was no longer permitted from Slovakia, I received packages from acquaintances who mailed them under a different name from Bohemia or Moravia. The prisoner's name and number were on each package. We were allowed to receive evaporated milk, jellies, and food supplies, but no bread. The relationship between prisoners depended on their character, political connections, and intelligence. Among the German prisoners were antisocial criminals and political prisoners. Personally, I had good relations with people of all nationalities as long as they acted like humans.

There was an orchestra that played on Sundays, in the Sauna in bad weather and outside in good weather.[34]

Once, when there had been an escape, everyone except the sick had to go to the yard in Birkenau (BI). Mala Zimetbaum had a razor blade and tried to slash her wrists. After a fight with some of the guards, they put her on a litter and the *Lagerführerin* [female camp commandant] decided to burn her alive. She never got to the hospital.[35]

In October 1944, we were moved from BI.[36] I don't know what the place was called. It might have been the "Gypsy [*Ziguener*] Lager." In the "Gypsy Lager" (BIIe) there were no women who were working, only sick ones. There were also children. I don't remember how many barracks there were. Thilo was the SS Arzt, and very often, men were in the hospital.[37] Organization and discipline broke down.[38]

As far as I know, there were no children in Birkenau before 1944. I know we used part of block 16 in BIa as a *Kinder revier*. That is where the sick children were, and a Russian female doctor, Olga Nikiticzna Klimenko, treated them. The children that were used by Mengele were in a *Revierblock*, but not a separate one.[39] They were never sent to work with us. With us were only young girls, but older twins came as well.

The SS asked for twins at the ramps. I can't remember their block number, but these twins were treated better than the rest of us and were not allowed to work. We had to inform Mengele when they were sick and when they died. From the camp came two Polish Jewish doctors.[40] They often drew blood from these people and took their measurements. An eye doctor examined them. Mengele wanted all the data on their measurements as he was interested in all "rarities."[41] Once a circus came to camp with misformed clowns—probably Jewish. They were not gassed right away, but experiments were conducted on them. I don't know what happened to them, but they were not gassed. Only women were gassed.

In Birkenau there were female twins from Czechoslovakia. Mengele looked for male twins approximately the same age. He wanted them to live together and have children, but this did not happen because they were evacuated. I can't remember their names.

I can't remember whether the numbers of the block were changed in 1944. Whether it was barrack 16, I'm not sure, but I do know it was a wooden barrack, and only sick children were there—mostly Polish and Russian. After 1944, there were also some Jewish children.

At Dr. Mengele's office we had to treat patients with "fleck fever" [typhus]. Every day we had to inject a red colored liquid.[42] We had to keep records of fever, appetite, cough, and what mood they were in. I became ill a few times: 1) I had a middle ear infection which left me with a loss of hearing in one ear; 2) During September, 1942, I contracted typhus. Angela Autsch took care of me. Medicines were not available. One day SS Dr. Koenig came by and told me, "You have been lying here for an eternity." This meant that if I was still in bed the next day, I would be gassed. I got up the next day and started to work. Dr. Meier and Dr. Koenig practiced in the women's camp only in 1944. During Dr. Koenig's stay, even Dr. Edith Borg was gassed. There were children, mostly three to four years old, who came with their families in the last transport from Slovakia. They were not gassed but put into the camps. There were no babies. The men were sent to a camp for men, and the women with the girls and boys.

Early in 1944, Jewish Hungarian women were not tattooed. Officially they did not exist in camps because they had no numbers. When they became sick, they had to go to a special infirmary where I also worked. Whenever they contracted contagious illnesses, they were gassed. Later they were placed in block 6, where they could lie down on bunks, approximately three or four to a bunk. Exact fever charts were kept, and when the patients were sick for a longer time or did not improve, they were gassed. At that time, we falsified the fever charts or started them all over again so the women would not be sent to the gas chambers.

In fall of 1944, mostly Russian and Polish Jewish children arrived. Sick children, not only Russian but also those of other nationalities, were in block 16, in the hospital *Frauen Koncentration Lager*. Men painted pictures from fairy tales on the walls for these kids. The doctor there was Olga Nikititschna Klimenko. She was a pediatrician and was a decent person. She is not living anymore, but I did meet her after the war. Her fate was sad because, like many of them, she could not take it and died.

In BIa there was a girl, a messenger, approximately fourteen or fifteen years old, named Elsinka Mamat. She now lives in Bratislava. Frau Teichnerowa was a nurse, then the *Blockälteste* in a *Revierblock.* She accepted some Polish Jewish girls who came to that camp and had to be hidden from the SS doctors. All five of these children survived. One of them she probably took home to her parents in Slovakia, where she went to school. After that a relative came from the U.S.A. and took her to America. Frau Teichnerowa is now living with this "daughter" in the United States.

• • •

Margita Schwalbova's testimony ends at this point. Regarding the work of the female physicians at Auschwitz, she states that surviving, especially for a professional healer, was very difficult. Although working in a place of care and healing within an extermination camp was indeed paradoxical, it, nevertheless, gave the caregiver a sense of purpose. The physicians and nurses, although hampered by lack of medications and equipment, to say nothing of sanitation, were able at least to alleviate some of the dreadful suffering. In addition, because the Revier was one of the few places of organized resistance, the medical personnel were, in some instances, actually able to save lives. The most distressing aspect was the overpowering feeling of helplessness in the face of rampant disease, selections, and death from starvation.

Despite the dreadful circumstances under which they existed, Schwalbova points out that every attempt to save lives, such as hiding one another, exchanging the files of the dead for those of the living, and performing clandestine abortions to save mothers from the gas chambers, required a great deal of courage. Betrayal meant death. She states, "It was our endeavor to be true to ourselves, to fulfill our humanitarian mission, even in this inferno, but also the knowledge that together with you and next to you there were women of many nationalities, each one of them determined to remain a human being in the death camp."[43]

Bergen-Belsen

THE BOWELS OF HELL

Certainly any tongue would have to fail:
man's memory and man's vocabulary
are not enough to comprehend such pain.
—Dante Alighieri, *Dante's Inferno*

When the British liberation troops entered Belsen, they realized immediately the horrors that occurred there. Although described as "the camp of camps, the bottom of the barrel, the dumping ground for the infirmaries of other camps, the death house, the gutter, the cesspool,"[1] Belsen had comparatively benign roots, since Himmler's original intention had been to build a show camp to document the "humanitarianism" of the Nazis. In Bergen-Belsen citizens of foreign countries joined other "privileged" prisoners who might be able to supply currency on the international market, such as medal holders, Dutch diamond cutters, Spanish Jews, and some medical personnel. Meant to serve the Reich as pawns for international blackmail, these "exchange Jews" were to remain alive. As a model camp, Bergen-Belsen could then be used to deflect external criticism and cover crimes the Nazis were committing elsewhere.[2]

The largest number of prisoners were Jews from Russia, Poland, Czechoslovakia, Belgium, France, and Italy.[3] Camp I was a series of worn huts that fell apart under the crush of dying humanity, a stark contrast to Camp II, which was a blend of newer buildings and hastily constructed shelters. The entire camp had originally been designed to hold seven thousand prisoners, the first of whom arrived in August, 1943. In December, 1944, after Josef Kramer was transferred from Birkenau to Bergen-Belsen, it became the dumping ground for those who were being shipped west from the eastern death camps in order to escape the advancing Russian army. As the Germans faced these Allied armies, forced evacuations from Auschwitz, Flossenberg, Nordhausen, and many labor camps stretched Bergen-Belsen's meager facilities beyond comprehension. For example, in an eleven-day period in April, 1945, twenty-eight thousand new prisoners arrived, increasing yet again the pressure within a camp that on March 19th already held sixty thousand people.

Food was in such short supply that reports of cannibalism were rampant.

There were water tanks, but the British found them contaminated; one even had a dead body floating in it.[4] Starvation, disease, exhaustion, neglect, and murderous guards increased the death rates to over one thousand per day. Although there were no gas chambers, there was a crematorium, but it was totally inadequate to accommodate the ever increasing number of corpses. For that reason, dead bodies lay all over the ground and in piles outside the huts. These bodies then had to be burned in funeral pyres, creating a stench that permeated the camp. The camp doctors knew that "cure was impossible because the hygiene was purposely horrifying . . . only minute quantities of medicine were supplied, because rations were half the vital minimum."[5]

When the British liberation forces arrived on April 15, 1945, they found ten thousand unburied bodies and forty thousand sick and dying prisoners. In fact, the whole camp was no more than a "dense mass of apathetic scarecrows." The women, in the worst condition of all, wore only "filthy rags."[6] With no running water or electricity, the camp was teeming with tuberculosis and typhus. Within ten days of their liberation, another five thousand people died from hunger, disease, and shock before they could enjoy their freedom.

The dead had to buried in mass graves, and on May 20, 1945, the British, in reaction to the terrible contamination, destroyed Bergen-Belsen by fire. Although the camp itself is gone, the mere mention of its name is synonymous with horror, murder by neglect, and inhumanity.

Hela Jafe, Dr. Ada Bimko, and Magda Herzberger were all liberated from Bergen-Belsen. Magda was close to death when the British forces arrived, yet gave unstintingly of herself by rendering physical care to the living and emotional comfort to the dying in the hospitals established by the liberating troops. Hela Jafe and Dr. Ada Bimko had been caring for a group of children. After liberation they established what became known as the *Kinderheim* of Bergen-Belsen for those children who had no surviving relatives. The needs of these children were in some ways greater than those of the adults who had been imprisoned in the camps, for they were less able to understand why they had been subjected to the loss of their parents and the emotional and physical security of their homes.

According to experts in pediatrics, in order to develop normally, children need positive social experiences in addition to physical and emotional support. Furthermore, authorities claim that children denied these experiences will develop psychological problems which may affect their ability to adapt and to learn.[7] Yet, despite emotional and physical deprivations which are by and large unimaginable to today's experts, the children who were cared for by Dr. Bimko, Hela Jafe, and eight other dedicated women not only thrived in the *Kinderheim*, but learned in the school created there and adapted well to their new lives in Israel.

Hela, who now lives in Israel, was a nurse in Bergen-Belsen. During the last few months prior to liberation, she worked with Dr. Bimko and subsequently went with some of the children to Palestine. Both she and Dr. Bimko, now Dr. Hadassah Rosensaft, remain in contact with those who were once in their care.

Not only does Hela Jafe's narrative tell of her experiences at Bergen-Belsen, it also provides an interesting history of her experiences in the Warsaw Ghetto. Written in Polish, Hela Jafe's memoirs are housed in the archives of the United States Holocaust Memorial Museum and are published here in translation with her and their permission.[8]

Chapter Ten

Hela Los Jafe

"PEOPLE DIDN'T GO WILLINGLY"

· · ·

Dear "sister" Hela . . . had an open ear for every request. I remember the defeat of the Germans in 1945. . . . The Jewish Brigade started assembling children and helping them in their rehabilitation, naturally with the assistance of the wonderful team—Dr. Hadassah, Mrs. Losh and "sister" Hela.[1]

My name is Hela Jafe, née Los. I was born in Warsaw in 1923. My father was a famous antique dealer in Warsaw. He had an antique store on Marszalkowska Street and made a good living. We had a big family—I had four sisters and three brothers. One brother is still alive, but all four of my sisters died. The Germans took them, two by two. We all went to school until 1939. I had finished elementary school but couldn't go on to the gymnasium because the war started.

When the Germans attacked Poland,[2] we were in a village near Niedzeszynie, on the other side of the river Vistula. This village was taken by the Germans two weeks before they occupied Warsaw. Then there was terrible bombing and hunger in Warsaw, but after the Germans occupied it, I walked back home. Naturally the houses and everything were destroyed, but because our apartment was partially spared, we all went back there. After that the Jewish people began to suffer terribly.

At first the Germans didn't know who was a Jew and who was not, but the Polish people began to point us out right away. There were lines for soup and bread, and the Polish people grabbed the Jewish people out of the lines. Many of the youth organized themselves to leave Warsaw and go to Russia instead of staying with the Germans, but my siblings and I stayed.

My father still had to deal with the merchants, but the store was immediately taken by the Germans because Marszalkowska Street was in the gentile area.[3] After that, although he had to give up the store, he still sold privately. Even though I looked non-Jewish and could have gone to the non-Jewish side, I felt I had to stay home and help him.

Because we lived on Sliska Street, which was within the so-called "small ghetto,"[4] we were lucky and didn't have to move from our apartment and stayed there until the end. It was bad, but we never imagined that the end would be as terrible as it was.

In the ghetto the Germans caught people on the street as well as those hiding in their apartments. For a while they were taking people from the city. Then came the terrible day when they told Czerniakow to give them a list of Jewish people from the ghetto. He didn't want to and killed himself.[5] After that the real hell started. The next day, right after his suicide, the Germans were telling us that all young people able to work were supposed to leave Warsaw and go to work camps which they had organized. They would get food on the way. A lot of young people went, and naturally nobody came back. Meanwhile, there were pamphlets advising us not to go to those camps because this was a trick of the Germans; these were killing camps.[6] But some went anyway.

After these announcements people didn't go willingly. No one from our family went, and we remained together until the final order to liquidate. I witnessed Korczak leaving with the children from Krochmalna Street. Even at the end, he didn't want to abandon them.[7]

In the city there were German factories called *szopy*. Two were owned by Toebbens and Schulz.[8] There were some other shops, but I don't remember their names.[9] People tried anything to get work because if they were laborers in those shops, they could stay in Warsaw. Somehow we managed to get work, but not all together in the same place. My sisters and I worked for Toebbens, sewing uniforms in the small ghetto.[10] My father, brothers, and mother worked for Schulz on Nowolipie Street.[11] Later it was impossible to be with them.

Only the people who worked in the shops could live in the area where we lived.[12] Most of the ghetto had already been liquidated, but we lived on the street where the shop was.[13] In the meantime, not all people were working, so those who did not hid in the apartments. All the time I was there, I witnessed the *Aktions* which took place day and night. There was a garden by the shop, and Toebbens said to the parents who worked there that their children could play in the garden. I saw him come and take all the children out.[14]

I worked for Toebbens on the sewing machines. We were ordered to make a certain number of uniforms. There was a system of assembly. When one person finished her portion, he or she would give the piece to the next. I had a very hard time because three healthy men passed me portions of pants which I had to sew together. I couldn't follow them well, and my feet were swollen. There wasn't exactly a specific number of hours to work, but if we didn't fill the order we didn't get any food. When the other people saw that I couldn't keep up, they came and helped me. If not, we would have had to work later. And besides, people gladly helped one another. Finally, when we filled the order—I don't remember exactly how many uniforms we had to sew—we went to the kitchen and ate. Naturally we didn't get paid for our work, but at the end of the day, we got a ration card.

I don't remember exactly how long I worked for Toebbens, but on Yom Kippur he said we could go to the big ghetto,[15] where he had a shop for finishers—the girls there sewed the buttons, buttonholes, etc.—and I would be able to join my parents. It seemed good for us because we hadn't been able to go from the small ghetto to the other, and many families were divided. We were happy that we could be together. But it was only a trick on his part. My two sisters, Sala and Pola, who worked as finishers, immediately went to our parents. Before the uprising they had worked in a shop in a different, closed area. The Germans conducted a *Selektion* during the day in the area where they lived. Their husbands were working at the time, but my sisters were not. They took everybody who wasn't in the shop to the *Umschlagplatz,* and we later had news that they went to Treblinka, where they died. They were taken with the 350 girls who were supposed to be finishers for Toebbens. My other two sisters died the same way.[16]

Although I had the same opportunity to return to the other ghetto, I worked on the machines, and they didn't let me leave. As it turned out, it was a miracle that I stayed that day. My boss was sick, and they told me I could go the next day. Toebbens's shops had, in the meantime, been moved from Walicow to Poniatow.[17] He transported his equipment and took his people to work there. There was propaganda that Poniatow was not really a labor camp and people shouldn't go because it would be like Treblinka, but people didn't believe those pamphlets because Toebbens spoke so nicely, permitting them to take all their belongings, and transporting them in normal railroad cars.[18]

After I was left alone, I wanted to be with my parents. At night I begged a German who guarded the exit to let me in, and after that I stayed in the big ghetto. By that time my father was no longer there. He and one brother had been taken to the *Umschlagplatz* in a *Selektion,* so my mother was left with my older brother. We stayed together until the end.

Before the uprising, the feelings in the area were terrible. We knew that something would happen, but we did not know exactly what and when. We saw a lot of pamphlets in the city. This wasn't in the ghetto. This was in the area of Walicow.[19] The ghetto was in another place: Dzika and Mila streets.[20]

In the ghetto they didn't have shops. I don't know what the people did when they went out. I later went to a dead end street, similar to Walicow, but the area was much bigger. We could walk from one place to the other along the rooftops, as all the houses were connected by roofs. We could see dead people on the street. It's a shame to say that some people were Jewish and worked with the Germans. They had pieces of paper pinned to them on which it was written that this would happen to everybody who collaborated.[21] They were pamphlets calling people to arise and fight.[22] I had a girlfriend from school who worked in the underground organization and knew who had executed the collaborators. I saw her there.

The uprising was later.[23] I remember as if it were today. I was working in the shop, sewing. The boys, dressed in German uniforms, went out on the street and began shooting. The Germans didn't know who was shooting whom because they didn't know these boys were Jews. Many Jewish fighters were standing on the roofs. I met my girlfriend standing there by herself. I was still with Mama and my brother, hiding in the bunkers. We had prepared ours in an attic above a shop because we thought the shop wouldn't get burned due to the number of uniforms there. From there we had the view of the street. All work stopped.

We were prepared to live there for months. We had beds, and people came bringing food and money. We listened to the radio and thought because it would only be a matter of days, we would survive. All the time we were all in the attic, we saw through the cracks that the Germans were so terribly afraid that they came with grenades, which they threw into an area before they entered it. In the meantime, our Jewish police came and called aloud to the people that they should come out; they would get amnesty. The Germans would do nothing to them; they would just send them to a Lager. Unfortunately, some of the people believed them and started to come out of the bunkers. In this way they gave away their location. Then the Germans killed them!

We stayed in the bunker as long as possible and ran out only when the stairs caught on fire. If we hadn't, we would have been burned to death. The Germans took us to the *Umschlagplatz*, where we went through a terrible two days. There were many Jews there, not only from Warsaw, but from Zbasyna and other cities. We had no food, no bread or water. The Germans beat the people terribly and hanged some of them. Then Toebbens came and took his workers,[24] so when the Germans carried out a *Selektion*, I was working and didn't have to go through it.

I was in Poniatow from May 5, 1943, to November. Then there was another *Selektion*. At that time I was working as a cleaning woman in the hotel for the Germans. My mother was in the Lager and not working. My brother worked the night shift outside the Lager and wasn't there when they took my mother. Someone came to tell me, and on impulse, instead of going to the hotel to ask someone to save my mother, I didn't think and ran to her. Naturally they took me right away and I had no one to turn to for help. My brother returned from work, and when he saw that Mother and I were to be transported, he didn't think and came to us, so they sent him too. I had another brother in Poniatow who worked the night shift. When they took us, he was still sleeping and didn't know. If he would have known, he would have come as well and might still be alive.

There were forty people, mostly older, but also a few young people with children. The Wehrmacht took us from Poniatow to the Biala Podlaska *Arbeitslager.*[25] The Polish people said, "Oh, they brought *Zydkuw* [Jews] again." When we were there, I learned that I had left in the beginning of November. At the end of November was the famous action during which they killed all the Jews in the camps. I'm certain my brother vanished then. The Jews dug their own graves, and the Germans killed them all. We miraculously escaped.[26]

Biala Podlaska was an *Arbeitslager,* and there were only a few of us. When we came there, we learned that the month previously they had killed all of those who had been there before us. We occupied their places. We knew that the same thing would happen to us, and for most of us it was so. But we still worked hard and were productive. The people who had jobs managed somehow to get a little food. There was a German community, and they didn't treat us badly there. In the construction area were people who worked as clerks and, because I knew a little sewing, I sewed for them. There was a group that worked in the airport, whom the Germans beat terribly. When I got to know some of the people better, I asked them to take my brother out of the airport, and he got work elsewhere as a mechanic.

The Wehrmacht were there only at the beginning. After that they left us to the SS. Schultz was the commandant of the Lager. He was a crazy German, a deviant who beat the people and made up terrible stories about them. After work he would go to the block and check to see that everyone's feet were clean. If they were not, he beat them terribly.

We lived in two houses surrounded by fences. There were boys there who were in contact with the Partisans in the forest, but I don't know with which group. Three of the boys ran away, and because of this the Germans shot the *Lagerführer,* a boy who was forced to volunteer to sacrifice himself. He was a lovely young boy from Slusk named Julek. He knew German perfectly and was able to talk with the Germans, but they held him responsible for what had happened. Next Schultz prepared a list of names, and they shot every third person. But those three boys were not caught. We knew that more people would have liked to escape, but we were a small group. We knew that for every one who attempted to run away they would kill ten of us.

My mother, brother, and I were in Biala Podlaska from November to February, 1944. Then, one day when we came back from work, the whole Lager was surrounded by Ukrainians holding automatic rifles and carbines. The cars came and they took us all. We thought we were going to the forest where they would kill us, but that time they weren't ordered to shoot us; they took us to Majdanek. When we came there it was completely empty; we didn't see any people. We thought we were the only Jews who were still alive. When we went to the office to register, we saw people there. I found out that there were Polish prisoners too, not only Jews. They were called *"czerwonne winkle."* They were political prisoners, guilty of sabotage. They had been arrested and brought to Majdanek, and from them we found out that in November there had been an *Aktion,* and the Germans had killed all the Jews. We were the first Jewish transport to come to the Lager after that, and there were very few of us.

At the beginning we didn't work hard. Then they took most of the men from Majdanek, leaving only the women. My brother went with that transport to Skarzysko, where he worked in an ammunition factory.[27] There were still some men left, but they were in large fields and I couldn't see them.

We were there until May, 1944, when it was bombarded by the Soviet planes. The Germans marched us out, escorted by dogs. Later I found out that a lot of people had remained hidden there and were rescued by the Russians. There was an underground organization and some people had contacts. Maybe they had heard the radio and knew that the front was close. If more people would have known that, maybe they would have hidden and been rescued earlier by the Russians.

We had a terrible time going from Majdanek to Oswiecim. We walked with the dogs following us. Anyone who couldn't walk anymore was attacked and killed by the dogs. We wore striped uniforms made of synthetic material, and when the rain fell, the uniforms became very heavy, as though they were made of iron. It was very difficult. I wanted to go to a German and ask him to shoot me because I wasn't able to walk anymore. Mama was very brave. On the way we got bread and canned food, which Mama took from me and carried. I don't remember how many days we walked until we came to Oswiecim. By then everybody knew what it was.

I wasn't in Oswiecim long. In the morning I was in a group of people who had to pass through the gate where the German guards beat us. We had to go into a field to cut pieces of sod forty centimeters each and bring them to the Lager by hand just to go through the gate and get hit, because every time we passed through the gate into the Lager we got beaten. The next day was the same. There were also people who worked in factories. They made believe they were doing something productive, but many of them didn't work too hard in order to save their strength. There was also a very active underground organization.

I was in the women's camp with my mother. She was in the same commando and did the same thing I did. One time, when we were working in a field outside the Lager cutting the grass, we heard a lot of shooting. A group of boys who worked in the *Sonderkommando* had tried to run away from Oswiecim. I know that a lot of people were killed.

My mother and I were in a block where the *blokova,* the *Schreibers,* and the whole staff were gentiles from Poland. One night, on Yom Kippur, my mother asked the *blokova* to save our soup until evening because the Jewish women wanted to fast. It would be very important to get the soup then because we hadn't eaten anything all day. That *blokova* agreed to it, saved the soup, and gave it to us in the evening. We were very surprised that there was such a good Pole. Usually in Oswiecim the *blokovas* were cruel, and the atmosphere was terrible. Everybody was beastly, but they didn't have to be like that. They didn't have to beat the Jews so much. In spite of this, the Polish *blokova* saved our soup, although she could have thrown it out. Instead she saved it for the evening, and we couldn't forget it. Later on I sewed for her and got bread and potatoes for that, which I shared with Mama and my friends. Years later in Israel, I was traveling in an autobus and saw her. I felt like I was seeing her in a dream; it had been so many years. I said, "Helenka from Oswiecim, what are you doing here?" I had always thought she was Polish, but I found out that she was a Jew. She was so good, and as a hidden Jew she shouldn't have done that.

In Oswiecim I was a witness to how they hanged Mala.[28] At the *Appell* we all had to stand and watch. They made it a special demonstration. When they caught her and hanged her, I saw how she cut the veins on her wrists. I heard how she slapped a German's face and said, "You finish me, but your end is close." She was still alive when the boys took her in the lorry to the crematorium, but I think they shot her there. We learned that she had run away, but at that time I didn't know. I thought she had just attempted to escape on her own, but later, in Israel, when I met Helenka, she told me that Mala had not run away on her own. It had been organized by the underground. Because she was a messenger, it was possible for her to go out of the Lager. She knew the German language very well, and the German men and women liked her very much. She helped everyone she could. Because she left the Lager frequently, the underground organization turned to her for help. Everything would have been all right if she hadn't fainted in the mountains. The boy who went with her wanted to save her, but when she fainted, he accidently lifted her arm out of her blouse. Somebody saw the number and turned her in. If it hadn't been for that, they wouldn't have been caught.

In autumn 1944, before liquidation, there was a very big selection and they took the first big transport of three thousand people to Bergen-Belsen. I don't know how they decided who should go. I don't remember exactly when it was, but I know there were *wrzos* [some kind of flowers] blooming. We came by railroad—only Jews from Poland and Hungary. Maybe there were Poles, but they were in another place and I didn't see them. In our area there were only women.[29]

In Bergen-Belsen there was nothing, just fields, so we started to build tents out of canvas. The first night was terrible. The rain and wind blew the tents over, so we were left on the field. Later they started to build barracks out of wood. There had been some kind of Lagers before, but we didn't see them. We did nothing and had nothing to eat. The kitchen was in another place, and men brought us what little food we got from another Lager. There was terrible hunger. Despite this, the Germans called it "a rest camp."[30]

After a while, when Oswiecim started to liquidate, they brought everything from there to Bergen-Belsen. The transport and the system were like the ones we had gone through in Oswiecim. They sorted shoes and clothing. Whenever they brought new people, they had to go through a shower. There were *Appells,* just as there had been in Oswecim, and it was just as bad. We stood at the *Appells* and starved. It was dirty and cold. During winter, there was nothing out of which we could make a fire.

Dr. Hadassah Bimko, called Ada, came from Oswiecim to Bergen at that time. I am very hurt that no one talks about her. Hadassah was a doctor and an educated woman. She knew a few languages and conducted herself so honorably that even the Germans respected her.

At that time they organized a *Kinderheim* (children's house) in Bergen-Belsen. Before then this had been a family home for the Jews from Holland.[31] They were separate from the rest of the camp, and I didn't see them. I found out about them later. The Dutch Jews had some papers as American citizens.[32] I don't know exactly how they got them, but they brought them from the Netherlands to Bergen-Belsen, and the Germans didn't treat them so badly. They lived together with their children and got some parcels from friends in Holland. The Red Cross cared for them.[33]

One day they came and took all the Dutch Jews—we didn't know where—and left all the children from age eight months to fourteen years.[34] When Hadassah Bimko came, the Germans organized a children's house which began with the Dutch children whose parents they had taken. There were forty-nine boys and girls, Jewish children from Holland. At that time they still looked good because they had been with their parents until then. At that time Bergen-Belsen started to be like Oswiecim. Transports came from all over, bringing thousands of people. Ada walked from block to block, found the children, took them, lived with them, and took care of them. There were some women who came with children, but transports came with just children as well, and Ada would bring them to the children's house. I don't remember how the Czech children came to us. They were small—two and three year olds. It was possible that the parents had died. Later there were about a hundred children.

I worked there as a nurse with Hermina Szwarz and Luba Tryszynska [*sic*]. Hermina is in Israel, and Luba is now in America. There were also three women named Faja, Hela, and Mala. We all lived there together. Although there were few nurses, we had a lot to do and all worked hard, and even in such terrible conditions, managed to keep the *Kinderheim* clean. The children were very small and sick, and we had to wash them, clothe them, calm them, and feed them. That they survived was due to Ada Bimko and her helpers.

At the beginning it was winter. It was cold and terrible there, and the children cried because they were cold. Luckily they had Ada Bimko. Most of them were orphans, and she was like a mother to them. Although the atmosphere was terrible and life seemed hopeless, Ada would sit by the fireplace and sing Jewish songs to them. Most of them were sick with terrible indigestion, dysentery, and diarrhea, and just lay on the bunks; they couldn't do anything else.

There was very little food, but somehow Ada managed to get some special food and white bread from the Germans. For them this was a *Musterlager* [show Lager], which they needed to impress the Red Cross. When they came to inspect the Lager from time to time, the Germans would bring them straight to the children's house, which was separate from the rest of the Lager. They needed the children to survive. We couldn't say anything because Germans accompanied them. They would ask us whether conditions were good, if we got food, and if the Germans beat them. The children said that everything was good. The fact is the Germans didn't hit them, and the children did get better food than people in the rest of the Lager thanks to Ada Bimko.[35] Although there was no water in the Lager, Ada somehow got water for us too.[36]

Later there was typhus among the children. Ada was the one who could get injections, chocolate, pills, and vitamins.[37] I don't know how she did it. Although most of the children were sick, thanks to Ada nearly all of them survived, although in the Lager itself, hundreds of people died. At that time she was the chief doctor in the Lager hospital,[38] but she stayed with us and the children. There really wasn't a hospital there because there were no medicines. Bergen-Belsen wasn't a death camp like the others because there were no crematoria,[39] but there were more deaths than in Oswiecim because of the hunger and dirt.

One time I got beaten terribly. In the beginning, as I mentioned, we had nothing for building a fire, and the children were crying because it was very cold. At that time they were building bunks in the rest of the Lager, and I took a few logs. We made a fire in the stove and were sitting around it. Ada wasn't in the hospital, and I was the only grownup with the children when a German came and claimed sabotage: "How could you take German wood and burn it?" Right in front of the children he started to beat me terribly with the log. The children ran and started to yell and cry. I don't remember what happened, but Ada arranged for us to get firewood, and we were warmer. Somehow we lived like that until April 15, 1945, when we were liberated by the English army, commanded by General Glyn Hughes.

We had heard shots a few days before we were liberated and knew that something was going on. The Germans wanted the whole Lager destroyed. There were so many dead people, and there wasn't a crematorium to burn them. Across from our children's house was a field in which a small white house served as a so-called *Leichenkeller* (corpse cellar). They put the dead people there. I don't know if they burned them or buried them because in a short time there were so many corpses that it wasn't possible to pick them all up.[40] Those dead people lay across from our children's house. It was a constant, terrible, gruesome scene before our eyes. There were stacks of dead people, and it wasn't possible to bury them because there was no one to do it. The Germans were afraid that when the English came they would see it.[41] They planned to poison the surviving prisoners. Later they had proof of that. A few days before, they didn't give bread at all and there was terrible hunger.[42] After we were liberated, one German SS man turned to the English and took them to the bakery, where they saw a lot of bread. People hadn't gotten anything to eat for two days. Then the SS man said that the bread had been poisoned, and they had been told not to give it to the people. The British analyzed the bread, and it had indeed been poisoned.[43]

The SS man stayed until the last minute and saved the whole Lager.[44] People were saying that the Germans put him in a bunker too because he was too good for the Jews. He was some kind of officer and had some kind of kommando. He took people to work, and when somebody was sick he excused them. I don't remember his name, but his name was in the records. People from Bergen-Belsen remembered him well. He was a doctor but not a Lager doctor.[45] He stayed in Bergen-Belsen until the end and worked as an eye doctor.

Right after liberation, among the first Englishmen who came with the army were many doctors and medical students.[46] It was known that Bergen-Belsen was a typhus Lager, and everyone was sick. There was typhus even among the children. At that time they transported us from that *Schmutzlager* (filthy Lager), from the barracks. Not far from Bergen-Belsen was a hospital which had formerly been for the SS men.[47] After liberation the English didn't let us nurses transport the children. They saw that we were very overworked, so they did the work themselves. Because the typhus was contagious, they contracted it from us, and many English people died.[48]

When I went to the block they had prepared for the children, there still was a German *Schwester* (nurse) there wearing a white coat.[49] I took that coat from her and still have it today. We took the rooms from them, and they organized a hospital for all the sick. Things had already changed. There were British personnel, and they had medicines. After Ada Bimko went to work in the newly organized hospital, I remained with the children. We had two blocks: the healthy children were in one, and the sick ones in the second. I worked with all of them. Right from the beginning there weren't that many who were sick because the Dutch children who had come to us had, until that time, been under Ada's care. There were now two blocks for children and one for maternity patients.[50]

Then Dr. Robert Collis came. I don't know what army rank he had, but he was an army doctor who specialized in pediatrics.[51] He went to the Lagers and looked for the children. Most of them were in terrible condition, skinny as skeletons. He took them to the children's house, to that clean block which we had built. What he did for those children is priceless because he didn't only work as a doctor for a few hours, which he should have done. He worked day and night, sitting with the children. There was one twelve-year-old girl who had a blood clot which went to her heart. Dr. Collis positioned her so everything would flow downward and things would normalize.[52] She seemed to be in a hopeless condition and lay separately in the hospital for ten weeks. He brought ten doctors for consultation. He brought medications from America and England. She survived because of Dr. Collis and is now a neighbor of mine in Israel, the mother of two children. There were many such cases. Days and nights he sacrificed for them and the children realized it. Forty such sick children were healed thanks to his angelic patience.

Those who survived and now live in Israel were happy that he came to visit them. They never forgot him. When he saw the girl who had suffered with the thrombosis blooming today, he cried.

There were also English women from the Red Cross and degreed nurses who came because he needed professional help. One was a nurse named Ania, from Holland, who worked with Dr. Collis the entire time. They worked together day and night, sacrificing themselves, and sent the children to recovery houses. They sent children with illnesses of the lungs who were somewhat healed to Sweden. Dr. Collis went with them, and there he married nurse Ania.

I was there as long as the hospital existed because there still were a lot of children, all of them orphans. After they had been liberated, the children who had been transported from Holland returned home. Some healthy ones went to England. Dr. Collis had taken some of the children to the hospital in Sweden, and later the Czech children back to Czechoslovakia. Hermina from Czechoslovakia went with Dr. Collis because the children were sick and he didn't want to leave them there by themselves. I stayed with healthy children who needed care until I went to Israel. The older ones were already going to school.[53]

When a transport of the ill went to Sweden, the Red Cross organized a committee whose leader was Josef Rosensaft. The English were clearly opposed to sending the children just to Israel; they wanted to send them all over. But the survivors were against their sending the children abroad; they felt that the children should be sent to Israel. Although I could have gone there illegally, the children could not. We had to get certificates for them. The British made a questionnaire for the children and talked to them, saying: "Listen, listen, in Palestine it is very hard and hot. There is nothing to eat. Palestine is terribly ugly. It is possible for you to go to England or Canada. Why do you want to go to Palestine?" Then a young boy stood up and said, "When we go to Palestine, we will make it beautiful."

Groups of children went. They came as an *Aliya-Hanoar* in 1946. Ada Bimko came with the first group.[54] They left Belsen on April 9, 1946. They went to Marseilles, France, and boarded the ship *Champollion* for Palestine. After their arrival, the children were separated and sent to kibbutzim. Some went to Dorot, others to Kiryat Anavim. Later the sick children whom Dr. Collis had sent to Sweden came. A group of forty children went to Deganya. All the children from the children's house in Bergen-Belsen are now in Israel.

I came in 1947. Right after we came, I was with a group of children at Kiryat Anavim. I had a very difficult time here, but the children showed me a lot of sympathy, a lot of heart, and I needed that. They told me that I had earned it. When the war started in 1948, the children naturally went into the army. They were no longer children. There were some who were already women who had children of their own. Because I know how to sew, I have sewn every girl a wedding dress. I always had contact with them and still do. They call me Sister Hela even today.

Two years ago [1963] one of the children who had been saved by Dr. Collis came here. From Sweden she had gone to England, and from there to Israel. I am in contact with her, and I organized a reunion in my house. They came from Ashkelon and Haifa.

When I saw the couple that had sacrificed their hearts for the children, who worked with the children day and night and fed them, coming with old, torn luggage, I wanted to cry. Their financial situation must be difficult. She [Ania] knew that the children were here in Israel. I asked them why they hadn't come for twenty years. She answered, "We didn't have the money." How could they have been forgotten? The only one who remembers that time is Hadassah Bimko. It is a mistake on our part. I feel it is unfair; we were supposed to be in contact with and remember Dr. Collis. Through the years, some of the children were in contact with him privately, but officially no one recognized or appreciated what he did.

Dr. and Mrs. Collis now live in Nigeria, Africa. They said that of one million people, there are ninety doctors working in Nigeria. His wife finished her studies and is also a doctor. They work under terrible conditions. They said that it is terribly hot. They have sacrificed their lives, like Dr. Schweitzer. Dr. Collis could live in England, but he had to go to Africa. This is the kind of person he is. If he had met a group of Jewish children before, not after the war, he would have done the same.

When he came to Israel, the children went to honor him and show him recognition. We brought beautiful flowers. I was afraid I wouldn't recognize him because it had been such a long time, twenty years, but I recognized him right away. The steward came to the plane and told him that there were children waiting for him. I and another from the Irgun came out to the airport. When he came out, I, in the name of the children who were living because of him, greeted him in the name of the Irgun. He cried. It was very emotional.

Both of them kissed all the children. They hadn't changed, and they remembered all the names. When I saw him, I told him about Sali (the child with the thrombus). He said, "What are you saying? She is alive and has children?" And when he saw her healthy and blooming, he wept. We were all very happy that Dr. Collis came here with his wife. He had saved us all, and we believed that person should be recognized in some way.

Today I still have my mother who is over seventy years old. She had gone through the war with me. I have one brother, a husband, and two children. One son is in the army in Nahal. He goes to *Hityashvut* (settlement). He could be in a kibbutz, but he says that it is not interesting for him. He wants to make something, to build something new. The other one is in sixth grade. I do not work.

• • •

Hela Jafe and her husband live in Jerusalem. She has maintained close contact with those she once cared for as well as with Dr. Hadassah Rosensaft.

"The tears come into my eyes as I think how, amidst scenes of loathsome disease and death, there rose above it all the innate dignity, gentleness and chivalry of men (for never surely was chivalry so strikingly exemplified) shining in the midst of what must be considered the lowest sinks of human misery. . . ."

—Florence Nightingale[55]

Chapter Eleven

Dr. Ada Bimko

"DON'T BE AFRAID, CHILD"

• • •

*A man must stand in fear of just those things
that truly have the power to do us harm,
of nothing else, for nothing else is fearsome.*

—Dante Alighieri, *Dante's Inferno*

Although Dr. Hadassah Rosensaft, formerly Ada Bimko, has been both cordial and helpful, she declined to give us a formal interview. Perhaps this is because she feels she can never adequately convey the horrors that she and so many millions of others endured during the Holocaust. As she stated to Anton Gill, "Nobody will ever be able to tell you the whole story, to describe the emotions: the fears, the anger, the shame—or the Germans' efforts to dehumanize you. All that is very hard for me to be able to express in words; . . . But if I told you every detail of every moment from 1939 right up to now, I would not have told you the whole story."[1] She was one of the physicians who cared for the women at Birkenau. In addition, she devoted herself to the health and well-being of many children who were imprisoned at Bergen-Belsen, and she later accompanied a group of them to Palestine. Therefore, in order to recognize her work as best we could, we have based this chapter upon her testimony at the Lüneburg Trials,[2] other documented sources, and excerpts from her interviews with these survivors, which are collected at the United States Holocaust Memorial Museum.[3]

The Belsen Trials

Forty-five persons were charged with war crimes in a trial that took place in a British court in Lüneburg, Germany, between September 17 and November 17, 1945. Three of the accused, Josef Kramer, Franz Hoessler, and Dr. Fritz Klein, were officers. Others, including the notoriously cruel Irma Grese, were NCOs of both sexes. Some were capos who had been inordinately cruel. Although the three officers and eight others were sentenced to death, there were at least nineteen acquittals, thereby resulting in a trial which was severely criticized by many. To make matters worse, five of the female guards and capos who had been sentenced to ten-year sentences were released on December 22, 1951. Nevertheless, no system of justice could ever adequately compensate for the horrors the victims of the Holocaust had experienced.[4]

According to the testimony of Brigadier General Hugh Llewellyn Glyn Hughes, C.B.E., D.S.O., M.C., vice director of Medical Services, British Army of the Rhine, as related to the court in the Lüneburg Trials of Josef Kramer and forty-four others,[5] British troops came to Bergen-Belsen on April 15, 1945, following a request for a truce by German officers. Accompanying Lieutenant Colonel Taylor, officer commander of the 63rd Anti-Tank Regimen, Hughes first interrogated Josef Kramer, commandant of the camp. In the evening he met with the German medical officer, Dr. Fritz Klein.

The camp, situated fifteen miles north of Celle, was divided into five compounds, three for men and two for women, with a main road running through the middle. General Hughes found conditions within the camp beyond description, stating that even photographs did not do justice to the horrors both within and outside the huts. He further told of corpses of all descriptions and sizes lying scattered on the ground, in the gutters, some "outside the wires and some in between the huts," as well as within the compounds, where the dead lay next to the living. There were mass graves near the crematorium, and "outside to the left of the bottom compound was an open grave, a pit rather, half full of corpses" which "had just been begun to be filled." There were bunks in some of the huts filled "to overflowing with prisoners in every state of emaciation and disease." Most did not have enough space to lie down at full length. The most crowded huts housed six hundred to one thousand people in a building large enough to accommodate one hundred at the most.[6]

Brigadier Hughes described the women's compound, which contained between twenty-two thousand and twenty-three thousand women, of whom approximately seventeen thousand were acutely ill. For these there were only 474 beds in huts that supposedly had been set aside as hospitals by the internees themselves. Supplies of medications and dressings were totally inadequate—"300 aspirin tablets for 17,000 sick people for one week"—although the British troops discovered large stores which had been supplied by the Red Cross but had not been administered to the prisoners.[7]

According to the deposition of Major General James Alexander Deans Johnston, "The females were in worse condition than the men and their clothing generally, if they had any, only filthy rags." The diseases that were prevalent were typhus, tuberculosis, and starvation in camp 1, and "enteric, Tuberculosis, and erysipelas," although no typhus, in camp 2.[8] There had been neither food nor water available for the previous two weeks. Johnston estimated that there were approximately thirteen thousand corpses in every state of decomposition lying about when the British arrived. Seventy percent of the liberated internees required hospitalization. Of these, at least ten thousand would die before they could be brought to the hospital.

Despite these horrifying conditions, Captain D. A. Sington of the British Intelligence Corps, who was the first to enter the camp, testified that when he asked Commandant Josef Kramer who comprised the body of prisoners, Kramer replied, "Habitual criminals, felons, and homosexuals."[9] Contrary to Kramer's statement, however, once the British liberated the camp, they "found 58,000 inmates, both men and women, 90 percent of whom were Jews. The vast majority were living skeletons; most of them were too ill and too weak even to walk. Within the following eight weeks, 13,944 more died."[10]

Questioned by the court as to whether there were any children in the compound, Brigadier Hughes replied, "There was a small compound of children who were in fairly good condition, and obviously the women had sacrificed themselves to look after them. . . . The hospital compound in that area was very well run by the internee doctors—very well run."[11] The woman who ran this compound for children was Dr. Ada (Hadassah) Bimko, now Dr. Hadassah Rosensaft.

Dr. Bimko's testimony marked a dramatic moment in the Lüneburg Trials and was described in one newspaper article as follows:

> A plump, black-haired Polish Jewess, her concentration camp number tattooed on her left forearm, today dramatically pointed out 15 of 45 Nazis on trial for mass murder and declared some of them selected Jewish inmates of the Belsen and Oswiecim camps for death and prostitution. . . .
>
> The identification of fifteen of the accused by Ada Bimko, 30-year-old woman physician who survived both Oswiecim and Belsen, was the climactic moment today of the trial which began here Monday.
>
> She had given the court her estimate that 4,000,000 Jews perished in the Oswiecim murder factory and testified with tears streaming down her face, that her father, mother, brother, two sisters, husband, and 6-year-old son[12] were among 4,500 Jews put to death the day they arrived.
>
> Major General H. P. M. Berney-Ficklin, presiding judge, suggested she step into the center of the courtroom to see the accused more clearly. . . . They shifted uneasily in their places. Dr. Bimko slowly walked the length of the dock.
>
> First she pointed out Kramer, called the "Beast of Belsen" for his record there. Then she moved down the line singling out others.[13]

When asked why she was not in a state of extreme emaciation after liberation, Dr. Bimko replied that she was in better condition because she had come to Bergen-Belsen directly from Auschwitz. Those internees who had come on transports had been traveling in cattle cars without food or water for the past three to six weeks. Hence they were already in worse condition than she and were more severely affected by the food, or lack thereof, in Bergen-Belsen. Second, physicians in the camps were in better physical condition because they had such things as beds to sleep in and better washing facilities than the thousands of ill and starving internees who came to them for care.[14]

Dr. Ada Bimko, whose degree was actually in dentistry, had been arrested in her community of Sosnowiec, Poland, on August 4, 1943, and sent with five thousand others to Auschwitz. Her father, mother, husband, and son (age six) were immediately sent to the gas chambers. Her brother, as a member of the underground, had been shot by the Germans. Other members of her family had already perished in Treblinka.[15] Dr. Bimko was one of the five hundred who were herded into the camp. Ten days later, having been told that all doctors should report, she did so. After another ten days she was put to work as a physician in the hospital—such as it was. There she was an unwilling witness to several selections. Hundreds of women, both sick and well, had to parade nude before the SS. Most were sent to the gas chambers; some were designated to report to the camp brothel where they were forced to serve as prostitutes. During the Lüneburg Trials, Dr. Bimko named the SS physicians who had conducted these selections: "Dr. Rhode, Dr. Tilot, Dr. Klein, Dr. Konig, and Dr. Mengele."[16]

At first Dr. Bimko had worked in the women's barracks BIII in Birkenau. There, for the most part, she treated wounds resulting from dog bites or beatings from the SS. Asked whether she herself had ever been beaten, she replied that she had been beaten on the face three times, twice by Dr. Mengele and once by "a supervisor named Kuch."[17] In May, 1944, a transport of women arrived from Hungary. Many suffered from scarlet fever, and on July 27 those who were ill or even suspected of being ill were sent to the gas chambers, making way for a large transport from Litzmannstadt (Lodz). In this group there were many women who suffered from typhoid fever. She stated that by the first week in October, 1944, this hospital was liquidated. All 359 patients were loaded onto trucks and taken to the gas chambers. As she testified, "I am quite sure about the number because I had to prepare the nominal roll."[18] She was then sent to camp C, the area called "Mexico," which was also liquidated a week later. In November, 1944, after having been imprisoned at Birkenau for fifteen months, she was transferred to Bergen-Belsen, arriving on November 23, 1944, with seven nurses and two doctors, one of whom was Ada Bimko.

They had been sent to work in what was ostensibly the camp "hospital." She described conditions in the camp as filthy beyond anyone's imagination. There was no place for the inmates to wash. Everybody was "hungry. It was a cold winter, and we were all freezing. Diseases were rampant. Conditions in the hospital were no better, and, in addition, there was no medication for the sick. We were desperate."[19]

Josef Kramer was transferred to Bergen-Belsen to become camp commandant in December. After he took command, conditions changed for the worse. Dr. Bimko recalled, "We had suddenly the feeling that Belsen is going to become a second Auschwitz; for instance they started with roll calls, *appells,* and those SS men who previously did not hit the prisoners started now to do so."[20] Nevertheless, she worked there for the entire time as a physician. As she replied to cross-examination by Captain Phillips:

Q: "Were you in a position to see prisoners arriving at Belsen?"

A: "Yes, I was always called to be present to take the sick, when a transport arrived . . . into the hospital."[21]

Conditions in block 28 in Bergen-Belsen were described by other witnesses at the Lüneburg Trials. Dora Szafran's testimony depicts a horrifying picture of six hundred to seven hundred people lying on the floor of a barrack that was covered with lice and vermin. Supplies of food they received depended upon the goodwill of the block senior. "If she was energetic we might get a quarter basin of soup at midday, if not we might get it at 3 o'clock. We received one bread for ten people every second week, and there was no bread for four weeks before the arrival of the British troops." People had not been given baths or clean clothes the entire time she had been at Belsen, and every day "towards morning there were several hundred corpses. . . ."[22]

In her work as physician in block 26 at Belsen, Dr. Bimko endeavored to help women who suffered from all manner of illnesses, including gangrene.[23] In order to help care for adult female prisoners, Dr. Bimko stated that the quantity of medication they received was totally inadequate for the twenty-two hundred patients who were in the hospital, to say nothing of the fifteen thousand sick women in the camp itself. Receiving a supply of only three hundred aspirin tablets for an entire week, they were desperate as to what they could do to alleviate the suffering. "Three or four days before the British troops entered the camp, at a time when the S.S. men had already white armlets around their arms . . . we discovered that there were enormous stores with medicines and other instruments of such quantity which we did not even see or think of, and suddenly whatever we asked for in the case of medicine we were given, and any amount we were asking was given to us."[24] Regarding these medical supplies, Brigadier General Glyn Hughes related, "All I can say is that we, within a very short time of going there, collected 45 three-ton loads of captured German medical supplies in that area."[25] Unfortunately, for tens of thousands it was far too late.

As to the horrible living conditions at Bergen-Belsen, Dr. Bimko stated that they had been the worst during the three weeks prior to liberation. While epidemics of all sorts raged through the camp, approximately one thousand people died per day, and only those who had already had the diseases were immune. Although there was a small crematorium, it could not accommodate the many bodies; therefore, unburied corpses lay all over the camp. The SS had cut off all water, and inmates were given "one piece of bread per person only three times a week, and a half pint of so-called turnip soup per day." Because inmates were told that the camp was mined, and because they suffered from the extremes of disease, starvation, despair, and fear, no one felt the slightest bit of hope.[26]

Of Brigadier Hughes's reaction to the sight, Dr. Bimko stated, "At the sight of the huts with their dead and near dead, General Glyn Hughes, a medical officer hardened to human suffering, cried unashamedly."[27]

In the midst of all these horrors, Dr. Bimko somehow managed to run a small hospital for children that was known as the *Kinderheim* (children's home). One December morning in 1944, at 3 A.M., she and the rest of her block, ostensibly an ambulance and treatment unit, were awakened by the noises of an automobile, forty-nine crying children from eight months to five years of age, and the shouting of the SS. Several weeks later they were joined by more children from Buchenwald and Theresienstadt. Men in the camp who worked in the SS stores and pharmacies stole food and other supplies for these children, and because of their efforts none of the children died, although many were ill with typhus and other diseases.[28] On April 15, 1945, they were liberated by British troops. In her testimony for the International Liberators Conference at the United States Holocaust Memorial Museum, she recalled the reaction of the children when the camp was liberated:

> It was a Sunday morning, April 15, 1945. It was very quiet, nobody was to be seen outside of the barracks. The camp seemed to have become abandoned, almost like a cemetery. I was sitting with the children, 101 of them, Dutch Jewish orphans who had come to us from the Belsen camp for "Internees" in December, 1944, and other Jewish orphans from Poland and Czechoslovakia that we found after their mothers died. I lived with them in the same barrack.
>
> Suddenly, we felt the tremors of the earth. Something was moving, and then we heard the sound of rolling tanks. . . . The children were frightened and crying. We had a hard time pacifying them, because we all believed that these were the last minutes of our lives. . . . at about 3 o'clock in the afternoon, we heard a loud voice in German and in English: "Hello, hello— you are free. We are British soldiers and we came to liberate you."[29]

To quote one of several who are alive today because of the efforts of Dr. Bimko and her dedicated staff:

> *Lonely, sad and helpless, I was approached by Dr. Hadassah Bimko-Rosensaft, an extremely impressive Jewish female physician, dressed in doctor's attire, caressing my shaven head and holding my hand she said to me: "Don't be afraid, child, we will take care of you." She transferred me to the children's house. . . . If not for her, I'm certain I would not have survived . . . because I was on the threshold of total collapse physically and spiritually.*
>
> *Life in the children's house was different—warm rooms, beds, showers and most important of all, a staff of dedicated workers. . . .*[30]

During the International Liberators Conference, which was held in 1987, one of the survivors of Bergen-Belsen recalled that although she was almost at the point of death, her sister was allowed to bring her to Dr. Bimko's infirmary, but only if her sister washed her. Although Dr. Bimko and the other attendants did not think the child would live through the night, she did and recalled, "Somehow, maybe because of this cold water that my sister washed me in, my temperature dropped. I did survive the night." Another survivor whose life had been saved by Dr. Bimko also pleaded to try to save this child, and it was permitted, although the girl was put into a cot with two other girls—"both unconscious, both having diarrhea. . . ." Stating that at the time there was very little else a person could have done, she said to Dr. (Bimko) Rosensaft, "I looked for you for many years—36 years."[31]

Major General James Johnston, in his recollections of Bergen-Belsen attesting to the efforts of the two physicians, stated that they had managed "without any assistance from the authorities and without any medical or other equipment, to maintain some sort of order out of the chaos that prevailed around them." Within the horrible mass of human squalor and degradation that surrounded them, Drs. Bimko and Gutman, "physically clean, mentally whole, calm, serene and dignified, stood out as a shining example to their fellow internees, a personification of the triumph of good over evil."[32]

After liberation, the acutely ill inmates were transferred to a well-equipped former German army hospital in Belsen camp 2. On May 21, after having completed the transfer of all the patients, the barracks of the concentration camp were burned down.[33] Appointed administrator, Dr. Bimko asked for doctors and nurses among the inmates to report to her. "Twenty-eight doctors and 590 female and 30 male nurses reported immediately." Although not all were qualified and many were still very weak, they devoted themselves to the care of the patients.[34]

Dr. Bimko, who remained as a physician following liberation, stated, "I think it would have been hard to abandon my charges after liberation." In July, 1945, the government and Red Cross of Sweden declared that they would accept six hundred patients for recuperation. Offered papers to go to London at the end of 1945, Dr. Bimko declined, commenting, " 'It hurt me very much to have to turn down such an opportunity. But how could I go and have a better life for myself when there were so many thousands in Bergen-Belsen who needed my help? . . . My duty still lay with my work at Belsen.' "[35]

Dr. Johnston appointed her to administer the medical staff in the hospital established by the British in Belsen, writing that she had been one of the few people among the fifty thousand or so incarcerated in Bergen-Belsen who, "in spite of the horrors she had undergone, was still capable and was doing a magnificent job amongst the thousands of sick and dying." He further commended her efforts on behalf of the prisoners, stating:

> *I cannot speak too highly of her work in this camp against difficulties which no doctor can have experienced before—a complete lack of instruments and medicaments, even of the absolute essentials—beds, blankets, clothing. She had organized her own staff of nurses and was quite outstanding amongst all the other doctors in this camp.*
>
> *I am convinced that whatever medical task is undertaken by Dr. Bimko, that task will be undertaken superbly.[36]*

Children from Kinderheim *boarding train for Marseilles. Courtesy Dr. Hadassah Rosensaft.*

Dr. Ada Bimko (now Hadassah Rosensaft) and Josef Rosensaft (first two on left) aboard the Champollion. *Courtesy Dr. Hadassah Rosensaft.*

After liberation the British medical officers went to German homes and confiscated toys to bring into the camp, telling the mothers to explain the reason for this to their own children. Homes were set up for the Jewish children at Blankenese and Lüneburg, where they were cared for and educated. On April 9, 1946, Dr. Bimko accompanied the first transport of a thousand children and twenty expectant mothers to Palestine aboard the *Champollion.* At Lyon local Jews who came to offer bread cried as they saw the surviving children. In Marseilles they celebrated a Passover Seder, after which they left for Haifa. Two babies were born before they reached Palestine.

They were greeted at Bizerta, Tunis by a delegation of local Jews who gave them fruit and the rabbi who blessed them and gave them wine. In Palestine the children were distributed among various kibbutzim and schools, the Belsen group of 98 children divided among Dorot, Kiryat Anavim, and Ben Shemen.[37]

In April, 1946, the anniversary of the liberation of Bergen-Belsen, the Central Jewish Committee erected a monument on the mass graves of the former concentration camp. It reads: "Israel and the World shall remember the 30,000 Jews exterminated in the concentration camp in Bergen-Belsen at the hands of the murderous Nazis. Earth conceal not the blood shed on thee."[38]

Three days after their liberation, Josef Rosensaft was elected by the Jewish survivors to be their spokesman to the British authorities, and in 1945 was elected chairman of the Central Jewish Committee. In 1946, he and Dr. Bimko were married in the Belsen DP camp, where she gave birth to their son, Menachem, on May 1, 1948. The Rosensafts remained at the camp until it closed in 1950, after which they moved to Switzerland. They later immigrated to the United States, where they made their home in New York.

Josef Rosensaft remained president of the Federation of Bergen-Belsen Associations until his death on September 10, 1975. During his lifetime, he and Hadassah had devoted themselves to perpetuating the memories of the victims of the Holocaust and contributing to the well-being of its survivors. Their son, Menachem Rosensaft, an attorney in New York, is the founding chairman of the International Network of Children of Jewish Holocaust Survivors. On the twenty-fifth anniversary of the liberation of Bergen-Belsen, Josef and Hadassah Rosensaft were cited "for their devotion and untiring endeavors for the cause of the survivors of Bergen-Belsen and of Nazi oppression."

On November 9, 1978, Dr. Hadassah Rosensaft was appointed by President Carter to serve on the United States Commission on the Holocaust. In 1980, she was appointed by President Reagan to the United States Holocaust Memorial Council, which subsequently established the United States Holocaust Museum in Washington, D.C. She remained active on the Council until January 1994, when Menachem was appointed in her stead. Others who have commemorated her work include Presidents Reagan and Bush. She received letters on her eightieth birthday from President Bush, former New York City mayor Dinkins, former president of Israel Chaim Herzog, and former mayor of Jerusalem, Teddy Kollek.

On May 8, 1985, she received an award of appreciation and recognition from the United States Holocaust Memorial Museum, honoring her "for her extraordinary efforts as an organizer of the medical workers among Jewish survivors of Bergen-Belsen following liberation. She provided hope and dignity to the survivors of the Holocaust."[39]

Despite all the honors bestowed upon her, however, she still grieves for those she and so many others lost in the Holocaust. As she addressed those attending the International Liberators' Conference in Washington, D.C.:

"For the greatest part of the liberated Jews of Bergen-Belsen, there was no ecstasy, no joy at our liberation. We had lost our families, our homes. We had no place to go to, nobody to hug. Nobody was waiting for us anywhere. We had been liberated from death and the fear of death, but not from the fear of life."[40]

Chapter Twelve

Magda Herzberger

"GOD SAVED ME FOR A PURPOSE"

· · ·

My guide and I entered that hidden road
To make our way back up to the bright world.
We never thought of resting while we climbed.

We climbed, he first and I behind, until,
through a small round opening ahead of us
I saw the lovely things the heavens hold,

and we came out to see once more the stars.
                                    —Dante Alighieri, *Dante's Inferno*

I was born in Rumania on February 20, 1926, in the city of Cluj, in Transylvania.[1]
Like most Jews then, I had lived with persecution since I was very young. My father
loved books, and he was a great reader. We had books all the time. Books were
cherished. We had leather jackets on them. He had a library with a glass cabinet
which displayed the beautiful books. He always said, "A good book is like a sacred
thing. You have to take care of them."

I grew up with lots of music. My father loved music and played three instruments. When he was young, he played in an orchestra with my uncle. I have always
had a love for music. As a teenager I wanted to learn to play the piano at an earlier
age, but we could not afford it. Finally I got a very good piano teacher. I also liked to
fence and to ice skate.

We were very ignorant about sex. When I was growing up, discussing sex was a
no-no. At my age, when I was a growing teenager and even when I came back after
the war, I was like today's seventh graders! Even now seventh graders know more
about sex! Those were different times. I didn't have a normal teenager's life—like
you would go out and dance at a prom. No, as a teenager I always had to be very
serious; I had to fight for my grades.

Magda Herzberger, Dubuque, Iowa, June 14, 1994.
Photo by Diane Plotkin.

We had four elementary schools and eight gymnasiums. Each had a very heavy curriculum. You had to pass an entrance examination to the gymnasium. Then, in the fourth gymnasium year, you had to pass another entrance examination. If you didn't pass that one, you couldn't get further education because the four years of gymnasium were dedicated towards selecting your profession. You had to decide whether you want to earn a bachelor of arts or science degree. At the end of the eight gymnasiums, you got a bachelor of science or bachelor of arts degree.

My father advised me very well when he said, "You are Jewish; you have to take a profession which is needed." I wanted to study medicine at a very early age. I knew by the time I was finishing my fourth gymnasium that I had to pass this exam. Since I was Jewish, I would need very high grades in order to get to the fifth gymnasium. If you wanted to go to medical school, you had to pass the medical school entrance examination.

Father, my dear father,
I can never forget you—
Your words are deeply carved
Into my memory.
Beloved father, rest peacefully.[2]

It wasn't just my father's decision; it was my wish. It was my dream, and I worked towards it. I did get into medical school on a full scholarship after I came back from the German concentration camps.

When times were good, my father was a manager in a large engine factory, *Energia,* which means energy. Naturally, when the persecution started, there were difficulties in his job. Jews were not allowed to maintain managerial positions. When the Germans occupied our city on March 19, 1944, we had to wear the Star of David and, therefore, could be molested on the streets. We were scared. My father accompanied me at all times, and we went out just for the absolute necessities. At that time, some of my father's friends were able to get him some work, working until 3 o'clock or midnight. He had three jobs in order to make ends meet. This wasn't legal, but they wanted to help him. This was a very scary period.

Things started to be bad in the mid-1930s, and slowly became worse. By 1938 and 1939 things were really bad. Prior to the Germans' arrival, we were gradually robbed, first by the Hungarian government and then by the Germans. The Jewish people had to give them all our radios, so we could not hear any news. They did not want us to know what was going on in other parts of the world, and there were severe penalties if you didn't surrender your radio. Then we had to give certain jewelry items; and gradually, there were more and more restrictions. Then, in 1944, when Hitler occupied our city of Cluj, we knew something very bad was about to happen. But we didn't realize how bad it was going to be.

My father had always respected the German culture. He admired Beethoven and Mozart. Since he had grown up with Germans and Hungarians, he spoke both languages. He talked like a German. Since we had no idea about the German concentration camps, my father thought we could trust them. He had a low paying job so we could have something to eat; we had a little apartment. Why should we go? The German army occupied my home town on March 19, 1944. In April, all the Jewish people had to wear the Star of David pinned on our clothing at all times. The word *JUDE* was written on the Star of David; it means "Jew" in German.

So that everyone could see
From far
The stamp of our religion—

We were avoided
Like the plague.[3]

Cut from a canvaslike material, it had to be yellow. Why yellow? Because it repre-
sented the tarnished, the filthy Star of David, symbol of the filthy Jews. In March
and April, when it was cool, we had to wear it on the left side of our outer clothing.
It was very humiliating, very painful. Sometimes I felt that it was so unjust and
unfair that I took off my Star of David and went outside. My parents were very
upset because if I had been caught, I probably would have been put in prison.

We had to walk the streets with this Star of David pinned on us. It was very
dangerous because many of the special Hungarian police and local citizens were
anti-Semitic. Naturally, not all people were anti-Semitic, but there were some who
did not like Jews. And, from their viewpoint, with good reason, because Jewish
people were holding good positions; they were ambitious. Some of them wouldn't
have minded having a Jew's job. We were always persecuted. Even though we too
were citizens like they were, we never had the same rights. It's sad, but that's the
truth.

Everyone could see the sign of our religion. They also had a special nickname
for Jews, very degrading. In Rumanian, they called us *Jewdan.* This lasted through
March, April, and May.

Everything happened fast from then on. May was the worst part. In Rumania
and in Hungary, when you registered, you had to specify your religion. Therefore,
City Hall had a list of the Jewish people. I was registered as a Jew; it was on my
identification card. In May we were taken out of our homes. It was easy for them;
the SS and German soldiers with a special Hungarian police took the list and went
from street to street, from home to home, pulling out the Jewish people. The Hungarian police wore boots with little bells on them—special bells. There was a special
police force which assisted the Nazis in taking the Jews from their homes. When
they started doing that, we knew that our street was going to come. There was no
way we could run away anymore; we would have been arrested.

We lived in an apartment house, but it had a yard and trees. We had some
cherished heirloom pieces which my father did not want to lose, like his pocket
watch, a little locket, the wedding rings, his rings. Hearing that they came from
street to street, he buried them in a box in the ground at night. That's how we could
retrieve them. I still have those, including a locket from my great grandmother. I
never knew her.

My father also gave some of our photographs to our Hungarian friends with
whom he played chess, to hold for us "just in case." I have these today, a selection of
meaningful photos of ourselves. We didn't know that we were going to be taken to

Germany. They said that we were going to be taken to labor camps within the country. Who would have thought that we would end up in Auschwitz? We hoped that we would come back, but it did not happen that way. We had to leave the house, and we knew what was happening to our house. When you walked out, you knew.

I will never forget that day. I could see that the going was bad. We lived on the second floor in a two bedroom apartment. I could see the Germans coming in with the civilian police. I could hear the bells. They were taking our neighbors, and then they came up—walking up the stairs.

I experienced brutality for the first time in my life. I was an only child. I grew up with lots of love. My father was a peace-loving person, and I never got corporal punishment. He always believed in the power of words and not of blows. I had very kind parents. We were a very close, loving family.

The Germans broke in and started pushing us. They were treating us like cattle who had to be taken out from the barn. "Fast, fast, fast; out, out, out." Beating us if we didn't move fast enough. To avoid the blows, we had to go fast.

They said that we can take only a small suitcase. We opened the drawer and pushed in whatever we could. All the rest remained in the house, which was totally looted.

When we came back after the war, our neighbors had some of our stuff, which we couldn't even retrieve. None of our neighbors tried to help us because they were scared. They would have been punished if they helped us. They couldn't. Nobody could. Nobody was coming to our aid. And I refer to the priest, I refer to the reverend, I refer to everybody in the city. They were silent. They had seen what was happening to us, but I think that they did not have any second thoughts about stealing some of our stuff. They took everything away. We had to leave our house with everything that my parents had worked for during their lifetimes. My mother was very good in crafts; she had beautiful needlework. We had personal pictures, family pictures. You lost everything that you had!

Open trucks took us from our apartment to the so-called ghetto, an open area at the site of an old abandoned brick factory on the outskirts of the city. We were put down there on the ground, not even a roof above our heads. We had a very poor diet. It was practically a starvation diet. Most of it was just a little bread and some water. Some of us packed food and took along some things like eggs and things that can be preserved. The conditions were horrible hygienically.

It was a big area guarded by Hungarian police. Some of the Hungarian police—not all of them—were just like Nazis. They were Jew-haters too. Sometimes they were very vulgar—the way they made us go to the restroom, for instance. We had outdoor privies. I knew one of the guards. I really wished they would have caught him. There was an older lady who had to go to the bathroom. He said, "You can make it in your pants." She could only go when he wanted. We couldn't get away; it was too late because we were guarded from all sides.

If we could wash at all, it was very primitive. We did not have showers. We did not have sinks; everything was outdoors. It was very hard. You even had to stand in line for water which was distributed in big containers. If you didn't have much water, you did what you could with a little. We had to wait for it. My parents had a little bar of soap which we treated like a sacred thing. But you could not use the soap because it required too much water. At that time, I had long hair. It was almost impossible to wash it unless you used cold water. It was inhuman the way we were treated. You had to do whatever you could to help yourself under those conditions.

Toilet paper was unheard of. We used whatever was around. If you had a newspaper, you used that, or whatever paper you could get hold of. It was not a luxury. This was really the preliminary German concentration camp. We slept on the ground. There were no buildings. No covering. The camp was surrounded by a metal fence with barbed wire. And this was surrounded by soldiers. There were thousands of people; they concentrated all the Jews just from Cluj. I don't know exactly what our number was, but it was quite a sizeable Jewish population. It was a big camp.

It had gates, but you could not go through them because they were guarded. We were told, "This situation is not going to last. It's a short period." They were feeding us all along with lies. "It's going to be just for a little while. Families are going to be together." That was a big thing—"Families are going to be together. The situation is going to be much better." Our situation lasted for a whole month.

Sometimes we had to form lines and go for water. The camp was in the out-skirts of the city and there was a water supply. We had to go there, get the water, and carry it back. I can't remember whether it was a well, a spring, or a faucet. I think it might have been an outdoor faucet. On those occasions when we carried the water, I said to my parents, "Let's run away; this isn't good." That's when I saw an oppor-tunity. "Let's get to the end of the line and maybe we can do something." We had Hungarian friends who lived in the vicinity. But I think my mother was too scared. I said, "Maybe we could run to her place. We must try something." You want to do something, but you're scared about what might happen to you. It was a no-win situation.

We did not know anything. We had no way of talking to people who were in Poland or Czechoslovakia. We could not imagine something horrible. We were kept in total darkness after losing our radios.

The camp was guarded by German and Hungarian guards. Most of the Ger-man guards were Wehrmacht. You could still find among the Wehrmacht some people who were humane. But the SS were totally loyal to Hitler and had a license to kill in the camps. They enjoyed torturing you. Torture can be emotional and physical, and they were skilled in both.

That was going on for a month. We still didn't know what was happening. The Jewish Committee had to make the lists to meet the quotas imposed on them. We were wondering where they were going. There were maybe five hundred people on each transport accompanied by several guards. They were transported in cattle wagons to German concentration camps, but we did not know where they went. It was just a gradual thing; you take five hundred people, again and again.

Our turn came on June 1, 1944. The whole camp was taken. We were marching for a while, accompanied out of the camps by Hungarian police and the German guards. Then we were taken to the cattle wagons. These cattle wagons had hardly any windows. They put us in compartments which were filled to their maximum. We could hardly move in there. Then the trains started moving. We did not get any food; we did not get any drink; we had no toilet. They locked us in by bolting the doors from outside. We traveled for three days and three nights. The situation inside the cattle wagons was horrible! All that excrement! Some people were in a horrible state. Imagine little kids and old people traveling like that.

Everyone was fighting for his or her own survival. We had to sleep on the floor of the wagon. My father was a very strong man, strong personality, and this was the first time I had seen him really crying. He said we made a grave mistake, but it was too late.

After three nights and three days, the train stopped and I heard German voices. I was scared. We didn't know that we were in Auschwitz. The biggest extermination in the history of Auschwitz was going on in 1944. Transports came day and night; twenty-seven thousand Jewish people were gassed and cremated each day. It was madness! I couldn't have come at a worse time.

The heavy doors of the cattle wagons were opened and the SS guards came in with short rubber sticks. They were hauling us out and beating us if we didn't go fast enough. They were really brutal. We were ordered to leave everything in the cattle wagon, even our small suitcases. We had to come down, "fast, fast, fast; *shnell, shnell, shnell;* get out, get out." Then we were standing on a platform, and I will never forget the first look at Auschwitz-Birkenau.

> *So many times*
> *I could have been selected*
> *For the gas chambers*
> *To meet the horrible fate*
> *Of all the infants, the children,*
> *The young, the old,*

The sick, the disabled
Who were executed
In the mysterious
"White House" of Auschwitz,
Whose naked bodies were thrown
To the furnaces
Of the huge crematoriums,
Whose ashes were used
On the fields and the gardens.[4]

I couldn't understand the great flames belching from chimneys and why the air was filled with a strange, sickening, sweetish odor. We didn't know then that it was burning flesh. It smelled like a slaughterhouse when they burn the fat. I couldn't imagine that my family members and innocent victims were burning there. I couldn't imagine something that horrible.

Auschwitz-Birkenau was a huge camp. I can still see the concrete posts connected with barbed wire fence charged with electrical current. On the top of each of these concrete posts, there was a light directed to the camp; it was a watching eye. The women's camp was behind the fence. I could see women, shaved, begging for food. They were dressed in rags. I thought that this was the mental asylum. I couldn't believe it, how horrifying this was—my first impression of Auschwitz-Birkenau. Cruelty all around.

The wagons stood there, and we had to leave everything in them. Then Polish prisoners took our things from the wagon and put them in the Canada warehouse. We didn't know that, but we found out later.

We were standing on the platform for a long time. Then the first separation took place. Women were separated from men. This first part of the selection was done by a medical committee. I found out later that the head of the committee was Dr. Josef Mengele. I did not know his name. He had very dark hair, dark eyes, dark eyebrows, and something of a cold, callous look in his eyes. He was impeccably clean. He was a well-built man—I would say even good looking. I looked especially at his highly polished boots. He held a stick in his hand. I can't remember whether it was made of wood or something else.

But I do remember Dr. Josef Mengele, and I found that the other one was Dr. Fritz Klein.[5] Dr. Mengele and Dr. Klein, two German high officials, did the selections when I came. Dr. Klein was shorter than Dr. Mengele, but I can't remember him that well. Dr. Josef Mengele pointed me to the right and many of my family members to the left. I remember him because he looked directly at me.

He was asking the age of the children, and the people were telling the right age.

They didn't know that children up to age fourteen were taken to the gas chambers along with the infants. They were sending all the old people—the aged—to the left. They were joined by pregnant women, the disabled, and others who were weak or injured. Sometimes they would take a child away from its mother. They enjoyed this emotional torture. There were instances when a grandmother and the children were taken away, and the mother said, "Please take care of my children." The Polish prisoners were telling the mothers, "Give us the child; they are going to have better treatment." They knew if the mother goes with the child, she's going to be gassed too.

It took hours to separate everybody. If you were pointed to the left, you went to the gas chambers; if you were pointed to the right, you went to the barracks. The gas chamber had a white fence around it. There was a forest next to our camp. People who were selected sometimes would stay in the forest and wait until two thousand could go into this underground viaduct. They probably knew what was happening to them. Most of the people working in the crematory ovens were men—Polish prisoners. Every four months the unit was exterminated and others were brought in.

Mengele did not say anything to me but pointed to the right. He was motioning, "left, right." He looks at you and assesses you, and then decides what he's going to do to you. He was talking to us, asking our ages. Sometimes he would ask the age of a fourteen or fifteen year old, and he would point to the gas chambers. That's what happened to my cousins. He did not talk to me. I was eighteen years old. I was very well developed and strong, and I was taller than many others. I'm five feet, three inches tall, but that was considered tall in my home town. I played a lot of sports, so I looked like I would be good for slave labor. They could leave me alive and use me later on.

We were pointed to the right. To the left, I could see families trying to run after each other. The SS guards were shooting in the air; there were beatings. I can never shut that horrible scene out of my mind. I was totally shocked. I thought that I must be dreaming. This could not happen. They separated families. Within a short period of time, my family was taken away from me. That was such emotional torture. Now I didn't have the emotional support of my family.

My father told me, "Please practice the art of love, forgiveness, and tolerance in your heart. Take care of your mother. Cherish and respect her. Don't forget your loving father." These were his last words when we were separated. I had made a vow to take care of my mother. I love her and I will always take care of her. I said, "Mother, I love you and I will do everything so that you are happy, regardless." She said, "I know. That's all I want to hear." Now she's in a nursing home, but my promise is a promise; it's a commitment. When you love somebody truly, then you don't let the person down when the person is in need.

Your last words
Still ring in my ears
After so many years—
"My child, my dear daughter,
Soon we will be separated
From each other.
I may never return—
Be strong, don't cry.
Let the candle of hope burn
In your heart
Take care of your mother,
Cherish and respect her."[6]

I went to the right. First we entered a room where we had to leave all our belongings, everything we had. We were just a bunch of women separated from the men. Two women whom I knew from our city were with me, but I was one of the youngest. We were all naked. We had to leave everything and enter the shaving room naked—naked in front of everybody. I tried to hide myself.

An SS woman ran the shaving room. Some of these SS women were snakes who enjoyed biting you. I had hair down to my knees. My hair was in a "Gretchen" hairdo: two sets of braids twirled around my head and fastened with pins. I did that because it was more hygienic. She was smiling when I came in. When she took the cutting shears, I said, "Please leave me a little hair." I never forgot that horrible feeling I had when somebody was pulling my hair with such force. She cut off *all* my hair. Then I was in a shock. She was enjoying herself, smiling and laughing while she did that. It was a horrible experience when I saw my hair fall down in one piece. The head was shaved, but not the pubic hair. They used the hair for different purposes, including hair from the victims of the gas chambers—from the dead. They used the hair for pillow cases and wigs, probably my hair also, which was beautiful long hair. I couldn't even cry because I said, "This is a nightmare. It couldn't happen. It's not happening."

The guards came in, and then I felt a pain on my naked back. They were hauling us into the shower room. I was in shock, and I got hit because I didn't move fast enough. This was a real shower room. I don't think it was heated water, but I can't remember that. You took a shower, but you were persecuted and harassed: "*shnell, shnell, shnell.*" Could you even take a decent shower when you were so shocked that you are in another world, a world of nightmare?

When we came out of the shower room and entered the dressing room, we got the most ridiculous clothing. Some of us got summer clothing. The good clothing was taken away, so we got the clothing that they probably wanted to discard but gave to us instead. I did not get prison clothing. I ended up with a long, dark blue dress that hung down to my ankles. I don't wear too much dark blue today because of that! I like blue, but not that color blue! It was probably about twice as big as I needed. Then I got an orthopedic shoe for a foot that needed it. I didn't. It was a high shoe with laces. I had pain walking in that shoe because I have normal feet. I didn't need that orthopedic thing, but who cared if it was my size, or if I needed an orthopedic shoe? I did not get any underwear. But I was lucky that I got that long dress. I realized that later because every day, in the morning before going to work, they counted us standing in line. We looked like people from comic strips—like clowns.

Next came the paint room where they painted our outer clothing with a red stripe about four to five inches wide. It went all the way down from the base of the neck. Why did they do that? Evidently so that if we ran away, we could be recognized.

Who could run away from Auschwitz? People tried, but in Auschwitz there were Doberman killer dogs; you could hear their barking in the morning. When somebody tried to escape, the alarm went off. The dogs were barking and going after the people. I don't know if anybody escaped from Auschwitz, but if you didn't succeed, you were better off if you were shot. Otherwise you were put in the torture cell, which was about three feet by three feet. You were chained and they could do anything—torture you. Or they would hang you in public. I realized I could never have gotten away. Nevertheless, the alarm sounded quite often because somebody else who couldn't stand the humiliation any more had tried to escape.

When we left the paint room we were led to our barracks. It's interesting, but when you are in shock, you experience contradictory emotional reactions; either you laugh or you cry. Some started laughing because we all looked so ridiculous. I personally couldn't laugh. I couldn't cry. I was in shock. I didn't know if it was real. I was confused.

I was not tattooed. None of our transport was tattooed for a good reason: in 1944 there were massive exterminations and maybe they did not want to invest that effort. Besides, the going wasn't exactly that great for the Germans. So I was lucky. If I had come earlier to Auschwitz, I would have been tattooed. So there's no record of me being in Auschwitz. We were not tattooed in Bremen; neither were we in Bergen-Belsen because when we got there, you had a three week life expectancy. We were infected with typhus and everything. But when I was liberated in Bergen-Belsen, I got a fingerprinted certificate.

There was a great extermination going on. In Auschwitz there were four crematory units.[7] Each consisted of an underground viaduct, gas chambers, and the crematory ovens. Two thousand could go into this underground viaduct, where they had to strip and were told that they should put everything together nicely—for what purpose? When everything was transported to the Canada warehouses, they could select and put it nicely in order. They were given soap and towels; they were accompanied with classical music to that point. Did they ever think that they were going to have this fate?

They distributed towels and soap and then they were pushed into the gas chamber—five hundred at one time. Because the door of the gas chamber said "BATH HOUSE," people went in voluntarily. The doors were closed. The gas chamber had fake shower heads. On the ceiling, there was an opening which was latticed with a glass window through which a lethal gas was administered—Zyklon B which resulted in cyanide. The gas chambers had porous walls. There were ducts from outside administering the gas through these holes. The gas came from above and below. People were defecating in it. It's a horrible thing to talk about. I just have nightmares; I never got rid of my nightmares. The gas chambers had peepholes so the guards could look in. People died in those gas chambers. You could see true love. They were holding hands in rigor mortis. They had terrible contortions. They had to use hook-tipped poles to separate them.

There was a special *sonderkommando*. Everybody who worked there was *sonderkommando*. We who dragged, we were *sonderkommando*, but so were the SS who administered the gas the *sonderkommando*.[8] Then the *sonderkommando* dragged the corpses outside. Naturally I was also selected for that gruesome task because I was young and strong—eighteen years old.

My first night in Auschwitz, my first night in the barrack—it was a very large barrack, and it had two entrances. They could accommodate, I think, about five hundred people. The barracks were very poorly constructed. I know that on my side were fewer windows. It was always dark. You could see some chimneys from the kitchen of the barrack. The food was terrible. The barracks had some wooden planks, and many people were on each plank. When I got there, those barracks with planks were filled, so we had nothing except the floor. We had to sleep with crouched knees, practically like sardines. In my barrack, I was one of the youngest. There were more mature women, or maybe even girls who were more like twenty or twenty-two. I was eighteen. I woke up with some other women; there were three women whom I knew from our city who were also with me.

There was a door in the middle of our barrack separating one side from the other. When it was raining, water ran through the crevices. We were given pails. The water accumulated, and we had to throw it out with pails. The barracks were inundated. I had a friend a little older than I, about twenty-three years old. She was very nice, a kind and very gentle person. One night, there was a horrible rain. Our barracks started to get water. We used pails to get the water out. The other side of the barrack was cleaner; they had water, but we had it worse. They thought our side was better, and they broke through that door to see. It was a nightmare. My friend was close to the door. In order to survive, she started strangling those people, attacking, so that she would stay alive. That night passed, but my friend never recovered. I think she snapped. Every time there was rain, she was actually trying to strangle people. She became violent. She was not a violent person. She had a mental breakdown. She was screaming. She was taken away. We never saw her again because she was a bother; she was probably killed.

It was cold in the barrack. Five people got one blanket, a wool blanket. These were kept in a corner. When people were coming back from work, the fight started for the blankets. I was very good at running into the barracks and getting at least one blanket because otherwise we remained without any. It was like a madhouse.

The first nightmare I faced the first day in Auschwitz must have been around 4 o'clock in the morning. We had no watches; we didn't know what time it was, but it was pitch dark. We had no electricity in our barracks. Then the guards came in with those sticks. "*Heraus, heraus, heraus,* fast, fast, fast." I woke up from a dream: I was home, combing my long hair. Then I heard "*heraus, heraus.*" It was a roll call which lasted for hours. We were surrounded by guards on high platforms with machine guns. That's when our torture started—with the roll call. We had to stand straight in line, erect, in the morning. It was cold at that hour. I was lucky. At least I had my long dress and my high shoes. If you deviated from your line and were so unlucky that the guard caught you, your whole line was punished. The whole line had to kneel, even though only one person was out of order, just to teach you. We had to kneel in clay or in stone as long as they wanted us to, with our hands up in the air. If you were unfortunate and couldn't keep up your hands, you were beaten.

I want to talk about physicians in the camp. People would think that physicians had privileges, but not all physicians were treated well. Many were treated very badly where I was. Sometimes they would line up physicians in order to persecute them more because they were intellectuals. Some of these guards with very little education now suddenly got power. They hated intellectuals.

It happened that in my barrack there was a physician. She got worse treatment than all of us. The guards and the *blockältesters* were very cruel. I hate to tell you that some were Jews, Polish Jews. I think they must have been in the camp for a longer period of time, and they sold themselves to the Germans. So they had to act like that; they had to be more cruel in order to maintain their positions and not to be gassed themselves. It's no excuse. But we had these *blockältesters* who were cruel enough. So sometimes you were better off not to reveal that you were a physician. I don't think people knew that.

One morning this physician—she was older, thirty-two, middle stature, and she had dark hair. She was with me in the barracks. She was always cold. In order to warm herself up, she tore a part of her blanket and put it around her chest. We advised her not to do that. She did that several times. She had, unfortunately, a thinner dress. It was the roll call. Not only did they number[9] you, they could also check you. You could not hide anything on you. If you were caught with anything, you were punished. So, there was the roll call and she had this little piece torn from the blanket wrapped around her chest.

The SS guards were usually wearing handguns and high boots; they were always well dressed. The SS guard on this day was very pretty. We called her the blond angel of death. She was very cruel and sadistic. If she felt like it, she could hack you up. Unfortunately, she saw that the physician looked more stuffed, and she pulled off that little piece of blanket that she was holding. And, my God, she started beating her, slapping her and slapping her and slapping her. Her face was all red. And what she did—the physician couldn't stand it. She attacked and tried to strangle the SS woman. She went for her neck. Naturally she was taken away and we are pretty sure she was shot.

If you got sick in Auschwitz, it was scarlet fever; it was scurvy; typhus was raging. As far as medications in Auschwitz, you got nothing. People were dying of scarlet fever, of scurvy. You would be sick and still have to drag the corpses. People were beaten to death because they couldn't drag the corpses anymore.

We were on a starvation diet. In the morning, the black coffee tasted like dishwater. We had foul water in Auschwitz. In the evening we got foul water. You had nothing during the whole day. In the evening, again they counted us after we came back to the camp. And you had to wait in line for that. The food was distributed. You got a six-and-a-half-ounce piece of bread. It was always stale bread, hard. It had something in it that tasted like sawdust, and it irritated our throats. We never got fresh bread, and always dark bread. Then you got a little soup with a few rutabagas floating in it. It smelled awful. You could feel the sand in it. The only way you could eat this was if you closed your nostrils. That's the way I did it; I closed my eyes. I had to eat that soup because that was all I would get. With this kind of nutrition, how could you survive? Occasionally they would give us a razor-thin slice of meat—some kind of a cold cut. And then a big delicacy sometimes—a spoon of jelly. We did not have any possibility for additional food.

I don't know the exact distance, but across from our camp was a men's camp. I think that they were Polish prisoners, Polish Jews. I remember that some of the women did something they shouldn't do. If they had a long dress, they would cut a part of it off, and they would put on a little bonnet to hide the baldness, hoping that the men would throw them a piece of bread or something. They were begging from the men.

Some prisoners defected. These Polish prisoners were there so long that they had access to other food. I could never beg food from them. I felt I'd rather die because it would be like prostituting myself. I said, "No, I am a proud person." But sometimes, those Polish men were able to cross over to the women's camp. I don't know how they did it, but they must have had some of the men working in the Canada warehouses. In the Canada warehouses you had jewelry, you had clothing, you had shoes. So some of them could bribe the guards. Loot has some benefits. We could not do this. I think the only people who could bribe the guards were the ones who were working in the Canada warehouses because they found jewelry. The guards were not supposed to take anything, but greed exists. That was going on in the camp. I felt I'd rather die in dignity. I have very strong principles and values which I never gave up regardless of circumstances. But I remember definitely that in the men's camp some people had more access to food and other things. But not us. We had to be satisfied with that coffee and with that miserable food.

Everyone in the barrack took care of herself. We got bread and soup in the evening. You had to hide it underneath your head because there were people in the barracks who would steal your bread. I found that it was the safest to eat it so nobody could steal it. I remember thinking what to do with my bread when I got it. When I got to the barrack, I said, "Well, I'm going to just take a few bites. I'll leave something for tomorrow." I got up in the middle of the night and said, "Maybe one bite." By the morning the bread was finished. I was a young person, so I used up my food. My luck was that God really protected me.

I did not see any infirmary. I never saw any kind of medical assistance. I did not get any medication whatsoever. I didn't see anyone get medication. There was no access to medication. There were some people with cancer who were not treated. They had terrible pain but still had to work. Our barracks had nothing. The only infirmary I saw was in my second camp in Bremen. You had to be half dead to get anything from there. But in Auschwitz I was confined. We were isolated. There were gates separating barracks. We were in the Hungarian camp. There were gates between the quarters. There was no way out. If you went out past a certain barrier, the guard could shoot you on the spot. So I did not go out of my environment.

There were outdoor toilets: just holes, that's all. Sometimes the guards didn't let you go when you wanted. Just to torture us, they made us shit in our pants. You had to do everything with others watching. You had no privacy in there.

We were just the women's camp, isolated from the men's camp. We had barbed wires. You had to go through a gate, but you could see the men's camp. The only people who went through gates were those transporting the food—that little black coffee. They were the *ess commando*. I'm glad I never was selected for that because it was another torture. It had to be boiled at night so that it could be transported early in the morning in a huge metal kettle with handles on both sides. There were a number of people assigned—not too many—and sometimes they got burned by carrying it. It was a nightmare when that coffee came. Sometimes the people carrying it were attacked; everyone feared they would get left out and not get their ration.

We didn't have utensils. No knives, forks, or anything. We had a kind of an armylike thing, metal containers, and had to drink our soup from that. They would take those metal containers and try to pour the coffee in that. Many times the coffee spilled. People who were too close got burned. You had to be very careful because it was like a revolution when that drink came. It was dangerous to be transporting that. The same thing happened to the people who transported the other food. But the other food was dished out. The guards were there. But in the morning, because of all the nights and the torture and the hunger, there was a craze. Every morning was an absolute madness! People were hysterical.

I have seen people who wanted to die and refused to eat. Why? It was easy after a while not to eat because they fell into depression. They didn't care. They didn't want soup. They didn't want coffee. That's when you knew that somebody is going to go down. If you started looking like a skeleton, you were called a *Mussulman*. You knew this is not going to be good; they are going to be taken away. You tried to prevent it. Sometimes you succeeded and sometimes you couldn't.

In my second or third week in Auschwitz, I started toying with the fence. I was trying to think whether it's worth living under those conditions. I felt that I had very little hope—just a slow torture and I am going to die ultimately. Something interesting happened to me on that night because I think really God protected me. Because of the things that happened to me, I believe in miracles. I have a deep faith in God because that's the only place I could turn for help.

On that night I couldn't sleep, and I was wondering what to do—whether I should live or I should die. And I said, "Well, what am I going to do?" I am going to just get up in the middle of the night and go close to the wires. I was toying with suicide on that night. We were so cramped. I got out by crawling over the others. They cursed me because I had to go over people who were sleeping in order to reach the door. I was standing there, thinking, "What's the reason for me to live?" Naturally I have parents. I am only eighteen years old; I want to do many things in my life, but then what kind of a life do I have here? Who knows, maybe my parents ended up in the gas chambers. Who am I going to have? I know many of our older people and children have not survived because they were pointed to the left. I knew what happened to them. Then I felt a hand on my shoulders. There was a girl in my barrack who was just one year older than I was, a schoolmate from elementary school. She and her sister were very poor. They were not very good students. She never got to go to that gymnasium. She put her hand on my shoulder. "Magda, what are you doing? Why did you come up?" I said, "How do you know?" She said, "I followed you." She recognized that there was something not okay with me because I would close my ears. I didn't want to hear anything. I lost the desire to swallow food. She had seen that something was happening to me and wanted to save me. She said, "Aren't you ashamed of yourself? What if your parents survived and you never come home? You are an only child." I went back and I was thinking, "What can I do?"

In the third week, my depression got worse. I didn't know if I could take this much longer. At age eighteen, I had to make the biggest decision. I was debating with myself: why do I want to live; why do I want to die? And I came up with the end result: I want to live regardless of circumstances. I was given that great, divine gift, a great miracle created by God, and I have to respect it, I have to cherish it, and I have to do everything in my power to fight for life. I asked God to help me. I knew I had to do something because I was very depressed. When you are depressed and there's nobody to help you, you have to extricate yourself. If you are not able to do that yourself, you are lost.

I got my first slap on the face from a guard. I never was beaten at home. Then you create an invisible shield and say, "I don't feel anything anymore." That happened to many prisoners. You anesthetize yourself emotionally in order to tolerate it because otherwise you know you are going to do something. Either you kill yourself or go into a deep depression. Then you don't eat; then you are not useful anymore. It's a vicious circle.

I had this shield over me. I didn't like it, but knew that I was the only one who could pull myself out of this. I had to do something to start with, to break the emotional anesthesia so that I feel something. I knew I had to inflict pain upon myself, to shock myself. I had to break the pattern, to shock myself out. I had to do some injury to myself, to wake up and feel—feel some pain, feel that I'm alive. I decided that I'm going to put my nails in my flesh so deep that I'm going to feel pain. I'm going to see my blood coming out, and I did it. And it surely hurt. I could see my blood flowing out. I said to myself, "Now this is you. I mean, you are not dead yet; you are alive, and you can feel." I knew that if I inflicted pain upon myself, I was going to feel it. If it was somebody else, I was anesthetized to that.

Naturally we didn't get any scissors; you had to bite off your fingernails. Also at the beginning, we didn't get any tampons or anything, so the blood was flowing in our menstrual periods. It was a horrible stench. They didn't want that. I think that they must have administered something in our food because gradually we lost our periods. We heard that a drug was administered in our soup; it's a type of powder.[10]

I don't actually know what they gave us, but we lost our periods for a whole year. They must have done something to us because it wasn't just me. It was my whole barrack, all the people, my fellow prisoners in my barracks. I don't know what happened in other barracks, but this happened to us. They must have used some medications or something, unless it was due to the stress and the poor nutrition. But it was a blessing because it was a horrible thing. You worked, you walked. I always had heavy periods, and I had nothing to protect myself. They didn't give us anything to protect ourselves. We were considered filthy; we were addressed names like you wouldn't believe. I got my period back after liberation.

We had tags. Each tag had a six digit number. You were a number. You lost your identity. You had no name. I had the tag in Auschwitz; I had the tag in Bremen; I had the tag in Bergen-Belsen. I wish I had kept my tag, but after liberation, people were throwing out and crushing their tags. Can you imagine the rage you feel when you are liberated? Do you want to see your prison tag? I did not realize that one day maybe it would be nice to have my prison tag. I wanted to crush it and burn it and wreck it. That was not only me, but all of us because you were so enraged. After wearing this tag for such a long time and being a prisoner, you didn't want to have anything that even remotely reminded you of that.

You were taken to the gas chambers when you were not useful, but while you were useful, you were in great danger because twice a week, you had to sit naked and march in front of an SS committee headed by Dr. Josef Mengele, the chief physician in Auschwitz. He also had the infamous laboratories for experiments. If you were considered useful, only then were you left alive. If you were not considered useful anymore, if you had any sign of weakness, you were pointed to the left and exterminated.

There were people selected for horrible experiments conducted in the infamous laboratories of Dr. Josef Mengele. Dr. Carl Clauberg was one of the other physicians working with Dr. Mengele.[11] He was a monster in my opinion. Anybody who collaborated with him was a monster. Dr. Mengele had pet projects. One was to do experiments on twins. My cousin was selected as one of the experimental children. For months Mengele castrated them; then he would inject chloroform in their hearts. He also wanted to turn their eyes blue. In order to do that, he injected some dye in the eyes, blinding many. Out of about two hundred twins, about twenty came back alive.[12] Some of them were not healthy, even after they were liberated.

My cousin had a terrible experience. He was fourteen years old, and I was very close to him. Mengele ordered him to go with the experimental children. My cousin was not a twin, but he said that some children went in with the twins. Mengele was a sadist because he had a horrible game for those who were not twins. My cousin told me this story. They were brought into a room for selections between the twins and those non-twins who were thirteen or fourteen years old. A pole was hung from the ceiling and lowered. Whoever could reach the pole was left alive for a while, for another good purpose, for experiments. The ones who couldn't [reach] were taken to the gas chambers. He enjoyed that—to see which child is going to reach or not to reach. My cousin said, "Magda, I reached it."

Then he was with the experimental twins. He said, "Do you know what it feels like, that you are going to be taken one day for some experiment? They come in and you don't know if you are next in line." My cousin was very lucky because before he was liberated, he was scheduled for experimental surgery. He was once, though, injected in his spine with something. He doesn't know what it was, but he was afraid all his life. He said, "Magda, I don't think I'm going to live a long life." I said, "Alex, how can you say something like that? I didn't know what will happen to me." They never knew what my cousin really had because he died suddenly. I think he was in his fifties. He was always scared, and maybe with good reason, who knows.

There was a woman, Margaret Swartz, a Hungarian from Transylvania. They were experimenting on her: the effects of starvation in the infamous laboratories of Auschwitz. They also mutilated her knees by sectioning them. They were dissecting people and when they were through, they would throw these horrible bodies in the gas chambers. There were skin grafts without septic care. I have about 130 slides; some of them show medical experiments, including vivisection, which were conducted in Auschwitz. Others are actual photographs from Auschwitz and Bergen-Belsen, which were given to me later by a liberating soldier. They were using young women, exposing them to radiation. They were sterilizing them and dissecting them to see the effects of the radiation, after which they were gassed. I have a relative in Israel, a cousin of my mother. He lost his two beautiful children and his wife—they were killed. He met this other woman in the camp after liberation and married her later. He knew that she never could have children because she had been sterilized. She was also beaten to the point where she lost her hearing in one ear.

There is another horrible thing that happened in Auschwitz. Pregnant women were taken to the gas chambers. There was a pregnant woman among us in the barrack, and we really had to guard her so they would not see her tummy. This was difficult, and if the guards found out you were pregnant, your fate was terrible. You were taken to the gas chambers because you were carrying another life within you and you were not useful anymore.

In another barrack was a Jewish physician who had access to medication. She would inject the mother, making it possible to abort the embryo in order to save the mother. If a woman somehow managed to give birth to a new life and a Jewish physician who had access to drugs was around, she would inject the baby with a lethal dose of medication in order to save the mother. Once the mother knew what was going to happen if that was not done, she was faced with a terrible decision: whether to perish with her baby or stay alive, in which case both would be killed.

Some people, due to stress, lost their humaneness. Others maintained that humaneness, that feeling of helping. You had that little piece of bread, and you didn't know where to hide it if you did not eat it because someone would take it from you while you were sleeping. Not everyone was doing that. There were many among us who could see the signs of depression. If we didn't help those in need, they would die. We tried to prevent it. In some instances it was possible; in other instances it was not.

My uncle had said, "You have to be able to tolerate pain to improve your endurance." Even today, I never neglect my physical fitness because of this promise. I was thinking of his words as I was dragging those corpses. You had to take the corpse and pull it; you drag one arm, then the other, and pull it. You always had to bend to pull these corpses. Some of them were still warm. Some of us had to hoist the corpses on lorries. Others had to drag the lorries. The prisoners dragged the lorries since we had no horses. The lorries traveled with the naked corpses stacked on them. No respect for the dead. Everything was stripped from the bodies: their hair, their artificial limbs, their golden teeth. Everything.

The crematory ovens had huge casks. Body fat melted at the high temperatures was used for soap. Ashes from the crematory units became fertilizer on the fields and in the gardens. Because I was strong, I had to dig death pits for the innocent victims of persecution. Then we had to throw the corpses in and incinerate them. We had no choice.

The ones who were working in the crematory ovens were executed every four months because the Germans, the SS, never wanted to be found out. So they were executed. They were lured by saying that if you worked there you would get better food. You were often lured into things. You didn't know exactly what you volunteered for. Food was an excellent lure because we were starving. Seeing my fellow prisoners beaten to death, I knew the only way I could survive, if I had the intelligence, was to have the strength to endure pain. And I did. That was the toughest work that we had to do. I saw good people go insane because they recognized a family member.

I saw many of my fellow prisoners getting the corpses out of the gas chambers and throwing them on the lorries to take them. I saw people beaten to death because they collapsed with the corpses. They were standing up, beaten, collapsed, standing up, beaten. There were people who were shot in the back of the gas chamber too. It was only luck that I survived seven weeks in Auschwitz. If it had been longer, I don't think I would be here today. Not that I went to such a beautiful place in my second camp, because I went for slave labor too. But at least I was on the streets. Maybe I could raid a garbage can.

In Auschwitz we had to drag the corpses from that wire fence almost daily. People who did not want to live anymore touched the barbed wire fences with electrical currents. Others went to the barbed wire fence to be shot by the guards.

We had two kinds of corpses in the barracks. There were those who tried to hang themselves and succeeded. They often used a piece of their clothing. Others who got typhus were not treated. If you got sick, you were not useful anymore. It was very dangerous to be sick; it was your death sentence.

You could see people get sick. There was scarlet fever—high fever—and scurvy. People were pulling out their teeth from vitamin deficiency. Every single day I tried my teeth to see if they were still in place. I survived three camps. In Bergen-Belsen I was starving, but when I came home, I didn't have a single cavity. This is a miracle.

There was a selection in the seventh week in Auschwitz, especially younger people and young women who looked strong. We didn't know where we were going to be taken, but we were taken out of Auschwitz. I thought that anything would be better than Auschwitz because there we had to face death every day.

After seven weeks of doing that horrible, nightmarish job, five hundred women were selected from Auschwitz for slave labor. We didn't know where we were going when we were selected. We were taken to Bremen in cattle wagons on a train. Bremen was the second largest port in Germany. At that time it was really the front line and was attacked day and night by the Allies. When we arrived, Bremen looked like a cemetery. We walked through a part of the city to our barracks. I had never seen anything like that in my life. Whole streets were gone. There were half ruins sticking out; walls looked like tombstones in a cemetery. You could see big caravans of people moving away because their city was bombed morning, noon, and night. We were in a war zone and were used as slave labor to clear the ruins. Then we had to drag the corpses of victims.

Our barracks in Bremen had bunks with mattresses. It was a primitive mattress filled with straw, maybe two or three inches thick. There were three bunks for five hundred women, the ones who were taken from Auschwitz. I was always on the top bunk because I could climb well. The mattress was checked every day by the guards to see if we hid anything. You could be shot immediately if they found paper and a pencil, which could be used to record these events.

We were allowed to heat the barracks only once a week for two hours on Sunday. We only had ice cold water for washing a little bit. We came from the streets all chilled, and then we went into the chilled barracks. We were shivering outside and inside. I had frostbite on all my fingers. All my fingers and toes were affected. We got thin blankets and shivered through the night.

> *We were five hundred*
> *Jewish prisoners,*
> *Women with lost identity,*
> *Captives of the Nazis,*
> *Transferred from Auschwitz*
> *To the port of Bremen,*
> *To clear the ruins*
> *And the charred bodies*
> *Of the devastated streets*
> *Of that doomed city . . .*
> *And destined to be annihilated*
> *After our last drops of strength*
> *Were extracted.*[13]

We had to get up early in the morning and then march for a while until we got to open trucks which took us to the part of the city we were supposed to clear. Usually after a great bombardment, we had to select things that could be reused, like whole bricks or big pipes. It was heavy labor. I was constantly in pain, back pain. All of us were because we had to lift all day. Winter caught us there, and we were very poorly clad. We didn't get winter clothes. We had wooden Dutch shoes and rags around our feet. We put rags around our hands. One SS guard, a woman we called "The Raven," even wanted us to strip so that we could work faster. She thought that cold workers worked faster!

I will never forget that winter in Bremen. The fact that I did not lose my extremities, which some of my fellow prisoners did, was because I was moving all the time. Frostbite was a great danger. You were taken away because you were not useful anymore. My training from fencing gave me tremendous endurance because I learned to move and jump all the time. I said that I was not going to die; I constantly moved my legs and everything so I did not freeze.

In Bremen, we could only get excess food from two sources. There was a garbage can if you had a good guard who would close his eyes. The other possibility was at the site of bombed factories or bombed-out houses.

One of my friends was named Ilus, a Hungarian name. She is now living in Israel, a survivor. She was quite a bit older than me, maybe forty, forty-one, or forty-two. She was a very strong woman and was very protective of me—like a mother to me. I grew up with good manners at home. I could not do certain things. I couldn't steal; I couldn't attack somebody and take away their food.

I remember we were working at the site of an old brick factory—an old cheese factory. Ilus was digging and came across something that looked like a piece of excrement. It was round. We were laughing; we said, "Ilus eats everything." And Ilus said, "When I clean it, I think we might want to eat it!" She was a very good woman. She cleaned it. The surface of the cheese was burned, but inside the cheese looked good. This was a delicacy. There were a number of them underground. And she pulled them, cleaned them, and shared with all of us.

To do this we had to have a good guard. On that day we had a Wehrmacht guard. Ilus cleaned it and asked, "Would you like to have a piece?" The guard ate a piece of that cheese with us because he didn't have much food. There was not much food in Germany during the war. He was like a friend of ours. He was unusual. There were a few Nazi guards who were humane. On that day if we found something, we could eat it. On that day he closed his eyes to something that we should not have. But when we had the SS guards, we could not raid the garbage cans. If they found we had taken anything, they would beat us. So we knew we would have a bad day. But on the good days we had some extra food, which was crucial, especially in winter. But we were in danger because we went into those holes that had incendiary bombs. They would explode.

In Bremen, they sold us as slave laborers to people who were in construction. They paid the Germans, but we didn't get anything. And if we died in the work or were bombed, they would bring more people from Auschwitz. We were dispensable. The only improvement was that occasionally we had access to food from the streets. One day there was a bombed house. I was poorly clad in the same blue dress I described before. Ilus found this little spring coat in one of the bombed basements. It became my winter coat. It was like a raincoat, but not the same material. It had two pockets, a real luxury. You could put your hands in the pockets. When "The Raven" came, I had to take off that coat. She said I had to be cold to work better. I lived in pain. I thought I would come home with a broken back.

One thing we could hope for was to have a good guard after one of the bombardments. There was a little SS guard, a short man. He was uneducated, vulgar. When we were marching to the open trucks, he could not contain himself; he had to kick somebody, to beat somebody, to be violent. He was very nasty. When he came we had a miserable day, a horrible day.

We were working on the streets in this bitter cold with no heat. My fellow prisoners came back with horrible frostbite on their extremities. We were assigned to lift a heavy pipe, really heavy. I speak German and asked the guard if we could get some more people to help. He said, "Oh, I can help you. What's the problem?" He came over and I said, "This is the problem. We need some more people. This is very heavy. We can't lift this." He said, "Oh, if you can't lift it, I'm going to help you. I'm going to count to three. One, two, three. If you don't lift it, I'm going to shoot all of you." I don't know how we did it; we lifted it because we had no choice. I was injured for a year. Naturally we never got rid of pain afterwards, but we knew we were going to die because he meant it. I lived with pain for the rest of the winter. So did every one of us. I thought I had a broken spine—fortunately not—but probably we strained our backs.

In Bremen there was a group of French prisoners who were working on the street next to ours. I don't know what they did. I think that they were political prisoners. These people were absolutely wonderful. There was one who was like an angel. The reason why we survived the winter—we can thank them. I don't know how they had access to some packages.

In Germany they were set for the war. There were two kinds of bunkers. One was a little bunker underground, and there were bunkers that had nine, ten stories. Those were safer than the smaller ones because they were very massively built. If there was a direct hit on the small ones, you perished. If we were working near the railroad station, we were put in the underground bunkers while the guards went to the big bunkers. They locked us in there so if something happened we couldn't get out. One of the Wehrmacht guards who stayed with us in the bunker said, "A bomb is not going to fall where the Jews are." He never wanted to go to the big bunkers because he said that "God protects the Jews." Can you imagine that?

The only place where I saw any medical facilities was in the infirmary in our camp in Bremen. The Germans in the infirmary wore white robes; maybe they were nurses. I think there were two or three of them in there. You could come up from the barracks and walk directly through a hall to this infirmary. It had two parts: one had the drugs, like painkillers or just aspirin. In the other part there were fifteen or twenty regular beds with mattresses which could accommodate the very sick. I can't remember if I saw blankets. You had to be very sick. If you had a strep throat, if you had anything minor, you had to go out to work. If you got scarlet fever or something else, you were finished. They took you to the infirmary and then, if you were there for a long period, they might take you to the gas chambers. Your only defense, your only chance of surviving was being able to work.

Even if we had bloody hands, we didn't get any disinfectants or anything. If you got scratched it was too bad, you lived with the scratch. You didn't get anything. You weren't sick enough. You never were sick enough. You were not given personal treatment or disinfectant. The next day you had to go to work, regardless of what you had. If you were lucky enough and had a good guard, you could put on some rags, take something from your clothes, use something from a bombed-out basement.

Among us, these five hundred women, there were no physicians or nurses. I don't think there were Jews in positions like that in that infirmary because we were taken to Bremen exclusively as slave labor. The only physician I had was in Auschwitz. That was the only physician I encountered through my captivity.

There was a miracle which happened to me on the eve of the Day of Atonement, Yom Kippur, that shows how much medication we got. I got up in the middle of the night with a severe pain in my throat. I knew I had a strep throat because as a youngster I suffered from strep throats very often. I knew I had high fever because I was a little confused. I had to come down from this third bunk, but finally I made it. I was so dizzy that I was hanging on to the wall. I went to the infirmary and asked for a painkiller. They looked at me and said that I wasn't sick enough. I looked horrible, but they threw me out. I wouldn't have minded sleeping on the bed in there because in the morning they would take us out for work. They said that I was not sick enough to get anything. I went back to my bunk, holding to the wall. I thought I was going to die. Finally I got next to my bunk. I couldn't eat my bread, that little piece of stale bread. I soaked my bread with a little soup so that I had some fluid. The next day—it was fall—was a really cold day in the northern part of Germany. I knew if I went out I would probably catch pneumonia.

The next morning the guards came in. In German I said, "I am sick and maybe I can stay in the barracks." They said I was not sick enough *not* to go out to work. I could hardly swallow, but I had to get up, totally dress, and work outside. I thought this was going to be the end of me. I was praying that the Allies would bomb so I could go into the shelter; anything was better than the streets.

On that day there was a bombardment. It lasted forty-five minutes and was the biggest bombardment that I experienced in Bremen. You could hear the whistle of these bombs falling and exploding, and you thought they were right next door. I had no idea. At one point was a huge detonation, and I knew it must have been close by. We had electrical lights in those bunkers, and they went out. They had heavy concrete doors. From this pressure the door was pushed open. The whole bunker was shaking. I remember I closed my eyes and said, "Oh God, if this is the end, please let me die. I don't want to end up in a gas chamber. Let me die on the spot if it's the day to die." Then it stopped. Later we heard the "All Clear" siren telling us the planes had gone, that we could go outside.

When I came out I was horrified. A car now looked like rubble. Houses were burning; people were burning and running out of their houses. It was a total kill. Half of the bunker—there were Russian prisoners in that bunker—all died. One side took a direct hit; the part that I was in stayed intact. Thirty or forty people survived in this one bunker. After that our guard also believed that the Jews are protected.

We worked outside for about forty-five minutes at the site of a bombed pre-serve factory. As I was digging there I found two little jars of jelly. It reminded me of Chanukah. I hid those two jars in my blue dress and in the pocket of the small spring coat. Finally we came back on the truck to the camp. Our camp was leveled. There was rubble everywhere. The infirmary was partly hit. If I had been in there or in the barracks, I would have been dead.

Now comes the other part of the miracle. They had to take us to another camp. During this confusion they were not checking when we entered, so I smuggled in my two little jars. I had to eat the jelly. I could not leave the jars in the barracks. I could not put them in mattresses because I would have been discovered, so I was praying that we wouldn't be checked. I ate all the jelly in the middle of the night. It was so soothing to my throat. When I woke up in the morning my sore throat was totally gone. I can never understand how this happened. I got those two little jars of jelly and my sore throat was cured. I was praying and there was no checking in the morn-ing, so I could discard the jars on the street. That was on the Day of Atonement. Ever since for me it is a sacred day. I go to the temple and say thanks to God that I was saved on that day.

Towards the end of March, 1945, we really looked bad. We lost a great deal of weight and did not look useful anymore. They wanted to take us away and get another transport from Auschwitz for slave labor. We didn't know at that time that we had been sentenced to death in Bergen-Belsen. We never knew where they were taking us—what they would do to us. They just pick you up. Do you know what it means to have to march on foot for thirty kilometers when you are weak, when you are poorly clad, when you don't have that much strength? We wore wooden shoes. We did not have trucks or anything. But it was their policy to get rid of some of us on the road. So whoever was not able to go was shot. Some couldn't go and fell by the wayside.

We had terrible SS guards. Two women were especially cruel; I don't know their names, but we called one "The Raven." When she came it was the Apocalypse. The other one was "The Angel of Death" [Irma Grese]. She was very pretty—blond, blue eyes, nice wavy hair. She was flirting with one of the SS officers there.

We had a stop at one point. It was the only stop we had during thirty kilome-ters. We were put in kind of a cottage—not even a cottage, more like a primitive hut. It didn't have anything in it except the floor. There were several huts, and "The Raven" locked us in. We could not get out. We used our metal containers for food. Since "The Raven" locked us in, we had to urinate and do everything else in these same metal bowls. Even if you had to go terribly, there was no choice. We could not defecate on the floor where we slept. We heard later on that she wanted to put our hut on fire, but somehow she was prevented.

The march continued the next day. I was so tired and weak, but if I stopped or sat down I would be finished. I saw many of my fellow prisoners falling on the wayside get shot because they couldn't go on. I knew that I was going to die. I was so exhausted at one point I felt that I was kind of napping—a sort of trance, but my feet kept moving. It was like somebody behind me kept me erect and moving.

There is a nice story which I read a long time ago. A man dreamt that he was walking with God on the beach and said, "Most of the time when we walked there were two sets of footprints in the sand. But now in the hardest times of my life I only see one set of footprints. Why did you abandon me? Why did you let me down?" And God replied, "No, my child, I didn't. The reason why you see only one footmark here is because on the very hardest times I was carrying you." This is what God was doing with me on the thirty kilometer march. At one point I felt like I was falling asleep, that I was dozing off. Yet my feet were carrying me automatically.

I reached Bergen-Belsen with others who survived the march. Thirty died. It was late at night, pitch dark. Naturally it was wartime; you couldn't make light. When we entered the camp I smelled the terrible stench of decay. I smelled the smell of death in Auschwitz; I recognized it in Bremen, and I knew there were dead bodies here. By now I knew the stench of decaying corpses. There was no doubt about it. I thought they had brought us here to execute us the next morning.

I was at the end of a long column of prisoners, and I could see barracks. I heard screaming from the barracks and wondered what was happening. People were pushed into the barrack, and it was so full that there was no more room. But they were pushing more people in. When it was impossible to push any more people in, the SS guards told the rest of us to lie down and sleep where we were.

I said, "Ilus, something terrible is happening here. I think we are going to be shot—no more place in the barracks." Ilus said, "You know, I can see some tents." She was so resourceful. She said, "Maybe we can go into the tents. Maybe there are people in there." I said, "Ilus, you try it. I don't know what is in that tent." She came out and said, "Magda, do you know what is in those tents? Dead bodies." Now we were sure that they were going to execute us. Ilus watched over me and took care of me.

We slept on the ground that night, and when morning came I saw my fellow prisoners. They looked like walking skeletons. They were in the last stages of starvation, their eyes sunk deep into the sockets. It's like you see the dead walking. What horrified me more was when I saw where we were sleeping. The ground of Bergen-Belsen was littered with corpses in all stages of decay. That was where the stench came from. What were we taken there for? To dig the graves, to dig the pits as long as we could dig them, and to bury the dead.

We were loaded, infested with lice. It was easy in those terrible conditions.

There was typhus raging in the camps, killing thousands; it's called typhus exanthematous and is transmitted by the infected lice. Once lice bite you, your life is in great danger because your resistance is very low. After liberation, thirteen thousand people died of typhus. I was very lucky.

Decaying corpses were piled up in a pyramid shape. Since there was no room for me to sleep in the barracks, I had to sleep next to the pile of dead bodies and look at them all around me. We were collapsing and dying of typhus, and the bodies built up. They were stacked, naked. Who would want to touch those bodies? Nobody touched them except us. We were the ones who had to drag the corpses, dig the graves, and bury the bodies. There were fewer and fewer grave diggers, so the dead bodies were on the ground in all stages of decay, in all colors. This breeds pestilence. Gradually, you would get exhausted from it. No food, just dragging and digging.

At night there was raiding. Some of the Russian prisoners would attack you, pulling your shoes off, even those wooden Dutch shoes. It was a monstrous environment. Not only the corpses. They said beware of the Russians because they were the most aggressive. They tried to strip you of everything that you had. We were always afraid.

There was a girl who had been with me through Auschwitz and was also selected for Bremen. We had worked side-by-side on the streets in Bremen and went together to Bergen-Belsen. We had gone through all this hardship together, and I really liked her. She had a sister who was my friend too. One night, a week or so before liberation, we heard shooting from afar, but we thought that they were shooting us. That's always what we were thinking. It was night and her sister had to go to the latrine. The latrines were out of doors. We said to her, "Don't go. Just do it here." She said, "I can't do that here." We said, "You must do it here." She didn't listen and went to the latrine. We heard a shot and a scream. We knew she was the one. She was shot in the lungs. My friend was absolutely hysterical.

We don't know who shot her. I think it must have been one of the guards. Those guards were very sadistic. We had to bring her body back and throw it on the ground. I still was dragging corpses when this happened. The guards forced her to carry her sister's corpse and throw it up on the pyramid of death. Then she had to sleep next to it and look at her sister. She wanted to scream, but we held her mouth. We were holding her down, "Please, please," because we were afraid if she yelled she would be shot herself. The night before that happened her dead sister said to me, "Magda, I'm not going to see the liberation." I said, "Shut up! How do you know? How can you say such a thing? Some of us will, others will not." She said, "I am going to die before liberation." And she did.

After being in Bergen-Belsen for a week and a half, there was another torture:

the deprivation of fluid and solid food. The little black coffee was not available anymore. Sometimes there was a little soup, and if you got it, someone tried to take it out of your hands. You never ended up with anything. They were attacking you. It was a fight for survival. They reached a stage when they didn't care about anything except trying to live. "If you die it's fine. I want to live; you can die."

After three weeks I was dying. I looked like a skeleton and was afraid to look at myself. I prepared for death. I never thought that I would survive. There was absolutely no caring, no medication. They did not want us to have anything. They wanted us to die. To get rid of us, to bury the dead. If we collapsed, it was fine. If we died of typhus, that was fine too. They didn't care how we died.

I thought there was no way I could escape from there alive, but I had to try. I was desperate. Up to then I had used my judgment. I knew the worst thing I could do was to try to escape. But at this point I said, "I'm going to die. So before I give myself to death, while I can still walk, I'm going to do something. I'm going to try to escape."

I was watching. The only people who had access to the gate were the ones who occasionally brought in the food. Most of the time we ended up with nothing. Then dehydration set in. Dehydration is worse than starvation because it can drive you insane. With dehydration and vitamin deficiency you start getting wounds on your tongue. You start having difficulty swallowing because you are so dry. Going through the torture of dehydration and starvation, you see yourself shrinking to the point that you become a living skeleton. I looked at myself and was scared of myself. Then you have abnormal water retention. Edema, swelling, and when you look at your fellow prisoners, they look like skeletons. You look at the ground, and you see the dead stretched out all over.

So I thought I have to do something. I was so desperate. If only I could pass through the gate; if only I could smuggle myself in with the people who occasionally brought some food. I actually tried to escape Bergen-Belsen twice. I wanted to live. I had lost my perspective. I snuck into a line of Polish women prisoners. But I didn't count on one thing—that at the gates an SS woman would come out and count them. I was number thirteen. There should be only twelve. The others were very scared. The guard asked, "Who is this, the thirteenth here? It doesn't belong here." If no one answered, she might have shot all of us, so I came out. She beat me and kicked me all the way to my camp.

My friends said, "You are crazy. You are going to be beaten to death." I was bruised; nevertheless I said, "What can I lose? I can't stand this anymore. I'm going to try it again." I speak French, so I joined some French prisoners. The Jewish French prisoners were absolutely great people. They said, "We are not going to give you away; we are going to say that you are a part of us." Fate. As we went through the gate, the same SS woman came out and recognized me. She pulled me out and was kicking and hitting me like I had never been beaten in my life. I thought she was going to beat me to death. At least she wasn't hitting my head. I came back and my fellow prisoners said, "Magda, you are crazy." She told me one thing, and I know German: "If I find you again, I will shoot you, I will kill you." And she meant it. So I had to accept it.

In my third week in Bergen-Belsen two SS women came and said, "We are going to take you from the ground into the barracks. It's going to be a lot better." I thought maybe things would get better; at least I wouldn't have to face the dead bodies. That day I was saved by God with the greatest miracle. Miracles happen to me. I have a very strong faith. I was raised with lots of Orthodox Jewish traditions, and I think my faith in God and my prayers were heard. I believe in the power of prayer.

We were marching through the camp, and I could see from afar the barrack where we were supposed to be taken. As we approached, I saw a woman being thrown out of that barrack. She looked like she had been kissed by death: red cheeks, glassy eyes. We were being taken to the typhus barracks, a death sentence. Once you entered the typhus barracks you were certain to be infected. Because we didn't look good anymore, we were put into the typhus barracks to perish with all the others. The barrack was full, so we were pushed in, crushed inside. I looked pretty bad at that time. There was this little SS woman with the comb on the side. As we entered the barrack she looked at me, "You, go up there." It was a third tier and I saw a woman dying of typhus up there. She wanted me to sleep next to that dying woman. It was a certain death. I did not want to die.

This was a huge barrack, holding three hundred prisoners. Desperately I started running from her. I started running down the middle. I defied her. She could have shot me, but I didn't care because I thought I would die for sure. She wanted to chase me, but as more prisoners were pushed in, she was prevented from running after me. I ran straight through the barracks to an open window and jumped out of it. I was hiding. I thought if I'm caught I'm going to be executed. She was trapped in the middle and couldn't do anything to me. My maiden name is Moses, and I felt like the waters split and then the Egyptians came and the water rose and they couldn't do anything. Really, this was a repetition of that. How do you explain these things?

After a while I was as close to death as I could be. It was the end of the third week. I could not stand up anymore. I was lying next to a pyramid of corpses and I was helpless. I weighed about seventy-five pounds; I looked like a living skeleton. At that point I felt that it might be the end of me. I said, "Oh God, I don't know what other miracle can happen. Only you can save me, but what miracle can happen now?" And He did it. I remember that day which I thought was going to be the last day of my life. I think that if you ever were that close to death, you are going to love life, and you are going to live it and be a doer in your life.

Physically I was in apathy. I did not feel hunger anymore. I was so weak that I was prepared to die. I gave up my fight on that day, and I felt very sad. It was April 15, 1945. It was a nice day, I thought, to say good-bye to life. I was thinking back. Like you have a movie in front of you, and you relive your whole life and you see how you acted at one point or another. I said, "Oh God, I want only three things and those are the most important things, the most valuable things that you can have: your life, your freedom, your family. I don't ask for any more. A little food, that's all I want." And I would like to do some things in my life yet, but I said, "If that's the time I have to go, I accept your will. But I have three wishes before I go, and if one of them is fulfilled, I know that the other two might come true too. My number one wish is to embrace life for the last time. I did not see how I was going to do it because I saw death around me. And help me to be buried next to a living thing so I can be a part of it. And then help me to escape my doomed body and let my spirit rise to heaven." I was not afraid of death. I was prepared for the first time to die.

I was very conscious, just very weak. I could not move. I don't know if I could talk, but I was thinking. I had myself. I could see very well. I could hear very well, and I was totally conscious of myself. I could still feel the smell of death. I could feel. We heard shots through the night and thought they were killing other prisoners; maybe some of us were being executed. We didn't know anything about the war or that the liberators were coming.

And then, as I was thinking, suddenly I looked at the birch tree which was very close to me. Since our camp was in a forest, I thought, "Oh God, I want to reach this old birch tree because I see something on it, the first bud, that's life. Please let me embrace this tree and feel life for the last time." I crawled, digging my fingernails into the ground. It seemed like it was an awfully long distance, but it was so close by. When I reached that tree, I embraced it. This tree personified all the life I ever encountered, all the trees in the orchard of my grandparents' yard. I have a love for trees. I said maybe I could be buried next to it, and I could be a part of a root of a tree. I would be just a part of a transformed life.

And then I hoped that my spirit would be liberated because the only freedom I had in that camp was my spiritual freedom. I could think what I wanted. In my imagination I could be everywhere I wanted to be. I could see myself liberated. I could see myself at home. I could see my mother lighting the candles on Shabbat, on Friday night. They can kill you physically, but they can never take away that spirit of freedom. Spiritual freedom has the most value. You change in the course of your life; you go through different stages, but this is something that never ages. It always stays with you; it's always fresh. You have to keep it fresh by doing things, by using your creativity, your imagination. That is something that's going to be there whether you are fifty or sixty or eighty years old.

Then I felt a feeling of peace because finally I accepted death. I even whispered, "Death, come and take me." I was ready. I closed my eyes and was wondering what it is like to die. As I was holding, crushing the tree trunk with my hands, suddenly I heard voices and commotion in the camp. I felt I must be on the other side; I'm dead now and there's another world that I have to face. I was scared because I didn't know what I was going to face. But the commotion looked like it was coming from the camps, and I said that maybe I'm in a delirium; I hear things that are nonexistent. I couldn't believe that I was going to be liberated. I said, "I'm opening my eyes. Whatever I see I have to see."

Then the picture I will never forget. First of all the guards had disappeared from the elevated tower where they kept the machine guns. I thought that maybe they were changing the guards. But then I saw British tanks coming in and heard a loud speaker, "We are the liberators; you are free, you are free." They threw cans of food from those tanks. They were horrified at what they saw. They came into a nightmare. They were in awe. They saw the ground was littered with corpses. They didn't come down from their tanks, but they were throwing food.

I said thanks to God for being liberated. But then I asked if my family made it. I looked at all those people around me—some were dead, some were dying, some were sick—and I felt that many of us were crushed by the unkind hand of fate. I knew one thing, that for them the rewards of victory were too late. I didn't know if I would survive, but I made a vow in that apathetic and weak state that if I do, I'm not going to let all those left behind be forgotten. I was so weak it took me three months to be able to wobble on my feet. But I saw the liberation of Bergen-Belsen.

The people who came after us and could still walk had what seemed to be a revolution. They were breaking into the warehouses. They brought out food, they brought out potatoes and kettles. They were cooking outside. I couldn't eat. That was my luck because many died from too much food. Then our whole camp was quarantined so disease wouldn't spread. They had to clear the corpses from the ground, so they brought in bulldozers to dig mass graves and to push the corpses in. We used the SS complexes for our living quarters.

The British soldiers were wonderful people, yet they were outraged at what they saw. They caught some of the German guards and put them in camps, in concentration camps. The guards had to drag the corpses and do the work that we did. They had to clean their crime, so they got their punishment in that sense. They were dragging corpses, digging the graves, and doing all the things that we had to do.

One of my friends came to tell me an SS guard who had beaten me up in Bergen-Belsen had been captured by the British. At that time I was recovering. She came and said, "You know whom I have seen? The guard who beat you is here, loading the corpses. You can go there now and beat her up. Remember what she did to you?" I was curious to see her. I wanted to look this guard straight in the eye. So I went there, but I could not beat her. God had punished her already. I could not be violent. I could not beat up somebody because I would be just like they were. I personally wouldn't behave like that.

There was another wicked guard, a woman who was hiding in prisoner clothing. She wanted to mingle with us. She was recognized by the prisoners, by the inmates, and was beaten to death by the crowd!

Two British soldiers lifted me up. I joined ten other women in a barrack. I couldn't even talk. When you are in a weak state you don't want to talk. You want to rejoice but are too weak. You don't even know how to really rejoice. You feel like you are dying. I was on a death bed. They didn't ask me any questions when they saw what state I was in.

Even though typhus was raging, I didn't get it. Because I didn't have typhus there was no bed for me. Only those with typhus were given beds. I slept on the floor. We had some sheets and blankets—a few things.

There were only British nurses; no more Germans after that. Everything was done by the British.[14] Immediately they had to delouse and disinfect us because we were littered with lice. There wasn't even enough disinfectant. It took several weeks. I know because I was already walking and still had lice. Always itching and scratching; it was very unpleasant. I was always afraid of typhus. Finally we got some kind of powder to get rid of the lice.

At that time I didn't have the fever. Those who had the fever had very strong symptoms. There's a temporary—I call it madness—with it. Each person is affected differently. There is a delirium, then they hallucinate. One of the girls in my room had that very high fever. The other is that change of moods: uncontrolled laughing, from one mood to the other. But the uncontrolled laughing is like a temporary madness. Two of my friends got it and survived. The third one, the one who was sleeping on the floor, developed this later. Nobody wanted to sleep next to her, and with good reason. I wanted to help her. She was incontinent and in a delirium. At that time I was better. I could walk and I took care of her. I was with this woman for a long time—half a year. She thought that I was her father, a missionary. She was Jewish, but she was telling me that he's a Christian missionary. It was very painful, but she got out of it.

We got packages from the Red Cross and the American Jewish Joint Distribution Committee [AJDC]. The girl I had helped wanted to give me the first package, but I didn't want to accept it. We had everything. We had cookies and canned food, but we never had coffee in those packages. We got fluids: juices and water. We had to eat, but you had to be very careful how much food you ate. People died by overeating. It was dangerous to give somebody a big meal. You couldn't digest it.

I started recovering gradually. When I started to get up and walk, I realized that I was not going to die. I wasn't sure, though, if I was getting typhus belatedly. It was a fear all along because I was exposed to so many people with typhus. I must have had an immunity because one day I felt like I was getting a fever and I didn't feel good, and I thought, "Oh, no. Oh, God, no, I'm getting typhus." But it passed.

The aftereffects of this illness are that your hair falls out. We had public showers and could see that some of the women became half bald. Many envied me because I never had that. My hair grew back. I never had wavy hair, but when my hair grew back, I had beautiful waves. When I went home the waves grew out, but for a while, it was beautiful wavy hair.

You could get extra food by cleaning the rooms specially assigned to some translators. When I was cleaning the room, I had one very trying and sad experience. When I was in Bremen and through Bergen-Belsen, I was with a girl and her mother, which was very special. She was the only one who had her mother with her. They were tremendously close to each other. Both of them were liberated and her mother got typhus. She didn't. I was cleaning the rooms. From the next room, she called me, "Magda, Magda, come, I think some food is caught in my mother's throat." When I came in she was feeding her mother; I could see she was dead. I had to tell her that, and it was just terrible. She had seen death, but she just couldn't believe it. We had British physicians there, and until the physician was called she just didn't believe me.

In Bergen-Belsen's hospital were those who had a chance to survive. They were not quite as bad as these others, and they were lucky enough to get into that accommodation. One of my fellow prisoners was in medical school before; I think she had one year of medical school. She and her sister had been with me through Auschwitz, through Bremen, and through Bergen-Belsen. One of the sisters got typhus and was taken to this hospital. The other one didn't. I did not see the inside of that hospital, but I know it was a two-story building. They said that was the death place. I never entered that one; I don't know how it looked. She had a very tragic end because she was recovering from typhus, but she still had this delirious state; she had fever. It's just like LSD; she visualized that she was flying. She thought she was a bird. She wanted to fly and jumped from the second floor. She was already recovering, but she died. So it was a dangerous unit. There was no guarantee; all of us were vulnerable.

After that I did something that everyone thought, "No, you are crazy." I volunteered for the typhus hospital—to help, and I really risked my life. After three months I didn't get typhus. They said, "You didn't get typhus; you are disinfected now. You don't have to come in contact with people who have typhus and get it from them." I said, "God protected me up until now. For that privilege I had to do something for the others." It was truly my desire to help. I wasn't thinking of myself. Nobody could stop me from doing that.

I worked in the typhus hospital for three months. Each person was in her own bed with linens, pillows, and blankets. There were two British nurses, and they had assistants. They had medication too. I was feeding the sick who were so weak they couldn't feed themselves and giving them comfort—maybe changing their things, maybe carrying the pot [bedpan] after them. I'm glad I did because I heard stories. I was like a rabbi. I closed the eyes of those who died, and I listened to their stories—confessions you make in the last moments of your life. It was terrible for me when they died because they were my fellow prisoners and I felt a great kinship to them. I think God rewarded me for that—helped me find my mom and granted me a new life. I heard secrets that you don't tell anybody, but when you are in the last hour of your life, you want to get them off your chest. I held their hands and comforted them and gave them hope when I knew it was hopeless. I tried to help them die in peace. There was nothing else I could do for them.

After liberation there was sex going on in the camp—in the forest area. Sometimes people found their mates there, and they came home and got married. They were young people, men and women of all ages thrown together. I was not interested. I grew up with certain values. Because of that sometimes some of the women were really nasty: "Oh, you act like an old maid. Here comes the old maid." It hurt me. I didn't like that, but they wanted me to conform.

I was in the camp six months. Then we were repatriated by the AJDC. We were disinfected and got other clothing. I don't know what happened to my blue dress. Probably it was thrown out. I don't think that anybody wanted to use it after I did.

I had to wait for the Hungarian quota. I had very important decisions to make. I could go to Israel, the United States, or Hungary. It was very confusing. But my intuition said to go home and track my relatives. So when my turn came, I decided to go home. We traveled by freight train, some of the same trains that took us to the concentration camps. It increases your suffering when you are in a cattle wagon that you were transported in with your family to the concentration camp. No luxuries. The cattle wagons still had the odor. Primitive accommodations. We had to sleep on the floor. The AJDC was extremely helpful to us. I don't know what we would have done without them. We traveled through German cities in ruins. It looked like a cemetery. I thought, how are they ever going to rebuild this country?

I went home with very little clothing. One thing I saved was my overcoat. The best clothing was my overcoat. I had nothing else, not a penny.

The train stopped in Budapest, which was about two or three hundred miles from my native city of Cluj. We were told that there would be no way to go further until the next morning. The Red Cross and Joint Organization provided us with primitive accommodations for the night. Then, in the afternoon, we had to pick up packages of food from a distribution center. This was all the food they provided for us.

I went with a group to pick up my package. After that I wanted to walk back by myself to gather my thoughts. Deep in thought, I lost my way. I did not know where I was. I went from one side street to another, and then I thought that I would ask directions from the first person who came. As he approached I said, "My God, this face looks familiar." As he came closer I realized that he was our next door neighbor from Cluj. He stopped, and I said, "My God, you are still alive!" The first thing he said was, "Your mother is going to be so happy to see you." I said, "My mother? Did you see my mother?" And he said, "Yes." I asked, "Where did you see her?" He said he came back earlier. His family was wiped out; therefore, he moved to Budapest. "I met your mother on the square in Cluj. I talked to her, and I know where she lives. She's moved." "Do you have the address of my mother?" And he said, "Sure, I have it." I was white as a sheet! I had found my mother. Isn't it a miracle? I had to get lost on a street. The first man I met, the first person to get directions from was my next door neighbor who had my mother's address!

When I came home to Cluj, I looked for my mother's address but was frightened to go there by myself, thinking that he may have been mistaken. I asked another woman who had been repatriated with me to accompany me for moral support.

We came to this big apartment house. There was a gate. You had to ring the bell. "Who is it?" "It's your daughter coming home." She said, "My daughter!" I heard my mother's voice, and I saw a window opening on the second floor. She ran down like crazy. I ran up and we couldn't believe what was happening. I went in. It was a small apartment, one room really. But it was a big room with a little kitchenette in the back. When we wanted to take a bath with warm water, we had one of those old-fashioned sinks—those wooden things.

My mother is a very neat person and is very good in crafts. She has homemade curtains and homemade tablecloths. Everything was homemade. On a chair secondhand clothing and secondhand shoes had been prepared for me when I came home. The neighbors said, "If you wouldn't have come home, we were worried that your mother would break down totally."

When I came home I really had to cope with loss and grief. I had lost my father. I had lost eighty percent of my family. I had frostbite on all my fingers and all my toes from the camps—gangrene, and at that time there was no antibiotic. My mother would fry some onions in the oven, then put them on me. They were supposed to extract pus. That didn't help. I needed treatment for a year on all my fingers and all my toes. After that I had such a sensitivity; when we go skiing my big nightmare is not to get frostbite. I had abnormal retention of water when I came back.

This was due to the starvation that I experienced in Bergen-Belsen when I was dying.

I did get into medical school after I came back from the German concentration camps. We had to study for a big exam. I met my husband at a lecture at the university; he was in his last year of medical school. I told him that I really wanted to go to medical school. We really didn't have any money, and he said I could borrow his books. He said there must have been 900 students for 150 places; I would have to fight if I wanted to get in. He got me some books on anatomy, physiology, biology, chemistry, and physics, and said, "I can give you some tutoring." Two days before the exam, he asked me to marry him. I passed the exam and got into medical school. It was my dream come true.

At that time Rumania was an authoritarian Communist state. It was getting worse, so we decided a year later, in December 1947, to immigrate to Israel. As a result I was unable to complete my medical training. The mass Jewish emigration took place at that time, sixteen thousand people on two cargo ships. Palestine was under British mandate. No free immigration was allowed. Our immigration was organized by the Mosad, the Committee of Illegal Jewish Immigration (Jewish Palestine Underground). Our ships were exiled on the island of Cyprus for a year. There we lived in tents on the seashore. Our camps were surrounded by barbed wire fences guarded by the British. My husband, Dr. Eugene Herzberger, worked as a physician and I as a nurse. In the spring of 1948, the Jewish State of Israel was proclaimed. In February, 1949, we entered Israel. Two weeks after our arrival my son Henry was born, and five years later, my daughter Monica was born. At the end of October, 1957, we, along with my mother, immigrated to the U.S.A., where my husband continued his neurosurgical practice.

After I was liberated from the German concentration camps, I said thanks to God. God had saved me for a purpose. I had made a vow in my very apathetic and weak state that if I survived, I was never going to forget all those left behind. I have to be their spokeswoman. I have to do things for them, not come back and feel sorry about myself. It's important that I keep their memory alive so that they shouldn't have died in vain. I'm not going to let that happen.

Wake up my friend,
Be thankful
That you are alive—[15]

Let's go outside
This room is small
The world is wide.[16]

• • •

"There are moments for all of us when we care quite naturally . . . no ethical effort is required. 'Want' and 'ought' are undistinguishable in such cases."[17]

Our experience with Magda has been and continues to be both rewarding and interesting. She is a lovely and talented lady who continues to call both of us just to see how we are and to express her gratitude for including her memoirs in our book. She had given Roger an interview over the telephone before I went to see her in Dubuque, Iowa. When I arrived, she greeted me cheerfully at the airport and began to speak of her experiences in the camps on the way to my hotel. The next day, as we sat down for her interview, she showed me her home, her books of poetry, her photographs, and every hospitality. After over three hours of taped narrative, during which she frequently changed the subject, we came to the end of her very descriptive oral history. I sent the tapes to Roger, whose secretary transcribed them and returned them to me for review. After I had corrected these transcriptions, I left them in Roger's capable hands for conversion into a narrative. He describes his experience as follows:

> *Magda's interview presented quite a challenge for me, as wishing to cover as much as she could, she often skipped from one subject to another. For this reason, it was difficult to attain a definite chronologic flow. I wanted to be accurate in the narrative, while at the same time doing justice to her many talents. For this reason, I decided to include some of her poetry within the text. Finally, after one month and much work, I sent quite a long manuscript to Diane for editing. After she had honed it down quite a bit and improved the chronologic flow to a degree, she returned it to me for further editing. Several exchanges later we sent it to Magda, who went over our work again with each of us, line by line, until all three of us were satisfied with the result. Magda's account accurately exemplifies her vibrant personality.*

Magda and her husband have recently moved from Dubuque, Iowa, to Arizona.

Liberation

INTO THE VOID

and that place is the lowest and the darkest
and the farthest from the sphere that circles all;
I know the road, and well, you can be sure.

This swamp that breathes with a prodigious stink
lies in a circle round the doleful city
that now we cannot enter without strife

—Dante Alighieri, *Dante's Inferno*

The Allied forces that came into the camps saw walking skeletons suffering from starvation and disease. Corpses lay all over, and the stench carried for miles. What they encountered was a virtual reality of Hell that was almost beyond their ability to comprehend. Because these horrors beggar description, witnesses' memories are best related in their own words. For example, as one young soldier who came into Ordruf on April 4, 1945, wrote to his family:

Dear Folks,

I am going to try in this letter to describe to you a little of what we saw this morning. . . . In the courtyard you are greeted by the awful smell of dead humans . . . on down the line there is a building piled half full of naked bodies . . . stacked just like cordwood . . . the place has a dirt aisle . . . patted hard as a rock by the bare feet of the people . . . along the sides are stretched burlap bags . . . a good couple hundred of them. . . . On each there is a bowl like a dog eats out of . . . you can see the marks of the tongues where these people cleaned out every bit of food.

I see by the home papers about the treatment of the Kraut P.O.W.s in the States and how important it was not to do them any harm. Sometimes I wonder.
Your Son,
Stan[1]

Irving Heymont, an army officer, wrote to his family regarding his view of Landsberg:

The camp is filthy beyond description. Sanitation is virtually unknown. Words fail me when I try to think of an adequate description. . . . With a few exceptions, the people of the camp themselves appear to be demoralized beyond hope of rehabilitation. They appear to be beaten both spiritually and physically, with no hopes or incentives for the future."[2]

And Marie Ellifritz, a young army nurse, recalls twenty-seven years later:

I cannot believe what I am seeing. My mind does not want to absorb the reality of my eyes. The nurses are hearing rumors from the medical personnel—Are the bodies really stacked 4 across and 4 feet high? Nazi genocide, a most terrifying network of slave labor and death camps, was almost more than I could envision or realize.[3]

Nevertheless, these Allied forces left doctors and nurses to care for the sick as best they could. Despite the condition they were in, these pitiful survivors, if they did not die immediately after liberation—which they often did because they could not tolerate the food they were given—slowly began to be rehabilitated.

Just as there had been female prisoners who, as physicians and nurses, had rendered care to one another while incarcerated, there were female nurses in the army who treated the liberated prisoners. One such nurse was Marie Ellifritz, who recounts her experiences in Mauthausen.

Chapter Thirteen

Marie Ellifritz

"MY SORROW IS CONTINUOUSLY BEFORE ME"

•   •   •

"Marie Knowles Ellifritz may be one of the few people who was obligated to visit the perimeters of hell, and yet, chose thirty-two years later to return and allow the ghosts of man's inhumanity to man to re-enter her consciousness.

"That is not to say that they ever truly leave, but as a registered nurse, she has had to learn control to separate that which can be avoided from that which must be faced.

"She acknowledges that death is a natural order of life, when it is in its natural order—age or disease. But when inhumanely caused by external agents, it ceases to be understandable or acceptable.

"Her story began in May, 1945, when she was a member of the 130th Evacuation Hospital assigned to care for the victims of Mauthausen Concentration Camp in Austria. Theoretically it ended, or more exactly reemerged, in December of 1977 when she returned to Mauthausen."[1]

In her interview at the Liberators' Conference in Washington, D.C., Mrs. Ellifritz related the information contained in the following paragraphs.[2]

I had trained during the war at a small private hospital in Newport News, Virginia. I was twenty-two years old when our unit liberated Mauthausen. By that time we knew about the existence of concentration camps, but Mauthausen was the only camp which our personnel were involved in. One of those places was enough. We were simply put in trucks, because evacuation hospitals moved from place to place, and told we were going to a liberated concentration camp. They did use that term. I do not remember the date, but it was in the spring of 1945. I was a registered nurse, attached to the 130th Evacuation Hospital Unit. Our unit included 205 enlisted men, thirty officers and administrative personnel, and forty nurses. . . . Because it was wartime, we were used to working twelve hour shifts, so the twelve hours didn't really bother me. It was the extra time you had to take.

In an evacuation unit, you simply arrive and pitch what we called a "tent city." Evacuation hospitals in those days lived out of tents. You slept in tents; you took your bath in your steel helmet, and bathroom facilities were dug for you. The trucks took us to a large wheat field in once-beautiful Austria. We were fairly close to the Black Forest, so guards were placed around the nurses' tents in case any of the people who had gone up into the Black Forest might come down and not know whether we were friend or foe. The nurses did warrant protection from that.

We arrived under the afternoon sun, dismounted and were told to pitch the hospital and the tents and patients would be brought to us. They would be sick, but we had no idea of the condition they were in and were very ill-prepared for the types of patients we were asked to care for. The term "survivor" or "inmate" was not used.

I couldn't say whether or not the number of men and women was equally divided; there were plenty of men in Mauthausen. We had something like 6000 Russian prisoners and 4000 French that had been incarcerated there, although a large percentage of the prisoners were Jewish. We had no knowledge of the Holocaust, no publicity that concerned the Jews, although there was a rumor that there were some. But it was nothing like the extent of what we found when we finally arrived.

There were Germans around soon after we arrived because we needed extra medical help. We took 1400 patients into a four hundred bed hospital, so the hospital itself had to be elasticized to accommodate that number of patients. "[T]he first couple of days in the camp were spent preparing for the survivors. 'And then they came—stinking, bewildered, staggering, naked human beings. They were almost like animals, without fur.

"'Cast aside by all involved . . . was concern for [our] own physical and emotional well-being. Some of us did get sick from the dysentery that the patients had . . . from the TB exposure—from the emotional trauma—but most of all it was from the sickness of the heart—of being a witness. . . .'"[3]

Because evacuation hospitals are used for American fighting troops, and we could have moved out at any given moment from a concentration camp back into the combat field, we were only allowed to use the German medical supplies we had captured on the concentration camp victims and were, therefore, very limited. We had plenty of x-ray; however, after the first three days, we stopped x-raying, mostly because ninety percent of the patients did have TB and because they were too weak to transport. To do this to them was one more thing they did not need at that time.

The patients were gaunt, very emaciated. "Clinically, it was a matter of sorting the dead from the living, deciding who would live for at least three days or more and to make all those we found comfortable and begin the process of treatment. A tent to keep the patient dry, an air mattress to give them a sense of dignity, a small amount of food to nourish them and plasma to preserve the remaining life and begin them on the road back to living . . ." (p. 75).

From a psychological viewpoint, I think the survivors suffered so much from the apathy and the horror they had been through. I like to think of man's eyes as being a reflection of his soul, and we wondered, when we looked into their eyes, if they really had a soul because their eyes were dead to the living. They would stare off at given times into untold space. Psychologically they had departed from us; it was a reaction over which they had no control. They had vitamin deficiencies; they had beriberi; they had typhus and TB. They had many diseases that Americans wouldn't survive.

When we tried to administer to them, some trusted us immediately. They were glad that the liberators had come; they knew that life would now have some meaning and that they could go away from this place. Others weren't sure. It would take two or three days to convince them that we were Americans and that they had been liberated and were free.

They had refused to die as prisoners and wanted to die in freedom. So after three days, when we had convinced them of who we were, why we were there, and that arrangements had been made for them to leave the camp, some of them simply lay down and died. Thus, "even for the patients who knew they would be dead in a few hours or days, liberation in May of 1945 was a joyous time—a time they were free of Nazism . . . a time of breathing fresh air outside the confining walls of the camp—a time of sharing with the American liberators the joy of sudden freedom" (p. 75).

My reaction to these patients was quite different from the way I reacted to patients on the battlefield. In the first place, there was the language barrier. In the second place, they were not the type of patients we were used to nursing. They suffered from different diseases and for different reasons than other patients, and each one of us nurses reacted differently. "I had to tell myself over and over again that these were human beings encased in what was left of a human body bringing with them only their faith in God and the storehouse of their brains" (p. 75).

Other patients had come to me in a hospital environment. Our own liberated prisoners at Moosberg, Germany, who were Air Force prisoners, who had also been in a camp for five years, came to us, and we were familiar with them.[4] They spoke our language. . . .

I was lucky that I had a Taber's dictionary that I was given in nurses' training. The back of the book was written in five languages, so I could read symptoms in the different languages. I sat down the first day and circled questions about diseases that I thought most of the patients would suffer from. I simply took the book with me, and when I wanted to ask the patient if he had diarrhea, I pointed to the word, and he had five languages to choose from. When he pointed to the answer, I looked at the English and knew what his problem was. It took a long time communicating with them because I don't speak any language other than "Americanese," and most of the patients didn't speak English.

There were many children in the camp. A little boy befriended me. I don't know his name. He called me "Sistra," I called him "Junior"—a good GI name that we gave to almost any child. When I transferred from the tent city into the larger hospital, which was down in the main camp, the permanent building, Junior would come down on the picket fence every morning when I went to work and wave me off to work and every night when I came home. I just thought that it was nice that he would see me off and come home with me. Twenty-two-year-old girls aren't really that clued into motherhood, and at that time, he was just a nice little kid who happened to be one of my patients.

One day I came home and Junior wasn't there. I asked, and they said that a lot of patients that day had been transferred to the displaced persons' camp, which was about thirty miles from us. However, the chaplain went up . . . a couple times a week, and Junior did send a message for me to come to see him. But I didn't go.

When I came out of the camp and began to look at my Christianity, I'm afraid I turned away from it because your God is my God, and I could not believe in that God. It took me many years, and the good Lord knocked my feet out from under me. My husband was killed in Korea twelve days before the truce. I lost my brother that year; I lost my husband's best friend that year; I got a body home from Korea that year, and I got his personal effects. I consider myself a survivor—not of a concentration camp, but of life.

"Liberators!" (p. 75) continues:

"[I]n December, 1977, upon her return [to Mauthausen], she once again tried to describe the incomprehensible which must lie just beyond the limits of the human vocabulary.

" 'As the train lumbered along from Vienna towards Linz, Austria, I wondered if I had made the right decision. Several people told me . . . that perhaps the emotional trauma I would subject myself to would not be worth it. But, then, those people had not been there 32 years ago. There was no way of telling them that it had been hell then and now perhaps I would find solace for my troubled conscience, troubled for I never understood how my world had let it happen.'

"In 1977 the walls of the camp were as she remembered them. The one difference then was the quiet. 'No Russian prisoners burning their barracks, no celebrations of Polish weddings, no moaning that goes with suffering, no gaunt, haunting faces searching for compassion. . . .'

"October 27, 1981, Ellifritz, R.N., as a member of a medical panel on the Holocaust for the U.S. State Department, had another time to express her feelings

Marie Ellifritz and "Junior" at right in 1945. From Reba Karp, "Liberators! A Nurse's Story," Renewal Magazine, *March 29, 1995, United Jewish Federation of Tidewater.*

as an American woman and nurse who had to deal with the full gamut of emotions.

"'The emotional trauma . . . was beyond belief—as Americans and as women never before had been subjected to such inhumanity. . . .'

"Other memories surfaced during that presentation. Pride at being an American and part of the liberation, and as such winning the immediate trust of many of the survivors. For others, it took the rest of their lives for them to accept their freedom, for in reality many died within a few days of entering the camp. . . .

"Now it is 1985, forty years since the twenty-three-year-old Second Lieutenant in the U.S. Army Nurse Corps stepped into the perimeter of hell and dared to look over the barrier through the eyes of her patients. But even as her memories are filled with the sharp blacks and greys of suffering, she sees the blue summer flowers gathered from the wheat fields which bordered the evacuation hospital. She terms it 'love at first sight' as she reaches for words to convey the tenderness of her association with a ten or twelve-year-old Jewish boy who called her 'Sistra.'

"He brought her flowers and helped her keep fragile sanity. They did not speak the same language, 'but the looks and deeds for a child are universally understood. His gentle offerings were a response to casual American friendliness. He never knew the years of stirring memory those small deeds would cause. . . .' Today, looking back from the vantage point of a mother, she realized his 'goodness, his kindness, his gentleness reflected, not the five years in a concentration camp, but rather in his mother's love and . . . teaching before she was put to death in a gas chamber.'

"And so a friendship out of mutual need developed—his for the surrogate mother he had lost, and hers for a bit of gentleness in a world that reflected the brutal side of man's nature. 'I promised myself that I would visit Junior—tomorrow. My tomorrow somehow became the hurried yesterdays of life.'

"Today that promise [to visit him] is a whiplash which still stirs within her. 'Was I too tired, too busy or too young and immature that I did not go?' she questions. 'I have looked for him for thirty-six years, and that guilt has lived with me all these years.'

"Today she has a photograph that is forty years old and shows her as a young woman between two camp survivors. One of them is Junior.

"'The photograph will brown with age, and the wonderful but sad memories . . . will fade, along with the horror of dying war victims. But my love for Junior lives on.'"

The Survivor's Purgatory

*I stood up straight to walk the way man should,
but, though my body was erect, my thoughts
were bowed and shrunken to humility.*

—Dante Alighieri,
The Divine Comedy

In addition to the horrible memories many, indeed most, of the survivors live with a sense of guilt. As for caregivers in the camps, Elie Cohen cannot escape the feeling that in some way he "did the Germans' job for them." As a physician in Westerbork, he was allowed to live in a barrack with his wife, had a red stamp on his identity card that exempted him from transport to the East, and examined incoming prisoners, having the power to declare them "unfit for transport." Nevertheless, because he often faked the diagnoses, he was warned that if this continued, he would be put on the next transport. Because of this, he bowed to authority. As he states, "I gave in to pressure and became the victim of my own selfishness."[1]

The memories of those brave women who resisted by doing what they could to alleviate the suffering of their sisters in sorrow have never left them. Neither has the pain. Of the horrible memories she retains regarding the deaths of so many that she could do nothing to prevent, Olga Lengyel states that she too yearns "for sunshine and peace and happiness. But it is not easy to erase the memories of Gehenna when the roots of life have been destroyed and one has nothing to go back to."[2] Nevertheless, frequently survivors feel that in relating their experiences, they not only offer a memorial to those who did not survive but carry out a mandate given them to be sure the world never forgets. Indeed, as Maria Rosenbloom comments, "More than death, they feared that the world would never know what they were enduring. . . . For some, the need to record and witness was as elemental as hunger. . . ."[3] Regarding this need to bear witness, Dr. Hadassah Rosensaft states: "There was no meaning to the Holocaust: it was horrible and pointless; but if you want to look for something positive that can come out of it, and you must, then it is for us who went through it to talk about it as a warning, a dire warning, of what happens when indifference is taken to the extreme that it was in the Thirties; and then the only positive effect of the Holocaust will be that the world learns from it."[4]

By relating their experiences, survivors do what they can to rebel against the Germans under whose authority they suffered and so many millions died. These feelings are beautifully but sorrowfully expressed in the following article by and about a female physician, Dr. Zina S., which appeared in *Le Monde*.[5]

Chapter Fourteen

Zina S.

REBEL THROUGH RECOLLECTION

• • •

"How could you express in a news article the fear and anguish that we felt? Sometimes, in Auschwitz, I thought: 'why doesn't my heart stop and explode?'"

Probably because it was necessary for her to hang on, to tell us the reason for this anguish: the careful dealing with her horror.

Zina S. is seventy-six years old and still has beautiful blond hair. In her comfortable living room, everything looks well prepared for a happy retirement: quiet and calm, the city vibrating a little farther out, but not threatening. On the piano, some classical music books, most of them in German. Beautiful furniture, a beautiful expression on this face which has maintained its beauty and does not reveal her age. Holding up like an aristocrat with precise and pure language. A modest story teller: "Don't tell my name, I don't want notoriety."

She can talk about Josef Mengele. She knew him and had to work for him. She followed the recent sad and macabre hunt for him, but with more reason than many others. Quietly she says: "I don't think it is he we found; as he saw the net drawing tighter, he may have set up this operation. However this is only my impression." Dead or alive, who cares. For Zina S., Dr. Mengele is still alive in her memory. Forty years did not change anything; his sinister presence will only disappear when she passes away.

The life of Zina S. followed this century's hellish route. While some may feel glorified by an established ancestry, her destiny is to live under the chaos of history. Jewish, of Russian origin, she was born in Lodz, Poland, when her country was under Russian occupation. Before World War I, her father, a manufacturer, emigrated west and moved to London with his family. She went to the London French School which had been created for Belgian refugees. She graduated from high school and then went to Paris to enter medical school. Jewish, born in Poland, Russian, a British citizen, she would become a French doctor. It was to be an extraordinary melting pot for creating the intelligence and character which would help her to bear what was to come.

After marrying a doctor, she moved with him to Correze, France, in 1940. Jewish doctors were victims of anti-Jewish movements and subject to *numerous clausus* (limited numbers). The welcoming committee of her peers was rather awkward. When, after the accidental death of her husband in 1941, Zina wanted to take over his practice in a rural town, the representative of the Medical Association raised his arm and shouted: "But we never had a woman doctor around here!" This was the obvious answer; the underlying concern was that she was Jewish. Despite that, she opened her practice. The village was split: There was another French family doctor, a *real* Frenchman. Over the next few months, patients were split between the two doctors for dubious reasons: The supporters of the Resistance went to her; those supporting Collaboration, those accepting German occupation, chose the other. As she attended to people from the Resistance, he [the other doctor] quietly waited for his opportunity to turn her in.

During the spring of 1944, the German army was to halt this unstable situation. They invaded the town of Correze as well as the rural areas. Zina felt the threat; she was not to sleep during her last night of freedom: "I had a lot of problems: A difficult delivery which lasted forever and the daughter of a member of the Resistance with appendicitis." Sure they were problems, but rather insignificant compared to what followed.

Doctor Mengele

Early one morning the German army arrived. An officer had a complete list of the local Jews, supplied by the other doctor. Zina was arrested and questioned briefly: "You know, I was a female doctor and blond! We felt like we were in a social club." She spent the night in the Treignac jail, during which time she learned that all the men who were arrested with her had been shot. Afterwards she was taken to Limoges, Paris, and Drancy. There she met a doctor from Marseilles who was weeping, "What bothers me is that I do not have my reflex hammer." "Later in Auschwitz," says Zina, "I always remembered that silly story of the reflex hammer."

At the end of April, 1944, the convoy was deported east to Auschwitz. After several days, the doors were brutally opened: "Screams, crowds, and hysteria." Mengele led the welcoming committee. "He was doing the selection right there on the platform with another doctor. He was impeccably dressed, as usual. I think he had white gloves. With his stick, he was showing the deported who passed in front of him which way they should go. On one side, the healthy, on the other the tired, the elderly, and the children. I told him that I was a doctor. He put me aside with a group of young women."

At the women's camp, the newcomers were worried about the members of the convoy. Some deported said, "What, you just arrived? We have been here for two years and you are complaining? Your families? They are burning." It was brutal but accurate. In Zina's convoy there were one thousand people. Only thirty-seven would make it back from the camps.

After three weeks, Zina was sent to the women's hospital as the head doctor. Mengele had divided them into specialized blocks: Germans, Polish, Russians, recovering patients, surgery, infectious diseases, Jewish, etc. She would spend eight months trying to practice medicine in a world in which logic was not survival. Mengele oversaw everything: "He would come to our block every day. Two prisoners watched the door. When he was announced, the floor had to be mopped. His visit was a true parade, very theatrical. He was escorted by many people. One of them, a prisoner, was Ella. She was a Slovak Jew, pretty and always well dressed. Some said she was his mistress. They joked together. He was not taking care of the patients at all. I never saw him perform any medical tasks. At the foot of the beds—without sheets, shared by two patients—we were to write the diagnosis and treatment. At the beginning I wrote those in French. Mengele went into a rage and requested that I write it in Latin. I did, inventing Latin words. Diagnoses had no value since we refrained from indicating any serious diseases which would send them to their deaths, such as tuberculosis, diabetes, etc. As for treatment, we did not have any medication!" Followed by his courtiers—half a dozen—Mengele contemplated his kingdom with pride. This M.D., Ph.D. had his principles: one day he became angry at some deported doctors who had used suction cups on the patients: "It is a barbaric treatment," he shouted.

Hygiene

Sometimes Mengele came to select—based on the quotas which were given to him—tens, hundreds of patients for the gas chambers. The "blockowas" (prisoners who were heads of blocks) shut all the exits. All the female patients, naked, emaciated, shaved, would walk in front of Mengele—always very elegant—who "inspected them like cattle." His secretary took note of the numbers tattooed on the arms of the ones selected, and then he would leave. Shortly thereafter, a commando of deported men came to take the women selected. "They were extremely brutal. With hooks, they would grab the ones hiding under their beds. They thought they would benefit from this attitude. They did not know that they would also end up in the gas chamber and that they would be replaced by others."

The last sight that Zina had of Mengele, at the beginning of 1945, was shortly before the camp was evacuated, and it demonstrated his cynicism. She was in a cell that she shared with a German female doctor. They slept there, but only Zina would eat the little food she was given there. Mengele, looking at a food bowl lying on the floor, said to Zina: "You eat in here," and then, turning to the German, said, "Those French people have no hygiene!"

Outside you could see carts full of bodies, with legs and arms hanging out. "I don't know why," said Zina, "but there was always a head hanging out of the cart which would get hit at each turn of the wheel." Hygiene. . . .

Transferred to Ravensbruck, she saw Berlin in ruins in the moonlight. "There is nothing to be proud of, but I have to tell you that when I saw that, I felt good and thought it wasn't even enough." At this time she weighed sixty pounds.

For forty years Zina has never returned to Germany. "I am not against reconciliation, but I would rather leave it to others. What shocks me the most is that Mengele could live like that for forty years, as if nothing had ever happened." Sometimes during her lonely walks in Paris, Zina walks by the Deportation Memorial to pray. "I don't know how to rebel any other way but by remembering." She rebels.

Chapter Fifteen

Conclusion

BEYOND THE PARADOX

• • •

The sounds of sighs of untormented grief burdening these groups, diverse and teeming,
made up of men and women and of infants

—Dante Alighieri, *Dante's Inferno*

According to Elie Cohen,[1] there were three stages of prisoners' adaptions to the concentration camp. "The first was what he terms 'The stage of initial reaction,' during which the prisoner developed a conception as to what would happen to him or her. If there was a sense of 'acute depersonalization,' the prisoner developed what Le Coultre describes as a 'triad of estrangement from one's ego, . . . one's body, . . . and one's surroundings.'"[2] Cohen goes on to say that this reaction was limited to those who seemed to be aware of what to expect in the concentration camp and were prepared for what was to happen; therefore, it was limited to a small group of new arrivals. Although the majority went through what he terms "an *acute fright reaction*" when faced with the realization of what awaited them,[3] most had only a vague notion of the reality of concentration camp life.

The second stage was "the stage of adaptation." During this period the prisoner's ability to adapt was severely tested and was often the deciding factor as to the prisoner's survival or death. During this time the prisoner was forced to adapt to the difficult working hours and labor to which he or she was subjected; the nauseating camp soup, bread, and ersatz coffee; the horrible sleeping conditions; and the poor hygiene.[4]

Because of the difficult conditions, most prisoners became irritable due to constant hunger, loss of sleep, and the omnipresence of death. There was a loss of identity that resulted in a lowered self-esteem. For those prisoners who did not give in to feelings of depression and suicide, nothing became as important as preserving one's own life. As a result, many underwent a loss of compassion for others. Nonetheless, Cohen stresses, just as many survivors have stated that those factors which most determined survival were beyond the prisoner's control. These included "luck, fate, [and] accident . . . which often caused the prisoner's life to take an unexpected turn."[5] Nevertheless, Viktor Frankl maintains that despite the loss of values that was often the norm, given the circumstances in which prisoners found themselves, some prisoners, even though subjected to these conditions, were able to preserve "a vestige of spiritual freedom, of independence of mind," thereby enabling them to "retain some sense of dignity."[6]

The third stage was "the stage of resignation." During this time the prisoner turned "from nobody into somebody." Able by now to attain sufficient food, better clothing, and easier labor, he or she had achieved some success in the constant struggle for existence, although one's survival was never assured in the concentration camp.[7] Depending on the needs of the SS, physicians and nurses were most likely to fall into this category.

Frankl maintains that one of the psychological weapons many survivors developed was the use of humor. Of this he states, "It is well known that humor, more than anything else in the human makeup, can afford an aloofness in an ability to rise above any situation, even if only for a few seconds. . . . to see things in a humorous light is some kind of trick learned while mastering the art of living . . . even in a concentration camp, although suffering is omnipresent."[8]

During their imprisonment, women were subjected to indignities peculiar to their gender, such as the ugliness they felt because of their shaven heads and the lack of femininity due to cessation of menses, although if they did menstruate there was nothing to absorb the menstrual blood and no way to cleanse themselves. Many who were forced to undergo involuntary sterilization still suffer because they were never able to create new life. Most could not even control what became of their own bodies due to constant danger of rape or other sexual, physical, and verbal abuse. Regarding women's conditions in the camps Ella Lingens-Reiner states: "The women prisoners would work the whole day, stand in the pouring rain for two hours or more during roll call, and go to bed in sweaty, wet clothes, to wake the next morning at five, chilled to the bone and forced to get on to their tired feet."[9]

Despite these factors, some of these prisoners were able to rise above their horrendous circumstances and devote what was left of themselves to the care of those with whom they suffered. In places where death seemed inevitable, and at times the only relief from pain and sorrow, there were many who remained dedicated to the preservation of life. When fear seemed to be the only reality, there were women who rebelled against it, and in so doing they restored to themselves and others a sense of self as well as a feeling of purpose. In not allowing themselves to give in to despair, these women, working under conditions which defy comprehension, with few supplies and meager rations, helped others to defy the reason for their incarceration: to serve as slaves until they were to be exterminated. And despite the memories of what they had undergone, each of the women in this book has risen above her personal nightmares. Each, in her own way, defied the system that sought to extinguish her people and has become a contributing member of society. Among the factors that link these women with many other survivors of the labor and death camps is a combination of the right set of circumstances and a great deal of personal courage. Each in her own way withstood the common enemies of disease, starvation, and terrors of the Nazi system. Nonetheless, none of them will deny that in every case survival depended upon the time they came into the camp, the whims of the SS personnel who greeted them, the help and advice they received from others, and/or any professional training they may have had before they were transported. As Hana Bruml succinctly stated, "It was fate. Just fate."

In addition to surviving through the right set of circumstances, some of these women survived because of their ability to "organize" food and supplies, while others had the nerve to step forth for transports out of Birkenau despite warnings never to volunteer. Some had the fortitude to stand up to the SS physicians and other personnel, while others had the courage to hide their fellow prisoners when their health was so frail that selection for death would have been inevitable. A few were willing and able to suffocate newborn infants in order to save the lives of the mothers when it was a choice between one or both going to the gas chamber. Most important, however, was the fact that they were often able to bond with one another, giving each other strength and the ability to withstand their common suffering.

Although physicians did their best to adhere to the tenets of the Hippocratic Oath, many, as mentioned above, were forced to contradict aspects of the physician's creed in order to preserve life. For nurses, however, patient care, even under the worst circumstances, was and is "a process that incorporates the elements of soul, mind, and imagination. Its very essence lies in . . . [a] sensitive spirit, and . . . intelligent understanding. . . ."[10] By and large, the personalities of those who rendered nursing care in the camps were comprised of these elements, as is evident in their efforts to attend to the needs of those who suffered. Furthermore, regarding nurses' responsibilities, one of the tenets of the International Code of Nursing Ethics, which was adapted by the International Council of Nurses in 1953, states that every nurse has a threefold obligation: "to conserve life, to alleviate suffering, and to promote health."[11] Even though this code had not yet been written, all of the women whose narratives we have related tried as best they could to adhere to these very responsibilities.

Carol Gilligan maintains that "Woman's place in man's life cycle has been that of nurturer, caretaker, and helpmate, the weaver of those networks of relationships on which she in turn relies."[12] These women, when imprisoned in the camps as well as after liberation, exhibited this nurturant behavior, and the majority went on to become helpmates in marriages and caretakers of their husbands and children. Indeed, when Dr. Rosensaft was asked if she continued to practice as a dentist, she replied, "No. I just wanted to be a good wife and mother."[13] Only a few continued in or went into the caring professions after liberation, and even fewer were officially recognized for their heroic actions.

Although while alive she never revealed what she had done for others in the camps, Dr. Ellen Loeb conducted research to find a cure for leukemia. Recognized for her contributions to medicine, she became the DAR Americanism Recipient for her "outstanding achievements in America, her adopted country" on April 5, 1968.[14] Ironically, in 1972, a generation after the Holocaust, Dr. Loeb was invited to speak to those who were currently conducting medical research at the Bayer Pharmaceutical Company in Wuppertal, Germany. As she addressed her distinguished audience, Dr. Loeb looked across from the lectern through the large windows facing her. Directly in her line of vision was the house in which her father had once practiced medicine.

Dr. Hadassah Rosensaft has perhaps been given the greatest amount of personal recognition for her lifesaving efforts during and immediately after the war. On the wall in her home is a recent picture around which each of the former children whose lives she saved expressed his or her best wishes. In addition there are plaques from the former mayor of Jerusalem, Teddy Kollek, and former president of Israel, Chaim Weitzmann. She has been recognized by Presidents Carter, Reagan, Bush, and Clinton and was awarded an honorary doctorate in humane letters by the Hebrew Union College, Jewish Institute of Religion, City of New York, on May 25, 1995, which reads:

> *Inspiring example of a woman governed by love and conscience, a woman of noble spirit, who in a life rich with service, gloriously fulfills the role of Ashat Cha'il [a noble woman], who has borne testimony with elegance in the nightmare of the Shoah, whose combination of courage, mirrored by her personal commitment and moral passion helped to sustain the lives of children in the darkest of Jewish history, who as a source of light, delivered the future to Israel and rejoiced that "her children had at last come home."*

Whether publicly recognized or not, all of the women about whom we have written, as well as many others whose efforts we were not able to include in this volume, helped others to survive. Each, in her own way, was a source of light and life to those for whom she cared. Despite a political system which sought to extinguish her generation through sterilization and murder, each has played an important role in helping others to live and to beget a new and healthy generation. In this way, each, in her own way, has contributed to the survival of the Jewish people.

Appendix A

Women Prisoners at KL Mauthausen

•   •   •

Record of Convoys to Lenzing

According to the entrance registration, 3,077 women and 176 children passed through KL Mauthausen in 9 arrivals, in regular intervals from the 15 of September 1944 to the 15 of April 1945.

- 1st convoy: Arrival: 15.9.1944—Numbers 1 to 59

38 were identifiable as Jehovah's Witnesses: Dutch, Czech, Polish, German, and Belgian

These 38 persons were ferreted from the direction of St. Lambrechts and Mittersill.

17 Germans and 3 Polish AZR (*Arbeitswang Reich work forces*) stayed at the camp.

1 German AZR transferred from Ravensbruck the 4.10.1944

- 2nd convoy: Arrival: 28.9.1944. Numbers 60 to 459

400 women ages in total of 18 to almost 30 years. Nationality: Russian (198), Italian (104), Polish (83 + 7 AZR), Croatians (2), and 1 Hungarian

The convoy seemed to have been directed through Hirtenberg.

During the entire time there was one successful massive escape from that place on 16.4.1945

Elsewhere 7 women helped to discover them out in an attempted escape on 10.4.1945

The commando at Mauthausen and a group of women occupying the "prominent" positions were permitted to leave for France and Belgium on 22.4.1945, leaving a vacancy on the 23 and 24.4.1945

- 3rd convoy: Arrival: 3.11.44. Came from K.L. Auschwitz—Numbers 460 to 959

They were composed of Hungarian Jews (321), Czechs (56), Slovaks (31), Polish (43), German (34), Dutch (12), stateless (2), and one Yugoslavian, aged from months to 50 years with the majority 18 to 30 years.

According to the second page of the register, the convoy was directed to the commando of Lenzing (manufacturing cartridges)?

Observation: 2 persons were transferred from K.L. to Bergen-Belsen on 17.3.1945.

• 4th convoy: Arrival: 27.11.44—Numbers 960 to 970

Coming from Auschwitz: 2 Hungarian Jews and 1 Slovak

Coming from Ravensbruck: 7 Polish *Schutzhaft* (detained for security) and 1 German.

Observation: One Polish *Schutzhaft* was hanged on 29.4.1945, one Polish *Schutzhaft* escaped from Hirtenberg the 16.4.1945, 2 Hungarian Jews and 1 Polish *Schutzhaft* filled the "prominent" positions of the Belgians and French on the 23 and 24.3.1945.

• 5th convoy: Arrival: 27.1.1945 Numbers 971 to 1048

Coming from Auschwitz, the convoy was composed of: 38 Russians, 4 Germans, 3 Poles, 2 Czechs, 1 French, and 1 Lithuanian. In this were 19 Jewish Poles, 4 Jewish Yugoslavians, and 1 Jewish Belgian.

With one exception, nearly the whole convoy was directed to the commando at Lenzing the day before—either early arrival or late registration???[*sic*]

4 Russian prisoners had escaped the 17.4.1945.

• 6th convoy: 28.2.1945 Number 1049—place of origin not indicated.

1 French remained at Mauthausen

• 7th convoy: Arrival: 28.2.1945 Numbers 1050–1052. Came from K.L. Auschwitz: 3 German AZR

• 8th convoy: Arrived 7 March 1945. They came from K.L. Ravensbruck

a) their group: Numbers 1053 to 1153

101 women who only wore a number and 174 children of both sexes (2 died at Mauthausen); they were directed to K.L. Bergen-Belsen the 17.3.1945

It was: 7 Hungarian

69 German

146 German Gypsies

53 Hungarian Gypsies

b) 2nd group: Numbers 1154 to 2856, it was 1,703 prisoners, (seen from far off).

• 9th convoy: Arrival: 15.4.1945 Numbers 2,857 to 3,077 or 221

Camp of origin: K.L. Mittelbau

2 Hungarian + 184 Hungarian Jews

33 Polish Jews

1 Jewish Belgian and 1 German Jew

According to Julie Delwiche *epse* Jean Hoffman *(nom de guerre: Paule)* that convoy had
been directed to the horse stable of Mauthausen. The majority were aged 17 to
30 years. 42 of those prisoners were discovered on 23.4.1945, pretending to be
in the interior commandos of the camp at Mauthausen, after the departure of
the western European prisoners (the majority were French and Belgian)

The number from the second group to the 8th convoy: 1,703 prisoners

Those 1,703 prisoners came from block 24, "Night and Fog," of Ravensbruck and
several other blocks.

The political prisoners N.N. were the large majority.[1]

Mushroom Sausage Experiments

$\bullet \qquad \bullet \qquad \bullet$

Production of Mushroom Sausage

A preparation could be made with the help of sulfa byproducts and the fermentation of yeast.[1] It produced sulfite. Production was economical only if pine wood shavings were used. These wood shavings produce sugar products which, because they blend with the yeast fungus, are not destroyed. There are mushrooms in which these sugars—so-called *Pontosen*—are present as a byproduct of the wood shavings. Because these sugars can be utilized as nourishment, the mushrooms grow on them. This produces, along with other things, a form of yeast called *Torula.* It is difficult to filter because it is shaped like a big ball. We were looking for a mushroom which filtered better, and it was found in the threadlike mushroom with the botanical name *Oidium lactis.* With this mushroom, and with the help of the research department of Zellwolle—and its silklike products—the wood sulfite byproduct was developed to the point that they could manufacture it on a regular basis as the so-called *Oidium mycel*[2] in the Lenzing or Zellwolle A.G. paper factory. This mushroom produces a very potent protein. This fact gave us the idea to use this large number of mushrooms as a food product. We thought of sausage—at least in the vicinity of Lenzing—which went under the name of *Biosyn-Wurst.* The production of this sausage resulted in some difficulties because growth of these mushrooms was hindered due to contamination with other mushrooms. Because it was costly to produce food from that mushroom, after the war factory production was discontinued.

After this was no longer manufactured, we sought different avenues in which to utilize these byproducts. *Biosyn-wurst* itself was never again produced. What had been planned was a production of about "3,5 t mycel-dry mass" per day. Whether they ever achieved that goal, one can no longer determine.

Lenzing, April 29, 1966

Copied from statute 245499-33/66   Made by von PR. MARSALEK

Mushroom-Protein Sausage Experiments
(Biosyn-wurst)

This paper deals with printed material of Dr. Hornke, director of the paper factory, to make a sulfa solution in the Lenzinger Textile A.G. A sausage-like product had probably been produced since 1943. The exact time and number of trial products is unknown. The product originated from the experiments of the SS Hygiene Institutes and the SS Business administration main office (WVHA).

The artificial sausages were given to the inmates in the lager, the laborers, and in the main camp of Mauthausen. The result of these experiments is presented in a report of O. Pohl and SS Chief Himmler, dated December 12, 1943, as "Entirely unsatisfactory for human consumption." In another report one learns that "The growth of these mushrooms was disturbed due to contamination from other mushrooms." From other reports we learn that sausage led to "various inflammations of the human intestinal tract."

According to the population, the sausage looked like soft, spreadable summer sausage and smelled spicy, sour. It had a good flavor and smelled like real sausage. In spite of a lack of nourishing food, people were more or less skeptical about using it. AKT B.f.I. Z.L. 245499-33/66

Notes

• • •

PREFACE

1. Epigraph is from Charlotte Delbo, "None of Us Will Return," p. 12.

CHAPTER ONE.
INTRODUCTION

1. Dante Aligheri, Canto III, in *Dante's Inferno*, trans. Mark Musa (Bloomington: Indiana University Press, 1971), p. 20.

2. Terrence Des Pres, *The Survivor: An Anatomy on Life in the Death Camps* (New York: Oxford University Press, 1976), p. 37.

3. Andrea Dworkin, "The Unremembered: Searching for Women at the Holocaust Memorial Museum," *Ms.* (Nov./Dec., 1994): 52–58.

4. Sybil Milton, "Women and the Holocaust: The Case of German and German-Jewish Women," in *When Biology Became Destiny: Women in Weimar and Nazi Germany*, pp. 279–333.

5. Joan Ringelheim, "Women and the Holocaust: A Reconsideration," in *Jewish Women in Historical Perspective*, ed. Judith R. Baskin (Detroit: Wayne State University Press, 1991), p. 243.

6. Mary Berg, *Warsaw Ghetto: A Diary by Mary Berg.*

7. Seweryna Szmaglewska, *Smoke over Birkenau.*

8. Published both as *Etty: A Diary 1941–1943*, intro. J. G. Gaarlandt, trans. Arnold J. Pomerans (London, Glasgow & Toronto: Triad Grafton Books, 1985; rpt. 1986) and as *An Interrupted Life: The Diaries of Etty Hillesum*, intro. Gaarlandt (New York: Washington Square Press, 1985).

9. Marlene E. Heineman, *Gender and Destiny: Women Writers and the Holocaust* (New York & Westport, Conn.: Greenwood Press, 1986).

10. Vera Laska, ed., *Women in the Resistance and in the Holocaust: The Voices of Eyewitnesses.*

11. Ruth Schwertfeger, *Women of Theresienstadt: Voices from a Concentration Camp.*

12. Carol Rittner and John Roth, eds., *Different Voices: Women and the Holocaust*, p. xi.

13. John Roth and Michael Berenbaum, *Holocaust: Religious and Philosophical Implications.*

14. Fania Fenelon, with Marcelle Routier, *The Musicians of Auschwitz.*

15. Delbo, "None of Us Will Return."

16. Isabella Leitner and Irving A. Leitner, *Isabella: From Auschwitz to Freedom.*

17. Sara Nomberg-Przytyk, *Auschwitz: True Tales from a Grotesque Land.*

18. *Hannah Senesh: Her Life and Diary,* intro. Abba Eban (New York: Schocken Books, 1973).

19. Liana Millu, *Smoke Over Birkenau,* trans. Lynne Sharon Schwartz (Philadelphia, New York, Jerusalem: The Jewish Publication Society, 5751/1991).

20. Gerda Klein, *All But My Life* (New York: Hill and Wang, 1957).

21. Corrie Ten Boom, *The Hiding Place.*

22. Bezwinska and Czech, *Auschwitz as Seen by the SS,* p. 75 (Hoss), as quoted in Rittner and Roth, *Different Voices: Women and the Holocaust,* p. 228.

23. See chap. 23, "Love in the Shadow of the Crematory," in Olga Lengyel, *Five Chimneys: The Story of Auschwitz,* pp. 181–86. Also see Tadeusz Borowski, *This Way for the Gas, Ladies and Gentlemen,* pp. 86–88.

24. See Reiser narrative.

25. Milton, "Women and the Holocaust," p. 311.

26. Hanna Levy-Hass, *Vielleicht war das alles erst der Amfang: Tagebuch aus dem KZ Bergen-Belsen, 1944–1945,* ed. Eikel Geisel (Berlin, 1979), pp. 10–11. Also I. BI, NY: Eva Noack-Mosse, "*Theresienstadter Tagebuch,* January–July 1945," unpubl. ms. (1945); and Hanna Schramm, *Menschen in Gurs: Erinnerungen au ein französisches Internieungslager, 1940–1941* (Worms, 1977), p. 88. As quoted in Milton, "Women and the Holocaust," p. 311.

27. Ringelheim, "Women and the Holocaust," p. 260.

28. See Reiser and Herzberger narratives.

29. Ringelheim,"Women and the Holocaust," p. 259.

30. Rosalie Schiff, Interview, Dallas, August 5, 1995.

31. Adina Blady Szwajger, *I Remember Nothing More: The Warsaw Children's Hospital and the Jewish Resistance.*

32. Gisella Perl, *I Was a Doctor in Auschwitz.*

33. Lengyel, *Five Chimneys.*

34. R. J. Minney, *I Shall Fear No Evil: The Story of Dr. Alina Brewda.*

35. Simha Naor, *Krankengymnastin in Auschwitz: Aufzeichnungen des Häftlings Nr. 80574.*

36. *Criminal Experiments on Human Beings in Auschwitz and War Research Laboratories: Twenty Women Prisoners' Accounts.*

37. Philippe Aziz, *Doctors of Death.*

38. Walter Poller, *Medical Block, Buchenwald: The Personal Testimony of Inmate 996, Block 36.*

39. Albert Haas, M.D., *The Doctor and the Damned.*

40. Dr. Miklos Nyiszli, *Auschwitz: A Doctor's Eyewitness Account.*

41. Michael Kater, *Doctors under Hitler.*

42. Robert Jay Lifton, *The Nazi Doctors: Medical Killing and the Psychology of Genocide.*

43. George J. Annas and Michael A. Grodin, *The Nazi Doctors and the Nuremberg Code: Human Rights in Human Experimentation.*

44. Alexander Mitschlerlich, M.D., *Doctors of Infamy: The Story of the Nazi Medical Crimes.*

45. Danuta Czech, "Role of the Men's Hospital at Camp KL-Auschwitz II (Birkenau)," in Czech, et. al., *From the History of KL-Auschwitz,* vol. 2, p. 91.

46. Louis J. Micheels, M.D., *Doctor 117641: A Holocaust Memoir.*

47. Christian Bernadac, *Doctors of Mercy.*

48. Dr. Frank Stiffel, *The Tale of the Ring: A Kaddish, A Personal Memoir of the Holocaust.*

49. Carol Gilligan, "Woman's Place in Man's Life Cycle," p. 440, as quoted in Nel Noddings, *Caring: A Feminist Approach to Ethics & Moral Education,* p. 96.

50. Anton Gill, *The Journey Back from Hell: An Oral History—Conversations with Concentration Camp Survivors,* p. 105.

51. Primo Levi, *Survival in Auschwitz: The Nazi Assault on Humanity,* p. 79.

CHAPTER TWO.
WOMEN TRAPPED WITHIN A MEDICAL PARADOX

1. Florence Nightingale, *Notes on Nursing: What It Is and What It Is Not,* p. 3.

2. Christian Bernadac, *Doctors of Mercy,* p. 13.

3. All italicized quotes in this section are from "The Oath of Hippocrates," in *The World Book Encyclopedia,* vol. 9 (Chicago: Field Enterprises Educational Corporation, 1977), p. 227.

4. Nyiszli, *Auschwitz,* p. 83.

5. Ibid., p. 50.

6. The Testimony of Mme. Vaillant-Couturier, *Trial of the Major War Criminals before the International Military Tribunal, Nuremberg, 14 November 1945–1 October 1946,* vol. 6, Proceedings Jan. 22, 1945–Feb. 4, 1946 (Nuremberg, 1946), p. 209.

7. Lengyel, *Five Chimneys,* p. 145.

8. Szwajger, *I Remember Nothing More,* p. 28.

9. Ibid., p. 42.

10. Ibid., p. 62.

11. Ibid., p. 57.

12. Dr. Esther Fox, "Jewish Doctors and their Work in the Ghetto (Lodz)."

13. Lucjan Dobrozycki, ed., *The Chronicle of the Lodz Ghetto,* pp. 57, 217–18.

14. Ibid., p. 535.

15. Rosalie Schiff, Interview.

16. Yitzhak Arad, *Ghetto in Flames: The Struggle and Destruction of the Jews in Vilna in the Holocaust,* p. 316.

17. Hermann Rauschning, *The Voice of Destruction,* p. 312.

18. Ibid.

19. Ibid., pp. 306–307.

20. Arad, *Ghetto in Flames,* pp. 315–18.

21. Schmeglevskaya testimony, *Nuremberg Trials,* vol. 3, p. 319.

22. Nomberg-Przytyk, *Auschwitz: True Tales from a Grotesque Land,* p. 69.

23. Ota Kraus and Erich Kulka, *The Death Factory: Document on Auschwitz,* p. 87.

24. Vaillant-Couturier testimony, *Nuremberg Trials,* vol. 6, pp. 209–10.

25. Szmaglewska, *Smoke over Birkenau,* p. 32.

26. Micheline Maurel, *An Ordinary Camp,* p. 51, as quoted in Des Pres, *The Survivor,* p. 140.

27. Lengyel, *Five Chimneys*, pp. 57–58.

28. Ibid., pp. 58–59.

29. Szmaglewska, *Smoke over Birkenau*, pp. 243, 260.

30. Susan Beer, telephone interview, August 3, 1995.

31. Perl, *I Was a Doctor in Auschwitz*, pp. 80, 83–84.

32. Vaillant-Couturier testimony, *Nuremberg Trials*, vol. 6, p. 212.

33. Susan Beer, telephone interviews, January 26, 1992, and August 2, 1995.

34. "The Last Days of Auschwitz, 50 Years Later: Untold Stories from the Death Camp," p. 54.

35. For a compelling narrative of one man's experience see Jack Oran's memoirs in Gene Church, *'80629' A Mengele Experiment* (Richardson, Tex.: Sharon Kimberly Damon, 1986).

36. Danuta Czech, ed., *Auschwitz Chronicles: 1939–1945, From the Archives of the Auschwitz Memorial and the German Federal Archives*, p. 172.

37. Suzkever testimony, *Nuremberg Trials*, vol. 8, p. 310.

38. Czech, *Auschwitz Chronicles*, pp. 262–63.

39. Suzkever testimony, *Nuremberg Trials*, vol. 8, pp. 310–14.

40. Vaillant-Couturier testimony, *Nuremberg Trials*, vol. 6, p. 220.

41. Ibid., p. 224.

42. Shelley, *Criminal Experiments*, p. 50.

43. Ibid., p. 267.

44. Jozef Marszalek, *Majdanek: The Concentration Camp in Lublin*, pp. 122–23.

45. Shelley, *Criminal Experiments*, p. 51.

46. Ibid.

47. For a record of the trial, see Mavis M. Hill and L. Norman Williams, *Auschwitz in England: A Record of a Libel Action*.

48. Minney, *I Shall Fear No Evil*, p. 135.

49. Gill, *Journey Back*, p. 369.

50. Haas, *Doctor*, p. 177.

51. Micheels, *Doctor 117641*, p. 70.

52. Ibid., pp. 76–77.

53. Ibid., p. 84.

54. Rabbi Dr. I. Epstein, *The Babylonian Talmud*, p. 234.

SECTION ONE.

THERESIENSTADT: LIMBO OF THE DAMNED

1. Konnilyn Feig, *Hitler's Death Camps: The Sanity of Madness*, p. 238.

2. Ibid., p. 238.

3. George E. Berkley, *Hitler's Gift: The Story of Theresienstadt*, pp. 23–24.

4. "Pamatnik Terezin."

5. Feig, *Hitler's Death Camps*, p. 238.

6. Libuse Krylova, *The Small Fortress of Terezin*, p. 5, as cited in Feig, *Hitler's Death Camps*, p. 238.

7. "Pamatnik Terezin."

8. Narrative constructed from the following sources: Hana Bruml, Interview by Radu Ionid, March 12, 1990, used with permission of United States Holocaust Memorial Museum, Washington, D.C.; Hana Bruml, telephone interview, March 6, 1992; Hana Bruml Interview, Arlington, VA, June 4, 1993.

CHAPTER THREE. HANA MULLER BRUML: "I WAS A NURSE IN THERESIENSTADT"

1. Acute, generalized illness caused by salmonella. Spread by contaminated food and water. Symptoms: fever, malaise, rash called "rose spots," abdominal pain, enlargement of the spleen, bradycardia, low white cell count. May lead to intestinal hemorrhages and perforation (*Dorland's Illustrated Medical Dictionary*, p. 623).

2. Acute infection caused by lice. Symptoms: severe headache, chills, fever, stupor, skin eruptions. Central nervous system involvement progresses from dullness to stupor, and sometimes coma and death (Ibid., p. 1780).

3. Healing gas: a mixture of antibacterial and astringent agents.

4. Acute superficial cellulitis involving dermal lymphatics, caused by infection. Symptoms: spreading, bright red, edematous, infiltrated, circumscribed plague with a raised border (Ibid., p. 577).

5. See Reiser narrative, re: Bialystok children.

6. Seigfried Seidl, the Obersturmführer (Ruth Bondy, *"Elder of the Jews": Jakob Edelstein of Theresienstadt*, p. 241).

CHAPTER FOUR. MARGRET LEHNER: "IF ANYONE HERE MENTIONS HUMANE TREATMENT"

1. Walter Laqueur, *The Terrible Secret: Suppression of the Truth about Hitler's "Final Solution,"* p. 17.

2. Lewis H. Weinstein, "A Living Nightmare: Liberation of the Death Camps Recalled," *Jewish News* (New Jersey), April 23, 1987, p. 51.

3. Bruce F. Pauley, *From Prejudice to Persecution: A History of Austrian Anti-Semitism*, p. 305.

4. Deborah Lipstadt, *Denying the Holocaust: The Growing Assault on Truth and Memory*, p. 21.

5. Lehner Interview, Vöcklabruck, Austria, March 11, 1994; telephone conversation, December 1, 1994.

6. The book by Hawle et al. was published in 1995.

7. All quotes and other material from letters and documents given to Margret Lehner and quoted here courtesy of the authors. Christian Hawle, et al., *Täter und Opfer, Nationalsozialistische Gewalt und Widerstand im Bezirk Vöcklabruck, 1939–1945*.

8. From documents supplied by Margret Lehner.

9. From documents supplied by Margret Lehner.

10. Appendix A, Record of Convoys to Lenzing, courtesy of Margret Lehner.

11. Documents supplied by Margret Lehner.

12. Anna Benjamin, Hanna Kohner, Walter Kohner, and Frederick Kohner, *Hanna and Walter—A Love Story.* Material supplied by Margret Lehner.

13. The documents from Margret Lehner do not specifically identify Frau H., Frau P., or Mrs. Holzweiser.

14. It is most likely that Mauthausen and its surrounding camps were liberated by Patton's Third Army, 11th Armored Division and 71st Division ("Army Divisions and the Concentration Camps that they Liberated," "The Seventy-First Came . . . To Gunskirchen Lager" [Augsberg: E. Klaeses, K. G. Druckerel v. Yadag], *G-2 Periodic Report dated May 6, 1945,* courtesy of Leo Serian).

15. Text of speech supplied by Margret Lehner, with permission to publish.

16. See Lehner, Appendix B, Production of Mushroom Sausages.

CHAPTER FIVE. RUTH REISER:
"THE ONLY MEDICINE WAS CHARCOAL"

1. Ruth Reiser, Interview, New York, March 5, 1994.

2. A grenz ray: very soft ray, lying between roentgen and ultraviolet rays in the electromagnetic spectrum, used to treat excema. Named for German-American roentgenologist Gustav P. Bucky (*Dorland's,* pp. 241, 1427).

3. German *Stadt:* trans. city, i.e., Theresa's city.

4. "A police prison of the Prague Gestapo was established in [a] Small Fortress in June, 1940, and a ghetto-concentration camp for Jews was founded in the min Fortress (the town of Terezin) in November, 1941. . . . It served three purposes simultaneously: a transit camp, a decimating one . . . and a propagandistic one" ("Museum of the Terezin Ghetto," text Pamatnik Terezin, trans. Giba Zbalitelova, photos Frantisek Maly, Pamatnik Terezin: OSWALD [*sic*], 1992).

5. The main hospital in the Hohenelbe barrack contained one thousand beds. There were also clinics and infirmaries in every barrack and block of houses. There was approximately one doctor for every 750 people, but a shortage of nurses and caretakers (Bondy, *"Elder of the Jews,"* p. 320).

6. Probably a chilblain, usually involving the fingertips, nose, ears, hands, calves, and heels and caused by microvascular injury secondary to exposure to cold (*Dorland's,* p. 958).

7. Hyperexcitability of nerves and muscles from decrease in concentration of extracellular ionized calcium (Ibid., p. 1700).

8. Chronic disease; symptoms: hypertrophy of skin and subcutaneous tissues. Begins with dermatitis and enlargement of part, accompanied by chills and fever. Followed by ulceration, thickening, discoloration, and fissuring of skin. Principally affects legs and external genitals (Ibid., p. 540).

9. "Sanitary cesspools were constructed . . . of concrete and topped with primitive but

sanitary latrines. Whenever possible, indoor privies with connections to the cess-pools were constructed. In front of every closed privy . . . would be a . . . wooden table with a tin washbasin on it containing a mixture of water and chlorine, with an elderly . . . ghetto resident sitting next to it as the privy guard. Every occupant—after leaving—would be reminded by the guard: 'please wash your hands'" (Norbert Troller, *Theresienstadt: Hitler's Gift to the Jews,* trans. Susan E. Cernyak-Spatz, ed. Joel Shatzky [Chapel Hill: University of North Carolina Press, 1991], p. 84).

10. Surgical creation of a fistula by puncturing the soft tissue and bone to provide drainage (*Dorland's,* p. 1748).

11. Pregnant women and newborns were usually taken to Auschwitz and gassed.

12. According to one account, infirmary patients did receive a special diet called "Reko." This consisted of "soup, tea, a roll that had . . . half the nutritional value of the bread ration, one potato more than normal, every second day a yeast dumpling." This food was especially prepared in the hospital kitchen (Troller, *Theresienstadt,* p. 128).

13. "One half loaf of bread, the noon soup, one or two potatoes; in the evenings, coffee without anything, sometimes the lentil soup without lentils" (Ibid., p. 134).

14. "Bohemian black bread with . . . dark brown, crunchy crust" (Ibid., p. 133).

15. Troller states that he shared his hospital room with forty to fifty patients (Ibid.).

16. "They visited the bank, the newly erected bane pavilion, the laundry, the living quarters of some Prominenten, the ground floor of a barracks, one or two hospital wards, the post office, the cafe, the pharmacy, and other sites" (George E. Berkley, *Hitler's Gift to the Jews: The Story of Theresienstadt,* p. 174).

17. On August 17, 1943, over twelve hundred children, ages six to sixteen, were rounded up and taken to Theresienstadt. No one there was allowed to talk to them. Terrified, having seen their parents shot, none uttered a word. They were bathed and lodged in houses surrounded by barbed wire. Many died of disease. Others were taken to the "Small Fortress section and beaten to death." Four weeks later those who survived were taken to Birkenau, along with fifty-three adults who had volunteered to accompany them (Martin Gilbert, *The Holocaust: A History of the Jews of Europe During the Second World War,* p. 601).

18. A small subcamp of Dachau (Gill, *Journey Back,* p. 226).

19. Czech Jews numbering 3,860, survivors of 6,000 Jews who had been brought to Birkenau from Theresienstadt in September, 1943, were gassed on March 7, 1944 (Gilbert, *Holocaust,* p. 658).

20. Block 25, the "anteroom of the gas chamber." Described as having "rats as big as cats running about." Whereas in most blocks there were eight hundred women, here fifteen hundred women were crowded in. Many could not sleep or lie down (Vaillant-Couturier testimony, *Nuremberg Trials,* vol. 6, pp. 208–209).

21. October 27, 1944, "497 female prisoners are transferred from the transit camp at Auschwitz II to another camp" (Czech, *Auschwitz Chronicle,* p. 739). This transit was brought to the labor camp at Lenzing (Hawle et al., p. 33).

22. The factory is still in operation today.

23. *Duese:* trans. nozzle. To begin the process, the nozzles with the fluid viscose had to be dipped into the acid. Besides the damage to the hands, the girls had to inhale the vapors all day long.

24. According to the memoirs of Ellen Loeb, four women were killed and a fifth severely injured.

25. German term for low-flying aircraft, most likely the North American B-25A Mitchell, Martin B-26B Marauder, or Douglas a-20G Havoc (Enzo Angelucci, *The Rand McNally Encyclopedia of Military Aircraft, 1914–1980*, pp. 265–66).

26. "*Letter, GSP, Jr. to Beatrice, April 21, 1945:* We go all out in the morning for a junction with the Russians near Linz" (Martin Blumenson, *The Patton Papers, 1940–1945*, p. 691).

27. According to the army reports for May 6, 1945, this would have been the 71st Infantry Division (Headquarters 71st Infantry Division, Office of the A C of S, G-2 APO 360, U.S. Army, G-2 Periodic Report), courtesy of the Army, Center of Military History, DAMH-RA/Drea, Washington, D.C.

SECTION TWO
WESTERBORK: JOURNEY TO THE UNDERWORLD

1. Dirk Mulder, "Camp Westerbork: Symbol of Destruction," pp. 1–2.

2. Dr. J. Presser, *Ashes in the Wind: The Destruction of Dutch Jewry*, pp. 429–31.

3. Ibid.

4. See Loeb narrative.

5. Presser, *Ashes*, p. 420.

6. Ibid., pp. 424–25.

7. Philip Mechanicus, *Year of Fear: A Jewish Prisoner Waits for Auschwitz*, pp. 38–39.

8. Etty Hillesum, *Etty, A Diary 1941–43*, p. 74.

9. Oral History of Hildegard Grau, Interviewed by Ruth Block, June 7, 1985, and Jessica Selbst, April 1, 1986, The Yaffa Eliach Collection, courtesy of the Center for Holocaust Studies, Museum of Jewish Heritage, New York, GH 1304.

10. Hillesum, *Etty, A Diary 1941–43*, p. 261.

11. Ibid., p. 438.

12. Mulder, "Camp Westerbork: Symbol of Destruction," p. 13.

13. Ibid., p. 11.

14. Ibid., p. 16.

CHAPTER SIX. TRUDY SHAKNO:
"I DON'T KNOW WHAT THIS ALL MEANS"

1. Trudy Shakno, Interview, Dallas, June 23, 1991, Letters and Diary, trans. Trudy Shakno.

2. Julius Loeb, born July 10, 1881, at Huffelsheim, Germany, passed away November 2,

1943, at Westerbork. Courtesy of the Local Archive Service, Amsteldjik 67, 1074 HZ Amsterdam.

3. Ingaz Philipp Semmelweis reduced infant mortality due to postchildbirth infection by instructing his students and colleagues to disinfect their hands with calcium chloride solution (Felix Marti-Ibañez, M.D., *The Epic of Medicine*, p. 231).

4. Trudy was never able to locate her father's grave.

5. "Wednesday, December 1, 1943: 'A heavy blow has fallen on us. The Commandant has laid out that, as from December 15th, men and women who are on their own can receive a parcel of foodstuffs of not more than two kg. Once every six weeks, families with not more than two children a parcel every fortnight, but only from Jewish relatives or from relatives who are partners in mixed marriages. Berlin has ordered this restriction on foodstuffs. In a German newspaper it was pointed out that the Jews at Westerbork lived far better than the German population'" (Mechanicus, *Year of Fear*, p. 201).

CHAPTER SEVEN. ELLEN LOEB:
"DEAR TRUDY, DEAR RUDY"

1. Each Tuesday one thousand people were shipped off to their deaths in Auschwitz or other camps (Mechanicus, *Year of Fear*, p. 7).

2. Mechanicus describes the arrival of fifty children on June 10, 1943, from Vught, a transit camp in northern Holland. Scattered throughout the hospital barracks, they suffered from such diseases as scarlet fever, measles, pneumonia, and mumps (*Year of Fear*, p. 43).

3. Purple lupins grew all around the camp (Ibid.)

4. For the visit of the Danish Red Cross, June 23, 1944, and the filming of the propaganda movie *The Führer Gives a City to the Jews* (Bondy, "Elder of the Jews," pp. 437–41).

5. "Healing gas," an antibacterial and astringent combination used for the treatment of wounds (Peter Loewenberg, M.D., Interview).

6. Balsam of Peru: a thick liquid from the *Myroxylon pereirae* tree, grown in El Salvador and Central and South America. Fragrant and reddish brown, it has soothing and tonic effects on the body. Used for skin irritations, an ingredient in cough syrup, and a tonic for indigestion (*World Book Encyclopedia*, vol. 2, p. 47).

7. Trench mouth: inflammation of the oral mucosa; may involve cheeks and lips, palate, tongue, floor of the mouth, and gums (*Dorland's*, p. 1585).

8. A black ointment put on developing abscesses. Supposed to help the abscess to open and drain, but irritated the skin, making things worse (Loewenberg Interview).

9. "An acute superficial form of cellulitis, characterized by the spread of a hot, bright red, infiltrated plaque . . ." (*Dorland's*, p. 577).

10. Acute inflammation usually occurring as a reaction to multiple provoking agents, including infection, tuberculosis, drugs, etc. (Ibid., p. 578).

11. A contagious purulent skin disease (Ibid., p. 824).

12. Painful nodules formed in the skin by circumscribed inflammation of the skin and subcutaneous tissue.

13. Used as an analgesic (Peter Loewenberg, M.D., Interview).

14. Thought to be effective against flu.

15. Ethly chloride, used to deaden pain.

16. Sulfanilamide powder.

17. Very caustic agent, can cause blindness.

18. Inflammation of the subcutaneous tissue, draining pus (*Dorland's*, p. 299).

19. Trans.: Used to be in the women's infirmary, concentration camp Lenzing.

SECTION THREE
LABOR CAMPS: CIRCLES OF SUFFERING

1. Lucy S. Dawidowicz, *The War Against the Jews 1933–1945*, p. 533.

2. *Obozy hitlerowska na ziemiach polskish 1939–1945*, Informator encyklopedyczny (Warsaw: Panstwowe Wydanick Naukowe, 1979), Summary, p. 664, trans. Leo Laufer, as cited in Diane Plotkin: "A Historiographic Analysis of a Survivor's Narrative: The Story of Leo Laufer," p. 92.

3. Martin Gilbert, *Atlas of the Holocaust*, p. 36.

4. Plotkin, "Historiographic Analysis," p. 95.

5. Benjamin B. Ferencz, *Less Than Slaves: Jewish Forced Labor and the Quest for Compensation*, p. 51.

6. Ibid., p. xvii.

7. "Communicable Diseases and the Physician's Obligation to Heal," in *Medicine and Jewish Law*, p. 65.

8. The subject of the negotiations is fully discussed in Yehuda Bauer, *Jews for Sale: Nazi-Jewish Negotiations, 1933–1945*, p. 230.

CHAPTER EIGHT.
DR. EDITH KRAMER: HELL AND REBIRTH

1. Used with permission from the United States Holocaust Research Institute Archives, Record Group 02, Survivor Testimonies, 037: "Hell and Rebirth: My Experiences During the Time of Persecution," by Dr. Edith Kramer.

2. Similar to other Nuremberg Laws, this was actually a new form of a decree which had been issued as a Canonical Law of the Trulanic Synod in 692, which stated that Christians were not permitted to patronize Jewish doctors (Raul Hilberg, *The Destruction of the European Jews*, p. 11).

3. On May 11, 1942, Joseph Goebbels noted in his diary that there were still forty thousand Jews in Berlin, many of whom were working in the munitions industries. By September 30, however, he wrote that Hitler had expressed his decision to evacuate the Jewish people, that they could be easily replaced by foreign workers. Over the

next five months, this Jewish population was severely diminished, some by deportation, others by suicide (Leonard Gross, *The Last Jews in Berlin*, p. 17).

4. Although the number of underground Jews still alive in Berlin at the end of the war is a matter of conjecture, the Berlin Jewish community estimates this number to be 1,123, while others state that it cannot be more than a few hundred (Ibid., p. 345).

5. November 9, 1938.

6. A work camp for Jewish women, opened in 1942 (*Obozy*, p. 400).

7. Due to primitive living conditions, there were few, if any, sanitary facilities. Hence inmates were plagued by lice and itch mites, which in turn led to such conditions as scabies and impetigo. Others suffered from tuberculosis (*Dokumenty I Materialy: Zczasow Okupacji Niemieckiej W Polsce*, p. 95, as cited in Plotkin, "Historiographic Analysis," pp. 94–95).

8. A contagious dermatitis caused by the itch mite and transmitted by close contact. Characterized by intense itching and sometimes associated with excema from scratching and secondary bacterial infection (*Dorland's*, p. 1487).

9. "In the women's camp of the city of Poznan, food rations contain about 800 calories: 200 grams of bread daily, 60 grams of margarine once a week, about 150 grams of marmalade once every two weeks" (*Dokumenty*, p. 296, as cited in Plotkin, "Historiographic Analysis," p. 95).

10. Although Dr. Kramer describes it differently, Antonienhof is listed as the German name for Camp Antoninek (Polish), a labor camp for Jewish women situated in the stadium in the city of Poznan (*Obozy*, no. 3623, p. 400).

11. "'On territory regarded as incorporated into the Reich, the Nazi authorities set up 2197 labour camps and work detachments for prisoners-of-war, including 19 camps for officers (*Oflag*) and 63 for NCO's (*Stalag*)'" (Ibid., p. 664, as cited in Plotkin, "Historiographic Analysis," p. 92).

12. Lodz ghetto "'announcement No. 166,'" dated November 19, 1940, issued by Chaim Rumkowski, stated: "'I am hereby announcing that healthy, strong men, age 18 to 40, can get work outside of the ghetto. They will receive salary, accommodation and full board for their work. The costs for board will be deducted from their salary. The rest of the salary they can send to their families in the ghetto . . .'" (Ibid., p. 96, as cited in Plotkin, "Historiographic Analysis," p. 91).

13. For examples of ghetto and concentration camp humor, see Steve Lipman, *Laughter in Hell: The Use of Humor during the Holocaust*.

14. According to the majority of sources on the subject, Jews were utilized as slaves. Ferencz states, "Concentration camp prisoners were being traded and transshipped like so many pieces of metal" (*Less than Slaves*, p. 28). Therefore, while Dr. Kramer's memories of the situation cannot be disproved, she could not possibly have seen the total picture, that being the ultimate aim to annihilate the Jews.

15. Leo Laufer survived at least four camps in the Posen area (Plotkin, "Historiographic Analysis," pp. 99–125).

16. There were eight transports in October, 1944, the last on October 28. While most of

those transported were brought to the gas chambers of Auschwitz, about twenty young men were secretly brought back to Theresienstadt, where, during the night, they exhumed and destroyed the remains of those hanged in executions which had taken place in 1942. Then they were taken to the Little Fortress and killed (Berkley, *Hitler's Gift*, pp. 189, 203).

17. The first transport, carrying 1,056 Jews from Prague, arrived on January 31, 1945. Over 5,000 were to follow (Ibid., p. 218).

18. Eichmann arrived March 5, 1945 (Ibid., p. 227).

19. In early February, 1945, two construction crews began work on what was said to be a place more suitable for storing vegetables and a poultry farm. However, airtight doors as well as lack of a ventilation system raised questions as to their real purpose. When suspicions mounted that the "vegetable storehouse" was actually to be a gas chamber and the "poultry farm" a site for mass executions, the camp engineers refused to work on the project. Although Commandant Rahm was furious and beat the head of the technical department, Erich Kohn, with his pistol, the project was abandoned. Other factors affecting this decision were rumors in Geneva that the Nazis intended to destroy the camp and Eichmann's fear of renewed scandal if the Russians discovered these executions after their having discovered the gas chambers and crematoria in Majdanek. It was later revealed that the entire ghetto population was to be executed by flame throwers in the "poultry farm" (Ibid., p. 225).

20. Former president of Switzerland Jean Marie Musy, although he had pro-Nazi leanings, wanted to cover his past by showing sympathy for the Jews. Following the request of Isaac Sternbruch, the Geneva representative of the Orthodox Rabbinical Association of America, to negotiate the release of the Jews, he and his son Benoit met with Himmler in Vienna. Himmler was offered five million Swiss francs to be deposited in a Swiss bank. The effort was supported by America's War Refugee Board. The agreement was reached in January that beginning in early February, Himmler would release 1,200 Jews to Switzerland every four days. The announcement to sign up was passed through Theresienstadt on February 3, and on February 5, at four o'clock in the afternoon, 1,210 well-dressed Theresienstadt Jews boarded a train for Switzerland. Kaltenbrunner, after having learned of the affair, informed Hitler, who removed Himmler from his job; therefore, there were no further transports to freedom (Ibid., pp. 221–23).

21. The transport of Bialystok orphans. See Reiser narrative.

22. As a result of Count Bernadotte's negotiations with the Nazis, the Danes were released on April 13, 1945 (Berkley, *Hitler's Gift*, p. 233).

23. Rahm assured everyone that they would be going to Switzerland, and no one was forced to go (Ibid., p. 221).

24. Each person was given the right to reject by signing a statement of renunciation. The group was disproportionately Dutch, as they were not used to the double dealing of camp life (Ibid., p. 222).

25. Dr. Nelly Stern, Leo Baeck's sister's daughter (Schwertfeger, *Women*, p. 76).

26. Capt. Hans Guenther, appointed by Eichmann in 1940 to be the overseer of the Protectorate Jews (Ibid., p. 22).

27. According to Berkley, those selected to go were told to wear their best clothing and carry " 'elegant suitcases' " (*Hitler's Gift*, p. 222).

28. "The train had hardly left the station when the Nazis began distributing generous supplies of bread, margarine, sugar, sausage, and milk. . . . Even vitamin tablets were given out" (Ibid.).

29. At dawn, when the train entered the Swiss town of Kreuzlingen, an SS man walked down the corridor and declared, " 'In the name of Reichsleiter Himmler, you are now free' " (Ibid.).

30. When the train stopped, women from the Swiss Red Cross came aboard and distributed apples, cigarettes, and chocolates. When one man declared that he smoked cigars, a Red Cross worker went to buy one for him (Ibid.).

31. Musy was a right wing politician with pro-Nazi leanings and, as such, was himself an anti-Semite (Ibid., p. 220).

32. Through postcards bearing Swiss postmarks, the ghetto learned that the transport had indeed arrived safely (Ibid., p. 223).

33. See note 21.

34. These accounts were carried not only by the press, but also by Swiss radio (Ibid., p. 223).

35. November 2, 1944: "Killing with Zyklon B gas in the gas chambers of Auschwitz is probably discontinued. The selected prisoners are shot to death in the gas chamber or on the grounds of Crematorium V" (Czech, *Auschwitz Chronicles*, p. 743).

36. October 1–31: "3,836 registered female prisoners die in Auschwitz II. 3,758 of these die in the gas chambers" (Ibid., p. 742).

37. According to Berkley, the exact count was 1,210 (*Hitler's Gift*, p. 220).

38. October 30, 1944: "2,038 Jews arrive in an RHSA transport from the Theresienstadt ghetto. There are 949 men and boys and 1,089 women and girls. . . . After the selection 217 men are sent to the camp . . . 132 are put in the transit camp. The remaining 1,689 people are killed in the gas chambers" (Czech, *Auschwitz Chronicles*, p. 742).

39. Hermann Hesse (1877–1962) was awarded the Nobel Prize for literature in 1946 (*The World Book Encyclopedia*, H, vol. 9, p. 204).

SECTION FOUR
AUSCHWITZ: THE DEPTH OF HELL'S ABYSS

1. Czech et al., "Role of the Men's Hospital," p. 112.

2. Yisrael Gutman and Michael Berenbaum, eds., *Anatomy of the Auschwitz Death Camp*, pp. 382–86.

3. Ibid., p. 381.

4. Ibid., p. 383.

5. Although she does not specifically mention block 3, Czech states that prisoners with "more interesting cases" sometimes received dietetic soup, white bread, and milk ("Role of the Men's Hospital," p. 51).

6. Ibid., p. 11

7. Ibid.

8. Feig, *Hitler's Death Camps*, pp. 180–81.

9. Vaillant-Couturier testimony, *Nuremberg Trials*, vol. 6, pp. 209–10.

10. Shmaglevskaya testimony, *Nuremberg Trials*, vol. 8, p. 319.

11. Vaillant-Couturier Testimony, *Nuremberg Trials*, vol. 6, p. 212.

12. These materials are the property of the Archives of the State Museum of Auschwitz-Birkenau. Permission to publish courtesy of Jerzy Wroblewski, Director. Trans. Manfred and Friedel Marx, ed. Diane Plotkin.

CHAPTER NINE. MARGITA SCHWALBOVA:
THEY WERE MURDERED IN THE INFIRMARY

1. According to Danuta Czech, the women's section in the base camp of Auschwitz was established in March, 1942. There were ten blocks, which were separated from the other blocks and assigned to women. The first female prisoners arrived on March 26, 1942. Between March 26 and August 15, 1942, 17,316 women were brought to Auschwitz. After that they were transferred to Birkenau, where a women's concentration camp (*Frauen Konzentrationslager—FKL*) was established in section Ia. ("Role of the Men's Hospital," p. 11).

2. The Jewish female prisoners received the uniforms that had belonged to murdered Russian POWs (Czech, *Auschwitz Chronicles*, p. 148).

3. He died May 25, 1945, in a field hospital at Markt Pongau (Czech, "Role of the Men's Hospital," n. 12, p. 11).

4. In spring, 1942, prisoner doctors were allowed to take over medical duties. Prisoners working in the pharmacy and the store of the SS men's medicines illegally supplied medicines to the prisoners' hospitals. Many other remedies were sent illegally from Kracow, such as some antityphus vaccines from the Bujwid Institute. In addition, some medicines were sent from Swiss firms to the Chief Tutelar Council. Prisoners working in squads outside the camp collected them and smuggled them into the camp, for which many were killed (Ibid., n. 21, p. 18).

5. "August 6, [1942]: A start has been made to move female prisoners out of the main camp to . . . camp B-Ia in Birkenau" (Czech, *Auschwitz Chronicles*, p. 212).

6. "The prisoners' hospital at KL Auschwitz was not a place of cure, ever since its establishment up to April, 1943; it was a place where people died or were killed. The prisoners called it 'the anteroom to the crematorium'" (Czech, "Role of the Men's Hospital," p. 19).

7. During August, September, November, and December, 1942, 3,610 prisoners, mainly those suffering from typhus, were selected in the prisoners' hospital at the base camp. Of these, 1,143 prisoners were killed in the gas chambers and 2,467 were killed by phenol injections into the heart (Ibid., n. 27, p. 22).

8. Czech notes that according to the deposition of former prisoner Kazimierz Smolen, SS Rottenführer Franz Schulz killed patients by injecting phenol into their hearts ("Role of the Men's Hospital," n. 37, p. 27).

9. Death certificates with fictitious descriptions of terminal illnesses were made out for those murdered in order to prevent the news that such things were being carried out in the camp (Czech, *Auschwitz Chronicles*, n.**, p. 178).

10. July 17–18, 1942.

11. July 18: "With Schmauser, Himmler visits the kitchens, the women's camp (which then includes Blocks 1–10). . . . In the women's camp he is shown the effect of a whipping. Himmler must personally approve the flogging of women. He is also present at the roll call" (Ibid., p. 199).

12. "[Himmler] sees the prisoners and makes precise inquiries about each prisoner category and the current occupancy level" (Ibid.).

13. On May 4, 1942, the first selection of prisoners to be gassed was made. They were driven to the *Isolierstation* and into the yard in front of the block. From there, those resisting and attempting to escape were taken in lorries, which at that time consisted of two country cottages which had been adapted to serve as gas chambers (Czech, "Role of the Men's Hospital," pp. 25–56, n. 33, p. 25).

14. According to Czech, in August, 1942, the hospital complex in Birkenau consisted of Blocks 22, 23, 24, 25, and 26 (Ibid., p. 34). The term "hospital" is a misnomer. These blocks were not equipped with sanitary facilities, medicines, or equipment. According to one description: "Block 24 is overpopulated. The especially lucky patients manage to squeeze into and share somebody else's bed. Some beds are shared by three people. It is cold and drafty here. No stove has yet been installed. The wind comes through the front and back doors, circulating hospital odors without removing them" (Szmaglewska, *Smoke over Birkenau*, p. 40).

15. She is either referring to Hamburg physician H. H. Meier, who wrote about "'the elimination of Jewry from physiciandom and other facets of health leadership' as a medical precaution for the collective health of the nation" (Kater, *Doctors*, p. 178), Second Camp Commander Franz Xavier Maier, SS second lieutenant, or Director of Administration Max Mayer, SS first lieutenant (Czech, *Auschwitz Chronicles*, p. 16).

16. October 2, [1942]: "At another selection in the women's camp in Birkenau, 1,800 female prisoners are selected. They are killed in the gas chambers" (Ibid., p. 248). Between October 1 and October 3, 1942, because the five hospital blocks (22, 23, 24, 25, and 26) could not cope with the numbers of patients stricken with typhus, 5,812 women were killed in the gas chambers (Czech, "Role of the Men's Hospital," p. 34).

17. "October 13, [1942]: SS Captain Helmuth Vetter comes to Auschwitz. From 1941 to

1944, Vetter carries out pharmacological experiments on prisoners of Auschwitz, Dachau, and Mauthausen concentration camps in order to test the effects of medicines and preparations" (Czech, *Auschwitz Chronicles*, p. 253).

18. In the second half of 1944, a ward for abortions was set up in Block 2. Abortions were performed on prisoners, on orders of SS physicians, even those in advanced stages of pregnancy, without the consent of the mothers (Czech, "Role of the Men's Hospital," p. 48).

19. According to a report of former prisoner Kazmiera Topor, a Roentgen apparatus had been installed in the experimental station in Block 30 in the women's camp Bia at Birkenau (Czech, "Role of the Men's Hospital," n. 118, p. 61).

20. July 7, 1942: Clauberg is informed by Himmler that Auschwitz is at his disposal for sterilization experiments (Czech, *Auschwitz Chronicles*, p. 192).

21. Horst Schumann, who first came to Auschwitz in July, 1941. He came next in November, 1942, in order to find a method of mass sterilization which would require little time. In April, 1944, he sent his report to Hitler's office, from where it was sent to Himmler. In June, 1944, he was sent to Ravensbruck, where he continued his experiments on gypsy children. He was not arrested until March, 1966. He was tried in September, 1970, but the trial was discontinued because he was ill (Czech, "Role of the Men's Hospital," n. 117, pp. 60–61).

22. *"The sterilization method using injections of an irritant fluid into the uterus was developed exclusively by Prof. Clauberg, Königshutte, Upper Silesia"* [*sic*]. According to a letter from Clauberg to Himmler, dated June 7, 1943: "'The method I have devised for effecting sterilization of the female organism without operation has been developed virtually to completion. It operates by a single injection from the cervix . . .'" (Mitschlerlich, *Doctors of Infamy*, p. 141).

23. The experimental block of the main camp of Auschwitz.

24. December 5, 1942: "In the women's camp in Birkenau, the SS carries out a large-scale selection, which lasts the entire day. Afterward, approximately 2,000 young, healthy, and able-bodied women are brought to the gas chambers in the bunkers" (Czech, *Auschwitz Chronicles*, p. 279).

25. SS First Lieutenant Bruno Kitt.

26. "Danielle Casanova was a dental surgeon and she was very active among the women. It was she who organized a resistance movement among the wives of prisoners" (Vaillant-Couturier testimony, *Nuremberg Trials*, vol. 6, p. 205).

27. August 1, 1942: "A so-called quarantine camp is set up in camp B-IIa of Birkenau for newly arrived male prisoners." "The quarantine camp consists of 16 wooden barracks in which 4,000 to 6,000 prisoners are housed. . . . from September, 1943, to November, 1944, 4,012 prisoners become so ill that they are moved to the prisoners' infirmary in camp B-IIIf, 1,902 prisoners die, and 6,717 prisoners are selected and killed in the gas chambers. The several week quarantine is supposed to accustom prisoners to camp life and to put their physical and psychological stamina to a severe test" (Czech, *Auschwitz Chronicles*, p. 452).

28. Medicines obtainable from the camp pharmacy, although in insufficient quantities, were aspirin, pyramidone, cough tablets, some analgesics, thanalbin and carbon, lime water, and sodium bicarbonate. At times Digitalis leaves were available, out of which the pharmacist prepared a liquid called *Infusum Folia Digitalis.* Other remedies, such as Prontosil, Oleodron, sulphonamides, glucose, calcium, ichtiol ointment, and Mitigal for scabies were more difficult to obtain. Patients got only a teaspoon of medicine in order to create the impression that they were being treated (Czech, "Role of the Men's Hospital," pp. 89–90).

29. The SS physicians stressed the importance of keeping formal records. Hence they wrote patients' disease histories and compiled statistics, among other formalities, all of which were to create the appearance of proper medical treatment (Czech, "Role of the Men's Hospital," p. 73).

30. In December, 1943, Lagerarzt SS Obersturmführer Thilo set aside Block 7 as a special block for patients of German nationality and for those who suffered from interesting clinical conditions that would augment his medical research. These patients received dietetic soup in addition to the camp soup, white bread, and sometimes milk (Czech, "Role of the Men's Hospital," p. 51).

31. Medicines from "Canada" were transmitted by prisoners and former patients to the pharmacy in Camp BIIf as well as to some doctors in exchange for small services or in order to help (Ibid., p. 90).

32. Danielle Casanova (No. 31655) and Maie Politzer were brought to Auschwitz from Romainville, France, on January 27, 1943 (Czech, *Auschwitz Chronicles,* p. 314).

33. October 6, 1944: 3,000 prisoners from Theresienstadt are gassed (Ibid., p. 724).

34. See Fenelon, *Musicians,* p. 197.

35. Czech relates this execution as having taken place on June 24, 1944 (*Auschwitz Chronicles,* pp. 650–51). This incident is also described in Fenelon, *Musicians,* pp. 158–64, as well as in several other sources.

36. October 1, 1944: "The Commandant's Office of Auschwitz I takes over a new camp for female prisoners, which arises on adjacent grounds. . . . The occupancy level in the women's camp in Auschwitz II, Camps B-Ia, B-Ib, and B-IIc, is 26,230" (Czech, *Auschwitz Chronicles,* p. 719).

37. Lagerarzt SS Obersturmführer Dr. Erwin von Helmersen was succeeded on December 5, 1943, by Lagerarzt SS Obersturmführer Heinz Thilo. He held the post until October or November, 1944, when Mengele replaced him. Thilo supervised the hospital barracks in the quarantine camp for men, BIIa, as well as BIIb, and BIId (Czech, "Role of the Men's Hospital," pp. 68–69).

38. October 7, 1944: There was a resistance in the camp. Prisoners set crematorium 4 on fire and threw several handmade grenades. Some of the prisoners of Squad 59B managed to escape to a nearby wooded area. When they saw this, prisoners of Squad 57B, who worked in crematorium 2, became active. They overpowered the head capo, a Reich German, and pushed him and an SS man into the burning crematorium, after which they beat to death a second SS man, tore up the fence surrounding the

crematorium area, and fled. All prisoners were caught and shot to death (Czech, *Auschwitz Chronicles*, pp. 725–26).

39. Twins, dwarfs, and physically underdeveloped people were taken to Block 2, which had been opened in October, 1943, for experimentation. Blood samples were drawn and sent to the laboratory at Rajsko (Czech, "Role of the Men's Hospital," pp. 46–47). In July, 1944, when the inhabitants of the family camp BIIb were being liquidated, Mengele had twins transferred from there to the hospital camp BIIf. There they were placed in a separate area of Block 15 along with twins, dwarfs, and cripples from newly arriving transports. They were first brought to camp BIIe (the *Ziguenerlager*, or Gypsy Camp) to be examined. Mengele had his experimental laboratory in Block 22. The Jewish laboratory manager was prisoner Dr. Bertold Epstein. After the gypsies had been liquidated on August 2, 1944, the laboratory was transferred to Block 15 in BIIf (Czech, "Role of the Men's Hospital," pp. 61–62).

40. Probably referring to Dr. Epstein, and perhaps to Dr. Miklos Nyiszli.

41. According to Myklos Nyiszli, soldiers scouted the ranks of arriving convoys to search for twins and dwarfs. Thinking that they would be given better treatment, mothers presented them willingly, and older ones presented themselves. They were indeed allowed to keep their clothes, given better food, and treated better than other prisoners. Placed in Barracks 14 of Camp F, the experimental barracks of the Gypsy camp, they were subjected to interminable medical examinations which included blood tests and blood exchanges between twins as well as lumbar punctures and comparative studies of facial and bone structure. They then had to die together "in the B section of Auschwitz's KZ barracks, at the hand of Dr. Mengele" so autopsies could be performed on both (*Auschwitz*, pp. 50–51).

42. January 27, 1943: "Dr. Bruno Weber and Dr. Konig from the firm of Bayer . . . write to Camp Dr. SS First Lieutenant Dr. Vetter, and recommend testing the tolerance among typhus fever patients for the nitroacridine preparation '3582.' If no typhus patients are available, the effect of the preparation should be observed on diarrhea patients." Dr. Vetter observed the effect of "3582," as well as of Rutenol on 50 typhus patients in the *Stammlager* (Czech, *Auschwitz Chronicles*, p. 314).

43. Shelley, *Criminal Experiments*, p. 17.

SECTION FIVE
BERGEN-BELSEN: THE BOWELS OF HELL

1. Bernadac, *Doctors of Mercy*, p. 335.
2. Feig, *Hitler's Death Camps*, p. 374.
3. Bernadac, *Doctors of Mercy*, p. 338.
4. Gilbert, *Holocaust*, p. 793.
5. W. R. F. Collis, "Belsen Camp: A Preliminary Report," *British Medical Journal* (June 9, 1945): 814–16.

6. Lüneburg War Crimes Trials, RG 153, Records of the Office of the Judge Advocate General (Army) War Crimes Branch, Declassification Review Project, NND 735027, Record Group 153, Entry 143, Case Files 1944–1949, 12-459, boxes 271, 272, 273, National Archives, Suitland, Maryland, Sington Testimony, vol. 1, folder 2, box 271, September 27, 1945, p. 22, National Archives, Suitland, Maryland.

7. "Problems of Development: Three Approaches," in Sheldon White and Barbara Notkin White, *Childhood: Pathways of Discovery*, p. 98.

8. Hela Jafe, Deposition, taken by M. Thau, October, 1965. United States Holocaust Memorial Museum Research Archives, ed. Diane Plotkin with inaccuracies in translation corrected by Dr. Hadassah Rosensaft. Permission to publish courtesy of Hela Jafe.

CHAPTER TEN. HELA LOS JAFE: "PEOPLE DIDN'T GO WILLINGLY"

1. United States Holocaust Memorial Museum/Hadassah Rosensaft Collection, United States Research Institute Archives, RG-50.266, Interview with Genia R. (Abstract), pp. 5–6.

2. September 1, 1939.

3. As of November 16, 1949, 1,170 Jewish grocery shops and 2,600 other shops owned by Jewish merchants on the "Aryan" side were sealed (*The Warsaw Ghetto Diary of Adam Czerniakow, Prelude to Doom*, ed. Raul Hilberg, Stanislaw Staron, and Josef Kermisz, trans. Stanislaw Staron and the staff of Yad Vashem [New York: Stein and Day, 1982], p. 222).

4. About seventy-five thousand people were forced into two ghettos that were connected by a bridge over the intersection of the "Aryan" Zelazna Street and Chlodna Street. (*The Ghetto Anthology: A Comprehensive Chronicle of the Extermination of Jewry in Nazi Death Camps and Ghettos in Poland*, p. 310). Czerniakow states that the Warsaw Ghetto was divided into "northern and southern sections, which were separated by an 'Aryan' street (Chlodna)" (*Warsaw Ghetto Diary*, p. 40).

5. July 23, 1943: "'It is 3 o'clock. So far there are 4,000 ready to go. According to orders, there are to be four thousand [more] by 4 o'clock. . . . I am powerless, my heart trembles in sorrow and compassion. I can no longer bear this. My act will show everyone the right thing to do'" (Czerniakow, *Warsaw Ghetto Diary*, p. 23).

6. Abraham Jacob Krzepicki, after being at Treblinka for eighteen days, escaped and published the truth about the camp in an underground newspaper which began: "'Today every Jew should know the fate of those resettled. . . . Don't let yourself be caught'" (Gilbert, *Holocaust*, p. 461).

7. Dr. Janusz Korczak, head of the Children's Orphanage on Krochmalna Street, accompanied the children to Treblinka on August 5, 1942 (Aaron Zeitlin, *Janusz Korczak: Ghetto Diary, The Last Walk of Janusz Korczak*).

8. Walther C. Toebbens K.G. (Clothing) and Schultz & Co., Danzig (mattresses and

furs) (Czerniakow, *Warsaw Ghetto Diary*, p. 51). Part of the *Deutsche Firmengemeinschaft Warschau m.b.H.*, which began in the second half of 1941, Toebbens employed without wages at least forty-five hundred Jewish workers. He came to control all Jewish undertakings in the ghetto (*Judische Produktiongesellschaft m.b.H.*), which operated under the auspices of the *Judenrat*. He received his orders, however, from the Gestapo (Yisrael Gutman, *The Jews of Warsaw, 1939–1943: Ghetto, Underground, Revolt*, p. 205).

9. Czerniakow lists five additional German firms: Waldemar Schmidt, Warsaw (straw shoes); A. Ney, Berlin (straw shoes); Metallwarnefabrik A.G., Bromberg (furniture); Fa. Brauer, Danzig (leather products); and Astra Werke, Chemnitz (adding machines), as well as eight Jewish companies which were licensed for district exports (*Warsaw Ghetto Diary*, pp. 51, 53).

10. On June 22, 1942, a third section of the ghetto was built which encompassed eighteen buildings, housing six hundred families (*Scroll of Agony: The Warsaw Ghetto Diary of Chaim A. Kaplan*, pp. 358–59). Toebbens operated a whole network of shops, some of which were on Ciepla, Twarda, Prosta, and Ceglana Streets (Berg, *Warsaw Ghetto*, p. 188).

11. A street in the larger area which was separated from the "small ghetto" by an "Aryan" area.

12. Approximately twenty thousand Jews lived in housing blocks attached to the factories in which they worked (Gutman, *Jews of Warsaw*, p. 269). One of the workers' streets was Walicow, which Jafe mentions. For other names of streets on which workers lived see *Ghetto Anthology*, pp. 315–16.

13. Mass deportations began in July, 1942, and continued through mid September. During that time at least 250,000–275,000 Jews were transported to their deaths. About 254,000 died in Treblinka, 11,000 were taken to other concentration camps, over 6,000 were shot, and about 3,600 died in the ghetto, including about 200 suicides (*In the Warsaw Ghetto Summer 1941, Photographs by Willy Georg with Passages from Warsaw Ghetto Diaries*, compiled, with an afterword, by Rafael F. Scharf [New York: Aperture, n.d.], p. 108, and *Ghetto Anthology*, p. 314).

14. August 14, 1942: Yitzhak Mier Levin: "'yesterday 2–4,000 people were taken from Toebbens's "shops" in the ghetto, mostly women and children'" (as cited in Gutman, *Jews of Warsaw*, p. 216).

15. September 22, 1942: "Yesterday was the Day of Atonement, and on this sacred day the Nazis . . . chose to blockade Ostrowska and Wolynska Streets. Out of the 2,500 policemen they singled out 380 for continued service, and more than 2,000 others were deported, together with their families" (Berg, *Warsaw Ghetto*, p. 186).

16. On April 3, 1943, German members of the *Werkschutz* surrounded three of Toebbens's workshops and transported about 400 people to Poniatow. Between April 6 and 12, 360 workers and 36 others were also forcibly removed (Gutman, *Jews of Warsaw*, p. 355).

17. On February 23, 1943, Toebbens had dispatched his first transport of Jews and equipment to Poniatow, a labor camp in which he told his workers they would be pro-

tected. No one believed him, as Najberg commented, "So this is a new trick of murderers!" (Gilbert, *Holocaust*, p. 560; Gutman, *Jews of Warsaw*, pp. 332–33).

18. In an attempt to counteract growing suspicion, Toebbens issued a notice: "*Place your faith solely on the heads of the German firms who, together with you, want to transfer the production to Poniatow and Trawniki.* Take your wives and children with you, for they will also be looked after." The notice was signed by Toebbens as "Supervisor of the Evacuation of Firms from the Jewish Quarter of Warsaw" (Marek Edelman, *geto walczy*, 1946, as cited in Gutman, *Jews of Warsaw*, p. 335).

19. A short, dead-end street in the "small ghetto." The factories with Jewish workers were outside the reduced ghetto, on Leszno, Karmelicka, Nowolipki, Smocza, Nowolipie, and Zelazna Streets (Berg, *Warsaw Ghettos*, 188). For a more complete description of the borders of the ghettos and the areas of shops that were owned by Schultz and Toebbens, see *Ghetto Anthology*, pp. 309–10, 314–16.

20. The residual ghetto was now in the northern district of the original area, bordered by Smocza, Gesia, Bonifraterska, Muranowska, Pokorna, Stawka, Dzika, and Szczesliwa Streets and Parisowski Square (*Ghetto Anthology*, p. 314; Berg, *Warsaw Ghetto*, p. 188). The main focus of the Warsaw Ghetto uprising was in a bunker at 18 Mila Street (Gilbert, *Holocaust*, p. 564).

21. The ZPB (Jewish Fighting Organization), after assassinating Jacob Leijkin, the policeman who symbolized Jewish collaboration with the Germans, issued handbills proclaiming that they had likewise convicted members of the Judenrat and managers of "shops" and members of the Werkschutz due to their cruel treatment of the workers (Gutman, *Jews of Warsaw*, p. 302).

22. "'Rise up and fight! Do not despair of the chance of rescue'"—text in the manifesto in Blumenthal and Kermish, *Ha-Meri ve ha-Mered*, January, 1943, pp. 122–23 (as cited in Gutman, *Jews of Warsaw*, p. 305).

23. April 19, 1943 (Gilbert, *Holocaust*, p. 557).

24. On April 21, 1943, in accordance with Stroop's demand to evacuate the area of shops, Toebbens issued a deportation order to the management of the sixteen major "shops" (Gutman, *Jews of Warsaw*, p. 385).

25. Formerly a prisoner of war camp for Russian soldiers.

26. By March, 1943, the Russians were advancing into Germany. Thus Himmler chose to close the death camps of Belzec, Sobibor, and Treblinka. During September and October, 1943, about one hundred Jewish prisoners, commanded by Franz Stangl, dismantled Treblinka. Only about thirty prisoners remained after that, and the last transport carrying equipment from the camp departed on November 17, 1943 (Yitzhak Arad, *Belzec, Sobibor, Treblinka: The Operation Reinhard Death Camps*, pp. 370–72).

27. According to Gilbert, the Skarzysko-Kamienna ammunition camp was one of the most ferocious labor camps in Poland (*Holocaust*, p. 635).

28. Many survivors relate this same event.

29. Although camps 1 and 2 were inhabited predominantly by Jews, they came from

various countries. Collis states that the prison population was of various nationalities: Russian, Polish, Czechoslovakian, Belgian, French, and Italian ("Belsen Camp," pp. 814–16).

30. According to Presser, "the Germans . . . referred to it as a recuperation centre" (*Ashes*, p. 515).

31. Regarding families, Herzberger states that "in Bergen-Belsen too the Germans . . . saw fit to 'keep families together'" (Herzberger, *Tweestroomland*, no other bibliographic data given, as cited in Presser, *Ashes*, p. 520).

32. According to a document issued in The Hague on September 21, 1943, those eligible to go to Bergen-Belsen included Jews with South American passports, as well as others with double nationality, Portuguese Jews, and those with Palestine stamps (Presser, *Ashes*, p. 514).

33. A German document of August 31, 1943, signed by Kaltenbrunner contained several directives for running the "Residential Camp of Bergen-Belsen near Celle (Hanover)." Because at first the Germans hoped that the inmates might be exchanged for German prisoners, several survived. At first it was considered a privilege to be sent there (Ibid., pp. 513–15).

34. Presser notes that at least two trains carrying Dutch Jews left the camp, one on Sunday, April 8, and the other on Tuesday, April 10, 1945 (*Ashes*, p. 522).

35. According to the testimony of Lidia Sunschein, children and sick people received such "special diets" as milk soups, but no special proteins, vegetables, or fruits (Lüneburg Trials, 12-459, vol. 1, folder 2, box 271, September 27, 1945, tenth day, p. 22).

36. There were water tanks in the Lager, but the British found them to be contaminated. They even found a dead body floating in one (Lüneburg Trials, Sington Testimony, vol. 1, folder 2, Saturday, September 22, 1945, p. 14).

37. Dr. Rosensaft recalls that all the items were obtained through the help of Jewish men and women who, as inmates, were assigned to work in the SS food stores and pharmacy. She also states that one time the children got a few pieces of chocolate when a transport of Jews from Holland arrived in Belsen. The female inmates who were assigned to confiscate their suitcases found some chocolate in them and were kind enough to give some to the children (Dr. Hadassah Rosensaft, telephone conversation with Diane Plotkin, August 31, 1995).

38. The word "hospital" is a horrible misnomer. As Dr. Collis describes it, "The dead lie all over the camp and in piles outside the huts which house the worst of the sick and are miscalled hospitals" ("Belsen Camp," p. 814).

39. Although there was no gas chamber in Bergen-Belsen, there was a crematorium, but it was inadequate to accommodate the number of corpses.

40. According to Dr. Collis's description, "The dead lie all over the camp and in piles outside the blocks of huts . . ." ("Belsen Camp," p. 814).

41. According to the testimony of Dr. Leo Fritz, about eight days before the arrival of the British troops, SS Dr. Horstmann "made some very strenuous attempts. It seems

that he was very keen on having all the corpses removed before the British troops arrived. He kept his watch in his hand and he looked at it hourly and chased the people to hurry to get the corpses away as soon as possible" (Lüneburg Trials, vol. 1, folder 2, box 271, Friday, September 28, 1945, p. 33).

42. Gen. Glyn Hughes testified that Kramer was "very vague" about the supply of bread, and Lieutenant Sington recalled Kramer as having said that the distribution of bread had become a "rare thing." Dr. Fritz testified that bread came to the camp in trucks, perhaps from Saltau. Although there were adequate supplies of bread, it had not been distributed (Ibid., Hughes Testimony, Saturday, September 22, 1945, p. 14; Sington Testimony, p. 22). Regarding the distribution of bread, Dr. Fritz testified, "in the last few weeks . . . no bread at all. Perhaps this led to the rumor that the bread had been poisoned, for according to the aforementioned testimonies, the British found no evidence of this (Lüneburg Trials, Fritz Testimony, vol. 1, folder 2, pp. 28, 31).

43. Although they could not find any testimony regarding the poisoning of bread, Helen Hammersmasch testified that there were medicine bottles which were labeled glucose but which actually contained petrol. These were opened in the presence of a British doctor (Lüneburg Trials, Hammersmasch Testimony, vol. 1, folder 2, pp. 18, 23).

44. Perhaps Mrs. Jafe is referring to Dr. Fritz, who, although he was a German physician, was himself an inmate.

45. Dr. Fritz testified that an SS Dr. Schnabel worked at Bergen-Belsen. Regarding the conditions, he said "He was terrified about it and said 'I shall not go on with this.'" Following that Dr. Horstmann came and attempted to clean the camp a bit (Lüneburg Trials, Fritz Testimony, vol. 1, folder 2, pp. 26, 33).

46. Army Medical Services were set up under the direction of S.M.O. Camp Lieut. Col. J. A. D. Johnston. About a week later a contingent of the British Red Cross came to help, and about two weeks after liberation, one hundred medical students arrived under the direction of Dr. Meiklejohn of UNRRA (Collis, "Belsen Camp," p. 814).

47. Gen. Glyn Hughes testified that there was a "beautiful military hospital" for treating battle casualties that could accommodate approximately five hundred patients (Lüneburg Trials, vol. 1, folder 2, box 271, p. 2).

48. Dr. Collis makes mention of the fact that a wing in the military hospital was being reserved for several orderlies and RAMC personnel who had themselves contracted typhus ("Belsen Camp," p. 815).

49. At first, due to a shortage of skilled medical personnel, the British had to employ German nurses and physicians (Ibid.).

50. "Three blocks at the back are kept for maternity patients and children" (Ibid.).

51. W. R. F. Collis, M.D., F.R.C.P., F.R.C.P.I., D.P.H.

52. According to Dr. Collis, typhus cases were most often complicated by "thrombosis, gangrene, and bronchopneumonia." It is most likely that he placed her in Trendelenberg (head down) position in order to help the lungs drain (Ibid.).

53. Under the leadership of Josef Rosensaft, the new Belsen became a community unto

itself in which the survivors built a children's school (Feig, *Hitler's Death Camps*, p. 388).

54. Dr. Bimko accompanied a group of ninety-eight children to Palestine on April 9, 1946 (Dr. Hadassah Rosensaft, telephone conversation with Diane Plotkin, August 22, 1995).

55. Elspeth Huxley, *Florence Nightingale* (New York: G. P. Putnam's Sons, 1975), p. 107.

CHAPTER ELEVEN. DR. ADA BIMKO: "DON'T BE AFRAID, CHILD"

1. Gill, *Journey Back*, pp. 394–95.

2. Lüneburg War Crimes Trials, RG 153, Records of the Office of the Judge Advocate General (Army) War Crimes Branch, Declassification Review Project, NND 735027, Record Group 153, Entry 143, Case Files 1944–1949, 12-459, boxes 271, 272, 273, National Archives, Suitland, Maryland.

3. United States Holocaust Memorial Museum/Hadassah Rosensaft Collection, United States Research Institute Archives, RG-50.260.

4. Gerald Reitlinger, *The Final Solution: An Attempt to Exterminate the Jews of Europe, 1939–1945*, pp. 469–70.

5. Lüneburg Trials, vol. 1, folder 3, September 18, 1945, Hughes Testimony, pp. 3 ff.

6. Ibid., p. 7.

7. Ibid., p. 10.

8. Lüneburg Trials, vol. 1, folder 2, box 271, Wednesday, September 19, 1945, Deposition of Maj. Gen. James Alexander Deans Johnston, R.A.M.O., p. 8.

9. Ibid., Saturday, September 22, 1945, p. 12.

10. "Dr. Hadassah Rosensaft," in *The Liberation of the Camps: Eyewitness Accounts of the Liberators*, ed. Brewster Chamberlin and Marcia Feldman, intro. Robert H. Abzug (Washington, D.C.: United States Holocaust Memorial Council, 1987), p. 153.

11. Ibid., p. 9.

12. According to Dr. Rosensaft, the reporter was incorrect. Her father, mother, *one sister*, husband, and six-year-old son were killed. Her brother Benjamin, six years younger than she, did not go with the family to Auschwitz but rather remained in the ghetto. He was a member of the underground youth resistance. He was caught with four others and shot by the Germans at the end of August, 1943 (Dr. Hadassah Rosensaft, telephone conversations with Diane Plotkin, August 17, 30, 1995).

13. Lüneburg Trials, vol. 1, folder 2, box 271, p. 9, "Jewess Names SS Criminals," *Sun*, September 22, 1945.

14. Ibid., vol. 1, folder 2, box 271, pp. 21–22, September, 1945, Bimko Testimony, p. 2.

15. *Liberation*, p. 152.

16. Lüneburg Trials, Bimko Testimony, p. 8.

17. Ibid., p. 9.

18. Ibid., p. 8.

19. *Liberation,* p. 152.

20. Lüneburg Trials, Bimko Testimony, p. 8.

21. Ibid., p. 9.

22. Ibid., vol. 1, folder 2, box 271, September 24, 1945, Testimony of Dora Szafrin, p. 26.

23. Ibid., vol. 1, folder 2, box 271, Bimko Testimony, p. 16.

24. Ibid., p. 10.

25. Ibid., vol. 1, folder 3, box 271, Hughes Testimony, p. 4.

26. *Liberation,* p. 152.

27. Ibid., p. 153.

28. Hadassah Bimko-Rosensaft, "The Children of Belsen," in *Belsen* (Israel: Irgun Sheeirt, Hapleita, Me'Haezor Habriti, 1957), pp. 98–100.

29. United States Holocaust Memorial Museum, Liberation, [1981 International Liberators Conference Collection of liberator testimonies], United States Research Archives, RG-09.005*26. Langenstein.

30. United States Holocaust Memorial Museum/Hadassah Rosensaft Collection, United States Research Institute Archives, RG-50.266, Interview with Genia R. (Abstract), pp. 5–6.

31. *Liberation,* pp. 65–66.

32. United States Holocaust Memorial Museum, United States Research Institute Archives, RG-04.020*01, "The Relief of Belsen Concentration Camp: Recollections & Reflections of a British Army Doctor," pp. 5–6.

33. Rosensaft Testimony, Liberators Conference.

34. *Liberation,* p. 153.

35. Gill, *Journey Back,* pp. 394–95.

36. Ibid., pp. 391–92.

37. Rosensaft, "Children," pp. 102–104.

38. Dr. Hadassah Rosensaft, telephone conversations, August 17, 30, 1995.

39. Rosensaft, "Children," pp. 102–104.

40. Rosensaft Testimony, Liberators Conference.

CHAPTER TWELVE. MAGDA HERZBERGER: "GOD SAVED ME FOR A PURPOSE"

1. Magda Herzberger, Interview, Dubuque, Iowa, June 14, 1993.

2. Magda Herzberger, "Eulogy (in memory of my father)," in *Eyewitness to Holocaust,* p. 74.

3. Magda Herzberger, "The Yellow Star," in *The Waltz of the Shadows,* p. 25.

4. Magda Herzberger, "Memorial," in *Eyewitness,* p. 15.

5. Dr. Fritz Klein, from Braschow, medical director of the camp. He was in charge of the women's camp at Auschwitz. He believed Jews were the equivalent of a "gangrenous appendix," according to references in Lifton, *Nazi Doctors,* pp. 1, 206.

6. Herzberger, "Eulogy," p. 30.

7. The main camp, Auschwitz I, had one gas chamber and crematory oven; Birkenau [Auschwitz II], the extermination camp to which Magda was brought, had four.

8. Actually the term *sonderkommando* refers to the group of men who removed the corpses from the gas chambers, examined them for hidden gold or jewelry, and put them into the crematory ovens. Every so often the *sonderkommando* were themselves exterminated, and a new group of men were designated as sonderkommando.

9. In this context, "number" means count.

10. This is a common misconception among Holocaust survivors. There is no historical evidence to support the claim that there was any such powder in the soup.

11. Clauberg conducted the sterilization experiments on women in Auschwitz, Block 10.

12. According to one account, when Auschwitz "was liberated by the Russians on January 27, 1945, approximately 160 twins were found. Later another 30 or 40 were found" (Lucette Matalon Lagnado and Sheila Cohn Dekel, *Children of the Flames: Dr. Joseph Mengele and the Untold Story of the Twins of Auschwitz,* p. 257).

13. Magda Herzberger, "The Streets of Bremen," in *Eyewitness,* pp. 18–19.

14. Maj. Gen. James Alexander Deans Johnston, Q.B.E., M.C., Q.H.P., describes a square area of barracks set up by the British army medical units that would be sufficient for ten thousand patients. This area consisted of a "series of square buildings . . . each square would accommodate 600 patients in barrack buildings" (*The Relief of Belsen Concentration Camp: Recollections & Reflections of a British Army Doctor,*" courtesy of U.S.H.M.M.).

15. Magda Herzberger, "Hymn of Gratitude," in *Waltz,* p. 84.

16. Magda Herzberger, "A Song is Born," in *Waltz,* p. 96.

17. Noddings, *Caring,* p. 81.

SECTION SIX

LIBERATION

1. A letter home, from a liberator's speech given by Jack Coulston.

2. Irving Heymont, *Among the Survivors of the Holocaust—1945: The Heymont Letters,* p. 5.

3. Marie Ellifritz, Speech, June 5, 1982, for Elizabeth Buxton Hospital Nurses Alumnae, Fort Monroe Officers Club, Fort Monroe, Virginia, USHMM Archives.

CHAPTER THIRTEEN. MARIE ELLIFRITZ:
"MY SORROW IS CONTINUOUSLY BEFORE ME"

This chapter adapted from Reba Karp, "Liberators! A Nurse's Story . . . ," *Renewal Magazine* 1 (Mar. 29, 1985): 25, 75; published by the United Jewish Federation of Tidewater. Permission to publish courtesy of Reba Karp, Director of Communications, and United States Holocaust Research Institute Archives, Record Group 50, Oral History Collection, 234*11, United States Holocaust Memorial Council/International Liberators Conference Collection, "Interview with Marie Ellifritz."

1. Karp, "Liberators!," p. 75.

2. Unless otherwise indicated, material is USHRIA, RG-50.234*11.

3. Karp, "Liberators!," p. 75; page numbers of subsequent quotes from this source will appear in parentheses in the text.

4. Stalag VII-A. Jewish prisoners of war were segregated from the others (Mitchell G. Bard, *Forgotten Victims: The Abandonment of Americans in Hitler's Camps*, p. 41).

SECTION SEVEN
SURVIVOR'S PURGATORY

1. Gill, *Journey Back*, pp. 369–70.

2. Lengyel, *Five Chimneys*, p. 208.

3. Maria Rosenbloom, "Bearing Witness by Holocaust Survivors: Implications for Mental Health Theory and Practice," in Alan L. Berg, ed. *Bearing Witness to the Holocaust 1939–1989*, (Lewiston, N.Y.: E. Mellen Press, 1991), p. 342.

4. Gill, *Journey Back*, p. 398.

5. Bruno Frappat, "Militant Du Souvenir," *Le Monde*, July 7–8, 1985, trans. Barbara Pequinot-Ganch and Martine Bastianelli. Printed with permission of *Le Monde*.

CHAPTER FIFTEEN.
CONCLUSION: BEYOND THE PARADOX

1. Elie Cohen, "Psychology of the Prisoner," in *Human Behavior in the Concentration Camp*, pp. 115–210.

2. Ibid., p. 116.

3. Ibid., p. 120.

4. Ibid., pp. 125–27.

5. Ella Lingens-Reiner, *Prisoners of Fear* (London, 1948), p. 43, as quoted in Cohen, *Human Behavior*, p. 127.

6. Viktor E. Frankl, *Man's Search for Meaning: An Introduction to Logotherapy*, pp. 104–105.

7. Cohen, *Human Behavior*, p. 179.

8. Frankl, *Man's Search*, pp. 68–69.

9. Cohen, *Human Behavior*, p. 127.

10. Janice B. Lindberg, R.N., M.A., Ph.D., Mary Love Hunter, R.N., M.S., C.S., and Ann Kruszewski, R.N., M.S.N., "Nursing as an Art," in *Introduction to Nursing: Concepts, Issues, & Opportunities* (Philadelphia: J. B. Lippincott, 1990), p. 28.

11. M. B. Etziony, *The Physician's Creed* (Springfield, Ill.: Charles C. Thomas, 1973), as quoted in Tom L. Beauchamp and LeRoy Walters, *Contemporary Issues in Bioethics*, p. 139.

12. Gilligan, *Woman's Place*, p. 11, as quoted in Noddings, *Caring*, p. 96.

13. Dr. Hadassah Rosensaft, Interview, New York, June 16, 1996.

14. Copy of DAR Americanism Award—Dr. Ellen Loeb, p. 284.

APPENDIX A.
WOMEN PRISONERS AT KL MAUTHAUSEN

1. Reprinted material from "Women Prisoners at KL Mauthausen," provided by Margret Lehner. Trans. from French by Diane Plotkin.

APPENDIX B.
MUSHROOM SAUSAGE EXPERIMENTS

1. During their research, Margret Lehner and her co-authors came upon this evidence of experimentation. Ellen Loeb writes of prisoners suffering from abdominal pain. Perhaps they had been fed this "mushroom sausage."
2. Mushrooms with mycelial threads (fruiting bodies) (*The Oxford-Duden German-English Dictionary* [Oxford: Clarendon Press, 1979; rpt. 1984], p. 670).

Bibliography

• • •

AKT B.f.I.Z.J. 245499-33/66. Letter to director of paperworks in Lenzing, Austria, Dr. Hornke. Supplied by Margret Lehner, Lenzing, Austria.

Alighieri, Dante. *Dante's Inferno.* Translated, with notes and commentary, by Mark Musa. Bloomington and London: Indiana University Press, 1974.

——. *The Divine Comedy.* Vol 2: *Purgatory.* Translated, with an introduction, notes, and commentary, by Mark Musa. New York: Penguin Books, 1981; rpt. 1985.

Angelucci, Enzo. *The Rand McNally Encyclopedia of Military Aircraft, 1914–1980.* New York: Military Press, 1983.

Annas, George J., and Michael A. Grodin. *The Nazi Doctors and the Nuremberg Code: Human Rights in Human Experimentation.* New York and Oxford: Oxford University Press, 1992.

Arad, Yitzhak. *Belzec, Sobibor, Treblinka: The Operation Reinhard Death Camps.* Bloomington and Indianapolis: Indiana University Press, 1987.

——. *Ghetto in Flames: The Struggle and Destruction of the Jews of Vilna in the Holocaust.* Jerusalem: Yad Vashem, 1980.

Aziz, Philippe. *Doctors of Death.* 4 vols. Translated by Edouard Bizub and Philip Haentzler, under the guidance of Linda Marie de Turenne. Geneva: Ferna Publishers, 1976.

Bard, Mitchell G. *Forgotten Victims: The Abandonment of Americans in Hitler's Death Camps.* Boulder, San Francisco, and London: Westview Press, 1994.

Bauer, Yehuda. *Jews for Sale: Nazi-Jewish Negotiations, 1933–1945.* London and New Haven: Yale University Press, 1994.

Bearing Witness to the Holocaust 1939–1989. Edited by Alan L. Berger. Lewiston, N.Y.: Edwin Mellon Press, 1991.

Beauchamp, Tom L., and LeRoy Walters. *Contemporary Issues in Bioethics.* Belmont, Calif.: Wadsworth Publishing Company, 1978.

Beer, Susan. "To Auschwitz and Back: An Odyssey." Hungary, 1945. Translated by Susan Beer, 1980.

Benjamin, Anna, Hanna Kohner, Walter Kohner, and Frederick Kohner. *Hanna and Walter—A Love Story.* Austria: Knaur-Taschen Books, 1954.

Berg, Mary. *Warsaw Ghetto: A Diary by Mary Berg.* Edited by S. L. Schneiderman. New York: L. B. Fischer, 1945.

Berkley, George F. *Hitler's Gift: The Story of Theresienstadt.* Boston: Branden Books, 1993.

Bernadac, Christian. *Doctors of Mercy.* Paris: France-Empire, 1968; Geneva: Ferni, 1977.

Bimko-Rosensaft, Hadassah. "The Children of Belsen." In *Belsen.* No editor listed. Israel: Irgun Sheerit, Hapleita, Me'Haezor Habriti, 1957.

Blumenson, Martin. *The Patton Papers, 1940–1945.* Illustrated with photographs and maps by Samuel H. Bryant. Boston: Houghton Mifflin, 1974.

Bondy, Ruth. *"Elder of the Jews": Jakob Edelstein of Theresienstadt.* Translated by Evelyn Abel. New York: Grove Press, 1989.

Borowski, Tadeusz. *This Way for the Gas, Ladies and Gentlemen.* Selected and translated by Barbara Vedder. Introduction by Jan Knott. Introduction translated by Michael Kandel. New York: Penguin Books, 1976; rpt. 1982.

Bruml, Hana. Telephone Interview, March 6, 1992. Interview. Alexandria, Virginia, June 4, 1993.

Caplan, Arthur L., ed. *When Medicine Went Mad: Bioethics and the Holocaust.* Totowa, N.J.: Humana Press, 1992.

Cohen, Elie A. *Human Behavior in the Concentration Camp.* Preface by the author. Foreword by Dinora Pines. London: Free Association Books, 1988.

Collis, W. R. F., M.D., F.R.C.P., F.R.C.P.I., D.P.H. "Belsen Camp: A Preliminary Report." *British Medical Journal* (June 9, 1945): 814–16.

Coulston, John B. United States Army Veteran. Convent Station, New Jersey. Liberator's Notes.

Criminal Experiments on Human Beings in Auschwitz and War Research Laboratories: Twenty Women Prisoners' Accounts. Compiled, translated, and edited by Lore Shelley. San Francisco: Mellen Research University Press, 1991.

Czech, Danuta, ed. *Auschwitz Chronicle: 1939–1945: From the Archives of the Auschwitz Memorial and the German Federal Archives.* Foreword by Walter Laquer. New York: Henry Holt and Company, 1990.

———. "Role of the Men's Hospital Camp at KL Auschwitz II (Birkenau)." In *From the History of KL-Auschwitz.* Vol 2. Auschwitz: Państwowe Muzeum W Oświecimu, 1976.

Dawidowicz, Lucy S. *The War Against the Jews, 1933–1949.* 10th ed. New York: Bantam Books, 1986.

Delbo, Charlotte. *Auschwitz and After.* Translated by Rosette C. Lamont. Introduction by Lawrence L. Langer. New Haven and London: Yale University Press, 1995.

Des Pres, Terrence. *The Survivor: An Anatomy on Life in the Death Camps.* New York and Oxford: Oxford University Press, 1980.

Dobroszycki, Lucjan, ed. *The Chronicle of the Lodz Ghetto, 1941–1944.* Translated by Richard Lourie, Joachim Neugroschel, and others. New Haven and London: Yale University Press, 1984.

Document No. M3-1610. "Chief of the SS WVHA. The SS-Economic Administration. Ch/Po/Ha. V.s. 700." Berlin. August 16, 1943. Lichterfeld-West. Unter den Linden 126–135. Pertaining to: Dort. Written from 2,8,43, Tgb.Mr. 38/109/ 43 g. Supplied by Margret Lehner, Lenzing, Austria.

Dokumenty I Materialy Zczasow Okupacji Niemieckiej W Polsce. O Obozy [Documented Material in the Time of the German Occupation in the Polish Camps]. Tom I. Translated by Eddie Gorecky. Opracowal Mgr. N. Blumenthal, 1946.

Dorland's Illustrated Medical Dictionary. 27th ed. Philadelphia, London, and Toronto: W. B. Saunders Company, Harcourt Brace Jovanovich.

Dworkin, Andrea. "The Unremembered: Searching for Women at the Holocaust Memorial Museum." *Ms.* (November/December 1994): 52–58.

Emmens-Knol, Mayor A. "Speech on the Fiftieth Anniversary of the Liberation of Westerbork." Westerbork, The Netherlands, May 3, 1995.

Epstein, Rabbi Dr. I. *The Babylonian Talmud.* Vol. 3. Tractate Sanhedrin. London: Soncino Press, 1935.

Feig, Konnilyn G. *Hitler's Death Camps: The Sanity of Madness.* New York and London: Holmes & Meier, 1981.

Fenelon, Fania, with Marcelle Routier. *The Musicians of Auschwitz.* Translated by Judith Landry. London: Sphere Books, Limited, 1979; rpt. 1980.

Ferencz, Benjamin B. *Less Than Slaves: Jewish Forced Labor and the Quest for Compensation.* London and Cambridge, Mass.: Harvard University Press, 1979.

Fox, Dr. Esther. "Jewish Doctors and Their Work in the Ghetto (Lodz)." Condensed translation of original Polish article RG 92 A92. Donated by the Center for Holocaust Studies. Museum of Jewish Heritage, New York.

Frankl, Viktor E. *Man's Search for Meaning: An Introduction to Logotherapy.* Part 1 translated by Ilse Lasch. Preface by Gordon W. Allport. New York: Simon & Schuster, 1959, rpt. 1963.

Frappát, Bruno. "Militante du souvenir." *Le Monde,* July 7, 1985. Translated by Barbara Pèquinot-Ganch and Martine Bastianelli. Printed with permission of *Le Monde.*

Gertie, S. Interview. Sydney, Australia. June 7, 1994.

The Ghetto Anthology: A Comprehensive Chronicle of the Extermination of Jewry in Nazi Death Camps and Ghettos in Poland. Compiled and edited by Roman Mogilanski. Revised and prepared for publication by Benjamin Grey. Los Angeles: American Congress of Jews from Poland and Survivors of Concentration Camps—Musia Mogilanski, 1985.

Gilbert, Martin. *Atlas of the Holocaust.* Jerusalem, Tel-Aviv, and Haifa: Steimatsky's Agency Limited, 1982.

———. *The Holocaust: A History of the Jews of Europe during the Second World War.* New York: Holt, Rinehart & Winston, 1985.

Gill, Anton. *The Journey Back from Hell: An Oral History—Conversations with Concentration Camp Survivors.* New York: William Morrow & Company, 1988.

Gilligan, Carol. "Woman's Place in Man's Life Cycle." *Harvard Educational Review* 49 (1979).

Grau, Hildegard. Interviewed by Ruth Block, June 7, 1985. Interviewed by Jessica Selbst, April 1, 1986. The Yaffa Eliach Collection. GH 1304. Donated by the Center for Holocaust Studies. Museum of Jewish Heritage, New York.

Gross, Leonard. *The Last Jews in Berlin.* New York: Simon & Schuster, 1982.

Gutman, Yisrael. *The Jews of Warsaw, 1939–1943: Ghetto, Underground, Revolt.* Translated by Ina Friedman. Bloomington and Indianapolis: Indiana University Press, 1989.

Gutman, Yisrael, and Michael Berenbaum, eds. *Anatomy of the Auschwitz Death Camp.* Published in association with the United States Holocaust Memorial Museum, Washington, D.C. Bloomington and Indianapolis: Indiana University Press, 1994.

Haas, Albert, M.D. *The Doctor and the Damned.* Foreword by Dr. Howard Rusk. New York: Avon Books, 1984.

Hawle, Christian, Gerhard Kreichbaum, and Margret Lehner. *Tater und Opfer: Nationalsozialistische Gewalt und Widerstand im Bezirk Vöcklabruck 1938–1945.* Eine Dokumentation. Herausgegeben von Mauthausen-Activ-Vöcklabruck. Bibliothek der Provinz. Publication PN 1. Austria: Denkmayr Katsdorf-Linz-Wels, 1995.

Headquarters of 71st Infantry. Office of the A C of S, G-2. APO 360, U.S. Army. "G-2 Periodic Report." May 6, 1945. Department of the Army. Center of Military History. Research and Analysis Division, Washington, D.C.

Herzberger, Magda. *Eyewitness To Holocaust.* Mattoon, Ill.: Modern Images, 1987.

———. Interview. Dubuque, Iowa. June 14, 1993. Telephone Interviews, 1993–95.

———. *The Waltz of the Shadows.* New York: Philosophical Library, 1983.

Heymont, Irving. *Among the Survivors of the Holocaust—1945: The Heymont Letters.* Cincinnati: American Jewish Archives, 1945.

Hilberg, Raul. *The Destruction of the European Jews.* 3 vols. Revised and definitive edition. New York and London: Holmes & Meier, 1985.

Hill, Mavis M., and L. Norman Williams. *Auschwitz in England: A Record of a Libel Action.* Foreword by Lord Denning. Introduction by Alan U. Schwartz. New York: Stein & Day, 1965.

Hill, Mavis M., Stanislaw Staron, and Josef Kermisz. *The Warsaw Ghetto Diary of Adam Czerniakow, Prelude to Doom.* Translated by Stanislaw Staron and the staff of Yad Vashem. New York: Stein & Day, 1982.

Hillesum, Etty. *Etty: A Diary, 1941–43.* Introduction by J. G. Gaarlandt. Translated by Arnold J. Pomerans. London, Glasgow, and Toronto: Triad Grafton Books, 1985; rpt. 1986.

———. *An Interrupted Life: The Diaries of Etty Hillesum, 1941–43.* Introduction by J. G. Gaarlandt. New York, London, and Toronto: Washington Square Press, 1981.

The Holy Scriptures According to the Masoretic Text. New translation, with aid and previous versions and with constant consultation of Jewish authorities. Philadelphia: Jewish Publication Society of America, 1955.

"Jewess Names SS Criminals." *Sun,* September 22, 1945. Lüneburg War Crimes Trial RG 153, Records of the Office of the Judge Advocate General (Army) War Crimes Branch Case Files 1944–49 12-459. 1-60, Box 271, Folder 1, p. 3.

Karp, Reba. "Liberators! A Nurse's Story . . . ." *Renewal Magazine* 1 (March 29, 1985): 25. United Jewish Federation of Tidewater.

Kater, Michael H. *Doctors under Hitler.* Chapel Hill and London: University of North Carolina Press, 1989.

Klein, Gerda Weissman. *All But My Life.* New York: Hill & Wang, 1957.

Korzhavin, Naum. "Children of Auschwitz." In *Voices within the Ark: The Modern Jewish Poets.*

Edited by Howard Schwartz and Anthony Rudolph. New York: Avon Books, 1980, p. 1102.

Kraus, Ota, and Erich Kulka. *The Death Factory: Document on Auschwitz.* Translated by Stephen Jolly. Oxford: Pergamon Press, 1966.

Krylova, Libuse. *The Small Fortress of Terezin.* Terezin, 1975. Quoted in Konnilyn Feig, *Hitler's Death Camps: The Sanity of Madness.* New York and London: Holmes & Meier, 1979, p. 238.

Laqueur, Walter. *The Terrible Secret: Suppression of the Truth about Hitler's Final Solution.* New York and Middlesex, U.K.: Penguin Books, 1980.

Laska, Vera, ed. *Women in the Resistance in the Holocaust: The Voices of Eyewitnesses.* Introduction by Vera Laska. Foreword by Simon Wiesenthal. Westport, Conn. and London: Greenwood Press, 1983.

"The Last Days of Auschwitz: 50 Years Later: Untold Stories from the Death Camp." *Newsweek,* January 16, 1995, p. 46.

Lehner, Margret. Interview. Lenzing, Austria. March 11, 1994.

Lengyel, Olga. *Five Chimneys: The Story of Auschwitz.* Chicago and New York: Ziff-Davis, 1947.

Levi, Primo. *Survival in Auschwitz: The Nazi Assault on Humanity.* Translated by Stuart Woolf. New York and London: Collier Macmillan, 1961.

Levin, Nora. *The Holocaust: The Destruction of European Jewry 1933–1945.* New York: Schocken Books, 1973.

Levy-Hass, Hanna. *Vielleicht war das alles erst der Amfang: Tagebuch aus dem KZ Bergen-Belsen, 1944–1945.* Edited by Eikel Geisel. Berlin, 1979. Quoted in Milton, p. 311.

The Liberation of the Nazi Concentration Camps 1945: Eyewitness Accounts of the Liberators. Edited by Brewster Chamberlin and Marcia Feldman. Introduction by Robert H. Abzug. Washington, D.C.: United States Holocaust Memorial Council, 1987.

Lifton, Robert Jay. *The Nazi Doctors: Medical Killing and the Psychology of Genocide.* New York: Basic Books, 1986.

Lipman, Steve. *Laughter in Hell: The Use of Humor during the Holocaust.* Northvale, N.J. and London: Jason Aronson, 1991.

Lipstadt, Deborah. *Denying the Holocaust: The Growing Assault on Truth and Memory.* New York: Free Press, A Division of Macmillan, Inc., 1993.

Loeb, Ellen, M.D. Memoirs. Amsterdam, The Netherlands, 1946. Translated by Trudi Shakno and Diane Plotkin, 1993.

Loewenberg, Peter, M.D. Interview. Dallas, Texas. May 20, 1993.

Lüneburg War Crimes Trial. RG 153. Records of the Office of the Judge Advocate General (Army) War Crimes Branch. Case Files 1944–49, 12-459. Boxes 271, 272, 273, Declassification Review Project NND 735027. Record Group 153, Entry 143. National Archives, Suitland, Maryland.

Map of the Terezin Ghetto. Pamatnik Terezin. Muzeum Ghettz, Dr. Jan Munk, Director.

Marszalek, Jozef. *Majdanek, The Concentration Camp in Lublin.* Warsaw: Interpress, 1986.

Marti-Ibañez, Felix, M.D., ed. *The Epic of Medicine.* New York: Clarkson N. Potter, 1995; rpt. 1960, 1961, 1962.

Matalon Lagnado, Lucette, and Sheila Cohn Dekel. *Children of the Flames: Dr. Joseph Mengele and the Untold Story of the Twins of Auschwitz.* New York: William Morrow, 1991.

Maurel, Micheline. *An Ordinary Camp.* Translated by Margaret S. Summers. New York: Simon & Schuster, 1958.

Mechanicus, Philip. *Year of Fear: A Jewish Prisoner Waits for Auschwitz.* Translated by Irene S. Gibbons. New York: Hawthorn Books, 1968.

Medical Record and Fever Charts. Archives of the State Museum of Auschwitz-Birkenau. Permission to publish courtesy of Jerzy Wroblewski, Director.

Medicine and Jewish Law. Vol. 1. Edited by Fred Rosner, M.D. Northvale, N.J.: Jason Aronson, 1993.

Micheels, Louis J., M.D. *Doctor 117641: A Holocaust Memoir.* Foreword by Albert J. Solnit, M.D. New Haven and London: Yale University Press, 1989.

Milton, Dr. Sybil. "Survival Patterns Inside the Camps after 1939." In *Different Voices: Women and the Holocaust,* edited by Carol Rittner and John Roth. New York: Paragon House, 1993, pp. 227–32.

———. "Women and the Holocaust: The Case of German and German-Jewish Women." In *When Biology Became Destiny: Women in Weimar and Nazi Germany,* edited by Renate Bridenthal, Atina Grossman, and Marion Kaplan. New York: Monthly Review Press, 1984, pp. 279–333.

Minney, R. J. *I Shall Fear No Evil: The Story of Dr. Alina Brewda.* London: William Kimber, 1966.

Mitschlerlich, Alexander, M.D. *Doctors of Infamy : The Story of Nazi Medical Crimes.* Translated by Heinz Norden. Statements by Andrew Ivy, M.D., Telford Taylor, Leo Alexander. Note by Albert Deutsch. New York: Henry Schuman, 1949.

Mulder, Dirk. "Camp Westerbork: Symbol of Destruction." Translated by S. Bruidegorn and Dr. L. A. J. R. Houwen. The Arts Shop of the Faculty of the University of Gröningen.

Nahon, Marco, M.D. *Birkenau, The Camp of Death.* Translated by Jacqueline Havaux Bowers. Edited, with an introduction, by Steven Bowman. Tuscaloosa and London: University of Alabama Press, 1989.

Naor, Simha. *Krankengymnastin in Auschwitz Aufseichungen des Häftlings Nr. 80574.* Vorwort: Tisa von der Schulenburg / Basel and Vienna: Freiburg Im Breisgau, 1986.

Nightingale, Florence. *Notes on Nursing: What It Is and What It Is Not.* Foreword by Virginia M. Dunbar. New preface by Margaret B. Dolan. New York: Dover Publications, 1969.

Noddings, Nel. *Caring: A Feminine Approach to Ethics & Moral Education.* Berkeley: University of California Press, 1984.

Nomberg-Przytyk, Sara. *True Tales from a Grotesque Land.* Translated by Roslyn Hirsch. Edited by Eli Pfefferkorn and David H. Hirsch. Chapel Hill and London: University of North Carolina Press, 1985.

Nyiszli, Dr. Miklos. *Auschwitz: A Doctor's Eyewitness Account.* Translated by Tibere Kremer and Richard Seaver. Foreword by Bruno Bettleheim. New York: Fawcett Crest, 1960.

"The Oath of Hippocrates." in *The World Book Encyclopedia.* Vol. 9. Chicago: Field Enterprises, 1977, p. 227.

Obozy Hitlerowski na Ziemach Polkich 1939–1945. Warsaw: Panstwowe Wydawnictwo Naukowe, 1979. Translated by Leo Laufer.

The Oxford-Duden Pictorial German-English Dictionary. Oxford: Clarendon Press, 1979; rpt. 1984.

"Pamatnik Terezin." Translated by Gita Zbavitelova. Photos by Frantisek Maly. Terezin: Pamatnik Terezin, 1992.

Pauley, Bruce F. *From Prejudice to Persecution: A History of Austrian Anti-Semitism.* Chapel Hill and London: University of North Carolina Press, 1992.

Perl, Dr. Gisella. *I Was a Doctor in Auschwitz.* Salem, N.H.: Ayer Company, 1992.

Plotkin, Diane M. "A Historiographic Analysis of a Survivor's Narrative: The Story of Leo Laufer." Ph.D. diss., The University of Texas at Arlington, 1990.

Poller, Walter. *Medical Block, Buchenwald: The Personal Testimony of Inmate 996, Block 36.* New York: A Lyle Stuart Book, 1960.

Presser, Dr. J. *Ashes in the Wind: The Destruction of Dutch Jewry.* Translated by Arnold Pomerans. Detroit: Wayne State University Press, 1988.

Rashke, Richard. *Escape from Sobibor.* New York: Avon Books, 1982.

Rauschning, Hermann. *The Voice of Destruction.* Quoted in the Testimony of Abram Gerzevitch Suzkever. *Trial of the Major War Criminals before the International Military Tribunal.* Nuremberg. November 14, 1945–October 1, 1946. Vol. 8. Proceedings February 20, 1946–March 7, 1946. Nuremberg, Germany, 1947, p. 312.

Reiser, Ruth. Interview. New York. March 5, 1994. Telephone Interviews 1994–95.

Reitlinger, Gerald. *The Final Solution: The Attempt to Exterminate the Jews of Europe 1939–1945.* Northvale, N.J. and London: Jason Aronson, 1987.

Ringelheim, Dr. Joan. "Thoughts about Women and the Holocaust." In *Thinking the Unthinkable: Meanings of the Holocaust,* edited by Roger S. Gottleib. New York: Paulist Press, 1990, pp. 141–49.

Rittner, Carol, and John Roth, eds. *Different Voices: Women and the Holocaust.* Introductions by Carol Rittner and John K. Roth. New York: Paragon House, 1993.

Rosensaft, Dr. Hadassah. Telephone Conversations. 1995.

Roth, John, and Michael Berenbaum. *Holocaust: Religious and Philosophical Implications.* New York: Paragon House, 1989.

Schiff, Rosalie. Interview. Dallas, Texas, August 5, 1995.

Schwalbova, Dr. Margita. Interview. Panstwowe Museum W Osweicimiu Archiwum. June 8, 1988. Translated by Helen Koch. Archives of the State Museum of Auschwitz-Birkenau. Permission to publish courtesy of Jerzy Wroblewski, Director.

Schwertfeger, Ruth. *Women of Theresienstadt: Voices from a Concentration Camp.* New York: St. Martin's Press, 1989.

Scroll of Agony: The Warsaw Ghetto of Chaim A. Kaplan. Revised, translated, and edited by Abraham I. Katsch. New York: Collier Books, 1965; rpt. 1973.

"The Seventy-First Came . . . To Gunskirchen Lager." Foreword by Willard G. Wyman, Major General, USA Commanding. Courtesy of Leo Serian.

Shakno, Trudi. Interview. Dallas, Texas. June 23, 1991.

Stiffel, Dr. Frank. Interview. Queens, New York. June 1, 1993.

————. *The Tale of the Ring: A Kaddish, A Personal Memoir of the Holocaust.* New York, Toronto, and London: Bantam Books, 1984.

Szmaglewska, Seweryna. *Smoke over Birkenau.* Translated by Jadwiga Rynas. New York: Henry Holt and Company, 1947.

Szwajger, Adina Blady. *I Remember Nothing More: The Warsaw Children's Hospital and the Jewish Resistance.* Translated by Tasja Darowska and Danusia Stok. New York: Pantheon Books, 1990.

Ten Boom, Corrie. *The Hiding Place: The Triumphant True Story of Corrie Ten Boom.* With John and Elizabeth Sherrill. New York: Bantam Books, 1971.

Trial of the Major War Criminals Before the International Military Tribunal. Nuremberg. November 14, 1945–October 1, 1946. 38 vols. Nuremberg, Germany, 1947.

United States Holocaust Research Institute Archives, Record Group 02, Survivor Testimonies, .037: United States Holocaust Memorial Museum Collection, "Hell and Rebirth: My Experiences during the Time of Persecution," by Edith Kramer.

————. Record Group 04, Concentration and other camps, .020*01: United States Holocaust Memorial Museum Collection. "The Relief of Belsen Concentration Camp: Recollections & Reflections of a British Army Doctor."

————. Record Group 04, Concentration and other camps, .021*01, United States Holocaust Memorial Museum Collection, Hela Jafe. Deposition taken by M. Thau, October, 1965.

————. Record Group 09, Liberation .005*26 [1981 International Liberators Conference] Holocaust Memorial Museum Collection. Dr. Hadassah Rosensaft, "Bergen-Belsen 1945–1950."

————. Record Group 50, Oral History Collection, .234*11: United States Holocaust Memorial Council/International Liberators Conference, "Interview with Marie Ellifritz."

————. Record Group 50, Oral History, .030*43 United States Holocaust Memorial Museum Collection. "Interview with Hana Bruml."

————. Record Group 50, United States Holocaust Memorial Museum/Hadassah Rosensaft Collection, .266, Interview with Genia R. (Abstract).

White, Sheldon, and Barbara Notkin White. *Childhood: Pathways of Discovery.* New York: Harper & Row, 1980.

Yahil, Leni. *The Holocaust: The Fate of European Jewry.* Translated by Ina Friedman and Haya Galai. New York and Oxford: Oxford University Press, 1990.

Zeitlin, Aaron. *Janusz Korczak: Ghetto Diary: The Last Walk of Janusz Korczak.* Translated by Hadassah Rosensaft and Gertrude Hirschler. New York: Holocaust Library, 1978.

Index

•   •   •